James Playsted Wood has served in the editorial, marketing research, and circulation departments of national magazines and has written for a number of them. He worked first on newspapers and in book publishing in New York City, and completed his undergraduate and graduate work in American literature at Columbia University. Mr. Wood taught for some years at Amherst College and is the author of many books, including *The Story of Advertising* and *The Curtis Magazines*, both published by The Ronald Press Company.

MAGAZINES IN THE UNITED STATES

JAMES PLAYSTED WOOD

Third Edition

THE RONALD PRESS COMPANY • NEW YORK

Library of Congress Catalog Card Number: 78–112464
PRINTED IN THE UNITED STATES OF AMERICA

Preface

This book attempts to show, from general magazines that were important in their time and from important nationally circulated magazines of today, what magazines are and in what directions they exert their social and economic influence. It traces and gauges the force of periodicals from Benjamin Franklin's *General Magazine* to the weeklies and monthlies of the present. It shows how magazines have both reflected and helped to mould American tastes, habits, manners, interests, and beliefs; how they have shaped opinion on public questions; how they have crusaded effectively for social and political reforms; and how magazine advertising, as well as magazine editorial content, has affected Americans.

Significant changes have taken place and are taking place in magazine ownership and financing, in editing, advertising, and circulation.

There are more magazines than ever in the past. Total magazine circulation is at peak. The average per issue circulation of all the magazines checked by the Audit Bureau of Circulations is nearly 240,000,000. Every time they are issued there are about 170 copies of magazines for every 100 adults in the country. Each of the 50 largest general and farm magazines has a circulation in excess of 1,000,000, and a dozen have circulations of over 5,000,000—some of them very much over. Magazine advertising revenue is at its highest point in history. It runs now at almost $1,250,000,000 annually.

Yet the position of the major national magazines as both communications and advertising media has changed fundamentally. Despite all the surface indications of prosperity, general indicators and specific case histories point to decline rather than to advance in magazine publishing as an industry.

The chief attempt in this considerably enlarged Third Edition of *Magazines in the United States* has been to examine and describe this changed magazine situation and to suggest what some of it may mean.

Like its predecessors, this edition is addressed to all students of communications, to practitioners in magazine publishing, editing, and advertising, and to all those who realize that what its magazines have been, what they are now, and what they may become constitute a vital part of the social and cultural history of the United States.

My thanks go always to Elizabeth Craig Wood. They go to Donald M. Hobart who encouraged the first writing of this book. For answering questions and providing requested data, sometimes for stimulating discussion, I also thank William B. Arthur, Douglas E. Benney, Fifi Booth, John Dower, Brice M. Draper, John E. Drewry, Bonni Fiedler, Robert M. Goshorn, James P. Haughton, Earl Lawson, John W. Limpert, Jr., Newton F. McKeon, S. Branson Marley, Jr., John K. Montmeat, George W. Morgan, Jr., Stewart M. Ogilvy, Kathryn Powers, Kent Rhodes, Terry Rice, Grace Rupertus, Peter Schrag, Harold W. Schriber, Hoyt Spelman, Frank Strohkarck, and Ralph Woodward.

JAMES PLAYSTED WOOD

Springfield, Massachusetts
December, 1970

For

W. T. W.

Contents

MAGAZINES
IN THE
UNITED STATES

Chapter I

English Magazine Origins

The English newspaper developed in the late seventeenth century out of the political pamphlet and the newsletter. The English magazine developed out of the newspaper within less than fifty years after the first newspaper was founded.

The first newspaper was the *London Gazette,* which had been founded as the *Oxford Gazette* in 1665. What is usually, and with considerable justification, described as the first magazine in English was started when an outspoken Nonconformist with too skillful a pen was sent to jail in 1703. The writer, described in the advertisements for his arrest as "a middle-sized spare man about forty years old of a brown complexion and dark brown-coloured hair, but wears a wig; a hooked nose, a sharp chin, grey eyes, and a large mole near his mouth," was pilloried for three days and then imprisoned for the ironic opinions he had expressed against the extreme position of the established Church of England in his *Shortest Way With Dissenters.* Daniel Defoe, who had not yet written *Robinson Crusoe* or his other picaresque novels, thereupon began to issue in February, 1704, from Newgate Prison or immediately after his release from it, a weekly periodical which he called *The Review.*

The journalistic idea, the idea of periodical publication, was still new. It is not always possible to distinguish absolutely between the newspaper and the magazine of this time. The form of neither was fixed. The provinces of both media for public communication overlapped as, to a lesser extent, they still do, but the *Gazette* and its rivals and imitators were concerned almost solely with the news. *The Review,* written in Defoe's accurate, straightforward style, printed the news, too, but it also printed articles on domestic affairs and on national policy. Defoe was *The Review's* sole editor and contributor during its nine-year history. In its four small pages, which appeared usually three times a week, he expressed and forcefully defended his views on all matters of public concern. He instituted a department, run monthly at first, called "Advice from the Scandalous Club," in which he discussed literature, manners, and morals. He made *The Review* recognizably a magazine. It was Defoe's "Advice from the Scandalous Club," turned after 1705 into the semi-weekly *Little Review,* which suggested theme and treatment to the famous periodical writers who followed Defoe. Before *The Review* ceased publication in 1712, Richard Steele had started *The Tatler.*

The first *Tatler* appeared in April, 1709. Ostensibly by Isaac Bickerstaff, a name which Swift had made famous, it contained political news. More varied material soon followed. In imitation of *The Review,* Steele, motivated by the desire of financial gain and by the equally strong wish to influence the men and women of his day—twin desires which still motivate magazine publishers and editors—began his characteristic essays. He printed foreign intelligence and theatrical news, but he wrote and published short articles attacking the fads and follies of the day. "Poor Dick Steele," as Thackeray describes him in one of the finest of his essays in *The English Humorists,* might stumble, fall, and get up again in his own life, but his intent was moral and so were the principles of conduct he preached. *The Tatler* spoke out against gambling, drinking, and dueling. It also gave the gossip of the coffeehouses; and gossip about people and places is still a characteristic of the magazine. As Jenny Bickerstaff—for magazines from the first have wooed women readers as well as men—Steele wrote on subjects of interest to women. These, with advertising, were the contents of *The Tatler.*

Advertising, a feature destined to become so characteristic of modern magazines, not only served its usual purposes but even provided the subject of a *Tatler* essay. In Number 224 of *The Tatler,* September 14, 1710, Addison wrote:

> It is my custom, in a dearth of news, to entertain myself with those collections of advertisements that appear at the end of all our public prints. . . . But to consider this subject in its most ridiculous lights, advertisements are of great use to the vulgar. . . . A man that is by no means big enough for the Gazette may easily creep into the ads. . . . A second use . . . has been the management of controversy. . . . The inventors of "strops for razors" have written against one another in this way for several years. . . . The third and last use of these writings is to inform the world, where they may be furnished with almost everything that is necessary for life. If a Man has pains in his head, cholics in his bowels, or spots in his clothes, he may here meet with proper cures and remedies. If a man would recover a wife or a horse that is stolen or strayed, if he wants new sermons, electuaries, asses milk, or anything else, either for his body or his mind, this is the place to look for them in.

Advising copywriters of the day, Addison continued:

> The great art in writing advertising is the finding out the proper method to catch the reader, without which a good thing may pass over unobserved, or be lost among commissions of bankrupts. Asterisks or hands were formerly of great use for this purpose. Of late years the *N.B.* has been much in fashion, as also little cuts and figures, the invention of which we must ascribe to the author of spring trusses. . . .
>
> By the remarks I have here made, it plainly appears, that a collection of advertisements is a kind of miscellany; the writers of which, contrary to all authors, except men of quality, give money to the booksellers who publish their copy.

Joseph Addison had joined Steele in writing *The Tatler* after about its eightieth number. They continued to work together and in March, 1711, published the first issue of the famous *Spectator.* The humorous coffeehouse sketches which Steele had originated and Addison perfected became the new magazine's daily contents; all other material, except short advertisements, was dropped. Together the genial, very human Steele and the urbane, scholarly Addison created the English informal essay and made it the first magazine contribution to literature.

In *The Spectator* they almost gave form to the short story. Steele introduced Sir Roger de Coverley and the other characters of the most famous club in English literature in the second issue. The stories of Sir Roger, most whimsical of knights, and of Will Honeycomb, Sir Andrew Freeport, Captain Sentry, Will Wimble, and other delightful eccentrics of the club may be said to be the first magazine fiction. The pleasant, colloquial essays of *The Tatler* gave way to more serious essays. Addison, a fine critic, taught appreciation of literature and of classical learning at the same time that he and Steele discoursed humorously on the topics of the day.

The Spectator, 274 of its issues by Addison, 236 by Steele, the remaining 45 by occasional contributors, was read with delight by the literate and sophisticated of polite London to whom it was addressed. Its circulation reached 3,000 in a city of about a half million. Some numbers are said to have had a sale of 20,000 copies. Addison and Steele meant to entertain, but their serious purpose, as the essays show and Steele affirmed, was "to expose the false arts of life, to pull off the disguises of cunning, vanity, and affectations, and to recommend a general simplicity in our dress, our discourse, and our behavior." As *The Review* had been for practical, clear-spoken Defoe, *The Spectator* was a means of expression for these sharpest and most graceful of Queen Anne wits and moralists. More than a means of expression, it was a means of reaching and influencing public opinion. As such, *The Tatler* and *The Spectator* succeeded both in moulding the ideas and tastes of urban England in the early years of the eighteenth century, and in establishing the magazine as a journalistic and literary form of marked social force.

Numerous imitators of *The Tatler* and *The Spectator* sprang up. The coffeehouses of London were filled with wits and journalists eager to write for the newssheets and the new periodicals. Steele himself fathered half a dozen later and less successful periodicals, most of them Whig political organs or gossip sheets: the *Guardian,* the *Englishman, Town Talk,* the *Tea Table, Chit Chat,* the *Plebeian.* Alexander Pope used the *Grub Street Journal* (1730–1738), a magazine which he had in all probability founded though he consistently denied connection with it, to say that his many enemies were nasty people and to pour a little boiling oil on them in each issue.

In 1731 appeared the first number of the first monthly periodical to describe itself by the word "magazine." Under the name of Sylvanus Urban, Edward Cave, a London printer and bookseller, began publication of what was actually conceived as a *museum, depository,* or *magazine* which, while it paid some attention to current events, was more concerned with collecting in more permanent form the best of the material appearing in the journals. Cave's *Gentleman's Magazine* soon ceased to be merely eclectic. As did *Harper's New Monthly Magazine,* which was founded more than a century later in New York, the *Literary Digest,* and *The Reader's Digest,* founded almost two centuries later, all of which started purely as reprint periodicals, *The Gentleman's Magazine* soon began to publish more varied materials. It printed both prose and verse, historical and biographical material, and obituaries. It listed other publications. It printed songs with music, much as *Godey's Lady's Book* did in the nineteenth century and as Edward Bok's *Ladies' Home Journal* did as late as 1910. Some features of the first monthly magazine have lasted a long time. *The Gentleman's Magazine* even offered engravings and maps, as does the *National Geographic Magazine* today.

Perhaps the best, and certainly the best-known, feature of *The Gentleman's Magazine* was its reports of the debates in Parliament. The magazine had reported these from 1732. Six years later this task was assigned to one of the most famous of all magazine contributors, Dr. Samuel Johnson, who was just beginning his London career. Johnson wrote voluminously for the magazine, but his chief job was to report activities in Parliament. From inaccurate and sketchy notes made by Cave's friends and from his own imagination he pieced together these reports for publication in the monthly. He really wrote the speeches he attributed to English statesmen of the day, and probably wrote them better than those who delivered them could have done. When the House of Commons declared that publication of its proceedings was illegal, Johnson reported them under the transparent disguise of "Reports of the Debates in the Senate of Magna Lilliputia." Names of the speakers were designated only by their initial and final letters.

Besides his political writing, Johnson wrote numerous essays, biographies, and literary notices for *The Gentleman's Magazine.* In the issue for August, 1743, he announced that his famous *Life of Richard Savage* was in preparation. It was published in 1744. The circulation of *The Gentleman's Magazine* was already a high 10,000 when Samuel Johnson became Cave's assistant. Johnson, the first important writer to ally himself with a popular monthly as a reporter, article writer, and editor, aided largely in pushing it up to an almost incredible 15,000. *The Gentleman's Magazine* had imitators, the most important of them the *London Magazine,* but it was the outstanding success of its time.

Dr. Johnson ceased to write for *The Gentleman's Magazine* in 1744, but his connection with magazines was to continue. From 1750 to 1752, he published *The Rambler,* a paper after the *Spectator* manner. Johnson's essays appeared in it regularly every Tuesday and Saturday. By this time England had about 150 periodicals. Later Johnson undertook another series of essays in *The Idler,* which, from 1758 to 1760, ran as a department of *The Universal Chronicle, or Weekly Gazette.*

Dr. Johnson also commented on what early established itself as a magazine feature in England. He devoted No. IX of the *Idler,* January 20, 1759, to discussion of the "Art of Advertising." There were so many advertisements, and the competition for attention was already so severe, that people were beginning to pay less attention to them. Advertisers had to make large, then larger inducements to attract purchasers. "Promise, large promise, is the soul of an advertisement," said Johnson.

He ridiculed the pretensions of some advertisers, particularly the claims that one toilet soap would give an edge to a razor, that a down bed covering was warmer than four or five blankets, and that an advertised lotion would wash away freckles and smooth the skin. He decided, somewhat prematurely perhaps, that, "The trade of advertising is now so near perfection that it is not easy to propose any improvement."

By the mid-eighteenth century the magazine form had begun to crystallize and the magazine pattern to make itself clear. Some magazines, such as *The Tatler, The Spectator,* and *The Rambler,* were of the periodical essay type, and others, such as *The Gentleman's Magazine,* the *London Magazine,* and *The Monthly Review,* displayed more varied contents; but they all had magazine intents and features in common. Such periodical writers as Defoe, Steele, Addison, and Johnson developed a vehicle of literary quality meant to be more durable than the newspaper, to carry less ephemeral material, to comment as well as to inform, to communicate pleasure as well as fact, to provoke speculation, and to influence belief and conduct.

Before this time the magazine idea had spread to the British possessions in America. Inspired by the success of *The Gentleman's Magazine* and its rival, the *London Magazine,* Benjamin Franklin decided to establish in Philadelphia a monthly magazine for all the Colonies.

Chapter 2

Magazine Beginnings in America

In the *Pennsylvania Gazette,* a weekly which he had published since 1729, Benjamin Franklin announced in November, 1740, his plans to publish *The General Magazine, and Historical Chronicle, for All the British Plantations in America.* Unfortunately Franklin offered the editorship of what was to be the pioneer American magazine to John Webbe, a Philadelphia lawyer, who quickly divulged his knowledge of the scheme to Andrew Bradford, son of Pennsylvania's first printer. Thereupon Bradford immediately announced a magazine of his own and, on February 13, 1741, with Webbe as editor, got out the first issue of his own *American Magazine, or a Monthly View of the Political State of the British Colonies.* Three days later, Franklin, acting now as his own editor, published the first issue of the *General Magazine.*

The *General Magazine* was what Franklin conceived a magazine to be, literally a magazine or storehouse of varied material, gathered mostly from books, pamphlets, newspapers, and political documents, and offered for edification and entertainment of his readers. His magazine contained seventy-five pages, twice as many as Bradford's, and sold for sixpence sterling the single copy. There were no subscribers, Franklin depending on single copy sales. The first issue, dated January, 1741, was typical of the six monthly numbers published. It contained a discussion of the currency, a vital subject in the

Colonies; "Accounts of and Extracts from New Books and Pamphlets Published in the Plantation"; included sermons by Mathew Byles and George Whitefield, the English evangelist whom Franklin admired;[1] ten pages of verse ("Poetical Essays"); and "The Historical Chronicle" or news section. The "Chronicle" in this first issue described the Grand Mogul's defeat by Thomas Koulikan, recorded events in Turkey and Russia, and revealed that the German Emperor had died the preceding October from "being poisoned by eating mushrooms stew'd in oil." A fire at Charleston was described, and the "Chronicle" gave the most vivid of the Philadelphia news.

Succeeding issues of the *General Magazine* described proceedings in Parliament that affected the American Colonies, the negotiations of New York with the Six Nations. They contained more discussions of the uncertain Colonial currency, offered more sermons—for this was the period of the Great Awakening, the religious revival led by Whitefield and by Jonathan Edwards in Northampton, Massachusetts, which swept the Colonies in the mid-eighteenth century—and more verse. An article in the February issue described life in an orphan asylum which Whitefield had founded in Georgia. A lead article in March was on "The Present State of Virginia"; another article, "Evolutions of the Foot," described infantry drill and maneuvers; and a third dealt with "A New Method of Making Molasses from the Summer Sweeting as Communicated to the Royal Society and Put in #374 of Philosophical Transactions." Franklin's scientific interests, which led him to found the American Philosophical Society in 1743, show in his magazine.

There were intimations of things to come in the April issue of the *General Magazine*. In that issue Franklin printed what was, even then, a not very convincing attempt of the New

[1] The frugal Franklin was, at least temporarily, much moved by Whitefield's persuasive powers. In his *Autobiography* he writes: "I happened . . . to attend one of his sermons, in the course of which I perceived he intended to finish with a collection, and I silently resolved he should get nothing from me. . . . As he proceeded I began to soften and decided to give the coppers. Another stroke of his oratory made me ashamed of that, and determin'd me to give the silver; and he finished so admirably, that I empty'd my pockets wholly into the collector's dish, gold and all."

York Assembly to allay the suspicions of that Colony's nervous lieutenant governor:

> To what is mentioned of a Jealousy in England, that the Plantations are not without Thoughts of throwing off their Dependence on the Crown of England, we shall say the less, as your Honour declares you hope and believe no Man in the Colony has such an Intention, and we dare vouch, that not one single Person in it has such an Intention.

Obviously Franklin was editing his magazine not for Philadelphia or for Pennsylvania, but for the Colonies as a whole. Unformed as they were, and of short duration, the first American magazines were not merely local in content and appeal. They showed from the first the magazine trend toward coverage of all the Colonies that developed a century and a half later into the nation-wide coverage of the national magazine.

From the beginning the magazine's intent was the widest possible dissemination of important information, a basic intent of today's national magazines. They were founded, too, with the very definite intent of influencing public opinion, particularly on one crucial subject. Bradford, who had beaten Franklin to the street with his monthly American magazine, said that one of his reasons for publishing the *American Magazine* was "That the parliament and People of Great Britain may be truly and clearly informed of the Constitution and Government in the Colonies, whose Great Distance from the Mother-country seems in some sense to have placed them out of her View."

The *American Magazine and Monthly Chronicle*, begun in 1757, was prefaced with:

> It has long been a matter of just complaint, among some of the best friends of our national commerce and safety, that the important concerns of these Colonies were but little studied and less understood in the mother-country, even by many of those, who have sustained the highest offices of trust and dignity in it. . . . The present war [the French war] has rendered this country, at length, the object of a very general attention, and it seems now become as much the mode among those who would be useful or conspicuous in the state, to seek an ac-

quaintance with these colonies, their constitutions, interests and commerce. . . . This favorable disposition, if duly cultivated, may have a happy influence. . . .

The earliest American magazines were out, then, to influence opinion in the Colonies and opinion in England. One of Franklin's purposes and accomplishments in the *General Magazine* was to present political information, knowledge of which he felt should be widespread among the thirteen Colonies. To this end he devoted about a third of the space in his magazine to the reprinting of state papers.

The shrewd Franklin was, of course, well aware of the wider audience he could reach and influence through the medium of his magazine. He was no stranger to journalism. As a printer's apprentice he had worked with his brother James in getting out in Boston the *New England Courant,* founded in 1721 as the second newspaper published in America, preceded only by the *Boston News Letter* in 1704.[2] By 1729 he was issuing weekly from his own press in Philadelphia the *Pennsylvania Gazette* purchased from Samuel Keimer, who had founded it as *The Universal Instructor in All Arts and Sciences and Pennsylvania Gazette* the year before, when he heard that the twenty-two-year-old Franklin was planning a similar weekly.

The *Gazette,* a reflection of its acute and ambitious publisher-editor, became perhaps the best paper in the Colonies. Besides the news, it contained in its early years some of Franklin's familiar essays, disputes with imaginary characters created by Franklin for the purpose, and weather reports which Franklin was the first to introduce as a journalistic feature. In 1754, at the time of the Albany Congress, the *Gazette* carried what is usually considered America's first cartoon, probably drawn by Franklin himself. The earliest plea for a United Colonies, if not a United States, it pictured a snake in eight parts and underneath the legend "Join or Die." Publication was suspended for two weeks in 1765 as a protest against

[2] Franklin calls it the second newspaper in his *Autobiography.* Actually the *Boston Gazette,* printed but not edited by James Franklin, dating from 1719, intervened.

THE

GENERAL MAGAZINE,

AND

Hiſtorical Chronicle,

For all the *Britiſh* Plantations in *America.*

[To be Continued Monthly.]

JANUARY 1741.

VOL. I.

PHILADELPHIA:

Printed and Sold by B. FRANKLIN.

Benjamin Franklin conceived the idea of a monthly magazine for the American Colonies. The first issue of his *General Magazine* appeared on February 16, 1741.

the Stamp Act, but was only twice interrupted during the Revolution.

Only three numbers of Bradford's monthly were published, six of Franklin's, but the magazine, once established, quickly took root in American soil. About a hundred were founded before the end of the eighteenth century. William Beer in his *Checklist of American Magazines, 1741–1800,* (Worcester: 1923), lists 98. The figure varies according to the source used. Some of these "magazines" were really weekly newspapers. These magazines contained essays, poetry and fiction, political writing, literary and dramatic criticism, articles on economics and religion, comments on slavery, women's dress, dueling, swearing. They contained the best American writing of their time and reflected, as the best of our national magazines reflect today, the world in which their readers lived.

Notable editors succeeded Franklin and Webbe. Mathew Carey, Thomas Paine, Charles Brockden Brown, Hugh Brackenridge were all eighteenth-century Philadelphia editors, for Philadelphia was the center of the magazine-publishing industry. Noah Webster, whose *Spelling Book* and *Dictionary* were to be so basic in American education and in the standardization of American spelling, was a New York editor by 1787. Isaiah Thomas was Boston's best eighteenth-century editor.[3]

One of the most important American magazines of the eighteenth century was published only from January, 1775, to July, 1776, but none of its contemporaries exceeded it in social force at a crucial period in American history. Thomas Paine, whose electrifying pamphlet *Common Sense* did so much to crystallize the sentiment toward separation from England and whose letter *The Crisis* ("These are the times that try men's souls . . .") inflamed readers with his own fiery patriotism, had been in America only three months before Robert Aitkin made him editor of the *Pennsylvania Magazine.* Though it had been started by the milder Aitkin as a quieter periodical, there was

[3] Thomas was also a printer and publisher. His *A Specimen* (of the types he used), 1785, and his *History of Printing in America,* 1810, are valuable sources on early American printing. Thomas founded the American Antiquarian Society in 1812.

soon no mistaking the sympathies of the *Pennsylvania Magazine*. The vignette of the magazine showed the goddess of Liberty holding a shield with the Pennsylvania arms emblazoned on it. A mortar labeled "The Congress," battle-axes and pikes, the word "Liberty" on a gorget hanging from a tree, surrounded the goddess.

Paine, who numbered David Rittenhouse, Benjamin Rush, Mathew Wilson, and President John Witherspoon of Princeton among his important contributors, gave the *Pennsylvania Magazine* its strong political bias and himself wrote much of the strongly revolutionary matter that made the magazine so powerful an instrument of the times. "Reflections on the Duty of Princes" and "On Liberty," the former signed only with initials, the latter with a classical pseudonym after the fashion of the time, which appeared in early issues were obviously written by Paine. His famous poem "The Liberty Tree" was published in June, 1775. Before that had appeared an Irish-dialect attack on the British troops in Boston and a poem in memory of the American volunteers killed at Lexington and Concord on April 19, 1775. Consistently there was non-political matter in the *Pennsylvania Magazine*—verse, essays, a series on "The Old Bachelor," and an "Occasional Letter on the Female Sex"—but the periodical took its color and gained its force from Thomas Paine's revolutionary ardor. A department called "Monthly Intelligence" recorded the war news each month, printed the letters of Washington and other Colonial leaders and the proceedings in Parliament and in the Continental Congress. "Substitutes for Tea" was run in February, 1775, and the "Dialogue on Liberty" in April, 1776. The war put an abrupt end to the *Pennsylvania Magazine*, but it went down defiantly, carrying in the issue of July, 1776, its last number, the Declaration of Independence which it had been a strong force in bringing about.

The Revolution was over when the same man founded four months apart what were to be the most successful American magazines of the late eighteenth century. Mathew Carey, jailed in Dublin for his pamphlets criticizing British policy, fled to

France, where Benjamin Franklin employed him for a time as a printer at Passy. Returning to Ireland, he was again jailed for his militant anti-British editing of the *Volunteer's Journal.* This time Carey fled to America where, less than six months after his arrival in Philadelphia, he started the *Pennsylvania Herald,* with $400 borrowed from Lafayette. It came to a sudden end when Carey was wounded in a duel.

In August, 1786, the *Pennsylvania Gazette* carried an announcement of the first new magazine Carey was to edit and print. *The Columbian Magazine, or Monthly Miscellany* was to be started, according to the announcement, at a time "when the genuine spirit of liberty has extended its benign influence over these independent and highly favored republics." It was to be a monthly of forty-eight pages, with copperplate engravings, sold to subscribers at twenty shillings a year. The first number appeared in October, 1786. By March, 1787, Carey, having established the second of his magazines, *The American Museum,* hired Francis Hopkinson as editor and Jeremy Belknap as contributor. A paid editor and a paid contributor were startling magazine innovations. The *Columbian* introduced other changes. It stressed publication of original contributions and obtained capable men to write them. Most magazines of the period contained many items clipped from English magazines, other American magazines, newspapers, and pamphlets. There were no copyright laws to infringe. Ownership of writing was not as important as getting the material before the public.

The new *Columbian,* a new magazine for a new nation, paid particular attention to politics, agriculture, inventions, science, and business. Its writings were concerned with these subjects as well as with purely literary offerings. So were the copperplate engravings, most of them done by James Trenchard, one of the magazine's publishers. An important contributor was Dr. Benjamin Rush, who, after obtaining his medical degree at Edinburgh, returned to his native Philadelphia where he became a professor in the medical school of the University of Pennsylvania. Dr. Rush, a member of the Continental Congress and a signer of the Declaration of Independence, was a strong Federalist with decided ideas about slavery, capital punishment, the use of liquor and tobacco, education, and the proper treatment for yellow fever. About all of these subjects he wrote vividly and forcefully in the *Columbian*. He showed his hatred of slavery in several *Columbian* articles, one of them "The Paradise of Negro-Slaves"; his dislike of whisky in "A Moral and Physical Thermometer"; his belief in free schools in "The Benefits of Charity"; his medical interests in "An Inquiry into the Methods of Preventing the Painful and Fatal Effect of Cold upon the Human Body"; and his political beliefs in "Causes Which Produced the Ruin of States."

Reprinted items gave *Columbian* readers matter from the pens of Franklin, Washington, General Israel Putnam, and David Ramsey. There were selections from writers abroad: Johnson, Burke, Voltaire, Montesquieu, and Rousseau. At the same time the *Columbian* was running in 1787 and 1788 *The Forresters: An Historical Romance*, in which Jeremy Belknap, one of America's first paid magazine writers, through humorous allegory narrated the founding and growth of the British colonies in America.[4] Belknap also contributed a series of biographies of "Heroic and Virtuous Men" of the United States, including sketches of John Winthrop, Sir Ferdinando Gorges, and Captain John Smith. He even contributed an article, earlier printed in *The Boston Magazine*, which endeavored to determine whether the discovery of America had been a blessing or a bane to man. It was Belknap who promoted the sale of the *Columbian* in Boston and who persuaded the young John Quincy Adams to publish in the magazine his oration at the Harvard commencement of 1787.

The *Columbian* was good, but in some ways *The American Museum* was even better. Running from 1787 to 1792, when the *Columbian* also was discontinued, its issues are now invaluable as historical source material. This was not accidental. In

[4] Jeremy Belknap was a Congregational clergyman and a historian of Boston and one of the founders of the Massachusetts Historical Society, the first society of its kind in America. He had been offered the editorship of the *Columbian* but refused it because a Boston church offered him a larger salary, 125 pounds a year.

contrast to the *Columbian,* which was to publish as much original material as possible, the *Museum* was planned by Carey as a repository of important American writing. It was to be a museum of American writing worthy of preservation—and a publishing bargain: one hundred pages a month at a "quarter dollar" a number, or eighteen shillings a year; $2.50 outside Pennsylvania. Few modern magazines give their readers as much solid worth for their money.

Carey sought out and reprinted the basic documents of the Revolution. His first volume contained Paine's *Common Sense,* Washington's *Circular Letter to the Army,* Humphreys' *Address to the Armies of America,* Trumbull's *M'Fingal,* Various issues of the *Museum* reprinted writing by Benjamin Franklin, Witherspoon, Hopkinson, Dr. Ladd, Noah Webster, Hancock, and many others eminent in statesmanship or literature. The *Museum* ran articles on scientific subjects by Rittenhouse, Benjamin West, James Bowdoin, John Winthrop of Harvard, Samuel Dexter, and many others. It published the poetry of Freneau, Trumbull, Hopkinson, Dwight, Godfrey. Paine's *Crisis,* Dickinson's *Letters from a Pennsylvania Farmer,* and Witherspoon's *Letters on Marriage* were all reprinted in the *Museum.*

Carey, an anti-Federalist himself, printed the writings on both sides of this central question of the day, including the *Federalist* papers. He published articles on industry, the currency, commerce, politics, science, education, agriculture, and many directed against slavery. Carey made perhaps no more important contribution to the thought of his time and the subsequent economic history of the United States than in his selection of writing dealing with American business. The articles he chose emphasized a conservative and practical approach to business problems. They stressed protection as necessary to assist the growth of American industry, advocated free trade among the states but a national tariff to combat tariffs imposed abroad on goods imported from America. Carey published the opinions on business of Dickinson, Franklin, Rush, and James M'Henry, but gave particular prominence to those of two Philadelphians, Coxe and Barton. Tench Coxe was president of the Pennsylvania Society for the Encouragement of Manufactures and the Useful Arts. His "Address to an Assembly of Friends of American Manufactures, Convened for the Purpose of Establishing a Society" emphasized the need for private enterprise and government to join forces in the encouragement of American industry. An address, arguing for the tariff, was read at Franklin's home and published in the *Museum.* Carey also printed an essay by William Barton, secretary of the Pennsylvania Society for the Encouragement of Manufactures, who expressed similar conservative business opinions on the powers of Congress to regulate trade.

With Carey the American magazine went beyond the mere proffering of entertainment and spreading of information. The ideas he placed before his readers helped them to form their opinions on social, political, and business affairs in the formative period of the new country.

The Boston printer Isaiah Thomas founded his newspaper, *The Spy,* in 1770 as a revolutionary Whig organ and propagandized so successfully against British rule that, along with Samuel Adams and John Hancock, he was placed on the royal list of those seditionists who were to be summarily executed when caught. Thomas adopted Franklin's device of the eight-part snake and ran it across the top of his front page with "JOIN OR DIE" printed below it. His fiery exhortations to rebellion blazed fiercely in *The Spy.* Thomas got his press and type across the Charles River two nights before Paul Revere made his famous ride, April 18, 1775, and continued publication of *The Spy* in Worcester.

Thomas, who became a successful book publisher on a large scale, also founded and published three magazines: the *Royal American Magazine,* which lasted only fifteen months, 1774–1775; the *Worcester Magazine,* which ran for two years, 1786–1788; and the *Massachusetts Magazine,* 1789–1796. One of but two eighteenth century American magazines to last for as long as eight years, the *Massachusetts Magazine* made what was then a significant and prophetic departure in magazine publishing. Thomas, an experienced book and newspaper publisher, directed his new monthly not only to the cultured, at whom most magazines of the period were aimed, but also to the intelligent if less intellectual readers who had not yet been a recognized magazine audience. As do the best of modern magazines, it appealed to those with journalistic as well as those with erudite tastes. It was projected emphatically to entertain as well as to inform. The new magazine intended, its first issue stated, to "gratify and excite the natural inquisitiveness of the human mind . . . rouse and strengthen the native powers of the soul . . . give birth to literary emulation and effort . . . enforce and reward studious application . . . improve the taste, the language and the manners of the age . . . increase an acquaintance with natural and civil history, with arts, manufactures and commerce, with law, physick and divinity . . ." It was an ambitious program, and in reaching to tap the large potential magazine audience which publishers and editors had to this time neglected, Thomas offered excellent and varied fare.

Besides articles of most of the types printed by his contemporaries and competitors, Thomas published plays, essays, engravings, and sentimental fiction. Joseph Dennie, to become one of the most famous Philadelphia editors and essayists during the first quarter of the next century, made his magazine debut in *The Massachusetts Magazine.* Mrs. Sarah Wentworth Morton, wife of a Massachusetts attorney general and long thought to be the author of the first American novel, *The Power of Sympathy,* which Thomas had published in his *Royal American Magazine,* was a contributor of poetry. Sentiment and sentimentality, melodrama replete with villains and seductions, appeared in the tales carried by *The Massachusetts Magazine,* along with poetry, essays, serious discussions of contemporary problems and selections from the writings of the omnipresent Franklin, Jefferson, Jedidiah Morse, Dr. Rush, William Livingston, and others.

Isaiah Thomas became one of the wealthiest men of his time—a fate which has overtaken more than one magazine publisher in the twentieth century United States.

In 1778, only five years after his graduation from Yale, Noah Webster published *A Grammatical Institute of the English Language*, the first part of which became his famous *Spelling Book*. Four years later he left his teaching of English and mathematics in the Episcopal Academy at Philadelphia, where he had gone from his native Connecticut, to establish New York's first monthly magazine, *The American Magazine*. This was in 1787, almost a half century after the beginning of magazine publication in Philadelphia, when Webster, already well known as a philologist and a Federalist, was twenty-nine years old. Webster, by nature a writer and a disputant, made the *American* a bright and spirited magazine. The magazine, as Webster saw it, was meant to be a vehicle for the expression of ideas, and doing much of the writing himself, he used it to express his own ideas on the subjects in which he was most interested. Webster was a strong Federalist, largely because attempts to obtain copyrights for his *Spelling Book* from each of the thirteen states showed him the necessity for a central government to control such matters. He wrote much about the new Constitution, discussing governmental affairs in each issue. He wrote much, and sensibly, about education. He thought the teaching of English should be emphasized, the teaching of Greek and Latin minimized. One teacher should not teach a number of diverse subjects. There should be electives. He believed girls should be taught English, arithmetic, and geography. He felt that the teaching of religion, with government approval, was dangerous.

Webster printed the poetry of his fellow Yale men, John Trumbull, Joel Barlow, and Timothy Dwight. He even sprang to Dwight's defense when an English review harshly criticized Dwight's verse. "The London Reviewers Reviewed," which appeared in July, 1788, was one of the first American retorts to what was long seen as the consistently prejudiced criticism of American writing by English critics. In yet another important department the young Webster showed himself an astute editor. He paid more attention to women as readers than any other magazine had done to this time. In the first issue of the *American* he promised that "his *fair readers* may be assured that no inconsiderable pains will be taken to furnish them entertainment," and he provided the kind of Gothic and sentimental fiction considered appealing to feminine taste. He also, and not too deftly, offered advice on female dress and behavior.

It was part of Webster's plan to make his magazine national in coverage and distribution. He planned at one time to have part owners in Boston, Connecticut, Philadelphia, Virginia, South Carolina, and in New Jersey, Maryland, or Georgia. These part owners were to serve also as correspondents, sending in material from their sections to the editor in New York. Copies of the magazine were to be sent out from New York to every part of the nation. He tried through Belknap to secure subscriptions in Boston, later projected a Boston-New York magazine with Isaiah Thomas of *The Massachusetts Magazine*. All of Webster's attempts at expansion failed. *The American Magazine,* for which its editor had once envisioned 5,000 subscribers, never obtained more than 500, and lasted only one year. Webster went back to Connecticut where he practiced law and continued his philological work, returning to become editor of the Federalist journals, the *American Minerva,* 1793, and the *Herald,* 1794.

A little more than a year after the demise of Webster's *American* came the *New-York Magazine* which, with the *Massachusetts Magazine,* was to last as long as eight years. It did not differ importantly from other magazines of the time except that it included a department of dramatic criticism by William Dunlap and had among its contributors, all of whose works appeared anonymously, Charles Brockden Brown and members of the Friendly Club, a group composed of New York business and professional men. Its importance in the development of American magazines lies in what was at the time its almost spectacular longevity.

The average life of the American magazines of the eighteenth century was only fourteen months. There was little advertising to support them; what there was appeared in most cases only on the covers, in supplements, and on the final pages. Publishers were almost wholly dependent upon subscriptions for the support of their ventures. With the price of most magazines about a shilling a copy, even when subscribers paid promptly, which they seldom did, there was barely sufficient income to keep the best of the magazines solvent. There were other hindrances.

The magazines were badly handicapped by 1792 postal regulations, though those were no handicap to Benjamin Franklin who used his position as Philadelphia postmaster to keep the *American Magazine* of his enemy, Bradford, out of the mails while he allowed postriders to carry his own *General Magazine*. The postal law of 1792, confused and inequitable in practice, operated to prevent mailing of the *Columbian* and the *Museum*, which thereupon suspended publication, while the *Massachusetts Magazine* and the *New-York Magazine* were not affected. A more liberal postal law of 1794, recognizing the importance which magazines had attained, ruled that a sixty-four-page magazine could be carried less than fifty miles for four cents, between fifty and one hundred miles for six, and more than one hundred miles for eight cents.

Magazines were seldom profitable ventures in these early days. It is proof of the earnestness of their publishers and editors and the eagerness of the colonial and early republican audiences that one magazine after another appeared and that many lasted as long as they did. Editors strove to make their magazines useful vehicles for the communication of ideas, repositories of writing that they thought should be preserved, and instruments that would affect the public mind and influence national decisions that had to be made.

These early magazines had a definite force in unifying the Colonies and in inciting, then sustaining, the Revolution. They fought effectively for the ratification of the Constitution, encouraged native literary and artistic expression, and helped to promote American industry and commerce. They discussed important national affairs, and by reprinting work which had first appeared in English periodicals they made Americans aware of thought and action abroad. They recorded the American political and social life of the period and offered their readers almost all of the most significant American writing of the second half of the eighteenth century.

Americans took a patriotic pride in their early magazines, knew their value, saw them as useful and pleasing, and felt that they were an important sign of America's dawning cultural as well as political independence, a concept that was to be emphasized in books and magazines through the first half of the next century. Lyon Richardson points out in his *A History of Early American Magazines* that a great many subscribers to magazines in the eighteenth century considered themselves patrons of an instrument that spread knowledge, advanced culture in the United States, and supported the literary and practical arts developing in the country. Though subscription lists seldom attained to the more than 1,600 recorded for Mathew Carey's *American Museum,* running on an average nearer the 500 maximum of Webster's *American Magazine,* the figures hardly indicate the scope of magazine circulation and readership before the year 1800. Frank Luther Mott says in his standard, *A History of American Magazines,* which won a Pulitzer Prize in 1939, that the influence of the early magazines was probably far greater than the number printed and circulated would indicate. Books and magazines were prized if only because comparatively few were available. Every page of every magazine was read carefully by a number of people. Thus the influence exerted by the early magazines was both intensive and extensive.

A mere list of a few of the contributors and subscribers to American magazines of Colonial, Revolutionary, and immediately post-Revolutionary years indicates something of the stature the first magazines could boast. Contributors included almost every eminent writer, poet, and statesman of the time: Washington, Franklin, Hamilton, John Jay, Fisher Ames,

Tench Coxe, Benjamin Rush, John Witherspoon, Noah Webster, Francis Hopkinson, Thomas Paine, Philip Freneau, Charles Brockden Brown, Jeremy Belknap, Edward Shippen, Thomas Godfrey, Joel Barlow, John Trumbull, Edmund Randolph, John Hancock, Richard Henry Lee, Roger Sherman, Hugh Williamson, Timothy Dwight, William Barton, James M'Henry, Albert Gallatin, William Livington, Isaac Bartram, John Ewing, Hugh Brackenridge, David Rittenhouse. Paul Revere was perhaps the most famous magazine illustrator.[5]

Heading the list of subscribers to the *New-York Magazine* were George Washington and John Adams. Washington subscribed also to *The American Museum,* as did Franklin, Dickinson, Hamilton, Jefferson, Madison, Humphreys, Hopkinson, Pinckney, Rush, Webster, Edmund Randolph, Edward Shippen, Robert Morris, Rufus King, Robert Molyneux, and even the British consul, Phineas Bond.

To Mathew Carey,[6] editor of *The American Museum,* George Washington wrote a letter which Carey used as an advertisement in the *Pennsylvania Gazette* issues of July 16 and August 20, 1788, and which has since been quoted by most American literary and magazine historians. Washington expressed his delight in magazines, his strong approval, and his concern for their success. Of the *Museum* he wrote: ". . . I am of the opinion that this work is not only eminently calculated to dissiminate [sic] political, agricultural, philosophical and other valuable information; but that it has been uniformly conducted with taste, attention, and propriety."

Of magazines in general Washington said: "I consider such easy vehicles of knowledge, more happily calculated than any other, to preserve the liberty, stimulate the industry and meliorate the morals of an enlightened and free people."

[5] Isaiah Thomas paid Paul Revere three pounds each for a series of twenty-two engravings for the *Royal American Magazine* of Boston.

[6] Mathew Carey is buried in Philadelphia, in the cemetery of St. Mary's Catholic Church on Fourth Street near Locust. A bronze plaque on the front of the church reads: "Mathew Carey, the leading publisher of the early years of the Republic and the chief force in the creation of early American literature."

Chapter 3

Magazines as National Educators: *The Port Folio* and Its Contemporaries

The Adamses, four generations of them—presidents, diplomats, lawyers, historians, educators, businessmen—were all writers. In 1794, George Washington appointed John Quincy Adams as minister to Berlin, largely because of a series of pamphlets he had written in support of this country's neutral position toward France and England. Later, President John Adams sent his son as minister to Berlin, where he completed a business treaty with Prussia in 1799. On Jefferson's election to the Presidency in 1800, Adams recalled his son who came back to the United States determined to be a professional writer. The low opinion Europeans had for American literary performance led John Quincy Adams to feel that he would be doing his country a service as well as following his own inclination and talents. Though he became a statesman instead, he was all his life a voluminous and capable writer of prose and verse. When he returned to the United States in 1801, his Harvard friend Joseph Dennie was just starting the brightest and most important magazine of the new century. In pursuit of his chosen career, Adams became one of the chief contributors to *The Port Folio* during its first year.

Joseph Dennie, bohemian, bibulous, a wit, a dandy, an Anglophile, a reactionary, a writer of sharp and polished prose, was called the "American Addison." Usually described as the second professional man of letters in America, he had already edited the *Tablet* in Boston and the *Farmer's Weekly Museum* in Walpole, New Hampshire, for which he wrote his characteristic "Lay Preacher" essays. Coming to Philadelphia first as a clerk to Timothy Pickering, who was then Secretary of State, he was soon one of the most colorful and most skillful magazine editors of his time.

J. T. Buckingham, later editor of *The New-England Magazine,* who had been a boy in Walpole during Dennie's editorship of the *Farmer's Weekly Museum,* described him as slipping along Chestnut Street in Philadelphia to the *Port Folio* office "in a pea-green coat, white vest, nankeen small-clothes, white silk stockings and pumps, fastened with silver buckles which covered at least half the foot from the instep to the toe." A determined individualist, perverse from the start—he had been rusticated from Harvard where he had studiously read everything he could find except the books assigned by his instructors—Dennie defiantly, perhaps artfully, for the flattery must have been irresistible, addressed his prospectus of *The Port Folio* to one class of readers only. It was, in large type, "Submitted to Men of Affluence, Men of Liberality, and Men of Letters." The brilliant literary weekly that he put out was a success from its first issue of January 3, 1801. Most of that first issue was written by two men, John Quincy Adams and the colorful Joseph Dennie himself.

Adams' *Tour Through Silesia,* afterward printed as a book in two volumes, ran through most of 1801. The first *Port Folio* also carried Adams' version of the thirteenth satire of Juvenal. Dennie's essays began in the first number with the first of a series called "An Author's Evenings" (from the shop of Messrs. Colon and Spondee); these were reviews and criticism with lengthy selections culled from his wide reading. During 1801 he began again with his "Lay Preacher" essays and with another series, "The Farrago," all satirical and witty essays modeled after Addison and Goldsmith. There was a theatrical review but no political article in the first issue of *The Port Folio.* There were many political articles in succeeding numbers.

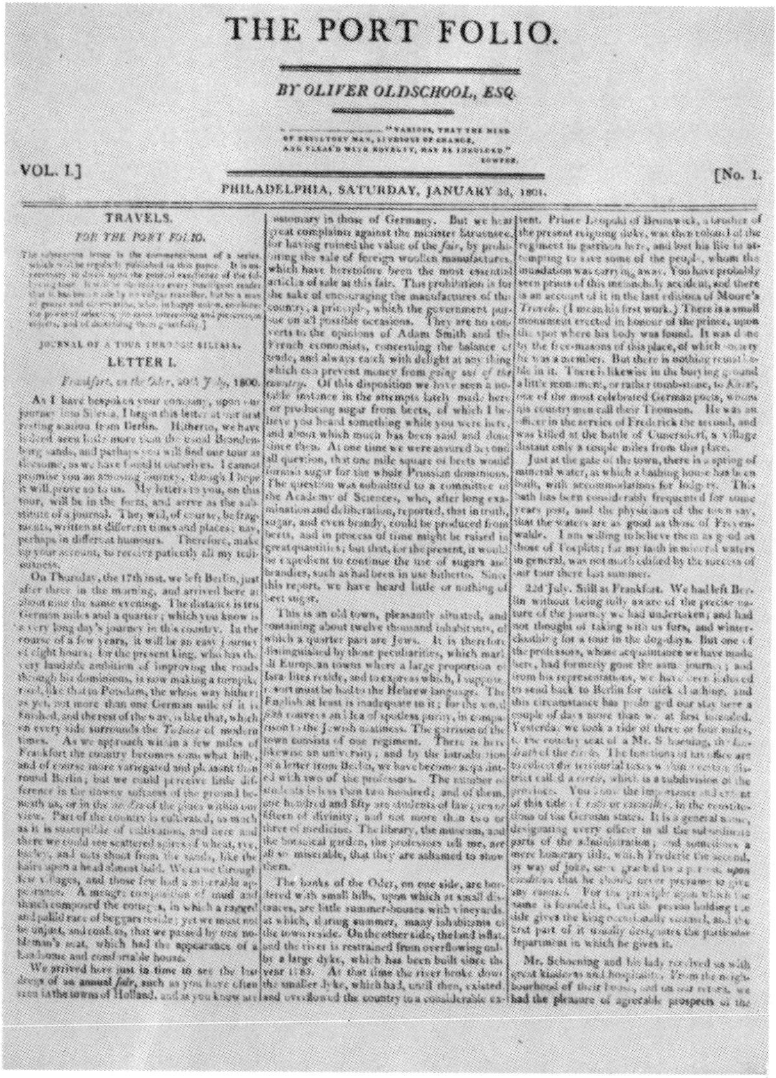

THE PORT FOLIO.

BY OLIVER OLDSCHOOL, ESQ.

——— "VARIOUS, THAT THE MIND
OF DESULTORY MAN, STUDIOUS OF CHANGE,
AND PLEAS'D WITH NOVELTY, MAY BE INDULGED."
COWPER.

VOL. I.] PHILADELPHIA, SATURDAY, JANUARY 3d, 1801. [No. 1.

TRAVELS.

FOR THE PORT FOLIO.

[The subsequent letter is the commencement of a series, which will be regularly published in this paper. It is unnecessary to dwell upon the general excellence of the following tour. It will be obvious to every intelligent reader that it has been made by no vulgar traveller, but by a man of genius and observation, who, in happy union, combines the power of selecting the most interesting and picturesque objects, and of describing them gracefully.]

JOURNAL OF A TOUR THROUGH SILESIA.

LETTER I.

Frankfort, on the Oder, 20th July, 1800.

As I have bespoken your company, upon our journey into Silesia, I begin this letter at our first resting station from Berlin. Hitherto, we have indeed seen little more than the usual Brandenburg sands, and perhaps you will find our tour as tiresome, as we have found it ourselves. I cannot promise you an amusing journey, though I hope it will prove so to us. My letters to you, on this tour, will be in the form, and serve as the substitute of a journal. They will, of course, be fragments, written at different times and places; nay, perhaps in different humours. Therefore, make up your account, to receive patiently all my tediousness.

On Thursday, the 17th inst. we left Berlin, just after three in the morning, and arrived here at about nine the same evening. The distance is ten German miles and a quarter; which you know is a very long day's journey in this country. In the course of a few years, it will be an easy journey of eight hours; for the present king, who has the very laudable ambition of improving the roads through his dominions, is now making a turnpike road, like that to Potsdam, the whole way hither; as yet, not more than one German mile of it is finished, and the rest of the way, is like that, which on every side surrounds the *Tadmor* of modern times. As we approach within a few miles of Frankfort the country becomes somewhat hilly, and of course more variegated and pleasant than round Berlin; but we could perceive little difference in the downy softness of the ground beneath us, or in the *verdure* of the pines within our view. Part of the country is cultivated, as much as it is susceptible of cultivation, and here and there we could see scattered spires of wheat, rye, barley, and oats shoot from the sands, like the hairs upon a head almost bald. We came through few villages, and those few had a miserable appearance. A meagre composition of mud and thatch composed the cottages, in which a ragged and pallid race of beggars reside; yet we must not be unjust, and confess, that we passed by one nobleman's seat, which had the appearance of a handsome and comfortable house.

We arrived here just in time to see the last dregs of an annual *fair*, such as you have often seen in the towns of Holland, and as you know are customary in those of Germany. But we hear great complaints against the minister Struensee, for having ruined the value of the *fair*, by prohibiting the sale of foreign woollen manufactures, which have heretofore been the most essential articles of sale at this fair. This prohibition is for the sake of encouraging the manufactures of the country, a principle, which the government pursue on all possible occasions. They are no converts to the opinions of Adam Smith and the French economists, concerning the balance of trade, and always catch with delight at any thing which can prevent money from *going out of the country*. Of this disposition we have seen a notable instance in the attempts lately made here for producing sugar from beets, of which I believe you heard something while you were here, and about which much has been said and done since then. At one time we were assured beyond all question, that one mile square of beets would furnish sugar for the whole Prussian dominions. The question was submitted to a committee of the Academy of Sciences, who, after long examination and deliberation, reported, that in truth, sugar, and even brandy, could be produced from beets, and in process of time might be raised in great quantities; but that, for the present, it would be expedient to continue the use of sugars and brandies, such as had been in use hitherto. Since this report, we have heard little or nothing of beet sugar.

This is an old town, pleasantly situated, and containing about twelve thousand inhabitants, of which a quarter part are Jews. It is therefore distinguished by those peculiarities, which mark all European towns where a large proportion of Israelites reside, and to express which, I suppose, resort must be had to the Hebrew language. The English at least is inadequate to it; for the word *filth* conveys an idea of spotless purity, in comparison to the Jewish neatness. The garrison of the town consists of one regiment. There is here likewise an university; and by the introduction of a letter from Berlin, we have become acquainted with two of the professors. The number of students is less than two hundred; and of them, one hundred and fifty are students of law; ten or fifteen of divinity; and not more than two or three of medicine. The library, the museum, and the botanical garden, the professors tell me, are all so miserable, that they are ashamed to show them.

The banks of the Oder, on one side, are bordered with small hills, upon which at small distances, are little summer-houses with vineyards, at which, during summer, many inhabitants of the town reside. On the other side, the land is flat, and the river is restrained from overflowing only by a large dyke, which has been built since the year 1785. At that time the river broke down the smaller dyke, which had, until then, existed, and overflowed the country to a considerable extent. Prince Leopold of Brunswick, a brother of the present reigning duke, was then colonel of the regiment in garrison here, and lost his life in attempting to save some of the people, whom the inundation was carrying away. You have probably seen prints of this melancholy accident, and there is an account of it in the last editions of Moore's *Travels*. (I mean his first work.) There is a small monument erected in honour of the prince, upon the spot where his body was found. It was done by the free-masons of this place, of which society he was a member. But there is nothing remarkable in it. There is likewise in the burying ground a little monument, or rather tomb-stone, to *Kleist*, one of the most celebrated German poets, whom his countrymen call their Thomson. He was an officer in the service of Frederick the second, and was killed at the battle of Cunersdorf, a village distant only a couple miles from this place.

Just at the gate of the town, there is a spring of mineral water, at which a bathing house has been built, with accommodations for lodgers. This bath has been considerably frequented for some years past, and the physicians of the town say, that the waters are as good as those of Freyenwalde. I am willing to believe them as good as those of Toeplitz; for my faith in mineral waters in general, was not much edified by the success of our tour there last summer.

22d July. Still at Frankfort. We had left Berlin without being fully aware of the precise nature of the journey we had undertaken; and had not thought of taking with us furs, and winter-clothing for a tour in the dog-days. But one of the professors, whose acquaintance we have made here, had formerly gone the same journey; and from his representations, we have been induced to send back to Berlin for thick clothing, and this circumstance has prolonged our stay here a couple of days more than we at first intended. Yesterday we took a ride of three or four miles, to the country seat of a Mr. Schoening, the *Landrath* of the *circle*. The functions of his office are to collect the territorial taxes within a certain district called a *circle*, which is a subdivision of the province. You know the importance and extent of this title of *rath* or *councillor*, in the constitutions of the German states. It is a general name, designating every officer in all the subordinate parts of the administration; and sometimes a mere honorary title, which Frederic the second, by way of joke, once granted to a person, upon *condition* that he should never presume to give any *counsel*. For the principle upon which the name is founded is, that the person holding the title gives the king occasionally counsel, and the first part of it usually designates the particular department in which he gives it.

Mr. Schoening and his lady received us with great kindness and hospitality. From the neighbourhood of their house, and on our return, we had the pleasure of agreeable prospects of the

The first issue of *The Port Folio*, the finest American magazine of the early nineteenth century, opened with "Journal of a Tour Through Silesia," by John Quincy Adams.

Dennie stated that one reason for founding his magazine was to combat revolutionary doctrines. He believed and said that the separation of the Colonies from England was a historical mistake. He was soon attacking President Jefferson, especially his literary pretensions, in almost every issue. The Declaration of Independence, he wrote, was filled with mistakes of grammar and diction. It was a "false and flatulent and foolish paper." In April, 1803, he declared in *The Port Folio* that democratic government itself was a mistake. Out of it could come only "civil war, desolation, and anarchy." As a result of this attack, Dennie was indicted on July 4 of the same year for seditious libel. Brilliantly defended by Joseph Hopkinson, he was acquitted in December, and Oliver Oldschool, Esq., as Dennie editorially called himself, went on with his attack. Most things American were bad; all things English were good. Next to Jefferson he seems most to have detested Noah Webster, whose effrontery in Americanizing the English language in his dictionary he saw as blasphemous—". . . let then the projected volume of *foul and unclean* things bear his own Christian name and be called NOAH'S ARK!" Dennie would have none of the *Republic* of letters. It was the *Monarchy* of letters to Oliver Oldschool, Esq. For their apparent lack of convictions, he would have despised many modern editors.

But there was more to this editor and more to his magazine than the prejudices and idiosyncrasies of Joseph Dennie. He made *The Port Folio* a force in American letters, an urbane magazine for an urbane and literate audience. He abused the freedom of the press in his political articles, but, as John Quincy Adams said in his epitaph, which is all but illegible now on Dennie's monument in the churchyard of St. Peter's in Philadelphia, "he contributed to chasten the morals, and to refine the taste of this nation." He made the magazine in this country the equal of similar productions in England at the time, and educated the most cultured section of the American public to look to magazines for the best writing of the day. He made the magazine an educational as well as a political force, gave it form, finish, variety, and literary excellence.

The Port Folio, well printed, well leaded, as readable and entertaining today as when its Saturday numbers appeared, published essays, travel articles, scholarly criticism of classical, English, and American writing, biographies of English authors and statesmen and of eminent Americans, much original poetry, and letters to Mr. Oldschool. At the bottom of the third column on page eight of each of the weekly eight-page issues the epigram was a regular feature,[1] and there were jokes, often risqué, in most numbers. The whole was well issued and well edited.

Dennie's own ironic style set the tone of his magazine. His "Lay Preacher" essay in the third number of 1801 was "A Lesson for Loungers." In it, writing as though he lived in Queen Anne's London, he advised: "If a coffee room be crowded, endeavour to fix yourself in a corner at the table, in such a manner that you prevent anyone from passing you to get seated on any other part of the bench; or, if that cannot conveniently be done, put one or both your legs, at full length upon the seat, lean back, whistle or pick your teeth. This will shew your consequence."

In 1804, there was much by and about Tom Moore who, visiting the United States after leaving his Bermuda post as Admiralty registrar, spent much time with Dennie and his coterie of Philadelphia wits. There was also one issue in which a black rule bordered every column on every page. "This paper,"

[1] Typical:

"Says a parson to Tipsey, 'I'm shocked at the sight,
So often your spirits are sinking;
In riot and folly so much you delight,
And still take such pleasure in drinking.'

"Says Tipsey to Parson, 'I'll puzzle you quick,
Of this paradox shew me the merits;
Gin now is so *cheap*, that though sometimes I'm sick,
I'm gayest when full of *low spirits.*' "

And, from the issue of March 13, 1802: "A gentleman, informed by a bill on a window of a house that *apartments were to let,* knocked at the door, and, attended by a pretty female took a survey of the premises. Pray, my dear, said he smiling, are you to be *let* with the lodgings?—No, replied the Fille de Chambre with vivacity, but I am to be *let alone.*"

read a notice on the front page, "is consecrated to the Memorial of Alexander Hamilton." In it Dennie, the Federalist, published all the Burr-Hamilton correspondence which led to the Weehawken duel, the full text of the funeral oration at Trinity Church in New York, a letter from Bishop Benjamin Moore, and all of the various newspaper tributes to Hamilton.

Contributions to *The Port Folio* were signed only with such pseudonyms as Amicus, Crito, Lucius Crassus, or with initials. Anonymity was the common magazine practice; the concept of the "name" writer had not yet arrived. Most of Dennie's contributors were members of the convivial Tuesday Club. These were university graduates, wits, Federalists, all of them men with literary tastes and abilities who met most often at the home of Joseph Hopkinson, author of "Hail Columbia," at Fourth and Chestnut Streets in Philadelphia. Prominent in the group, which Albert H. Smyth lists in *The Philadelphia Magazines and Their Contributors, 1741–1850,* were Charles Brockden Brown, Hopkinson, Thomas Cadwalader, Richard Rush, Philip Hamilton, Samuel Ewing, John Dorsey, Charles J. Ingersoll, William Meredith, and Thomas I. Wharton. Out-of-town contributors in Boston and New York included Royall Tyler, J. S. J. Gardner, Condy Raquet, Alexander Wilson, Thomas Fessenden, and William Dunlap, portrait painter, novelist, playwright, and biographer of Charles Brockden Brown.

But it was the lively Dennie himself who gave the weekly issue of *The Port Folio* from 1801 to 1809 its characteristic dash and brightness. His "To Readers and Correspondents" was always brisk and to the point. "We must earnestly caution our correspondents against *prolixity* a *deadly* sin. It is for the *interest* of all who wish to contribute to the Port Folio to be as *succinct* and *brief* as possible," he wrote in an early issue. "Write it in English" was repeated Dennie advice. Using the technique of the modern semanticist, he translated the Constitution into what he considered clear, logical English. In May, 1801, Oliver Oldschool took his public to task for its lack of interest in political affairs. "We regret that we have had such imperfect assistance in the *political* department of the *Port*

Folio. We had confidently expected *more* from *principals*. It is to be deplored that such supineness continues, that such a political palsy deadens the better half of our countrymen."

Dennie had started with a large circulation of 2,000. It mounted steadily, but in December, 1803, he was forced to write the type of appeal that all editors had to use in the days before advertising, when magazines were entirely dependent upon their income from subscriptions to continue publishing:

To Subscribers

In the course of the current and ensuing month every journalist has a right to remind his readers, that his claims must be cancelled. The Editor of the Port Folio has, for three years, conducted the miscellany, with an assiduity of labor, which deserves its stipulated price, and with a liberality of expense for the establishment that calls for a candid consideration. For some time his subscription list has been augmenting, and the circulation of his paper widens every week. But he is obliged to add that applications for his journal are, at some seasons, more frequent than payments, and that, though many are considerate and punctual, others are negligent.

The Port Folio, the best American magazine of its time and fascinating to read now, became a quieter monthly in 1809. Dennie died in 1812 at the age of forty-four. One of his assistants, Nicholas Biddle, later president of the Bank of the United States, succeeded him and made the magazine more and more a literary review. Politics were excluded now, and *The Port Folio* became patriotic in tone during the War of 1812. Biddle, who remained as editor only two years, was succeeded by others, and *The Port Folio* lasted until 1827.

The truth of Ralph Waldo Emerson's remark that an institution is but the lengthened shadow of a man is well illustrated by Joseph Dennie and *The Port Folio,* and throughout the whole story of American magazines. There is a corollary. A strong editor, even a strongly wrongheaded editor, has usually meant a strong and influential magazine; whereas intelligent editors of moderate views and no firm opinions have often produced colorless and comparatively ineffective magazines. Magazines have sickened and declined, sometimes disappeared, when an editor with a strongly marked character has been succeeded by someone as capable but not as distinct. *The Atlantic Monthly* has had a remarkable succession of able editors, but the magazine assumed a different character under such editors as James Russell Lowell, James T. Fields, William Dean Howells, Thomas Bailey Aldrich, Horace Scudder, Bliss Perry, and Ellery Sedgwick. Propriety and dullness almost accomplished its extinction at the beginning of this century. Such disparate individuals and editors as Sarah Josepha Hale of *Godey's,* S. S. McClure of *McClure's,* Harold Ross of *The New Yorker,* DeWitt Wallace of *The Reader's Digest,* and Henry Luce of *Time* and *Life* are other cases in point.

There were other magazines and magazine editors contemporary with Joseph Dennie and his *Port Folio.* One, edited by a *Port Folio* contributor, is of interest for the stature of its editor and for his distinctive conception of what a magazine should be.

Charles Brockden Brown is always called the first professional man of letters in America, as he was the first to devote himself wholly to writing as a profession. Born in Philadelphia in 1771, he had his first writing published in the *Columbian Magazine* in August, 1789. He studied law, but went to New York where he undertook the then risky experiment of earning his living by authorship. In rapid succession he produced five sentimental melodramas, important now because their author used American scenes and characters for the first time in native American fiction. The novels were *Wieland* (1798), *Arthur Mervyn* (1799), *Ormond* (1799), *Edgar Huntley* (1799), and *Clara Howard* (1801). In 1803, Brown returned to Philadelphia where he founded the *Literary Magazine and American Register.*

In the very long prospectus which filled the first three pages of this magazine's first issue, September, 1803, Brown said that he had gathered a group of friends who possessed literary talents and that, as editor, "my province shall be to hold the mirror up so as to assemble all their wit in its verge, and reflect them on the public in such manner as to warm and enlighten." Many magazines, he knew, had been started, had run for a number of issues, then had disappeared. This was not always because of lack of public interest and support. ". . . The public is always eager to encourage one who devotes himself to their rational amusement." Magazines disappeared usually because "those who managed the publication have commonly either changed their principles, remitted their zeal, or voluntarily relinquished their trade, or last of all, and like other men, have died."

Enlightenment and rational amusement were, then, prime purposes of a magazine. The magazine would also offer varied fare. The editor, Brown wrote, "will not forget that a work which solicits the attention of many readers, must build its claim on the variety as well as copiousness of its contents." The *Literary Magazine and American Register* would speculate and comment on foreign affairs, merely record domestic matters. It would contain materials from the newest foreign publications, but it would pay particular attention to American writing. "As to domestic publications, besides extracting from them anything serviceable to the public, he will give a critical account of them, and in this respect make his work an American Review, in which the history of our native literature shall be carefully detailed." Magazines were intent, from the founding of the United States, on developing and encouraging a native literature. Brown thus echoed a general magazine editorial concept. He was also careful to point out one significant distinction between the magazine and the newspaper. Each month he would give foreign and domestic news, but in magazine not in newspaper fashion. The *Literary Magazine and American Register* would handle "in a precise and systematic order, that intelligence which the common newspapers communicate in a vague and indiscriminate way." The magazine, he realized, has the time to judge and to comment on the news.

On the alert for promising young writers, Brown called on Washington Irving, who was running his Letters by "Jonathan Oldstyle, Gent." in the New York *Morning Chronicle* of which his older brother, Peter Irving, was editor, and asked him to write for the *Register*. Irving himself became editor of a Philadelphia magazine, the *Select Review*, in 1812. He changed its name to the *Analectic* and worked hard at his job for a year, then quit. A writer, he disliked editing.

The Port Folio was still appearing, but Brown's *Literary Magazine and American Register* had disappeared and a flood of new weekly and monthly magazines had been started when, on August 4, 1821, the first issue of *The Saturday Evening Post* was published in the office once occupied by Benjamin Franklin behind 53 Market Street, Philadelphia. The paper, edited by Thomas Cottrell Clarke and printed once a week on "a large royal sheet" folded to make four pages, was published by Atkinson & Alexander on Market Street "four doors below Second, where Subscriptions and Advertisements will be thankfully received." The cost of a year's subscription was a modest two dollars—in contrast to six dollars for *The Port Folio*—but the editors prudently made a condition that half the sum was payable in advance.

The issues of *The Saturday Evening Post* in 1821 contained essays, poetry, obituaries, a "Moral and Religious Column," a department called "The Ladies' Friend" which offered verse and articles deemed particularly appropriate to feminine taste, marine intelligence, editorials, an "Almanack," and news. The first issues ran two columns of short advertisements on the front page, two columns on the back, and a scattering of advertisements and notices on the inside pages. By 1822 poetry, both moral and sentimental, had replaced the advertisements on the front page, while page four was almost solid advertising. By the 1830's, *The Saturday Evening Post* was a larger and better periodical, more magazine and less newspaper, though the legend spread as a banner underneath the logotype read: "A Family Newspaper, Devoted to Literature, Morality, Science, News, Agriculture and Amusement."[2] It was still a

[2] By 1848, when it was one of the strongest weeklies of the day, *The Saturday Evening Post* described itself as "Neutral in Politics; Devoted to General News, Literature, Science, Morality, Agriculture, and Amusement." During the year a different order of importance was recognized; morality came first and

four-page sheet, but seven columns wide and illustrated. The subscription price in 1833 was "$2.50, if paid during the year; $2.00 if paid in advance; $3.00 if not paid during the year."

The *Post* quickly became, and remained for the next forty years, one of the most important weeklies in the United States. The issue of April 2, 1836, carried one of William Cullen Bryant's poems, "The Legend," on the front page. Edgar Allan Poe wrote his famous "The Black Cat" for its pages. Harriet Beecher Stowe, James Fenimore Cooper, Bayard Taylor, N. P. Willis, Emerson, James Russell Lowell, and Hawthorne were *Post* authors. Circulation before the Civil War mounted to an impressive 90,000. Other literary journals, *The Saturday News,* the *Saturday Bulletin,* and the *Saturday Chronicle,* were merged with the magazine. Among its early editors were Benjamin Mathias, Charles J. Peterson, Rufus W. Griswold,[3] H. Hastings Weld, and Henry Peterson.

Only three years after appearance of *The Saturday Evening Post,* magazines had become so numerous in the United States that a writer in the *Cincinnati Literary Gazette* was moved to express his amazement in verse:

"This is the age of Magazines
 Even Skeptics must confess it:
Where is the town of much renown
 That has not one to bless it?"

Magazines were numerous, and they were read. Emanating from Philadelphia, until past the middle of the century the un-

---

business was included. Beginning with the issue of March 4, 1848, the legend read: "Devoted to Morality, Pure Literature, Foreign and Domestic News, Agriculture, The Commercial Interests, Science, Art and Amusement." By 1874 the *Post* was simply "The Great Family Paper for Half a Century." In 1889, the magazine described itself as "The Great Pioneer Family Paper of America."

[3] Rufus Griswold was the most important of these men. He became editor, 1842–1843, of the splendid *Graham's Magazine,* of which Charles J. Peterson and Poe had also been editors. He later edited the *International Magazine* in New York which, in 1852, was merged into *Harper's Magazine.* His greatest service to American letters was in compiling and editing the first important anthologies of American writing: *Poets and Poetry of America* (1842) and *The Prose Writers of America* (1847). Charles Peterson in 1842 founded, in imitation of *Godey's,* the very popular *Peterson's Magazine* which lasted until 1898.

disputed "magazine city," they were read eagerly by a busy people concerned necessarily with the practical problems of agriculture, commerce, industry, and geographical expansion. Readers looked to magazines for information, for news and intelligent comment on the news, for guidance in their political thinking, and for entertainment.

The Port Folio, intellectual, satirical, almost wholly literary and political in content, appealed to the educated and cultured. The less artistic *Saturday Evening Post* and the other weeklies and monthlies of its kind undertook and accomplished a different service for a far wider audience. Their pages were devoted to a wide range of subjects—to any and every subject conceivably of interest to their readers, and almost everything was. Unlike the intellectual reviews, their purpose was not critical but educational in the widest sense. They popularized art and literature, instructed in matters of morals, manners, and taste. There were no public libraries in the United States of the 1820's and 1830's. The country's few colleges along the Eastern seaboard were for the very few. Even ordinary schooling, when obtainable, was limited in scope. Magazines served as schools and mentors, as instructors and advisers, for those who could obtain and read a copy.

News and analysis of the news were, as they are today, important features of these magazines. Newspapers were local only in their circulation. Books, less common then than now, were read by comparatively few. The magazine had become, as the *Pennsylvania Gazette* originally described itself, the "universal instructor."

Europe was experiencing in the 1820's the liberal impulses that were to result in England in the Reform Bill of 1832. Greece was struggling toward nationalism. In Germany and the Italian Peninsula were already apparent the stirrings of liberal thought that were to culminate in the revolutions of 1848. The Industrial Revolution was beginning to make itself felt in England. In English poetry this was the Romantic period of Wordsworth—disapproved by Joseph Dennie for his revolutionary and democratic tastes, but admired as a poet—

Coleridge, Byron, Shelley, and Keats. America's was still a primarily agrarian economy, with commerce brisk but industry hardly beginning to expand toward a dominant position. Rough Jacksonian democracy displaced aristocratic federalism and the milder Jeffersonian democracy when Andrew Jackson became President in 1828.

All the ferment in Europe, all the events and tendencies in political, social, and economic life in the early nationalistic period of the United States, were reported directly to its people in the magazines. The magazines did more. Editors of both the intellectual and the popular magazines resented the imputations, more often the loud declarations, of European, particularly English, writers and travelers that the United States was a barbaric region whose people were devoid of culture, taste, intelligence, or any semblance of good manners. Determined to give the lie to such English magazine writers as Sidney Smith, who had expressed his scorn of American writing, and to such travelers in the United States as Mrs. Frances Trollope whose *Domestic Manners of the Americans* (1832) was merely the most notorious of many such attacks, they filled their magazines with didactic and sentimental verse[4] and with essays designed to improve the taste of their readers as well as to inculcate approved morals and manners.

"Neutral in politics" as was *The Saturday Evening Post,* it and its contemporaries could leave factional disputes to the newspapers while they carried out their more fundamental informational and educational programs. They could offer, too, in quantity and quality, what the newspaper medium could not supply—entertainment. They were the great and, for a great part of the population, the sole source of literate entertainment. Their verse, humor, lighter essays, and tales were directed at the little leisure that Americans had in the first part of the nineteenth century. It was because of these accomplishments that the "dean of American magazine editors," Henry Mills Alden, editor of *Harper's Magazine* from 1869 to 1919,

[4] It must be remembered that poetry was the popular literary form. The novel was still fairly new. The short story had not been developed.

could say: "Periodical literature has done more for the American people than for any other. It had a considerable development before there was an American literature, meeting the intellectual needs of a sturdy race which, while its energies were engaged in the solution of difficult practical problems . . . was yet intelligent and keenly curious." [5]

By the mid-1830's magazines were a strong force in American life. A prolific contributor of verse, short stories, and literary criticism to many magazines, Edgar Allan Poe was the very type of the new magazine journalist. At various times he served in editorial capacities on *The Southern Literary Messenger* in Richmond, Burton's *Gentleman's Magazine* and *Graham's Magazine* in Philadelphia, and the *New-York Mirror* and the *Broadway Journal* in New York. He cherished plans for new magazines—*The Penn Magazine* and later *The Stylus*—which never materialized. In *Marginalia,* No. XXV, he wrote:

> The whole tendency of the age is Magazineward. The magazine in the end will be the most influential of all departments of letters. . . . In a few years its importance will be found to have increased in geometrical ratio.
>
> We now demand the light artillery of the intellect; we need the curt, the condensed, the readily diffused—in place of the verbose, the detailed, the voluminous, the inaccessible. On the other hand, the lightness of the artillery should not degenerate into pop-gunnery—by which term we may designate the character of the greater portion of the newspaper press—their sole legitimate object being the discussion of ephemeral matters in an ephemeral way.[6]

[5] Henry Mills Alden, *Magazine Writing and the New Literature* (New York: Harper & Bros., 1908), p. 49.

[6] Another acute if seldom charitable observer was less favorably impressed. Mother of the English novelist Anthony Trollope, Mrs. Frances Trollope was exiled in the United States from 1827 to 1830 when her husband ran a shop in Cincinnati. In *Domestic Manners of the Americans,* 1832, she deplored American bad taste and knew one reason for it. "The immense exhalation of periodical trash, which penetrates into every cot and corner of the country, and which is greedily sucked in by all ranks, is unquestionably one great cause of its inferiority."

Chapter 4

Early General Magazines as a Literary and Crusading Force

Charles Francis Adams, son of John Quincy Adams, graduated from Harvard, spent three years in Washington while his father was President, studied law in the Boston office of Daniel Webster, then turned to writing. Like his father, he wrote for the magazines, publishing articles on American history in *The North American Review*. He later edited the ten-volume *Works of John Adams,* wrote a sound biography of his grandfather, and edited the unique letters of his unique grandmother, Abigail Adams, and the very important *Memoirs of John Quincy Adams*. He published other writing, but his greatest service was as a capable minister to Great Britain during the Civil War, when his diplomacy prevented recognition of the South by England and stopped Britain's supplying ironclad vessels to the South. One son, Henry Adams, served as his secretary in London. Another son, three years older, a second Charles Francis Adams, served as colonel of a regiment of Negro cavalry and emerged from the war a brevet brigadier general. When at the close of the war the two young Adamses looked about for a place to start their war-interrupted careers, it was to magazines that both turned, and they turned first to the same *North American Review* which had published their father's first efforts.

John Gorham Palfrey, its editor, suggested that Henry Adams write for the *North American* an article on Captain John

Smith's relations with Pocahontas. It appeared in 1867, and the future historian of the administrations of Jefferson and Madison, the autobiographer whose *Education of Henry Adams* has become an American classic, was pleased because "for fifty years *The North American Review* had been the stage coach which carried literary Bostonians to such distinctions as they had achieved." He was soon writing more *North American* articles and articles for the powerful English magazines. Within a few years Henry Adams became the editor of the *North American*, which he was proud to be able to describe as "the first literary power in America."

Henry's brother, Charles Francis Adams, was also successful in his own magazine venture. After separation from the army, he considered various occupations, selected what he thought the most important activity of his day, and started to make his place in it by writing an article on railroads for the *North American*. He wrote more articles on railroads, and in July, 1869, his "Chapter of Erie" appeared in the *North American*. That same month, largely because of his magazine articles, the Massachusetts Railroad Commission was formed, and he was appointed one of the commissioners, later its chairman. The Massachusetts Commission, as Henry Cabot Lodge points out in the Memorial Address prefixed to Charles Francis Adams' *Autobiography*, was the first effective railroad commission. It served as a model for the system of similar commissions adopted by other states and eventually culminated in the Interstate Commerce Commission.

The North American Review started the two outstanding members of the fourth generation of the Adams family on their important careers. It is indicative of the force of this magazine that two such men could use it as a vehicle for their ideas, and that the articles which one of them published in it had a deep political and economic effect at a time when direction and regulation of railroad enterprise in this country were badly needed.

The North American Review, one of the longest-lived and most distinguished of American magazines, was founded in

1815 with the deliberate purpose of achieving greater national scope than any previous American magazine. Never a popular magazine, it was largely a literary, historical, and critical review from the time of its founding until it ceased publication in 1939. Though national in editorial coverage, it was a parochial Boston-Harvard magazine in the early days of its greatness, but this was hardly a handicap when that small part of New England could provide as contributors almost all the great names in American literature. It never had a large circulation, but soon after its founding it became, and continued to be, throughout its existence, a publication of real power and influence because it was read and studied by the leading men of the country. Poets, historians, scholars, said what they had to say in the *North American*, which thus made "the best that has been said and thought" available to those who affected the thinking of their fellows.

A roster of *North American* contributors would include almost every good American writer from Bryant, Longfellow, Emerson, and Irving through Mark Twain; historians such as Parkman, Motley, and Prescott; critics from E. P. Whipple to H. G. Wells; such novelists as Henry James and William Dean Howells; public men from John Adams himself, who wrote for the *North American* in 1817, to Theodore Roosevelt and Charles G. Dawes. Editors of the *North American* included William Tudor, the first editor, who was assisted by Edward Tyrell Channing and Richard Henry Dana; Jared Sparks, Edward Everett, James Russell Lowell, Charles Eliot Norton, Henry Adams (1870–1877), Henry Cabot Lodge, and Colonel George Harvey.

A major purpose of William Tudor, and one that prevailed in many minds at the time, was to free the United States of literary dependence on England. During its best years, or until about 1878 when the magazine moved to New York and tried for a brightness of a kind it never quite attained, the *North American* did perhaps more than any other magazine of its time to implement Emerson's plea for a native American literature in "The American Scholar," 1837, a Harvard Phi Beta

Kappa oration which Dr. Oliver Wendell Holmes described as our "Intellectual Declaration of Independence."

Neither *The Knickerbocker* in New York nor *Graham's* in Philadelphia was started with such lofty aims or written with such high intents. Both were meant primarily to be readable, and they were. They were addressed not to the intelligentsia but to the entire literate public. They were bright, alert, diversified, and *Graham's* in particular pointed the direction that general popular magazines were to take.

The Knickerbocker, as its name indicates, was peculiarly of New York, and a list of its leading contributors emphasizes that it was essentially a New York magazine. As the *North American* was doing for New England and the *Atlantic* was to do later, it brought to an appreciative public the best writers of what is now generally called the Knickerbocker school. There were occasional contributors from New England, but Irving, Cooper, Paulding, Halleck, Sands, Verplanck, were its characteristic writers. Charles Fenno Hoffman was the first editor of the *Knickerbocker* when it was founded in 1833. Its most famous and its best editor was the genial Lewis Gaylord Clark. Through his Philadelphia brother, Willis Gaylord Clark, such Philadelphia writers as Richard Rush, William Dunlap, and William E. Burton were brought into the *Knickerbocker* fold. The most prominent of the New England contributors were Hawthorne, Whittier, Holmes, and Longfellow. One Clark innovation marked the extension of the magazines' field of interest. In 1846 *The Knickerbocker* ran serially Francis Parkman's *The Oregon Trail.* Clark published other western writers and western copy, western humor, a series by H. R. Schoolcraft on the Lake Superior region, and stories of the West, including some by the incredible Ned Buntline.[1]

Graham's Magazine was in oblique fashion an offshoot of *The Saturday Evening Post.* Samuel C. Atkinson and Charles

[1] Ned Buntline, whose real name was Edward Zane Carroll Judson, hunted and trapped in the Far West, was a founder of the Know-Nothing party, the leader of the Astor Place riots against the British actor Macready in 1849, and impressario for Buffalo Bill. One of the inventors of the dime novel, he wrote some 400 of them.

Alexander in 1826 began to publish from the *Post* offices a monthly magazine called the *Casket*. Some of the stories in its early issues were merely reprinted from the *Post*. In 1839 George R. Graham of the *Post* bought the *Casket*, combined it with Burton's *Gentleman's Magazine*, which he bought the same year, and issued the first *Graham's Lady's and Gentleman's Magazine* in 1840, when he also became part owner of the *Post*.

Graham hired good editors. At various times his staff included Edgar Allan Poe, Rufus Wilmot Griswold, and Bayard Taylor in addition to those already mentioned. He made it his practice to pay contributors well and in this way obtained some of the best works of Longfellow, Lowell, Poe, Bryant, Cooper, R. H. Dana, J. K. Paulding, and other "name" writers. Where magazine contributions had been anonymous in the earlier magazines, and the ultra-conservative periodicals like the *North American* were not printing authors' names until late in the nineteenth century, Graham in his magazine inaugurated today's practice of advertising the names of famous writers on the front cover.

Graham made another important departure in magazine publication by stressing the use of illustrations. By employing John Sartain [2] to work exclusively for *Graham's* he made pictorial illustration a distinctive feature of American magazines. Magazines had carried a few illustrations before this time, but often these were merely reprints from plates already used in other publications. A Sartain mezzotint and a fashion plate—published in competition with those already being issued by *Godey's Lady's Book*—appeared in every issue of *Graham's* and other engravers brought their work to *Graham's*. It was these illustrations which were in large part responsible for the popularity and wide circulation which *Graham's* achieved.

[2] London-born John Sartain was one of the best-known painters and engravers of his time. After the failure of Graham in 1848, he purchased the *Union Magazine* and established *Sartain's Union Magazine of Literature and Art* in Philadelphia. It ran only until 1852, but published notable writing, including Thoreau's *Ktaadn* and Poe's "The Bells," and his important critical writing, "The Poetic Principle."

Graham's was notable for its pioneer use of fine illustrations. This Sartain engraving after Landseer's "Return from Hawking," appeared in April, 1842.

Still another reason for the success of *Graham's* was the appeal of its astute publisher to women readers. The fashion plates and other illustrations of domestic scenes were part of this appeal. So were the sentimental love stories which *Graham's* ran. It published material from the pens of well-known women writers of the time: Mrs. Seba Smith, Mrs. Frances Osgood, Mrs. Ann Stephens, and others. There was, of course, the poetry of Mrs. Lydia Huntley Sigourney; the sentimental poetry of the omnipresent Mrs. Sigourney appeared in almost every magazine of the mid-nineteenth century. These features, though some of them disgusted Poe, brought *Graham's* its feminine audience. Its short stories, particularly those of Poe, its criticism by Griswold and Poe, its essays by Nathaniel Parker Willis, Bayard Taylor, and similar writers, its verse by the established poets of the day, gave the magazine substance and quality. By 1842, Graham could claim a circulation of 40,000, no mean circulation when the population of the entire country was only 17,000,000, when facilities for shipping magazines were inadequate, and when the price of a magazine was a much larger part of a subscriber's income than it is today.

The January, 1842, issue of *Graham's Lady and Gentleman's Magazine,* as its title read in that year, was a typical *Graham's,* handsomely printed and illustrated. Its contents were varied, interesting, and highly readable. The hand-colored fashion plate with which each issue began was followed by a beautiful Sartain engraving, "The Shepherd's Love," as the illustration for a story by R. H. Dana. There were also, in order, "Goblet of Life" by Longfellow, a sonnet by Thomas Noon Talfourd, and "Highland Beauty," a story in camp by "Oliver Oldfellow," with an engraving of the Scottish beauty herself by E. T. Parris. There were pages more of poetry by Park Benjamin, Lowell, Louis Fitzgerald Tasistro, George Morris, Lydia H. Sigourney, and "Lines Written on a Portrait of William Henry Harrison" by Mrs. Amelia B. Welby. Stories and prose sketches appeared in profusion: "The Snow Storm," by Jeremy Short, Esq.; "Dreams of Land and Sea" by Dr. Reynell Coats; "The False Ladye" by "The Author of 'The Britishers,'

'Cromwell,' Etc."; a nautical story, "Harry Cavendish," by "The Author of 'Cruising in the Last War,' 'The Reefer of '76,' Etc., Etc."; and "Cousin Agatha" by Mrs. Emma C. Embury.

The most entertaining feature article in this issue was "An Appendix of Autographs" by Poe. In it Poe analyzed the signatures, reproduced in facsimile, of Charles Sprague, Cornelius Mathews, Horace Greeley, Charles Fenno Hoffman, Prosper M. Wetmore, Epes Sargent, Oliver Wendell Holmes, Ralph Waldo Emerson, and a dozen others. From the handwriting of each he deduced—quite a feat even for Poe—a sentence or two descriptive of the man's character and a sharp critical estimate of his writing. Under the reproduction of Emerson's signature—Poe's dislike of the New England writers was, of course, notorious—he wrote:

> Mr. Ralph Waldo Emerson belongs to a class of gentleman with whom we have no patience whatever—the mystics for mysticism's sake. . . . His present rôle seems to be out-Carlyling Carlyle. . . . His MS is bad, sprawling, illegible, irregular—although sufficiently bold. The latter trait may be, and no doubt is, only a portion of his general affectation.

The serial which started in this January issue was "The Daughters of Dr. Byles, A Sketch of Reality" by Miss Leslie. Ann S. Stephens contributed a short story, "The Two Dukes." Preceding five pages of well-written book reviews, evidently by Poe, who was literary editor, came another *Graham's* monthly feature, an inset of sheet music. This one was a ballad, "Thy Name Was Once a Magic Spell." It was presented as written by the Hon. Mrs. Norton and "as sung by Mr. Dempster."

In June, 1842, *Graham's* cover listed George R. Graham and Rufus W. Griswold as editors and the following, divided by sex, as "principal contributors": William Cullen Bryant, James Fenimore Cooper, R. H. Dana, Henry Wadsworth Longfellow, Charles Fenno Hoffman, Theodore S. Fay, J. H. Moncure, Mrs. Emma C. Embury, Mrs. Seba Smith, Mrs. "Mary Clavers," Mrs. E. F. Ellet, Mrs. Ann S. Stephens, Mrs. Frances Osgood. Though Lowell was not listed among the principal contributors, his poems appeared often during the year. Any magazine could well be proud of such a list of authors.

Graham's Magazine came to its end not through its own fault but because Graham invested heavily in newspaper ventures and in other speculations and lost control of the magazine in 1848. Before its demise, under other hands, in 1852, it had suffered from another cause. American magazines and, consequently, American letters all suffered by the policy of *Harper's Magazine* of reprinting English writing. As no international copyright laws were in force until 1891, it could do this with impunity, printing for an eager American audience the most popular English work almost as soon as it appeared in England.

A recurrent advertisement in *The Saturday Evening Post* at this time—similar advertisements had run in the *Post* before 1848 and were to run for many more years—was this one:

To the Ladies of the United States. It being now conceded that

GODEY'S LADY'S BOOK

Stands at the Head of American Magazines, it becomes the duty of the publisher to show what amount of reading, and how many embellishments she will receive for $3. . . . The coloring of our Fashion Plates—we say nothing of the Flowers and Cottages, costs us over

$2,000 in One Year.

To omit this is certainly a savings, but is it just to subscribers? Is it honorable? We cannot practice such a deception! . . .

The advertisement continued for another four inches of small type. Chatty, entertaining, persuasive, it extolled the beauty, the elegance, the virtue, the wonder of one of the most famous of all American magazines. It was signed, as were all such advertisements, by L. A. Godey himself.

In the opinion of Fred L. Pattee, a pioneer historian of American literature, the era of the magazine can be said to have begun with *Godey's Lady's Book* which, founded in 1830, three years before *The Knickerbocker* and ten before

Godey's Lady's Book, famous for its hand-colored fashion plates and the rest of its ornate "embellishments," deeply influenced feminine taste, dress, and manners.

Graham's, ran almost to the end of the nineteenth century. *Godey's,* like the fat and happy little man who owned it and like Mrs. Sarah Josepha Hale, the stalwart feminist from Boston, who edited it from 1837 to 1877, was marvelous. Far removed from the academic and often arid *North American* of the 1830's and 1840's, but lacking the brilliance and charm of *Graham's* or the alertness and readableness of *The Knickerbocker,* the popular *Godey's Lady's Book* under the militant Sarah Josepha Hale [3] had more real influence on American life than any of these basically superior magazines.

Though *Godey's* was directed entirely to women, *Graham's* and many lesser magazines imitated many of its features. *Godey's* became an American institution in the nineteenth century It affected the manners, morals, tastes, fashions in clothes, homes, and diet of generations of American readers. It did much to form the American woman's idea of what she was like, how she should act, and how she should insist that she be treated. *Godey's* had no interest in political matters or in intellectual subjects. It published nothing of either. It published Emerson, Longfellow, Hawthorne, Simms, and some of Poe's critical writing, but their contributions were not the most important *Godey's* features. T. S. Arthur [4] was a more characteristic *Godey's* writer than Hawthorne. More characteristic than even Arthur were the admired women writers of the day! Mrs. Sigourney, Miss Leslie, Mrs. Stephens, Mrs. Seba Smith, Harriet Beecher Stowe, and hordes of other women writers whose names no one would recognize today.

Fashions first, then moral stories, elegant tales of the chaste and the pure which were meant to instruct as well as to enter-

[3] In softer poetic mood she wrote an American classic:

"Mary had a little lamb;
Its fleece was white as snow;
And everywhere that Mary went
The lamb was sure to go."

[4] T. S. Arthur was a very popular magazine writer of the mid-century. He wrote in most of the Philadelphia magazines, including *The Saturday Evening Post* and *Graham's* as well as *Godey's.* Of his almost 100 moral tales and tracts only one is now generally remembered: "Ten Nights in a Barroom and What I Saw There" (1854).

tain, sentimental, didactic, and moral verse were the Hale-Godey staples. Much of the verse and more of the fiction reads like drivel now, but they must have been adored in their day, for Godey claimed a circulation of 25,000 in 1839—which might well mean 100,000 readers—and his magazine reached a circulation of 100,000 before the Civil War.

Besides fashions, shown in black-and-white line drawings and engravings as well as in the justly famous hand-colored plates, fiction, and feminine verse, *Godey's* published recipes, embroidery patterns and instructions, beauty and health hints, and elaborate illustrations—"embellishments," as both *Graham's* and *Godey's* called them. Its appeal was both practical and aesthetic. Small wonder that Louis Godey could claim in the *Post* advertisement that his magazine stood at the head of American magazines at the time. In popular acceptance and influence it did.

In 1848, T. S. Arthur, "Grace Greenwood" (Sarah Jane Lippincott), William Gilmore Simms, and Longfellow were prominent in *Godey's* along with the usual run of "female scribblers," as Hawthorne called them. "Hints on Equestrianism for the Fair Sex" ran as an illustrated feature through several issues. Every issue contained—a feature profitably rediscovered by the *Ladies' Home Journal* a half century later—complete plans and illustrations for a model cottage, together with prices of materials needed in its construction. Only one advertisement seems to have been run during the year. This was a full-page advertisement for *The Saturday Evening Post,* run perhaps as an exchange for the *Godey's* advertisement which the *Post* carried.[5]

Mrs. Hale's influence was apparent through all of *Godey's*. It was her tastes and her ideas of what was or was not proper material to be spread before the eyes of American womanhood

[5] The *Post* was described as "Always in Advance! Truly a Mammoth Sheet!" A portion of the advertisement headed "Our Contributors" read: "Our original contributors are the AUTHORS OF AMERICA. We always hold ourselves ready to purchase articles offered to us at a price proportionate to their merits. But authors whose writings are of a ridiculously exaggerated and immoral character may save themselves and us the trouble of sending them for examination. The Post is a family paper—and no article not calculated to enter the family circle can be admitted to its columns."

This advertisement for *The Saturday Evening Post,* "the very pearl of literary weeklies," ran, with minor variations, in *Godey's Lady's Book* and other magazines in the 1840's.

that determined the magazine's contents. A strong editor, she made her magazine a distinct force in American life, just as she and Godey made it a remarkable publishing success. Mrs. Hale campaigned for the recognition of women writers. Before her time women had either used masculine pseudonyms or initials or had hidden coyly behind anonymity. She had them boldly sign their names. She insisted on the simple and familiar as against the foreign and extravagant fiction. She introduced Harriet Beecher Stowe, who was still an unknown writer. She advocated educational opportunities and physical exercise for women. She argued in *Godey's* for national recognition of Thanksgiving Day until Lincoln proclaimed it on October 20, 1864.

Mrs. Hale gave up its editorship two years before her death, and Louis A. Godey died in 1878, but *Godey's Lady's Book* lasted until almost the end of the nineteenth century, vanishing finally in 1898. By 1883, when the *Ladies' Home Journal* was founded, the magazine had deteriorated. Its illustrations were crude, its makeup ugly, the quality of its paper bad. It featured "Gothic Country Houses," incredible monstrosities, instead of cottages, and there were several pages of small advertisements in the back of each issue; but despite these changes it was still functioning distinctively as *Godey's*.

Godey's, with *Graham's, Sartain's,* and *Peterson's,* maintained Philadelphia as the center of successful popular-magazine publishing. In the face of this competition from Philadelphia there was doubt in 1850 whether another popular magazine, *Harper's,* could be successfully established in New York. *Harper's Monthly,* founded in 1850, and *The Atlantic Monthly,* founded in 1857, both of them still current, were important and powerful magazines in the second half of the nineteenth century, but those which have just been discussed were the magazines which exerted the most marked influence in the mid-century. Other magazines which were distinctive and effective during the early nineteenth century include *The Southern Literary Messenger, The Dial, The United States Magazine and Democratic Review,* and *The Youth's*

Companion. The Southern Literary Messenger, founded in 1834, is important both because Poe was its editor from 1835 to 1837, and because of the literature, most of it by Southern authors, which first appeared in its pages. *The United States Magazine and Democratic Review,* a favorite magazine of Andrew Jackson's, published many of Hawthorne's early tales. *The Youth's Companion,*[6] founded in 1827, delighted millions of avid youthful readers for more than a hundred years before it disappeared in 1929.

Students of letters and of the cultural history of the United States must always look back with respect and affection on *The Dial.* Sponsored with his characteristic generosity of spirit by Ralph Waldo Emerson, named by Amos Bronson Alcott, edited during its first two years by the belligerently feministic Margaret Fuller, *The Dial* was the "little magazine" itself. It was out to reform the world nearer to the heart's desire of New England transcendentalism and the Concord group of mid-nineteenth century idealists.

The first page of the first issue of *The Dial* made the quarterly's intent clear. It was published, its editor said, in obedience to a strong current of thought and feeling "which, for a few years past, has led many sincere persons in New England to make new demands on literature, and to reprobate the rigor of our conventions of religion and education which is turning us to stone, which renounces hope, which looks only backward, which asks only such a future as the past, which suspects improvement, and holds nothing so much in horror as new views and the dreams of youth."

The Dial published some of the best of Emerson's poetry ("Forbearance," "Woodnotes," "Fate," "The Sphinx"). It gave stubbornly independent young Henry Thoreau his start as a

[6] Founded in Boston by Nathaniel Willis, father of N. P. Willis, *The Youth's Companion* was first intended to amuse and instruct children. Under Daniel Sharp Ford, who purchased it in 1857 and ran it until his death in 1899, it was made a magazine for adults as well. Harriet Beecher Stowe, Gladstone, Kipling, Tennyson, Whittier, Hardy, William Henry Huxley, James Bryce, Jules Verne, Jack London, Hamlin Garland and T. B. Aldrich all wrote for the *Companion* which at one time had the largest circulation (about half a million) of any American magazine.

poet and prose writer. Issue after issue, in blocks of fifty each time, it presented the startled world with the "Orphic Sayings" of Alcott.

Thoreau polished his verse and essays for *The Dial.* Alcott inundated it with more mystic and mystifying profundity than it could use. Margaret Fuller used it as a platform for her favorite subject of women *v.* men in the world, all her indignation on the side of the women. George Ripley, who was assistant editor, William Ellery Channing, whose sentimental raptures in verse were in most issues, Theodore Parker, Christopher Cranch, and most of the other transcendentalists all had their say—some at great length—in *The Dial.*

When George Ripley left to head the idealistic Brook Farm community and Margaret Fuller moved up in the journalistic world to Horace Greeley's *New-York Tribune,* Thoreau became assistant editor and Emerson took over the editorship himself. Margaret Fuller, who had been promised $200 a year as editor, had never been paid. The magazine's publisher, Weeks, Jordan and Company of Boston, had failed. Elizabeth Peabody began to print *The Dial* on a press behind her Boston bookshop. With only 300 subscribers, it was barely making expenses.

Thomas Carlyle scolded Emerson for wasting precious time on *The Dial* when he should be getting on with his own important writing, but Emerson persisted. He admitted that the magazine was not all that he had hoped but told Carlyle that it was serving its purposes usefully for the young writers he wished to encourage. He also admitted that *The Dial* was being viciously attacked by almost every newspaper and every other magazine. It was.

The publishers and editors of commercial periodicals seldom approve the "little magazines." Their very existence is a threat and a taunt. Such magazines are generally well written by young new writers who use them to disseminate new, strange, and therefore dangerous ideas. The contemporary press accused *The Dial* of being irreligious and irreverent. It attacked it for its mysticism and its feminism. It ridiculed the often ridiculous Bronson Alcott. It declared that *The Dial* was edited by zanies and bedlamites.

Emerson, who may well have agreed privately with some of these strictures, strengthened his magazine. He published some of his own lectures in it. He reprinted "The Natural History of Massachusetts" which had just been issued by the Zoological and Botanical Society of the Commonwealth. He printed "A Leaf from 'A Voyage to Porto Rico' " by his younger brother, Charles. He accepted a piece on Immanuel Kant as a transcendentalist by James Eliot Cabot and published extracts from *The White Lotus of the Good Law* in an essay, "The Preaching of Buddha."

Encouraged by his patron to seek wider experience in the literary and journalistic world of New York, Thoreau—who jested wryly that he was "private secretary to the President of *The Dial*"—took off for Staten Island to tutor William Emerson's children.

To the great relief of its tired editor, who said he felt as if he had been wrestling with a work of encyclopedic proportions instead of with "our poor little pamphlet," *The Dial* ceased publication with its issue for April, 1844. It was a brave venture which left its own monument.

The newspapers of the 1830's and 1840's were filled with bitter political disputes. They gave the news, but in news columns as well as in editorials they spent much of their energy and space in acrimonious party attack, shrill dispute, and violent abuse. Even the better newspapers, though in 1842 Charles Dickens exempted them from his bitter condemnation of what he saw as America's "licentious press,"[7] were continuously and rancorously involved in party controversy. Dickens seems not to have looked at magazines while he was here for six months of that year, except the *Lowell Offering*, published

[7] Though he praised some things American, Dickens in his *American Notes* (1842) attacked slavery, using a profusion of newspaper accounts of cruelty and maltreatment to prove his point, criticized American manners, emphasized the lack of cleanliness and sanitation he found here, and saw the position of letters as hopeless because of American preoccupation with trade. Dickens, who had suffered great financial loss through pirating of his work, was incensed by the lack of adequate international copyright laws.

by girl employees of the Lowell, Massachusetts, textile factories, and this he saw as a social phenomenon rather than as a magazine. Had he looked, he might have had more hope for American democracy and American culture.

The North American Review performed well the function for which it was intended. It provided a vehicle for the expression of critical literary thought and its dissemination to the comparatively restricted audience which could appreciate the ideas expressed. It provided magazine publication for poetry, fiction, travel, history, biography, economics, political science, and other scholarly writing. It compared favorably with the English quarterlies and reviews of the time.

The Knickerbocker and the Philadelphia magazines reached far wider audiences with less erudite materials and more popular writers, though often they brought to the general public the same great literary figures who appeared in the *North American* before a more select group of readers.[8] This was part of the distinct service which these magazines rendered. It was certainly a part of the educational force which they exerted.

There were general magazines now for the classes and the masses. Magazines were beginning to cover the field. Though by modern standards they were small, the circulations, particularly of *Godey's*, *Graham's* and *The Saturday Evening Post,* were large for the time, and circulation is a primary index of a periodical's strength. The contents of a magazine may give it great potential influence on the lives of the individual and the group, but with only a limited audience its actual persuasiveness may be nil.

Literary matter predominated in the magazines of the 1840's and 1850's. This was the period of the greatest development of

[8] It is of interest to note that many *North American* writers, a number of them the founders of *The Atlantic Monthly* and its chief contributors during its first greatness, were, before that, contributors to the popular magazines. Bryant, Poe, Hawthorne, and Emerson all appeared in the early *Saturday Evening Post.* Emerson, Holmes, Longfellow, Lowell, and Bryant were all published in *Graham's* and, most of them, in *Godey's.* Poe, of course, died before the *Atlantic* was founded. It is doubtful that, given his literary sentiments and his animosities, he would ever have been an *Atlantic* contributor.

a native American literature, and American magazines aided greatly in its growth. It is not improbable that the prose writings of Emerson and the verses of Longfellow have had as much to do with forming American character and ethical concepts as the more technical psychological and sociological articles in twentieth-century magazines.

These magazines also brought information, intelligent discussion, and entertainment into the home. They provided in verse and in stories what Dickens said in his *American Notes:* "The stern utilitarian joys of trade" in the United States made impossible "cheerful recreation and wholesome fancies" to a people who needed them in almost direct proportion to their immersion in the more practical problems of building a nation. The criticism of Dickens and of other travelers from Europe and its older civilization are in themselves enough to show just how vital was the service of the magazines in spreading awareness of manners, morals, taste, and a mild "culture" throughout the States. The superior illustrations in *Graham's* not only aided in the success of that impressive magazine, but also made Americans conscious of better art than they had been accustomed to see in newspapers, other magazines, or even in most books of the time. They foreshadowed the increased use of illustrations in magazines that reached full development in the late nineteenth century and appeared anew in the pictorial magazines founded in the mid-1930's.

Godey's early campaigns for education for women and for child welfare made people aware of the importance of the subjects and brought eventual results. Such campaigns were a portent of magazine crusades, such as those carried on by *Harper's Weekly,* by Edward Bok in the later *Ladies' Home Journal* of the 1890's and the early 1900's, and by the muckrakers in *McClure's Magazine,* which brought about important social reforms in American life.

Chapter 5

Emergence of the Magazine Journalist

Horace Greeley and Henry David Thoreau met in 1843 when Thoreau spent a year on Staten Island as tutor to the sons of Ralph Waldo Emerson's brother, William Emerson. Greeley, acting virtually as the younger man's literary agent, helped Thoreau to place his manuscripts with *Graham's, Putnam's,* the *Union Magazine,* and other periodicals. After Thoreau had returned to his beloved Concord the powerful editor of the *The New-York Tribune* wrote him shrewdly:

> This is the best kind of advertisement for you. Though you may write with an angel's pen yet your work will have no mercantile value unless you are known as an author. Emerson would be twice as well known if he had written for the magazines a little just to let common people know of his existence.[1]

Horace Greeley, one of the great journalistic figures of the nineteenth century, knew what he was talking about when he urged Thoreau to write for the magazines. He himself had been a magazine editor and publisher before he established the *Tribune.* In 1834, with Park Benjamin, Rufus Wilmot Griswold, and Henry J. Raymond, later editor of the *New York Times,* as his assistants, he had established the *New-Yorker,* "a

[1] Emerson had written more for the magazines than Greeley realized. He was editing *The Dial* at this time and was to help found the *Atlantic* in 1857, but Greeley evidently was talking of magazines with a wide general circulation.

weekly journal of literature, politics, statistics, and general intelligence." It was the *New-Yorker* which first gave Greeley his wide reputation. Strongly attached to his magazine, Greeley continued to edit it even while he edited the Whig papers, the *Jeffersonian* and the *Log Cabin,* for Thurlow Weed and William H. Seward. In 1841, the *New-Yorker* became the weekly edition of the *Tribune.*

For such writers as Lowell, Hawthorne, Cooper, Irving, and those others now recognized as classic American authors, the magazines provided just the service which Greeley indicated they would render for Thoreau. They offered an attractive vehicle for their work, extended and added to their reputations, and provided financial means of subsistence. Magazines were also beginning to develop a class of writers who were facile and deft, and who possessed a light touch and a sense of the dramatic and the timely that fitted the particular needs of periodical publication and matched the writing skills of the men and women themselves.

Poe invented the term "magazinist"—"magazine writer" would be a modern equivalent—to describe one of them. Almost everything Poe wrote, short stories, verse, critical articles, was written for the magazines. It was for magazines that he, with Hawthorne, developed the peculiarly American form of short fiction characterized by its conciseness, plot, and single action, a form essentially different from the earlier simple tale and later known as the short story. Rufus Wilmot Griswold, anthologist and critic, developed his distinctive editorial and literary talents for the magazines with which he was connected—the *New-Yorker, The Saturday Evening Post, Graham's,* and the others.

The writer whom Poe described as the very type of the magazinist was the exciting and romantic Nathaniel Parker Willis, a great and glamorous journalistic and literary figure in the last century. Willis was hailed as a leading American poet while still a Yale undergraduate. By the time he was twenty-three he had established in Boston his own magazine, the *American Monthly Magazine.* Before long, already known as a fluent and graceful writer of prose as well as verse, he was in New York helping Samuel Woodworth (author of "The Old Oaken Bucket") to edit the *New York Mirror.* The *Mirror* daringly sent Willis abroad as its foreign correspondent. The letters which Willis sent back to the *Mirror* during his five years of travel were compiled into *Pencillings by the Way* (1844) and made him one of the best-known American men of letters abroad. When, elegant, assured, and famous, he returned to the United States in 1840, he commanded the highest prices paid by *Godey's* and the other magazines.

Graham's paid Willis eleven dollars a page and Poe only four or five dollars. Willis in his best years is said to have had a magazine income of several thousand dollars, while his many books of verse, short stories, and travel sketches, almost all of them compilations of his magazine work, brought him additional sums. Willis, a prolific and successful magazine writer, forerunner of such other magazine correspondents as Richard Harding Davis, though his only war reporting was from Washington during the Civil War for the *Home Journal,*[2] was greatly admired in his generation both by the literati and the public. Oliver Wendell Holmes in a much-quoted passage recalled the twenty-five-year-old Willis: "young . . . and already famous . . . he was tall; his hair, of light brown color, waved in luxuriant abundance. . . . He was something between a remembrance of Count D'Orsay and an anticipation of Oscar Wilde." When Willis was in England, only the intervention of seconds prevented a duel with Captain Marryat, the nautical novelist, following a dispute caused by Willis' alleged indiscretions in some of his published magazine reports. Later he was involved in the divorce trial of the Shakespearean actor Edwin Forrest.

Bayard Taylor, an equally brilliant figure in the magazine world of the last century, got his start when in 1844 *The Saturday Evening Post* and the *United States Gazette* advanced

[2] The *Home Journal,* which Willis and George Pope Morris founded in 1846, as an elegant magazine which would be an arbiter of culture in the United States, became *Town and Country* and is still a luxury-class magazine. In 1946 it celebrated its centennial with a 350-page issue.

him money for travel letters he was to send back for publication. Taylor, who was then only nineteen, but who, like Willis, had early shown his ability as a writer, spent two years abroad. After travel in England, Scotland, Germany, France, he returned to the United States and in 1846 published his *Views A-Foot.* He became a staff member of the *New York Tribune* and, in 1849, was sent by Greeley to cover the California Gold Rush; *Eldorado* resulted in 1850. Taylor soon became the most famous American world traveler of his day, and most of the accounts of his travels in Europe, including Russia, and in Syria, Turkey, China, and Africa saw magazine publication before they were put into book form. Later Taylor, who was a facile poet as well as a writer of travel sketches and of fiction, held a number of diplomatic posts. He was minister to Germany when, still in his early fifties, he died in 1878.

Poe, Griswold, Willis, and Taylor are only examples of the best known among the host of characteristic writers developed by the advancing and developing magazines of the middle years of the last century. The competent, adequate to mediocre, magazine writers of our day are their professional descendants. The magazines were a natural outlet too for the major American writers of this period. *Godey's* and *Graham's,* as already noted, published the works of many of them. After *The Atlantic Monthly* was founded in 1857, they had still another periodical vehicle for their literary productions.

The *Atlantic* paid Thoreau $198 for his "Chesuncook," thirty-three pages at the rate of six dollars a page. It was the most money Thoreau had ever earned by publication of his writing in a magazine. Until the publication of *The Scarlet Letter* in 1850, what little income Hawthorne received outside his salary from the various political jobs obtained for him by his Bowdoin classmate Franklin Pierce came from the magazines and the Christmas annuals. His *Legends of the Province House,* for example, was first published in *The United States Magazine and Democratic Review.* This magazine, edited by the colorful John L. O'Sullivan, who had founded it in 1837, also published writings of Poe, Whitman, Bryant, Epes Sargent, and Paulding. Many of Hawthorne's other short tales appeared in the *Token,* the gift book which S. G. Goodrich published in Boston.

The close connection between the magazines and the best writers of this time is shown by the number of these writers who, at one period or another in their careers, were magazine editors as well as contributors. Poe's magazine alliances have been described. In 1836 the shy Hawthorne emerged from his seclusion in Salem to edit the *American Magazine of Useful and Entertaining Knowledge.* Thoreau and Margaret Fuller were, with Emerson, *Dial* editors. One of James Russell Lowell's first literary ventures was to found and edit the short-lived *Pioneer.* A few years later Lowell was a contributing editor of the *National Anti-Slavery Standard.* He was the first editor of *The Atlantic Monthly* and then the editor of *The North American Review.*

The magazines published the works of other, less notable, writers. Even the *Atlantic* was not solely the province of the Concord and Cambridge writers of the New England group. It printed Bayard Taylor as well as Longfellow, Holmes, Emerson, and the others. The magazines had their T. S. Arthurs and their Fanny Ferns, and Lydia Sigourney, the almost indecently prolific poetess, was a more popular and better-known magazine writer than Emerson. The articulate magazine journalist, able to turn a ready pen from subject to subject and to write competently about most of them, was active and admired in this period. It is doubtful that Emerson's essays and poems, Hawthorne's stories, or the longer novels of William Dean Howells, for example, would be accepted by any of the popular magazines today; but N. P. Willis and Bayard Taylor, if they were alive now, with their flair for the timely and their skill in the manufacture of salable copy, probably would turn from the romantic and write psychological articles on economics with an international slant—or international articles with a geophysical slant—and almost certainly would be feature writers in our best-paying magazines.

That there were both types of writers in the magazines then, as there are now, was recognized at the time. Boston alone in 1860 had nearly 150 periodicals, about one third of them described by a contemporary writer as "legitimate magazines." In April of that year *The Atlantic Monthly* said proudly:

> Among us . . . the magazine-writer, as he existed in the last century [the pamphleteer and the penny-a-liner] has left few, if any representatives. He is fading silently away into a forgotten antiquity; his works are not on the publishers' counters,—they linger only among the dust and cobwebs of old libraries, listlessly thumbed by the exploring reader or occasionally consulted by the curious antiquary. His place is occupied by those who in the multiplication of books, the diffusion of information, and the general alteration of public taste, manners, and habits, though revolving in a similar orbit, move on quite another plane,—who have found in the pages of the periodicals a theatre of special activity, a way to the instruction and entertainment of the many; and though much of what is produced may bear . . . a character more or less ephemeral, we are sometimes presented also with the earlier blossoms and the fresher odors of a rich and perennial growth of genius, everywhere known and acknowledged, in the realms of belles-lettres, philosophy, and science, crowded here as in a nursery, to be soon transplanted to other and better abodes.

The language is a trifle elegant for twentieth-century taste, but the points are clear. The many magazines of the mid-nineteenth century were achieving what have been twin magazine objectives from the start: providing information and entertainment for many people. Their contents were vastly superior to those of American magazines a century earlier. Much of the writing was merely the ephemeral work of competent hacks and journalists, but some was the best writing of a splendid period in American literary history.

Chapter 6

Magazines and the Abolition of Slavery

The mid-nineteenth century in the United States was a time of ferment. The political liberalism sweeping Europe, largely as a result of the revolutions in America and France, brought their repercussions in American life, and after the 1848 revolutions in Germany, Italy, and France, hordes of immigrants came to swell the rapidly mounting population of this country and to aid in its westward expansion and industrial growth. Three million immigrants entered the United States in the ten years from 1845 to 1855.

New means of transportation, the steamboat, the great canals, the railroads, and new means of communication—the telegraph in 1844, and the steam-driven printing press in 1847—were speeding the tempo of American life. The development of power machinery in the mills of New England, the invention of the sewing machine in 1844, the opening of new markets in the West by the railroads, and in the Far East by treaty with China in 1844 and Perry's persuasion of Japan a decade later, were emphasizing the change-over from an agrarian to an industrial economy which gathered new impetus between the administrations of Jackson and Lincoln. In 1850 the annual value of the products of American factories was for the first time greater than the value of agricultural products.

Paradoxically, even improvements in agricultural implements and machinery hastened the advance of industrialism. The McCormick reaper, first patented in 1831, freed men from northern fields to work in the factories—as later it freed men to fight in the Union armies. At the same time that industry was gaining strength and power in the North, the Southern cotton crop was year by year increasing in importance in the world market and in monetary value, reaching $105,000,000 in 1850. The very success of both the factories and the plantations widened the sectional split between the industrial North and the agrarian South. One needed and fought for a high protective tariff; the other fought as bitterly for the low tariff that would favor its position as a seller of raw materials and an importer of manufactured articles. And as the value of cotton rose, the value of the slaves who produced it rose steadily.

New and revolutionary ideas in science, ideas that were to culminate in Sir Charles Lyell's *Principles of Geology* (1830–1833) and in Charles Darwin's *The Origin of Species* (1859) were changing men's social and political, as well as their religious, ideas.[1] In 1847 the American Association for the Advancement of Science was formed in Boston, and in the same year Louis Agassiz left Prussia to begin his scientific work at Harvard.

There were more political ideas seething in the mid-nineteenth century than the Whigs and Democrats dreamed of. Horace Greeley opened the columns of *The New York Tribune* to Karl Marx. Greeley had already avowed his own interest in Fourierism and socialism. George Ripley and his fellow transcendentalists, whom Greeley admired, had tried at Brook Farm to put their idealistic socialism into practice in what was merely the most famous of numerous community experiments.

There were other ideas and ideals in swirling circulation. There was agitation for more education. Public school education, through the efforts of such leaders as Horace Mann and Henry Barnard, was already widespread and spreading fur-

[1] Darwin stated that the two most intelligent reviews of the *Origin of Species* were published in American periodicals; one in *The North American Review*, the other in *The New York Times*.

ther. Between 1819 and 1850, fifteen state universities were founded. The cries of Sarah Josepha Hale in *Godey's* and of others who demanded more education for women were being answered. Mary Lyon's Female Seminary, the first woman's institution of collegiate rank, was opened in South Hadley, Massachusetts, in 1837. Oberlin College was opened in Ohio as a coeducational college in 1833. The University of Iowa admitted women in 1858. There was agitation for temperance, for greater advantages for labor, for religious reform, diet reform, for dozens of other movements, some of them valid, some mere fads. Emerson, shrewd practical thinker as well as mystic and idealist, upon whom most reformers of the time seem to have descended with demands for his support, saw the swirling scene as populated with "madmen and women, men with beards, Dunkers, Muggletonians, Come-outers, Groaners, Agrarians, Seventh-Day Baptists, Quakers, Abolitionists, Unitarians, and Philosophers."

The imperialistic ambitions of the country, stirred by "manifest destiny," helped to bring on the Mexican War, and added California and vast territories—now Arizona, Utah, and New Mexico—to the United States in 1848. Texas had already been annexed in 1845. The discovery of gold in California in 1848 added to the general excitement and posed new problems. In the single year of 1849 some 80,000 immigrants landed in California.

This was hardly the Federalist United States of Joseph Dennie and *The Port Folio*. The "common man" of Jackson's time was becoming literate and articulate. Magazines by the score, most of them short-lived, sprang up to defend the opinions of one group or attack those of another. Frank Luther Mott, using various sources, estimates that there were about a hundred magazines other than newspapers in 1827. The census of 1850 enumerated 214 monthlies, semi-monthlies, and quarterlies, and 1,902 weeklies. Mott further estimates that 2,500 periodicals, not including newspapers, were issued, some for only a short time, others for several years, between 1850 and 1865. The growing urbanization brought about by industrialism was putting more and more people within the reach of magazines. These new magazines, brought into being as the result of social change, were the implements of more change.

There were still no truly national general magazines. Had there been, it is at least possible that their discussions of vital issues might have aided in the peaceful solution of sectional differences which even in the 1830's and 1840's were threatening the democratic experiment in America. South Carolina threatened secession as early as 1832. Compromise after compromise on the slavery issue was to prove ineffective for more than a few years or months. War seemed imminent when, after the Clay-Webster-Calhoun debates, the Compromise of 1850 was reached. Slavery was the basic issue underlying the political, economic, and sectional dispute; and on this issue the influence of the magazines was strong.

In 1831, a year before the threatened secession of South Carolina, William Lloyd Garrison, using borrowed type on a hand press set up in a mean back room in Boston, issued the first number of *The Liberator*. Like Wendell Phillips, Garrison was a complete and determined abolitionist who had no patience with compromise of any kind, who would not countenance the gradual emancipation by political methods favored by more conservative anti-slavery advocates. He stood radically and unequivocally for the immediate and complete abolition of slavery, no matter what the political result for the country. In the first number of *The Liberator* he wrote: "I am in earnest—I will not equivocate—I will not excuse—I will not retreat a single inch—and *I will be heard.*" Insistent, undaunted even when Georgia advertised a reward for the arrest and conviction of its editor who was mobbed on the streets of Boston, harsh, violent, even abusive, *The Liberator* for thirty-five years fought slavery with every weapon it could find or devise. In January, 1865, Garrison declined a twenty-third term as president of the American Anti-Slavery Society. On December 29, 1865, his great objective having been attained when the Thirteenth Amendment to the Constitution was ratified, Garrison put the final issue of *The Liberator* to bed.

The cause of abolition claimed the services and devoured the energies of great writers of the time. Emerson, Thoreau, Lowell, and Whittier, though more moderate in their views and temperate in their expression than Garrison in *The Liberator,* were as intense in their hatred of slavery. Thoreau used his Walden cabin as a station in the Underground Railway by which slaves were rushed northward to freedom. Lowell, whose burning interest in aboltion was intensified by the abolitionist fervor of the poet Maria White whom he married in 1844, wrote with vehemence and enthusiasm for the cause. His anti-slavery papers, collected now in two volumes, were written mostly for the *Pennsylvania Freeman* and for the *National Anti-Slavery Standard,* of which he was associate editor from 1845 to 1850. The Second Series of Lowell's *Biglow Papers,* supporting the North and attacking slavery, ran in the *Atlantic* during the war. Lowell, a liberal thinker who was against tyranny in any form, saw slavery as the worst tyranny of all. Moral indignation informed his denunciatory attacks on the institution he and his fellows were determined to uproot.

The *Pennsylvania Freeman* was edited in 1838 and 1839 by John Greenleaf Whittier, the gentle Quaker poet who gave so much of his life and of his literary talent to the fight against slavery. The offices of the *Freeman* were burned to the ground by a Philadelphia mob while he was its editor. Like Garrison, who was his friend, he was mobbed when he and George Thompson, an English lecturer, spoke in Concord, New Hampshire. In 1846 his anti-slavery poems were collected and printed as *Voices of Freedom,* and in 1848 he became contributing editor of the *National Era,* which was published as an anti-slavery paper in Washington. In 1852 the *National Era* published serially the one book which is universally acknowledged to have accomplished more for the cause of abolition—and done more to provoke the Civil War—than any other anti-slavery writing. This was Harriet Beecher Stowe's *Uncle Tom's Cabin.*

There were numerous other anti-slavery magazines: the *Anti-Slavery Record,* the *Anti-Slavery Examiner,* the *Massa-*

chusetts Abolitionist, the *Emancipator,* and the *Anti-Slavery Reporter.* Despite violence and threats of violence, depredation, and even murder, these magazines carried on their unrelenting warfare against slavery. *The Liberator's* presses were destroyed. In 1835 a mob in South Carolina broke into the United States mails and burned copies of the magazine and effigies of its editor. The press of the *Observer* in Alton, Illinois, was several times smashed by mobs. Attempting to protect a new press sent him by the Ohio Anti-Slavery Society, its determined editor, Elijah Lovejoy, an abolitionist of the uncompromising Garrison type, was shot and killed on the night of November 7, 1837.

Other general magazines took a definite, though less radical, stand against slavery, as did most of the denominational church magazines. The more conservative anti-slavery position of some magazines, whose first consideration was preservation of the Union, was best represented perhaps by *The North American Review.* Though it condemned slavery on humanitarian grounds, it deprecated the dangerous clamor of those who demanded immediate, unplanned abolition without regard to the political consequences. In October, 1848, it said: ". . . If any change takes place, it will be accomplished, not by the declamation and agitation of strangers, but by practical expedients, deliberately considered and spontaneously adopted by the public sentiment and the lawful authority of the States concerned."

Events were moving too fast, however, for the thoughtful approach of the more conservative magazines to check the speed with which the issue was headed for an explosive climax. It was the fiery exhortations of the abolitionist magazines which had the greater effect. These certainly aroused and intensified sectional hatred, incited to violence, worked to bring feelings to fever pitch that precipitated the final conflict—and, happily, achieved their objective.

Chapter 7

Innovation and Expansion in Coverage

The editors and publishers of early general magazines might look with awe and considerable envy on products of the periodical press today. Successors to Poe, Willis, Taylor, and the other "magazinists" of the 1840's have greatly developed the art of writing articles and stories particularly adapted to magazine publication. Magazine editing as it was developed by such later editors as Henry Mills Alden, Gertrude Battles Lane, Ellery Sedgwick, Edward Bok, S. S. McClure, and George Horace Lorimer, and as practiced today has become a far more complicated profession than magazine editing as understood and deftly practiced by Joseph Dennie, Charles Brockden Brown, and Sarah Josepha Hale.

The rise of advertising and improvements in printing and in the reproduction of illustrations were partly responsible for this advance. Improved methods of distribution also contributed greatly. Editorial, mechanical, and business skills all combined to make the national magazine into the medium that today functions to bring simultaneously to readers in all parts of the country information and opinion that exert their social force in almost direct ratio to the many millions of people that these magazines reach weekly and monthly. But the best magazines of 1850 could list contributors at least as distinguished and accomplished as those of the best magazines today. As vehicles for the communication of news, ideas, and entertainment those magazines were forceful and effective. The vital magazines of 1850 had form and substantial content. Each was possessed of its own validity and carried its own emphasis. Singly and as a group they exerted their strong force in American thought and American activity. Some of today's "new" ideas in magazine publishing were to have their inception at this time, attain full development before the end of the century, and then practically disappear before their renascence under different conditions and with improved editorial and mechanical techniques in the 1920's and 1930's.

Harper's New Monthly Magazine was founded in 1850 purely as a magazine to present a selection of material first published in other magazines, both American and foreign. *Harper's* published little or no original material.[1] Its first issue stated that, as the best writers in every nation were then writing for magazine publication, and as no one could possibly read all the magazines, *Harper's* would select and publish a 144-page "monthly compendium of the periodical publications of the day." It promised to "transfer to its pages as rapidly as they may be issued all the continuous tales of DICKENS, BULWER, CROLY, LEVER, WARREN . . ."[2] It also promised, with the success of *Godey's, Graham's,* and *Peterson's* evidently in mind, that "a carefully prepared Fashion Plate, and other pictorial illustrations will accompany each number." There was

1 An important consideration with Harper & Brothers, the book publishers, in founding the eclectic magazine was that it would serve as an advertising medium for their books. For many years it refused all other advertising. George P. Rowell, founder both of the first American Newspaper Directory and of *Printers' Ink,* writes in his autobiography, *Forty Years An Advertising Agent* (New York: Franklin Publishing Co., 1926): ". . . The writer remembers listening with staring eyes, while Fletcher Harper the younger related that he had that week refused an offer of $18,000 for the use of the last page for a year for an advertisement of the Howe Sewing Machine."

2 So normal and financially successful was this practice that N. P. Willis wrote in the prospectus to the *Corsair,* a literary weekly which he proposed at first to call *The Pirate,* that its editors intended "to take advantage . . . of the privilege assured us by our piratical law of copyright and, in the name of American authors (for our own benefit) 'convey' to our columns, for the amusement of our readers, the cream and spirit of everything that ventures to light in England, France, and Germany." Quoted by Frank Luther Mott, *A History of American Magazines, 1741–1850* (Cambridge, Mass. Harvard University Press, 1938), pp. 356–357. American writers naturally were resentful of *Harper's* initial policy. Later the magazine began to include original contributions by American authors.

the usual "monthly record of current events." This feature, which was still running in the late 1880's, was prepared until 1856 by Henry J. Raymond, *Harper's* managing editor who in 1851 founded the *New York Daily Times.*

At the end of its first half year of publication *Harper's,* which was immediately successful, could reiterate its purpose, declare its accomplishment, and firmly restate its basic intent:

> It was presented in the belief, that it might be the means of bringing within the reach of the great mass of the American people, an immense amount of useful and entertaining reading matter, to which, on account of the great number and expense of the books and periodicals in which it originally appears, they have hitherto had no access.

It could boast that it had already achieved a monthly issue of 50,000 copies, with circulation increase still unchecked. The publishers hoped for a popular circulation "unequalled by that of any similar periodical ever published in the world." The basic appeal of the early *Harper's* was the same as the present-day appeal of the digest magazines, though selections were not condensed but usually reprinted in full. Editors were already envisioning the kind of mass circulation which did not become a reality until Cyrus Curtis harnessed the force of advertising to magazines.

Harper's in 1850 "transferred" to its pages material on exploration, travel, science, art, on social and domestic life, as well as poetry and fiction. It drew heavily on the English magazines, wholesale from Dickens' *Household Words.* Other magazines whose names reappeared continually were the *Eclectic Review, Sharpes' London Magazine, Howitt's Country Yearbook, Chambers' Edinburgh Journal,* and the *Dublin University Magazine.* It drew on old and new books as well as on the magazines. An 1850 serial was Ik Marvel's (Donald G. Mitchell) best seller, *Reveries of a Bachelor,* "from a new work soon to be issued by Baker & Scribners." The magazine title was "A Bachelor's Reverie." The names of Lord Chesterfield, Harriet Martineau, Southey, Guizot, and Coleridge appeared as authors during the year, and Leigh Hunt, evidently a favorite with *Harper's,* was represented in almost every issue.

American writers might complain bitterly, and publishers like Graham might well protest such competition, but *Harper's* did its job of selection well, and the form proved almost as popular in its time as it is proving in its streamlined counterparts today. By expanding and intensifying the range of periodical materials available, *Harper's* accomplished a distinct service for its readers. After the 1850's it began to publish more American material but always relied heavily on English fiction. It published serially Dickens' *Bleak House* and *Little Dorrit,* Thackeray's *Virginians* and *The Newcomes,* and George Eliot's *Romola.* In January, 1893, at the height of its excellence as a literary magazine under Henry Mills Alden, it began serial publication of Du Maurier's *Trilby,* one of the most popular English novels of modern times. With the *Trilby* text were reproduced Du Maurier's original illustrations. Fine illustrating was by this time a *Harper's* tradition, and part of the magazine's great success was due to the work of its artists. In 1885 and 1886, with Alden as editor, and with George William Curtis in the "Editor's Easy Chair" and William Dean Howells occupying the "Editor's Study"—two famous *Harper's* departments—the monthly was running Oliver Goldsmith's *She Stoops to Conquer* with illustrations by Edwin Abbey. Though most stories and articles were still unsigned even in the 1880's, Brander Matthews, Helen Hunt Jackson, Elizabeth Stuart Phelps, Mary E. Wilkins, James Lane Allen, Thomas Nelson Page, Charles Dudley Warner, and "Charles Egbert Craddock" were prominent American contributors in 1885 and 1886. C. S. Reinhart and later Howard Pyle, A. E. Sterner, and William T. Smedley were, with Edwin Abbey, among *Harper's* best-known artists.

Harper's published Mark Twain and Thomas Hardy. For many years it brought the best in English letters and some of the most popular American writing to its readers. In the 1880's and 1890's the fiction and verse by present-day standards were thin, but they were the best of their kind at the time. Frederick Lewis Allen, editor of *Harper's,* 1941–1953, analyzed the defects of the magazines of this period, pointing out that the

"AH ME! WHEN SHALL I MARRY ME?"

Edwin Abbey's finely executed illustrations for *She Stoops to Conquer* were a leading feature in *Harper's New Monthly Magazine* for a half-dozen issues during 1886.

very excellence of *Harper's* and its competitors in 1891 marked the limitations of these magazines as a social force:

> Fifty years ago a small group of magazines, including the *Century, Harper's,* the four-year-old *Scribner's* and the unillustrated *Atlantic Monthly,* not only led the magazines of the country in literary and artistic quality, but were also among the big sellers. The circulation records of those days are hard to come by, but it is my impression that in 1891 *Harper's* had between 100,000 and 200,000 readers, and that few, if any, periodicals in America had more than that. To us today some of the *Harper's* fiction of 1891 seems naive, some of its verse weakly sentimental, some of its pen-and-ink illustrations too daintily photographic; we wonder at its comparative neglect of the vital social and economic issues of the day, at its preoccupation with the safely remote, the respectably classical, the second-hand literary; and at its careful propriety. We have to remind ourselves that the public for which it was edited was the victim of an attractive but academic and timorous genteelism. . . .[3]

The same limitations that Allen indicated in *Harper's* of the nineteenth century applied to the other famous magazines which he mentioned.

The Atlantic Monthly was founded in Boston in 1857 when Moses Dresser Phillips of Phillips, Sampson, & Company invited Emerson, Longfellow, Cabot, Holmes, and Motley to a dinner to discuss Francis H. Underwood's idea for a magazine. E. P. Whipple, the critic whose work appears in almost all the best literary magazines of the second half of the century, was invited to another dinner held the next day. Lowell was made editor and, at his insistence, Holmes, who named the new magazine, chief contributor. These founders became, with others of the New England group, the important and regular contributors to the *Atlantic* during its first and best years.

No American magazine has ever had more distinguished original contributors. Though none of their productions were signed, Emerson, Lowell, Charles Eliot Norton, Harriet Beecher Stowe, Parke Godwin, and Whittier all contributed to the 128-page first issue of *The Atlantic Monthly,* published in

[3] Frederick Lewis Allen, "American Magazines, 1741–1941," *Bulletin of The New York Public Library,* June, 1941.

November, 1857. That famous issue contained the first installment of Oliver Wendell Holmes' *The Autocrat of the Breakfast Table* (Every Man His Own Boswell)—which it is amazing to remember now was bitterly attacked by the evangelical press for its unorthodox remarks. There were several of Emerson's finest poems, including "Days," "The Rommany [sic] Girl," and "Brahma"; several short stories; the first part of a serial, "Akin By Marriage"; a discussion of "The Origin of Didactic Poetry"; a long description of the Manchester Art Exhibition; an article on "British India" and another on the currency; and departments devoted to "Literary Notes" and "Music." Surprisingly, the lead article in this issue was an appreciative essay on Douglas Jerrold, the great "Q" of *Punch,* who had died during the year. Although Holmes was a humorist and Lowell paraded a punning humor of a kind, it is difficult to associate the dignified *Atlantic* with the satirical wit and epigrammatic humor of the English comic weekly.

Whittier's "Skipper Ireson's Ride," which, on Lowell's advice, he wrote in New England dialect, was in the second number of the *Atlantic.* Lowell, always sure of himself, was a sound though arbitrary editor, quite willing to change what he did not like. Sometimes his changes improved a manuscript; sometimes he merely antagonized better writers than he. Thoreau's "Chesuncook," the narrative of his second journey into the Maine woods, was published in June and July, 1858. Without consulting Thoreau, Lowell, who had solicited the manuscript, deleted a passage whose philosophy he disapproved. After writing Lowell a stinging rebuke which was not answered, Thoreau thereupon refused to write again for the *Atlantic* while Lowell remained its editor. Thoreau did not appear again in the *Atlantic* during his lifetime. Though he arranged with James T. Fields, Lowell's successor and a member of the publishing firm of Ticknor & Fields which purchased the magazine in 1859, to publish a part of his *Excursions,* Thoreau died before it appeared. Almost all of his posthumous work, edited from his manuscripts, was published in the *Atlantic.*

The list of *Atlantic* literary triumphs is long; a full list of its early contributors would include almost every revered name of New England in American letters of the nineteenth century. Unlike *Harper's,* which in its first years simply exploited English writers, the *Atlantic* offered the finest American imaginative and critical writers a suitable, periodical vehicle for their work and consequently made great contributions to American literature. In so far as its belletristic product influences the spirit of a country, no American magazine has been more influential than *The Atlantic Monthly.*

One limitation has often been pointed out. The *Atlantic* was meant to be as broad in coverage as its name suggested. In reality, during its first years it confined itself almost entirely to publishing the Boston, Cambridge, and Concord writers. There was some justification for this. Though critics and historians jealous of the literary pretensions of other regions of the country may cavil, and many have cavilled loudly, the fact remains that the best writers of the mid-nineteenth century were concentrated about Boston.

There was another limitation. The *Atlantic* described itself as "a magazine of literature, art, and politics." In actuality, it presented the literary and acknowledged the artistic, but avoided the political and the social. Like *Harper's* of the same period, it suffered from the same restriction that produced its excellence. Neither magazine paid much attention to the Civil War, though the *Atlantic* published Julia Ward Howe's "Battle Hymn of the Republic" (Fields is said to have affixed the title), and the Second Series of Lowell's *Biglow Papers.* Both magazines stressed the literary and the cultural, largely neglecting other fundamental aspects of American life.

William Dean Howells was the best of the nineteenth-century *Atlantic* editors who succeeded Fields. His was still a literary *Atlantic,* but more a national than a provincial magazine. Thomas Bailey Aldrich, editor from 1881 to 1890, carefully gave the *Atlantic* the same academic, genteel propriety which Richard Watson Gilder guarded so jealously in *The Century.* The next three editors, Horace Scudder, Walter Hines Page, and Bliss Perry, injected more articles on social subjects into the magazine, and the *Atlantic* even indulged in some mild muckraking when the reform movement of the first decade of the twentieth century was in full swing. Yet it was not until 1909, when Ellery Sedgwick, a young editor trained on *The Youth's Companion, Leslie's Monthly* (Sedgwick changed the title from *Frank Leslie's Popular Monthly*), the *American Magazine,* and *McClure's,* bought the magazine, that the *Atlantic* fully recognized the importance of social and political material. Without neglecting the literary, always pre-eminent in the magazine, it broadened its coverage and sharpened its perceptions of the contemporary scene. When Sedgwick bought the magazine for $50,000, it was about to fail. It had a circulation of only 15,000 and was losing $4,000 a year. In his first year as owner and editor Sedgwick showed a profit of $4,000.

Under Sedgwick's direction the influence of *The Atlantic Monthly,* always strong in literature, was reinforced in other directions. The new editor's mail, he later said proudly in *The Happy Profession,* soon bore witness to its expansion and greater strength. Men of national reputation and eminence began to contribute articles. Woodrow Wilson, while President, sent the *Atlantic* an unsolicited article. Later Al Smith, still later Wendell Willkie, appeared in its pages. Ellery Sedgwick used these illustrations to show that such men deliberately chose *The Atlantic Monthly* as an effective medium for dissemination of their ideas. Every editor likes to believe that his magazine is, for one reason or another, pre-eminent in influence with the public. With more justification than some, Ellery Sedgwick could say: "To inoculate the few who influence the many is the *Atlantic's* perpetual formula." Edward Weeks, editor of the *Atlantic,* 1938–1966, successfully applied this inherited formula, publishing a literate and lively magazine.

It was another magazine, also founded in 1857, which became a strong political and social force and accomplished much toward the advance of the American magazine. *Harper's Weekly,* through its development of illustrations into vivid pictorial journalism and through its news coverage and comments as well as its feature articles, can easily be seen as the precursor of today's weekly pictorial and news magazines. *Harper's Weekly,* "a journal of civilization," as the line under the logotype read, was founded largely as a vehicle to carry the kind of political writing eschewed by the literary *Harper's Monthly.* From its first number in 1857 to its last in 1916, it was a bright, alert, well-illustrated weekly, offering fiction, both short stories and serials, essays, editorials, news, advertising, poetry, and humor. It began to run full-page pictures in its first year. These full-page pictures that always told a story became one of the best and most characteristic *Harper's Weekly* features.

There had been illustrated magazines before this time. The first of them, *Gleason's Pictorial,* was founded in 1851. Under the guidance of Henry Carter, the English-born engraver and publisher who later changed his name to Frank Leslie, it was a successful weekly for most of the 1850's. *Frank Leslie's Illustrated Newspaper,* founded a year before *Harper's Weekly,* was a sensational sheet. Leslie distributed the wood blocks among a force of engravers, then assembled the parts so as to hit the streets quickly with his eight-page tabloid of murders, fires, railroad disasters, lynchings, morgue scenes. By 1868 he was running a two-page spread of such cultural occasions as the grand dress rehearsal at Pike's New Opera House at 23rd Street and Eighth Avenue—which Jim Fisk bought and over which he and Jay Gould had their resplendent offices—in order to give variety to his enticing displays of home accidents, charred bodies, gun fights, and spectacular street accidents.

Undoubtedly *Leslie's Illustrated Newspaper* suggested the pictorial idea to the Harpers, and some of Leslie's artists, notably the young Thomas Nast, joined the new magazine, but well before 1868 *Harper's Weekly* had brought pictorial journalism to a kind of perfection never achieved by Leslie's newspaper. Its aim was not sensationalism but accurate graphic reporting, and that is what it provided. The Civil War was its great opportunity. Just as today's magazines sent their corps of correspondents and photographers to cover World Wars I and II, *Harper's Weekly* sent a staff of writers and artists to the Civil War battle fronts. William Waud, Theodore Davis, Thomas Nast, A. W. Warren, and Andrew McCallum sent back pencil or pen-and-ink drawings of battle and camp scenes which were published as half-page, full-page, and sometimes double-page engravings. The magazine so admirably succeeded in its reporting of the war that its files for the period are well known as a vivid pictorial and authentic news source for Civil War history. Besides engravings, *Harper's Weekly* by 1863 was publishing reproductions of Brady photographs, though these were usually portraits of the various Union generals and naval commanders.

The accomplishments of *Harper's Weekly* during the war were recognized at the time. Fletcher Harper, working editor of the *Weekly* as he was of *Harper's Monthly*, went to Washington during the war to defend the magazine against Secretary of War Stanton's accusation that it had given aid and comfort to the enemy by publishing pictures of Union fortifications, and to fight the Secretary's order for the magazine's suspension. Harper obtained both a revocation of the order and Stanton's thanks for the services his paper was performing. Lincoln later was reported to have said that Thomas Nast, through his cartoons and drawings in *Harper's Weekly*, had been the country's most effective recruiting sergeant.

The most spectacular magazine success of the mid-century showed, in other directions, ways in which the mass magazine was to develop. *The New York Ledger*, which Robert Bonner began to publish in 1855, was sensational in its day on several counts. Five years after its founding it had attained the then unheard of circulation of 400,000—at a time when the population of the entire country was only 31,000,000. It paid tremendous sums to "name" contributors. It made its publisher a millionaire. And, though Bonner would admit no advertising to the columns of the *Ledger*, he made uninhibited use of advertising to sell his magazine. Bonner, like those who publish the magazines of large circulation today, aimed at mass readership.

What he gave his readers in a well-printed eight-page magazine was the work of the best-known magazine fiction writers of the day, the work of the most popular poets, and special features written by all the literate figures in public life whom he could persuade to write for him.

In 1859 the masthead of the *Ledger* listed among "regular contributors": George D. Prentice, John G. Saxe, Col. W. B. Dunlap, Fanny Fern, Mrs. Sigourney, Mrs. Southworth, Alice Cary, Augusta Moore, Sylvanus Cobb, Jr., and Emerson Bennett. Bonner ran one after another that year and for many years afterward the melodramatic serials of Sylvanus Cobb, Jr., and all the stories and essays of the sprightly Fanny Fern. "The Hidden Hand" by Emma D. Southworth, "The Little Foxes" by the omnipresent T. S. Arthur, "Raphael; or The Fugitives of Paris" by Dr. Henry W. Wadsworth, and similar fiction were continued all through 1859.

But Bonner, a shrewd magazine publisher who had begun his career as a Hartford printer, also began to publish in 1859 "The Mount Vernon Papers" by Edward Everett, Harvard president and professor, *North American* editor, statesman and writer. For the series Everett, who was also president of the Ladies' Mount Vernon Society, received $10,000 which he contributed to the fund for the preservation of Washington's home. Later, in 1870, Bonner was featuring weekly articles by the popular and admired preacher Henry Ward Beecher and autobiographical writing by Horace Greeley. Along with the inevitable Cobb thrillers and the "Fern Leaves" was highly reputable biographical writing by James Parton, and with the mawkish verse of women poets Bonner ran serious articles by "twelve distinguished Senators of the United States." By paying liberally for them Bonner was able to obtain poems from Longfellow and Bryant, prose from Harriet Beecher Stowe, work from leading college presidents and scholars.

According to Bonner himself, as he is quoted by George Rowell, again and again he would gather all the money he could obtain and spend it in advertising his magazine. Before he returned to his office, it seemed, all his money had come back and more with it. What Bonner did was to publish a page or two of *Gun Maker of Moscow* by Sylvanus Cobb, Jr., or some similar *Ledger* story in the pages of a newspaper, then break it off with "Continued in *The New York Ledger!*" The idea was new then. Or he would buy whole newspaper pages and fill them with display advertising after this fashion:

THE NEW YORK LEDGER
THE NEW YORK LEDGER
THE NEW YORK LEDGER
WILL BE FOR SALE
WILL BE FOR SALE
WILL BE FOR SALE
TO-MORROW MORNING
TO-MORROW MORNING
TO-MORROW MORNING
THROUGHOUT THE
THROUGHOUT THE
THROUGHOUT THE
UNITED STATES
UNITED STATES
UNITED STATES
AND NEW JERSEY
AND NEW JERSEY
AND NEW JERSEY

Bonner is said to have paid as high as $27,000 for one week's advertising of his magazine, and up to $150,000 in a year. These were large figures at that time. Bonner could claim with some accuracy in an editorial in one issue of the *Ledger:* "More money is spent upon the *Ledger* to make it a good paper than is spent upon any other paper in the world. . . . It has the largest number of great and distinguished writers. . . . The principal Bishops, Doctors of Divinity, and Clergymen write for it. . . . Distinguished public men, including Foreign Ministers, Members of the Cabinet and Senators in Congress write for the *Ledger*. . . ."

Bonner reveled in the success of his magazine and bought famous race horses with part of his profits. He did not believe in stake racing but enjoyed a match race with some other horse fancier like Commodore Vanderbilt on a country road. Bonner liked to talk brightly and briskly to his readers and in one editorial, with the mixture of effrontery, complacency, and trust that were part of his charm, he quoted the Commodore. People were continually stopping him on the street, Bonner said, to express their approval of the newest *Ledger*. He was reminded of Vanderbilt's retort to those who had exclaimed that they liked a new ocean steamer. "Well," said the Commodore, "you'd be confounded fools if you didn't!" [4]

Robert Bonner's conception of a profitable magazine was very modern. The body of the *Ledger* was staff-written by popular writers whose work was produced exclusively for the *Ledger*. He gathered in special articles from writers whose names would add luster to the magazine. His uninhibited and successful use of advertising was in advance of his time. If it seems an anomaly that he would print none himself, it must be remembered that many other editors of the time also refused it. The wily Bonner may have felt that its absence gave his *Ledger* a certain *cachet* and respectability in the eyes of those who viewed the prolific outpourings of Sylvanus Cobb, Jr., Fanny Fern, and their fellows with something less than complete critical approval.

[4] Robert Bonner always kept his readers informed and advised. He did not call a spade by prettier names. "We employ no traveling agents," he wrote in 1859. "If any party pretends to act as such, you can put him down as a swindler." He suggested in another editorial that people stop bothering him. "We are," he wrote, "constantly receiving letters from parties whom we highly esteem and would be glad to oblige, but . . . we are so loaded with labors that every moment of our time has to carry double . . . our friends . . . will see how impossible it is for us to act upon our friendly impulses and answer their letters. Don't expect it of us; and don't send us any manuscripts."

Chapter 8

Magazines as a Weapon Against Political Corruption

If, under the determined leadership of crusading editors, magazines were made a dynamic force for social betterment in the opening years of the twentieth century, it was the rival illustrated weeklies founded just before the Civil War, *Leslie's* and *Harper's Weekly*, which first demonstrated the effectiveness of the American magazine as an instrument of civic and social reform.

In 1858 *Leslie's* began a bitter campaign against "swill milk" in New York City. Cows in dairies supplying New York's milk were being fed distillery mash and refuse. The diet stimulated the milk production of the animals, but they developed sores, their tails rotted off, and the milk was filled with disease germs. *Leslie's* described the situation in vivid editorials, ran pictures of filthy conditions in the dairies and of the diseased and dying cows. "For the midnight assassin," Leslie wrote, "we have the rope and the gallows; for the robber, the penitentiary; but for those who murder our children by the thousands we have neither reprobation nor punishment."

But both distilleries and dairies were protected by the politicians in power. An investigation by the board of health found no alarming conditions, and so reported. *Leslie's* pressed the fight. It had milk carts followed, and addresses where deliveries were made were published in the magazine, together with a warning that the buyers were feeding poisoned milk to their children. Another investigation showed that dairies and distilleries were blameless, whereupon the attack in *Leslie's* grew more virulent. The chairman of the exonerating committee *Leslie's* described as "a barefaced, shameless rascal." Another alderman was described as his superior "in all that constitutes the scurrilous blackguard and mouthy poltroon."

Leslie's printed cartoons now as well as pictures. It attacked the entire city administration which was responsible for the milk scandal. The report of the committee of the New York Academy of Medicine, which the mayor was forced to appoint, found the abuses as bad as the magazine had pictured them. An attempt was made to indict Frank Leslie for criminal libel, but the action was thrown out by the grand jury. The exposé in *Leslie's* put an end to the sale of milk from herds fed with waste from the distilleries. The New York State legislature was acknowledging a magazine-accomplished fact when it acted to forbid the traffic in 1861.

Harper's Weekly, under the idealistic leadership of George William Curtis [1] and with the devastating cartoons of Thomas Nast as the principal weapon, entered on the far more formidable task of overthrowing Tammany and smashing the notorious Tweed Ring. J. Henry Harper in *The House of Harper* (New York: 1912), tells in full a story of magazine courage which other magazine and social historians have noted and approved.

In 1870 the Tweed Ring, composed of William Marcy Tweed, Peter Barr Sweeny, Richard B. Connolly, and A. Oakey

[1] George William Curtis, like Charles A. Dana, famous editor of the *New York Sun,* was a product of Brook Farm, the transcendentalist community near Boston which Emerson had helped found and where Hawthorne lived for a year before his marriage. Like George Ripley, the community's president, he later joined the staff of Horace Greeley's *New York Tribune.* Curtis traveled in the Far East as a *Tribune* correspondent, wrote amusing travel books, several sentimental novels, and then became a strong reform editor, writing both in *Harper's Weekly* and in the "Editor's Easy Chair" in *Harper's Monthly.* Unlike Dana he remained an idealist, fighting first against slavery, then for women's rights, civil service reform, and industrial harmony. It is hard to reconcile *Harper's Weekly's* brutal ridicule of Horace Greeley during the presidential campaign of 1872 with Curtis' character and principles.

Hall, completely controlled not only the New York City administration but the Tammany governor of New York and a working majority of the state legislature.[2] Elated by their success in Manhattan, they were gleefully preparing extension of their very remunerative activities on a national scale. "Next year we shall be in Washington," Hall is reported to have asserted confidently. When the investigation into its intricate and widespread activities was completed, it was proved that the Tweed Ring had robbed the city of $200,000,000 by tax-dodging, blackmail, and extortion, by floating vast issues of fraudulent bonds, by selling favors and franchises, and by a multitude of other assorted swindles. Yet so deeply entrenched was it that when *Harper's Weekly,* joined later by *The New York Times,* began its exposure Tweed could coolly ask, "What are you going to do about it?"

For one thing, records of the city's expenditures were conveniently missing.

The opening attack in *Harper's Weekly* was mild by comparison with what followed. Editorially on October 29, 1870, it said:

> Tammany Hall, which absolutely controls the city by the most notoriously criminal means, and which, under popular forms, has annihilated popular government, justly excites the apprehension of all good citizens. Unless its power can be broken the most disastrous results and the most desperate civil convulsions are sure to come. Tammany Hall governs by terrorism and corruption. It relies upon cheating at the polls. And no free people can long tolerate such a system, when its character is exposed, as that of Tammany now is.

Later editorials described Tammany as "the rule of corruption by money and fear," and as a "plague spot in the center of the American system." *Harper's Weekly* pointed to its control of the state government and the city courts and to its avowed aim of conducting its depredations on a national scale.

The editorial language of *Harper's Weekly* was strong and grew stronger, but Nast's caricatures were ruthlessly destruc-

[2] The Ring members were known by names reminiscent of those popularized by the comic strips of a later date. Tweed was known as "the Boss," Sweeny as "the Brains," Connolly as "Slippery Dick," and Hall as "O.K. Haul." It was Nast who invented the last alias.

tive. Nast, the German-born cartoonist and illustrator, who through his work in the magazines helped develop American public opinion for more than a quarter of a century, had begun his attack on Tammany in *Harper's Weekly* in 1869. Among the most devastating of his later cartoons in the war on the Ring were "Tweedledee and Sweedledum," which showed Tweed and Sweeny dispensing funds to greedy henchmen and setting aside their own generous take; "The Boss," which showed the city flattened under a gigantic thumb; "The Only Thing They Respect or Fear," which showed the four Ring members cowering under four nooses dangling from a gibbet; "Let Us Prey," which showed the four perched as waiting vultures on a mountainside while lightning flashed about them; and "The Tammany Tiger Loose," in which Tweed, cast as Nero looked happily on while a tiger in a Roman arena tore into the prone figure of the republic.[3]

It was the cartoons that woke the Ring. "Let's stop them damned pictures," J. Henry Harper reports Tweed as saying. "I don't care so much what the papers write about me—my constituents can't read; but, damn it, they can see pictures!" Alarmed now, Tweed and his fellow statesmen tried threats, intimidation, and physical violence. All Harper books used as texts in New York City schools were thrown out and texts published by the New York Printing Company, a Tammany-owned business, were substituted. Tweed threatened to horsewhip Nast, but did not when they met. Mayor Hall forbade the sale of *Harper's Weekly* on the newsstands.

By a clever trick the missing city records were obtained. Samuel Tilden infiltrated the office of the comptroller, placing there as an employee one of his adherents, William Copeland, who carefully transcribed the damning accounts. Another investigator, Matthew O'Rourke, a county bookkeeper, gathered in further proof of enormous frauds. The records were turned over to the *Times* for publication. Begging and pleading,

[3] Use of a tiger's head as the symbol for Tammany stemmed from the picture on Americus No. 6, engine of the volunteer fire company Tweed had helped organize as a young man. Nast himself invented and used in cartoons the elephant as a symbol of the Republican party, and the donkey as the Democrats' symbol.

"Let Us Prey" was one of the most devastating Nast cartoons which *Harper's Weekly* loosed in its successful fight to demolish the Tweed Ring in New York City.

Comptroller Connolly called on George Jones, proprietor of the newspaper. He offered Jones $5,000,000 not to publish the records. Jones refused. The records, when they appeared in July, 1871, told an almost incredible story. The Ring had employed devices of every kind in its gouging of the people. One of its happiest ventures, the records showed, was a courthouse being built in 1870. One plasterer on this job, according to the city's accounts, had received $2,870,464.06. During one month he had been paid $50,000 a day.

The Nast cartoons continued. "'Twas Him" showed a group of the looters each pointing to one of the others when asked "Who Stole the People's Money?" "Shadows of Coming Events" prophesied the rioting that such misrule would cause. On July 12, 1871, the rioting broke out when Tammany-inspired ruffians, vowing vengeance on everything they disliked, especially on Nast, who was marching with the Seventh Regiment, and on *Harper's Weekly,* attacked marchers and onlookers in an Orangemen's parade. One hundred people were killed or wounded.

As the Ring had, in desperation, attempted to bribe Jones, it also approached Nast. An officer of the bank in which the Ring kept its funds offered him $200,000 to study art abroad. According to Albert Bigelow Paine, biographer of the cartoonist, Nast considered the matter a few moments, then asked if the Ring could not do better. The offer was immediately raised to half a million in gold if he would drop his attack on the Ring and leave the country. Nast said that, instead, he would remain where he was and bend his further efforts to placing the Ring members behind bars. The emissary left with the warning that he might first put himself in a coffin.

Though the Tweed-controlled papers, especially the *New York World,* continued to support the Ring, other newspapers and magazines which had dared not take the lead joined in the attack. The *Tribune* was first. Charles Nordhoff, managing editor of the *Evening Post,* which William Cullen Bryant owned and published, lost his job as the result of his onslaughts on the Ring. Charles A. Dana's *Sun* printed one or two damaging indictments but did little more. Among the magazines which allied themselves with *Harper's Weekly, The Nation,* edited by the militant E. L. Godkin, came out strongly for its distinctive solution to the problem. It advocated hanging. On September 2, 1871, *The Nation* said:

> . . . In our opinion Hall, Connolly, Tweed, Barnard, and all the class to which they belong . . . fear no penalty for their misdeeds except a violent death. They are indifferent to public opinion and have matters so arranged that the prison pen has no terrors for them, and a natural death they calculate upon. But the prospect of a violent death, which would suddenly stop their champagne, knock the satin sofas from under them, shut out the velvet carpets from their view, cause their fast horses to vanish into thin air, and launch them into the cold unknown would terrify them exceedingly; and such a death, we repeat, a large and growing body of respectable citizens think they ought to die—first and foremost in order to stop their thieving and rid the community of them, and secondly, to prevent an unwholesome influence on public and private morals of the spectacle of the peaceful close of their career in the enjoyment of their stealings.

Tammany was defeated in the elections of 1871, and the Ring was smashed. William Marcy Tweed was arrested, freed on a million-dollar bond supplied by his friend and Erie associate, Jay Gould. He served a short prison term was rearrested, and escaped. He fled to Spain disguised as a seaman. Spanish officials identified him from a Nast cartoon, and Tweed died in New York's Ludlow Street jail in 1878. Other members of the Ring fled into exile or died in jail, though Sweeny returned from France, made restitution to the city of $400,000 of what he had stolen, and was allowed to go free.

The circulation of *Harper's Weekly,* 160,000 in 1872, trebled as a result of the magazine's bold and successful fight against the Ring. Though it centered in a struggle against corrupt municipal administration, the drama received nationwide attention because of the fundamental issues of government involved. The whole country had an opportunity of watching a magazine match its force against a powerful enemy of the people and saw it prove its strength.

Chapter 9

Emergence of the National Magazine

The need for adequate communication of facts and ideas to all parts of the country at the same time was a lesson taught forcibly by the Civil War and emphasized by the sectional animosities and misunderstandings that persisted in the postwar years. Congress in the 1870's fully realized that the circulation of news, information, and intelligent discussion by reliable means was vitally necessary for the maintenance and strengthening of national unity.

The magazine could now be distributed nationally. Machinery for speedier distribution had been built up to meet war necessities. It was available now for the distribution of magazines as well as all other commodities. The magazine was a vehicle which could present simultaneously identical facts, uniformly treated, in every locality. Men and women, North, South, East, and West, could read and judge the same materials, instead of forming their beliefs and reaching their decisions on the basis of varied accounts published in different sections and often distorted by regional prejudice. Such at least, was the ideal possibility.

Realizing that in the magazine, which had already proved its effect on public opinion, the United States had a solid instrument for developing and reinforcing national sentiment, Congress passed legislation which established favorable mailing privileges for the periodical press. In a House debate on the subject, Representative H. D. Money, who incidentally was a newspaper publisher, voiced the considerations that prompted the measure:

> Mr. Speaker, the object of the government in establishing a postal service was for the dissemination of useful knowledge for the public good and to promote communication between its citizens in the several sections of the country. . . . The Post-Office Department, looked at in that light, may be considered as a great educator of people in all parts of the country. . . . That highest class of literature in which are ranked all monthly, bi-monthly, and quarterly publications, is excluded from the privileged rate, although they are in their very nature the highest educators that reach the people in that way. . . . Take all the monthlies of the country and I say if you examine the character of those monthlies you will find more than two-thirds of the monthlies of the country are not the mere vehicles of literature to the people, but are instructors in the highest sense of the term. (Congressional *Record,* January 23, 1879)

The postal act of March 3, 1879, which gave second-class mailing privileges to magazines "originated and published for the dissemination of information of a public character, or devoted to literature, the sciences, arts, or some special industry," was recognition of the stature which magazines were achieving in the years of accelerated industrial and economic growth in America that began with the Civil War and continued through the remainder of the nineteenth century. Of these years, Edward Atkinson, the economist, wrote in 1891: "There has never been in the history of civilization a period, or a place, or a section of the earth in which science and invention have worked such progress or have created such opportunity for material welfare as in these United States in the period which has elapsed since the end of the Civil War." [1]

East and West coasts had been joined by rail when in 1869 tracks laid from the east by the Union Pacific were joined at Promontory Point near Ogden, Utah, to those laid from the west by the Central Pacific. Chicago was growing almost incredibly as the principal rail center of the Middle West. Pitts-

[1] From Arthur M. Schlesinger, *Political and Social Growth of the American People,* 3rd ed. (Copyright, 1941 by The Macmillan Company and used with their permission.) P. 42.

burgh was rapidly becoming the great steel and iron center that it is today. Other cities were developing as manufacturing and distribution, given tremendous impetus by the war, were intensified to meet the demands of a population that grew from 31,000,000 in 1860 to 50,000,000 in 1880, to 76,000,000 in 1900. And it was a population increasingly urban and industrialized.

Less than 62,000 patents had been granted before 1865. The number during the remainder of the nineteenth century reached nearly 638,000. The value of manufactures in the United States trebled from 1860, when it was less than two billions of dollars, to 1880 when it was over five billions. By 1890 it had reached nine billions and the United States ranked as the first manufacturing nation in the world, its output exceeding that of Great Britain and Germany combined.

American engineering and production methods were speeding the vast and fundamental changes sweeping over the nation. Steel, oil, the application of steam to machinery, brought material progress, but in its wake new social and economic problems. This was the period of the Robber Barons and the Gilded Age, of new social patterns, of political corruption and economic conflict, as well as a period of material advance for the middle class that was growing in power. It was this class, made literate through public school education, that formed a new and wider audience of readers not reached by the rather staid monthly and quarterly magazines.

To reach this audience—and to take profitable advantage of the 1879 Postal Act which, in effect, was government subsidy of magazine distribution—a whole new group of magazines sprang up: *McCall's,* 1870; *Popular Science,* 1872; *Woman's Home Companion,* 1873; *Leslie's Monthly,* 1876, *Farm Journal,* 1877; *Good Housekeeping,* 1885; *Cosmopolitan,* 1886; *Collier's,* 1888; *National Geographic,* 1888; *Capper's Farmer,* 1889; *Vogue,* 1892; *Outdoor Life,* 1898, and many others.

From 1860 to 1900 the number of monthly magazines alone rose from 280 to over 1,800. "Never before," says Schlesinger, "had they [the magazines] reached so high a plane of general excellence, or represented so well the diversified interests of the public." Mott gives some 700 periodicals of all kinds for 1865; over 1,200 for 1870; more than 2,400 for 1880; and some 3,300 by 1885.

Improvements in printing, the roller press, the halftone engraving, the use of the linotype machine which Ottmar Mergenthaler perfected in 1885, and the increased use of advertising made lower magazine prices possible, thus insuring vastly larger circulations. *McClure's Magazine* appeared in May, 1893, at fifteen cents a copy, *Cosmopolitan* in July, at twelve and a half cents, then *Munsey's* in September, at ten cents. By 1898 there were some 750,000 regular magazine-reading families in the United States. By 1900 there were at least fifty well-known national magazines, a number of them with circulations of over a hundred thousand. There was one magazine with a circulation of a million. This was the *Ladies' Home Journal*, founded by Cyrus Curtis only seventeen years before.

The *Journal's* circulation accomplishment marked more than the unprecedented achievement of one magazine. It marked the beginning of new concepts in the publication and distribution of national magazines, with circulations running into the millions, that were to be characteristic of successful magazine publishing in the twentieth century. The change was largely brought about by one man, Cyrus H. K. Curtis, who "developed the magical possibilities of national advertising, and demonstrated more clearly than anyone else that you could lose millions of dollars on your circulation by selling at a low price yet make more millions out of your advertising, and build up such a mammoth enterprise you could pay unprecedented prices to contributors and thus command the market for writers and illustrators." [2] Curtis was the first to apply the intensive use of promotion to obtain a large circulation, and the first to weld the editorial force of magazines to the growing force of advertising.

[2] Frederick Lewis Allen, "American Magazines, 1741–1941," *Bulletin of the New York Public Library*, June, 1941.

Chapter 10

Edward Bok and the American Home

Cyrus H. K. Curtis, born in Portland, Maine, in 1850, evinced an early interest in magazines when as a thirteen-year-old schoolboy he commenced publication of *Young America*. Setting type himself and using an aged hand press which he purchased for two dollars and a half, he brought out his two-cent weekly for more than a year, selling advertising space in his magazine and doing job printing on the side. His schooling finished, Curtis became a dry-goods clerk in Portland and then went to Boston where in 1872, after several years' work as an advertising solicitor for obscure papers, he and another young man founded *The People's Ledger*. Curtis moved to Philadelphia and in 1879 began publication of *The Tribune and Farmer*, a four-page weekly with a subscription rate of fifty cents a year.

The *Ladies' Home Journal* originated from a department of *The Tribune and Farmer* which was devoted to subjects of interest to women. Noting the popularity of this department, which was written by his wife, the former Louisa Knapp, he decided to publish it as a separate monthly supplement to his magazine. The first issue of the *Ladies Journal and Practical Housekeeper*, the magazine's original title,[1] consisting of eight pages of domestic articles, appeared in December, 1883. It

[1] The artist drew a sentimental sketch of a happy family in their sylvan bower between the black-lettered "Ladies" and "Journal" in the logotype, and labeled the drawing "Home," thus adding that word to the title.

THE LADIES' HOME JOURNAL AND PRACTICAL HOUSEKEEPER.

VOL. I, NO. 12. PHILADELPHIA, NOVEMBER, 1884.

THANKSGIVING DAY IN THE OLDEN TIME

By reading the artist's label for his scene in the heading into the magazine's title, the public of 1883 changed Cyrus Curtis' *Ladies' Journal* into the *Ladies' Home Journal*.

contained an illustrated serial, articles on flower culture, fashion notes, advice on the care of children, and articles on cooking, needlework, and handicrafts—substantially the same material which, expanded and improved, characterizes the *Ladies' Home Journal* today.

The supplement, under the editorship of Mrs. Curtis, was immediately successful. While it took five years for *The Tribune and Farmer* to reach a circulation of 48,000, the *Ladies' Home Journal,* as the new magazine came to be called, had 25,000 subscribers by the end of its first year. Curtis thereupon relinquished his interest in *The Tribune and Farmer* and devoted all his attention to the new magazine.

At this point Curtis put into action some of the methods by which his success and the success of mass magazines in general were attained. Seeking well-known contributors for the *Journal,* he got Louisa M. Alcott, though it was hard for a comparatively unknown publisher to obtain writers already tied to other magazines. His success with Miss Alcott attracted other popular authors. He advertised the new magazine extensively; F. Wayland Ayer of N. W. Ayer & Sons extended him liberal credit for this purpose and obtained other credit for him. Curtis allowed club rates for women banding together to subscribe to the magazine. Within six months the circulation of the *Ladies' Home Journal* reached 50,000. In another six months it reached 100,000, equaling and even surpassing the circulation of many of the established magazines of the period. Curtis doubled the size of his magazine, raised his advertising rates, and circulation climbed to 700,000. In 1889 he raised the subscription price again, this time to one dollar a year, deliberately losing thousands of subscribers in order to stabilize circulation and consolidate his gains. He continued to pour money into advertising, spending more than a half million dollars in the first five years of the *Journal's* existence.

In 1889 Curtis hired as editor of the *Journal* Edward Bok, an employee of Charles Scribner's Sons in New York, whose syndicated literary letter he had seen and admired in the *Philadelphia Times.* Bok, who had been brought to this country from Holland as a child, was young, ambitious, didactic, and self-assured. For the next thirty years the *Ladies' Home Journal* was Edward Bok, backed in every one of his varied and often daring ventures for the magazine by his shrewd employer. *Godey's Lady's Book,* though it continued to be published in Philadelphia until 1892, had declined after the death of Sarah Josepha Hale in 1879. *Peterson's Magazine,* also in Philadelphia, was still going strong, but the *Ladies' Home Journal* was beginning to supplant both these earlier women's magazines when Edward Bok—with fanfare and wide publicity which spotlighted him as the youngest and highest-paid magazine editor of the time, and which made the most of the loud astonishment that a man should become the guiding light of a woman's magazine—took over its editorial direction.

The same sixteen-page issue of January, 1889, which announced the rise in price from fifty cents to one dollar a year, carried a signed announcement by Cyrus Curtis offering a prize of $500 to the person sending in the largest number of subscriptions by July 1. There were second and third prizes of $400 and $300. There was also a plentitude of advertisements for organs, watches, corsets—many kinds of them—hair curlers, self-wringing mops, jewelry, ornamental hairpins, linen, books, dolls, tools, and many other products, mostly for household use. It was "Rubifoam for the Teeth" in one dentifrice advertisement. Another advertisement read:

1,000 Gentlemen Want You

to take an interest in their well-fare and comfort. You cannot commence better than by urging them to shampoo regularly with Packer's Tar Soap, a remarkable remedy for, and preventive of, Dandruff and Baldness.

A half-page advertisement in the March, 1889, issue, its lead lines in large type, read:

Braided Wire Bustles Have Come to Stay
For Women Understand that they Cannot Afford
to Let Them Go

If a woman has too large hips, the Bustle relieves them of the protuberance; if she have no hips at all apparently, the Bustle supplies the lack; if she have too large an abdomen, the Bustle gives her symmetry, if she be too tall and thin, the Bustle helps her, if she be too short and broad, the Bustle helps her none the less. Of course, there are women so divinely moulded, so exquisitely symmetrical, that they do not need it and may not wear it; but there is only one in a thousand so perfectly proportioned, and the other nine hundred and ninety-nine will still avail themselves of its usefulness.

Edward Bok made his first appearance in the *Ladies' Home Journal* in the issue of September, 1889, with his syndicated column "Literary Leaves." Part of this gossip read:

> It is estimated by reliable judges that one out of every thirty novels printed in this country pays the author for his trouble. This will not be encouraging to those who are writing novels, but the statistics are authoritative. . . .
>
> The family of General Grant have thus far received $90,000 from the sale of the General's "Memoirs."
>
> Mark Twain's new book will be out in December. It is called "A Yankee at the Court of King Arthur," and is said to be a satire on the English nobility.
>
> Boston will again be the residence of Mr. W. D. Howells. His brief stay in New York, it is said, did not please him.
>
> Robert Louis Stevenson will not return to America for fully six months yet, unless he changes his mind, which is not an infrequent thing with him. At present the novelist is in Samoa.
>
> Jean Ingelow's health is so precarious as to prevent her from doing any literary work of moment.
>
> The widow of E. P. Roe has come to New York to reside.

A Bok article on "Forgotten Graves of Famous Authors" appeared in October; one on "Gladstone's Love for Reading and Bismarck's Literary Tastes," in December. Bok's accession was announced and his name appeared in the *Journal* masthead as editor in the issue of January, 1890; Mrs. Louisa Knapp Curtis, pleading that domestic duties no longer permitted her to give full services to the magazine, was to remain on the staff. A characteristic Bok innovation came in this number. Bok, undeterred by modesty or tradition, believed both in making himself as editor well known, in contrast to the anonymity of most magazine editors at the time, and in establishing the closest possible relationship between the editor and his readers. "The method of editorial expression in the magazines of 1889," he wrote years later, "was distinctly vague and prohibitively impersonal. The public knew the name of scarcely a single editor of a magazine; there was no personality that stood out in the mind. . . . He felt that the time had come . . . for the editor of some magazine to project his personality through the printed page." [2]

To stimulate reader response Bok, immediately on assuming the *Journal* editorship, turned to what is now called the "survey technique," offering a series of prizes for the best answers to questions he put to his readers. What in the magazine did they like least? Why? What did they like best? Why? What new features would they like to see started? Thousands of answers were returned, and the editor acted on the reader advice thus obtained. Bok had, he says, "divined the fact that in thousands of cases the American mother was not the confidante of her daughter, and reasoned if any inviting human personality could be created on the printed page that would supply this lamentable lack of family life, girls would flock to such a figure." Implementing this belief he wrote under the pseudonym of "Ruth Ashmore" and printed in the January, 1889, issue of the *Ladies' Home Journal* the first of his "Side Talks to Girls." In it he advised girls to "learn to say no. There is in that little word much that will protect you from evil tongues." He circumspectly warned his young readers not to give their photographs to every Tom, Dick, and Harry. In February, "Ruth Ashmore" wrote about "The Girl Who Hints,"

[2] Edward Bok, *The Americanization of Edward Bok* (New York: Charles Scribner's Sons, 1923), p. 162.

the wearing of jewelry, neatness in dress, and when dancing is wrong. "It's all very well to say that there is no harm in dancing. There isn't. But there is harm in having about you, a sweet, pure girl, kept as much as possible from the wickedness of the world, the arm of a man who may be a profligate, and not possess the first instinct of a gentleman."

Letters asking advice and describing problems of the feminine heart began to pour in. "Ruth Ashmore" became a woman writer to whom Bok turned over what rapidly became one of the most popular features of the *Journal,* and he went on to develop other features that would cause readers to write in to the editor. Determined to establish a warm rapport between his magazine and American women, he urged his readers to make it a clearing house for information of all kinds. He used many devices to stimulate personal contact between the magazine and its audience. To many, the twenty-six-year-old Bok seemed brash. There was jeering as well as praise. He encouraged both, for both meant attention to him and his magazine, and Bok adored attention.

Bok was derided for some of his novel undertakings. As late as 1916 Algernon Tassin [3] wrote that it seemed Bok's intention to place the two hemispheres on a family basis by introducing everybody in the world to everybody else. No sooner had "Unknown Wives of Well-Known Men" run its course than along came "Unknown Husbands" or "Famous Daughters of Famous Men." But Tassin also pointed out that the editors of the new popular magazines and of some of the conservative older magazines were quick to imitate Bok, seeking to emerge from their traditional editorial anonymity into places in the limelight.

By 1893 the *Ladies' Home Journal* was a magazine of thirty-four pages with a differently illustrated cover each month, new features, many illustrations. It was running William Dean Howells' *The Coast of Bohemia* as a serial and Mamie Dickens' *My Father As I Knew Him,* in addition to all the domes-

[3] See his *The Magazine in America* (New York: Dodd, Mead & Co., 1916), p. 354. *Cf.* John E. Drewry, *Some Magazines and Their Makers* (Boston: The Stratford Co., 1924).

tic departments and other literary offerings of the Laura Jean Libbey type. Ella Wheeler Wilcox was in almost every 1893 issue. Mrs. Lyman Abbott was contributing "Just Among Ourselves," and "Clever Daughters of Clever Men" was appearing month after month. Pages of sheet music were another new feature. In April, 1893, there were six pages of the "Magnolia Blossom Waltzes" by Reginald de Koven. "The Manhattan Beach March" by John Philip Sousa was in the Christmas issue; so was "A Pioneer Christmas" by Hamlin Garland. "Name" writers were usual in the *Journal* by this time. Bok in his "At Home With the Editor" columns was writing on such subjects as women in business. He was against it:

> The atmosphere of commercial life has never been conducive to the best interests of women engaged in it. The number of women in business who lose their gentleness and womanliness is far greater than those who retain what, after all, are woman's best and chief qualities. To be in an office where there are only men has never yet done a single girl any good; and it has done harm to thousands. . . . I know whereof I speak, and I deal not in generalities.

Many of Bok's readers were office workers by this time, but even they must have approved Bok's stand. It was characteristic of the 1890's to place women on a pedestal. Women themselves did all they could to encourage the flattery. In the same 1893 issue "Ruth Ashmore" wrote "My Sweetheart and I." Despite the saccharinity with which it was written, her advice was practical and probably palatable. The gist of it was—hang on to him.

Five years later, with the magazine marking its fifteenth year of publication, the *Ladies' Home Journal* was forty-eight pages instead of the original eight. It was printed on "slick" paper, profusely illustrated. Its circulation, 440,000 when Bok assumed the editorship, was now 850,000. In an editorial Bok wrote proudly, "Wherever the mail goes, the *Journal* goes. . . . The *Journal* crosses every sea and ocean." It was being circulated to fifty-nine of the sixty-five civilized nations of the globe. In the same editorial Bok wrote:

> The fact must never be forgotten that no magazine published in the United States could give what it is giving to the reader each

month if it were not for the revenue which the advertiser brings the magazine. It is the growth of advertising in this country which, more than any other single element, has brought the American magazine to its present enviable position in points of literary, illustrative, and mechanical excellence. The American advertiser has made the superior American magazine of today possible.

Bok could honestly describe the American magazine as having achieved literary and illustrative excellence. His contributors included Kipling, Howells, Mark Twain, Conan Doyle, Sarah Orne Jewett, John Kendrick Bangs, Kate Douglas Wiggin, Joel Chandler Harris, Jerome K. Jerome, Eugene Field, James Whitcomb Riley, and others of the best writers of the day. He had published work by Grover Cleveland and Benjamin Harrison, and was later to publish William Howard Taft and both Theodore and Franklin D. Roosevelt.

As illustrators the *Journal* had Edwin Abbey, Howard Pyle, Charles Dana Gibson, Will Low, W. T. Smedley, and W. L. Taylor. In the late 1890's it was running full pages of photographs which made good picture stories even by present-day standards. Typical picture stories showed the home and life of Mary Anderson, then living in England; Lew Wallace, the author of *Ben Hur,* writing at his home in Indiana; Joe Jefferson, the actor who achieved his greatest fame in the role of Rip Van Winkle, playing the amateur painter at his home in Buzzard's Bay. Bok could claim to be one of those editors who realized a picture can sometimes tell more than pages of print.[4]

At the same time the *Journal* stressed in every issue the domestic concerns of particular interest to its women readers, and Bok published all the true-life story material he could obtain. He got Mrs. Henry Ward Beecher to write "Mr. Beecher As I Knew Him," and had Dwight L. Moody conduct "Mr.

[4] Bok's ideas on the use of pictures in magazines were decidedly modern. In the November, 1898, editorial which he headed briskly "Fifteen Years of Mistakes," he wrote: "After the editorial part, the picture side of a magazine naturally always receives the most thought. The *Journal's* pictorial aim is to give its readers not only good pictures, so far as their art value is concerned, but interesting pictures from the standpoint of composition. The modern tendency is to illustrate almost everything. . . . But the danger has been to overdo illustrating—to push it into disrepute. Pictures are valuable only where they illustrate something or tell something. . . . A picture must tell something, it must, if possible, tell a story apart from what it seeks to illustrate."

Moody's Bible Class" in the *Journal.* He published one entire issue written by "Famous Daughters of Famous Men." In it were contributions by the daughters of Dickens, Hawthorne, Harrison, Greeley, Thackeray, Howells, Gladstone, and Jefferson Davis.

By 1898 Curtis and the energetic, confident, crusading Bok had built a magazine with a large and loyal audience which felt itself closely connected to the editor and his paper. The *Ladies' Home Journal* had become known as "the monthly Bible of the American home." "And," said Mark Sullivan in *Our Times,* "there was a measure of allegorical truth in what was sometimes jeeringly spoken."

Edward Bok was determined not only to make the *Ladies' Home Journal* a magazine which provided intimate and personal service to its readers, but also to bring about changes for the better in American home life. He intended to improve standards in everything that pertained to the home, and he went about realizing this large ambition in a direct and practical manner. At the same time that he was advising women about affairs of the heart, telling them how to dress, how to conduct themselves, how to feed their families, even how to bring up their children, he strove to effect changes in home architecture and in home decoration. He employed physicians and nurses to write on health long before this practice was adopted by the newspapers. Their duties included both the writing of material for publication and the answering of letters from readers provoked by their articles. He employed other experts, experts on cooking, nursing, beauty care, household management.

In 1895 he set out to wean American taste away from the ornate in home construction and furnishing and to direct it toward the simpler, more attractive, and more practical. He began publication of plans for a series of houses that could be built for from $1,500 to $5,000. Complete scale plans and specifications, together with estimates from builders, were offered at five dollars a set. *Ladies' Home Journal* houses began to go up in all parts of the country. Building promoters built whole

A Special Word to Subscribers

WHEN you receive notice that your subscription has expired renew at once, using the blank inclosed in your final copy. Sometimes a subscriber who has already renewed may receive this blank. That does not mean that the renewal has not been received. We begin to pack in mail-bags two weeks or more before mailing, and the renewal may have reached us after the copy containing the blank has been packed. In requesting change of address please give us four weeks' notice.

If your subscription expires with this issue your renewal must reach us before the tenth of October to avoid missing the next issue. We cannot begin subscriptions with back numbers. Subscribers should use Postal or Express money orders in remitting. All Rural Free Delivery carriers can supply Postal money orders.

THE LADIES' HOME JOURNAL

Registered in United States Patent Office

Published on the Twenty-fifth of each month preceding date of issuance by

THE CURTIS PUBLISHING COMPANY

421-427 Arch Street, Philadelphia, Pennsylvania

EDITED BY EDWARD W. BOK

Cyrus H. K. Curtis, President — Edward W. Bok, Vice-President and Editor

C. H. Ludington, Jr., Secretary and Treasurer — William V. Alexander, Managing Editor

The Price of The Journal

By subscription: One Dollar and Fifty Cents a year, postage free in the United States, Alaska, Cuba, Porto Rico, Mexico, and the Hawaiian and Philippine Islands. Single copies: 15 cents each. In Canada, $2 a year, except in Toronto, where the price is $1.50 a year. Single copies: 20 cents each, except in Montreal and Toronto, where the price is 15 cents.

In Foreign Countries in the International Postal Union other than those named above: Subscription, postpaid, per year, 10 shillings 3 pence, payable by international money order ($2.50 in American money); Single copies, 11 pence each (22 cents in American money).

Our Branch Offices

(For advertising business only. Subscriptions not received.)

NEW YORK: Madison Avenue and 23d Street
BOSTON: Barristers Hall.
CHICAGO: Home Insurance Building
LONDON: 5, Henrietta Street, Covent Garden, W. C.

The Editor's Personal Page

The time has come to turn the light on an existing condition touching the American fireside that will appal the average woman and girl. It is the knowledge of this condition that led this magazine, now nearly two years ago, to insist upon a greater parental frankness with children about their physical selves.

The Condition:

BECAUSE of the secrecy with which the whole question is enshrouded it is practically impossible to obtain absolute figures. But so far as the highest authorities have been able, through the most careful inquiries, to secure accurate figures, it is a conservative statement to make that at least 60 out of every 100 young men are today "sowing their wild oats." Of these 60 young men a startling number are either already making or will make a tragedy of marriage. They produce either childless homes: dead-born or blind babies: children with lifelong disease with them: or they will send thousands of women to the operating-table. Exactly what percentage of these 60 young men escape the lifelong perils of their early indiscretions it is impossible to tell.

These statements are made not upon theory, but facts that are proved and demonstrated at thousands of domestic bedsides and in the autopsy rooms of hundreds of hospitals. They are facts that are known to every physician.

This frightful condition has been brought about, largely, by two contributing factors:

First: The parental policy of mock-modesty and silence with their sons and daughters about their physical selves, and

Second: The condoning in men what is condemned in women. Fathers and mothers, and, in consequence, girls have condoned in a young man this sowing of his "wild oats" because it was considered a physical necessity; that "it would do him good"; that "it would make a man of him"; that "it would show him the world"—all arguments absolutely baseless.

With hundreds of girls the young man who has most promiscuously and profusely scattered his "wild oats" has been looked upon as the most favored one among possible husbands. To many a girl there is always something alluring to marry a man with a past because it appealed to her vanity to "remake" or "reform" him. The peril to herself she has never known, for silence has been the portion meted out to her by her parents.

The Five Results:

THE FIRST: The lifelong invalidism or the surgical mutilation of thousands of women;

THE SECOND: The deaths of untold thousands of unborn or new-born infants;

THE THIRD: The lifelong taint of disease upon children who do live;

THE FOURTH: The blindness of over 60 out of every 100 new-born blind babies;

THE FIFTH: The domestic unhappiness of tens of thousands of homes because of the absence of children.

Over 70 out of every 100 special surgical operations on women are the direct or indirect result of one cause

This statement is made on the highest medical authority

The Remedy:

NOW thousands will naturally ask: Is there a remedy for this slaughter and maiming of babies and the surgical mutilation of women? There is not only a remedy, but a remedy as potent as it is simple. It is this, and it is distinctly "up to" the parents:

First: We parents must first of all get it into our heads firm and fast to do away with the policy of silence with our children that has done so much to bring about this condition. Our sons and daughters must be told what they are, and they must be told lovingly and frankly. But told they must be.

Second: We fathers of daughters must rid ourselves of the notion that has worked such diabolical havoc of a double moral standard. There can be but one standard: that of moral equality. Instead of being so painfully anxious about the "financial prospects" of a young man who seeks the hand of our daughter in marriage, and making that the first question, it is time that we put health first and money second: that we find out, first of all, if the young man comes to court, as the lawyers say, with clean hands. Let a father ask the young man, as his leading question, whether he is physically clean: insist that he shall go to his family physician, and if he gives him a clean bill of health, then his financial prospects can be gone into. But his physical self first. That much every father would do in the case of a horse or a dog that he bought with a view to mating. Yet he does less for his daughter: his own flesh and blood.

Once let young men realize that such a question would be asked them by the fathers of the young women whom they would marry: that a physical standard would be demanded—and that knowledge would be more effective for morality among young men than all the preaching and moralizing and exhortations of the past thousand years.

Thus, and thus only, can we save our daughters and their unborn children. But in no other way.

The Darkened Sight of Thousands of Babies

Over 60 out of every 100 new-born blind babies are blinded, soon after birth, from one cause. One cause kills outright before, or shortly after, birth, 3 out of 4 children affected.

"A child dying, leaving this good world of ours, seems to have had so small a chance for itself. There is something in all of us struggling against oblivion, striving vainly to make a real impress on the current of time, and a child dying can only clutch the hands about it and go down—forever. It seems so merciless, so unfair. Perhaps that is why, all over the world, the little graves are cared for best. It is to the little graves that we turn, and not to the larger mounds, in our keenest anguish: to the little graves that our hearts are drawn in our hours of triumph; and so the child, though dead, lives its appointed time and dies only in the fullness of its years. The little shoes, the little dresses, the 'little tin soldiers, covered with rust,' and the memories sweeter than dreams of a honeymoon—these are life's immortelles that never fade."

—WILLIAM ALLEN WHITE.

Risking cancellation of advertising and thousands of subscriptions, Edward Bok dared discussion of venereal disease in the *Ladies' Home Journal.*

suburban communities according to *Journal* plans. Bok, who believed always in the concrete and visual, published pictures of the completed houses offering prizes for the best interior pictures of homes built on *Journal* specifications. The Victorian parlors were left out of these plans. Two windows were placed in the maids' rooms. Kitchens were made more compact, and built-in cupboards were substituted for pantries. Cupolas, balconies, gingerbread decorations, were discarded. Other practical and aesthetic improvements were made. Architects, among them Stanford White, acknowledged leader of the profession, opposed Bok's plans at first, but later White said: "I firmly believe that Edward Bok has more completely influenced American domestic architecture for the better than any man in this generation." Bok quoted the admission proudly in his autobiography.

The *Ladies' Home Journal* then turned its attention inside the house. It ran pictures of home interiors in every issue, labeling this living room, dining room, bedroom, as either good or bad. A photographic series run all through 1898 was the "Inside of One Hundred Homes." A similar series, "Outside of One Hundred Homes," ran in 1899. Bok printed pictures of furniture. Captions read, "This chair is ugly" or "This table is beautiful." These comparisons of the ugly and the aesthetically pleasing covered tables, beds, curtains, carpets, and other household furniture. The very pictures on the wall were changed by *Journal* teachings. Bok published pictures by Abbey, Pyle, Gibson, and others, and the *Journal* conducted art exhibitions of 250 originals in full color. Those which readers chose as their ten favorites were then sold in portfolios for use in their homes. Two hundred thousand pictures were thus introduced into American homes. "For certain elevation in the taste of houses and housefurnishings," said Mark Sullivan, "he is more to be thanked than any other one man."

Bok went on to exert the continually growing influence of the *Ladies' Home Journal* far beyond the domestic sphere, though he started in its immediate neighborhood. He began a campaign to clean up and beautify American communities. He showed "how much can be done with little" through pictures of back yards before and after planting of flowers and shrubbery. In a department called "Beautiful America" he printed pictures of localities cluttered with disfiguring billboards and advertising; then pictures of the same places with the objectionable signs removed. Bok succeeded in getting rid of a huge billboard erected at Niagara Falls and, by the mere threat of publication, prevented erection of another sign, described as "the largest advertisement in the world," on the rim of the Grand Canyon. Lynn, Massachusetts; Trenton, New Jersey; and Memphis, Tennessee, were featured in that order as "dirty cities," and the *Journal* published photographs to uphold the accuracy of its choice. Municipal authorities threatened suit, and local newspapers were virulent in their abuse of Bok and his magazine, but the cities were cleaned up, and other cities, fearing like publicity, swept and scoured.

In 1892 the *Ladies' Home Journal* announced that it would no longer accept advertisements for patent medicines. It was the first magazine to refuse advertising of this type, though within the next two years seven other newspapers and periodicals did likewise. In 1904 and 1905 Bok attacked the entire patent-medicine industry with every weapon at his command. In a series of exposures he attacked the evils of the industry from all angles. Bok tells the story graphically in his autobiography:

> The Editor got the Women's Christian Temperance Union into action against the periodicals for publishing advertisements of medicines containing as high as forty per cent alcohol. He showed that the most confidential letters written by women with private ailments were opened by young clerks of both sexes, laughed at and gossiped over, and that afterward their names and addresses, which they had been told were held in the strictest confidence, were sold to other lines of business for five cents each. He held the religious press up to the scorn of church members for accepting advertisements which the publishers knew and which he proved to be not only fraudulent, but actually harmful. He called the United States Post Office authorities to account for accepting and distributing obscene circular matter.[5]

[5] Bok, *The Americanization of Edward Bok,* pp. 340–41.

Bok reprinted in the *Journal* a patent-medicine advertisement which urged ailing women to write for advice to a woman represented as working in her laboratory to lessen their suffering. Next to the advertisement Bok ran a photograph of this woman's gravestone which showed that she had died some twenty years before. Bok likewise reproduced the American and English labels for a medicine used for quieting fretful infants. They were identical except that the English label, acceding to the provisions of the English Pharmacy Act, read: "This preparation, containing, among other valuable ingredients, a small amount of morphine, is, in accordance with the Pharmacy Act, hereby labelled 'poison.'" The American manufacturers of the remedy thereafter cooperated by publishing their formula.

The *Journal* then published a list of twenty-two patent medicines and told what each contained. An expert's mistake backfired in the case of one and The Curtis Publishing Company lost a suit brought by its manufacturer, but Bok and the *Journal* kept on arousing public opinion against a vicious social abuse. He hired Mark Sullivan, recently graduated from Harvard Law School, who unearthed and published in the *Journal* more damning evidence of abuses wrought by patent-medicine companies. The *Journal* had kept up the fight singlehandedly for two years when *Collier's Weekly* joined in. Other periodicals and various groups broke into the conflict. An exhibition of adulterated canned and bottled foods was shown at the St. Louis Exposition in 1904. In 1905 President Theodore Roosevelt recommended to Congress passage of an act regulating interstate commerce in misbranded and adulterated foods, drinks, and drugs. Despite the bitter organized opposition of Bok's antagonists, the Food and Drug Act was passed in 1906.

Chapter 11

Further Activities of the Women's Magazines

Edward Bok was not always successful in the many crusades which his energy and reformer's zeal led him to undertake in the *Ladies' Home Journal.* Ironically he succeeded where it was of national importance, but failed where the object of his attack was a matter of purely feminine concern.

Bok preached dignity and modesty in women's dress. In 1909 and 1910 he undertook to demolish Paris as the dictator of women's fashions, a state of affairs in dressmaking which he believed unpatriotic, economically unsound, and sometimes basically fraudulent. The *Journal* employed experts to design frocks and hats, inaugurated contests, and in every issue banged away with the slogan "American Fashions for American Women." Bok had designers visit the Metropolitan Museum of Art in New York. The designs they worked out were judged by a board of women experts in New York, then published in the *Journal.* It was proved that many Paris models which would have been rejected by European women of taste were concocted for the "barbaric" American trade. It was also proved that Paris labels made in this country were attached to goods of American manufacture. The *Journal's* campaign failed completely. Thanks to the free advertising, more Paris models were sold than previously, and the trade in spurious labels increased.

Bok was likewise defeated when, on humanitarian grounds, he urged women not to wear the aigrettes then considered fashionable millinery adornments. The *Journal* printed photographs of the killing of the mother birds to obtain the plumes, and pictured the bird's starving young. The articles and pictures drew the attention of women who had not before realized the need of aigrettes for their hats. Sales of the feathers more than quadrupled before the *Ladies' Home Journal* dropped the campaign.

In a more important and more spectacular undertaking, Bok and the *Journal* dared to violate a taboo. Lyman Abbott, successor to Henry Ward Beecher both as minister of the Plymouth Congregational Church in Brooklyn and as editor of *The Outlook*, a magazine which had started as *The Christian Union*, convinced Bok that he should take up the fight against venereal disease. More cautious friends advised against such a radical and dangerous attempt. Cyrus Curtis told Bok to go ahead if he thought he was right. Bok published an editorial on venereal disease in 1906. Immediately the protests began to arrive at the *Journal* offices. Thousands of subscriptions were stopped. Advertisers notified Curtis that they would cancel their advertising. Outraged *Journal* readers refused to admit the offending magazine to their homes, and some of the editor's own friends tore the wicked pages from the *Journal* before allowing it to be seen by their families. Despite losing about 75,000 subscribers, the *Journal* persisted. Finally such writers and public figures as Jane Addams, Cardinal Gibbons, Henry Van Dyke, President Eliot of Harvard, and the Bishop of London came to the aid of the indomitable Bok. They risked public indignation and wrote *Journal* articles supporting the magazine's position.

The *Journal* published article after article. A full-page editorial declared that seventy of every one hundred special surgical operations on women were directly or indirectly necessitated by venereal disease; and that sixty of every one hundred babies blinded soon after birth lost their sight from the same cause. Piously shocked men added their protests to those of the horrified women. The subject was not one to be talked of. If talked of at all, it was a subject for males only. But Bok insisted "that the time had come when women should learn the truth, and that, so far as it lay in his power, he intended to see that they did know."

Though completely open discussion of venereal disease did not become common for perhaps another twenty-five years, the *Ladies' Home Journal* made the facts known, made a forbidden topic a possible subject of open and sensible discussion in the press, in books, in schools and colleges.

In 1935, fifteen years after the resignation of Edward Bok and following a succession of short-term incumbents, Bruce and Beatrice Blackmar Gould, husband and wife, both Iowa-born and educated, were made co-editors of the *Ladies' Home Journal.* Under their vigorous and regal editorship the *Journal,* which had slipped in popularity and lost ground to its stronger competitors, was restored to the preeminence which it had held under Bok. Until the late 1950's the *Ladies' Home Journal* had the largest circulation of any women's magazine and one of the largest newsstand circulations of any general American magazine.

It was the Goulds' stated belief when they took over the *Journal* "that the working intelligence of the average American woman was far greater than generally believed." It was the new editors' aim "to bring our readers not only the most accurate and honest information possible in the traditional areas: health, nutrition, education, and the moral guidance of children; community, social and cultural activities . . . but also to widen the boundaries of her traditional areas of interest."

In pursuance of this policy, the Gould *Journal* carried articles on politics, foreign affairs, medicine, education, and social welfare. In 1947 it established a forceful "Public Affairs Department." In 1940 it started its "How America Lives" series, articles on the lives and homes of "typical" American families. The series was planned to run for a year. Title and emphasis changed to "How Young America Lives," it ran for many years.

Typical of the magazine's contents were the *Journal's* more intimate offerings: "Tell Me Doctor," "Dr. Spock's Talks to Mothers," "Can This Marriage Be Saved?" and other features of carefully designed interest to women exclusively.

The *Journal* was also consistent in the publication of best-seller fiction. Year after year the magazine ran either as serials or in versions edited for complete presentation in one issue romantic and sentimental novels that later attained wide if transient popularity in book form. It did almost as well with its biographies and autobiographies of prominent women—entertainers or royalty, with aristocracy at the very least seeming the preferred subjects.

The *Ladies' Home Journal* was persuasive and flattering. It was seductive. It thrilled its readers by describing and picturing fashions and household decor ordinarily beyond their means and slickly transporting them into the world of glamor which most of them did not inhabit. Calling itself "The Magazine Women Believe In," and coyly, insistently, and complacently warning the male world that it must "Never Underestimate the Power of a Woman," the editors professed an inability to define the achievement by which they were awed or to comprehend the full magic of the *Journal's* appeal. A statement of editorial philosophy read in part: "Primarily it is what goes into the editorial pages of a magazine that makes the magazine live and breathe and sing . . . A magazine like ours is . . . a moral force. It must have integrity and respect for American principles as well as entertainment and utility value. No formula will help us, no balancing of pictures or text, long articles or short, reprints or new. There is no possibility of laying down a pattern and then following through."

Yet there was a pattern. Readers could see it even if the editors could not. *Ladies' Home Journal* had become obviously a formula magazine. Femaleness rather than femininity gave a feverish warmth to each issue. Obstetrics and feminine hygiene set the tone. Every issue contained some carefully selected piece which, for purposes of circulation promotion, could be touted over the air, on posters, and in newspaper markets as especially glamorous or sensationally revealing. Almost every issue featured a brand-new, sure-fire diet. Consistently the diets advocated were for taking off rather than putting on weight. It seemed as if, all by itself, the *Journal* had assumed the moral responsibility for reducing the tonnage of American womanhood.

Ladies' Home Journal began to deteriorate well before the resignation of Bruce and Beatrice Gould as editors in 1962. The fresh ideas of the 1930's had gone limp and frayed, and no new ones were injected. The *Journal* had lost out to *McCall's* in the race for the greatest multimillion circulation. Advertising was falling off. Prestige slipping, the dowager of Independence Square in Philadelphia began to look dowdy.

As if it heeded some of its own diet advice, the *Journal* slimmed down as it lost more pages of advertising. Hoping that imitation of the monosyllabic titles of very popular magazines would bring it some of their success, the magazine began to print JOURNAL in huge block letters on its cover, making "Ladies" and "Home" almost invisible. In search of a more salubrious climate or of the lost youth she was continually telling her readers how to regain, the *Journal* moved to New York. The move did not noticeably improve her health, and the spectacular deterioration of The Curtis Publishing Company, in which the magazine was caught, did not help. From thin the *Journal* went haggard as advertising and profits further declined during the middle and late 1960's. The miracles that it was promised would be worked on behalf of *Ladies' Home Journal* either never materialized or did not prove miraculous enough.

Possibly the *Journal* was just too old. Eighty-five is a considerable age for a magazine as well as for a woman. The circulation was nearly 6,800,000, topped in size among women's magazines only by the victorious *McCall's* and *Family Circle.* First of all the Curtis family of publications, it was certainly the mother of *The Saturday Evening Post* and at least the stepmother of *Country Gentleman, Holiday,* and *American Home;* the grandmother, so to speak, of *Jack and Jill* and *Sta-*

tus. Ladies' Home Journal was still widely read and highly respected, but in August, 1968, the distressed Curtis Publishing Company sold *Ladies' Home Journal* at the price of distress merchandise. No separate price was announced for the *Journal,* but *Ladies' Home Journal* and *American Home* together brought only a reported $5,400,000 in the stock of the purchasing organization, Downe Communications, Inc.

Chapter 12

Fiction, Fashion, and Sex

The women's magazines were the first to achieve the vast circulations characteristic of the mass magazines. Like all consumer magazines they were conceived and founded for one purpose—to make money for their owners. To this praiseworthy end they were developed upon the idea of service to women and the home, and they provided what they claimed to provide.

Through their crusades and campaigns they wrought improvements in the domestic sphere. They gave women, not yet politically enfranchised, a chance to see the opinions and desires of women expressed and acted upon. They acknowledged the importance of women, which gratified their readers. Paradoxically, though they were first directed to women as housewives and homemakers, their development accompanied the emergence of women from the confines of the domestic sphere into the world of jobs, community activities, and politics; in fact, the magazines were largely instrumental in forwarding it. Bok, as reactionary in some directions as he was modern in others, protested against the entrance of women into what he considered masculine affairs, but his magazine and other women's periodicals did more perhaps to make it possible and even inevitable than any other single factor. They applied a social force and achieved a fundamental social change on which some of them at least had not counted.

Collier's, as has been indicated, fought valiantly beside the *Journal* in the battle for pure food and drug legislation. Dr. H. W. Wiley, chief chemist of the United States Department of Agriculture, was so vigorous a proponent of this legislation that the measures were for a time known as the "Wiley Laws." Shortly afterward Dr. Wiley became the head of the famed Good Housekeeping Bureau.

Good Housekeeping had been founded in Holyoke, Massachusetts, in 1885 by Clark W. Bryan, who described it as "conducted in the interests of the higher life of the household," designed "to produce or perpetuate perfection, or as near unto perfection, as may be obtained in the household." In 1901, a year after the magazine was purchased by the Phelps Publishing Company, the Good Housekeeping Institute was inaugurated as an editorial department which could provide detailed and accurate information on home economics subjects. It developed laboratories and kitchens for the testing of household appliances, textiles, home cleansing agents, and similar consumer products. In its many busy years of activity the Good Housekeeping Institute has become justly one of the most famous operations of its kind in the world.

In 1912, shortly after *Good Housekeeping* had been moved to New York as the property of Hearst Magazines, Inc., the Good Housekeeping Bureau was instituted with Dr. Wiley as its director. Almost immediately it began the investigation of food and drug products, of pharmaceuticals and cosmetics, which, on a much larger scale, it carries on today. Both the Good Housekeeping Institute and the Good Housekeeping Bureau have accomplished much in raising standards and improving products for the home, as well as in providing their readers with home information and ideas in the best traditions of the women's service magazine. Fashions, beauty advice, and baby and child care were added at various times to *Good Housekeeping* as editorial departments backed by Institute or Bureau findings or by work in specially devised clinics and centers for study of the problems. A building forum, devoted to home and community planning, was established in 1945.

As a property of the huge Hearst Corporation, which has a string of other magazines to appeal to the other interests of women (among them *Bride & Home, eye, Harper's Bazaar,* and *House Beautiful*), *Good Housekeeping* continues to emphasize and sell its practical utility to the housewife. The Good Housekeeping Institute and the "Consumers' Guarantee Seal" are featured in the magazine and in the publisher's advertising. The magazine's approach is more prosaic than that of its competitors. It offers its readers guidance toward making buying decisions and its advertisers a market of women conditioned by its editorial findings.

The *Woman's Home Companion* was founded ten years before *Ladies' Home Journal,* beginning life in Cleveland as the *Home Companion,* changing its name to the *Ladies' Home Companion* in 1866, and adopting its final title in 1897. Developing in much the same manner as *Good Housekeeping* and the *Ladies' Home Journal*—that is, as a service magazine for women—it was long edited (1911–1940) by the well-known Gertrude Battles Lane. It was she who, decrying "the cat in the cracker barrel," crusaded in her magazine for packaged groceries, created the *Companion*'s Better Babies Bureau, and in 1935 set up a reader–editor service through which readers were asked periodically for editorial service. During her long editorship the circulation of this Crowell-Collier magazine rose from 727,000 to more than 3,500,000.

The *Companion* was a typical woman's magazine comparing very favorably with its peers except in one all-important respect—advertising revenue. It published many of the leading women fiction writers. It offered articles, public affairs, fiction, help for love and marriage, features, home service center, fashions, beauty and grooming, teens, children, homemaking, and workshop. This run-down of the table of contents largely describes the attempt at editorial coverage of all the surviving women's magazines. Any difference there is lies in the phrasing of titles, the selection of diversified subjects for a given issue, and in the physical presentation of the material. From 1953 through 1955 the following were among the names appearing either as writers or as subjects of articles in *Woman's Home Companion:* Jack Benny, Pearl Buck, Queen Elizabeth, Mrs. Norman Vincent Peale, Thomas Costain, Marlene Dietrich, Mamie Eisenhower, Daphne du Maurier, the Duchess of Windsor, Joan Crawford, Arnold Toynbee, Alfred H. Kinsey, and Lloyd Douglas. They typify the writers and the types of people written about not only in the *Companion* but in the mass women's magazines still.

The eighty-three-year-old *Woman's Home Companion* had a circulation of well over 4,000,000, but it vanished unhappily in December, 1956, when the Crowell-Collier Publishing Company terminated it along with *Collier's* and the *American Magazine.*

McCall's Magazine assumed that name in 1897. In the 1870's and 1880's it had been *The Queen,* and in the early 1890's, *The Queen of Fashion,* indicating that *McCall's* was originally a fashion journal. It still emphasizes fashions but also includes all the service departments characteristic of its sister magazines: beauty, children, home, food, feature articles. It does more. In May, 1954, *McCall's* announced major changes in editorial policy. Prompted perhaps by the success of the so-called "shelter magazines" like *Better Homes and Gardens,* it announced that it would no longer look upon itself simply as a woman's service magazine, but that it would devote itself to the American woman and her family, becoming a publication for the entire household. Advertisements at the time stated that the new *McCall's* melody would be "togetherness." Neither the appearance nor the contents changed, and the promotion was soon dropped. Evidently the decision was reached that the female remains a more susceptible and profitable market than the male.

In the *McCall's* of this period there was usually an article on sex, often a complete novel. Always there were fashions, recipes, housekeeping hints. The names that appeared and reappeared were much the same as those that appeared in the other women's magazines. Once a *Ladies' Home Journal* regular, Eleanor Roosevelt wrote monthly in *McCall's.* Other writers included Alfred H. Kinsey, Mary Pickford, Dr. Norman Vincent Peale, Taylor Caldwell, Edward R. Murrow, Anthony J. Drexel Biddle, Audrey Hepburn, and the Duchess of Windsor. The women's magazines seldom go in for unknown names.

They do go in for the strenuous, often vicious, competition which characterizes mass magazine publishing. The female may or may not be deadlier than the male, but certainly the scratching, screaming, and hair-pulling among consumer publications devoted to the gentler sex is notable. Out of the melee *McCall's* has sprung triumphant.

Herbert R. Mayes is usually credited with the spectacular competitive triumph of *McCall's.* Editor of *Good Housekeeping* for twenty years, Mayes was made *McCall's* editor in November, 1958. Quickly he threw out the seductive but unworkable "togetherness." He made sweeping changes in both the content and appearance of his magazine, adding more and brighter color pages and featuring more fiction. Billing itself as the "First Magazine for Women," *McCall's* quickly surpassed its rivals in both circulation and advertising linage.

Mayes used Allen Drury, John Steinbeck, Ogden Nash, Phyllis McGinley, Herman Wouk, Anne Morrow Lindbergh, and writers of comparable achievement and reputation. A typical 1962 issue featured hairdos, chastity, diet, and the Hollywood story of Hedda Hopper. *McCall's* became vital and vigorous. As circulation increased rapidly, it raised its base circulation guarantees to advertisers but not always its advertising rates at the same time, making the magazine an attractive buy. Breaking with the practice of the other mass magazines, it did away with any premium charge for bleed pages (no margins on the page, giving the advertiser that much more space for display) and charged the same for black and white or full-color bleed as for its regular page.

Herbert Mayes was made president of the entire McCall Corporation in 1961. He retired from that position in 1965. Since that time, top McCall editors and executives have come and gone quickly, sometimes very quickly.

In November, 1966, to great fanfare in its promotion and in the press, it hired twenty-three-year-old Lynda Bird Johnson, older daughter of the then President, as writer and consultant on a new section of the magazine dealing with youth and the college campus. The first article of this recent graduate of the University of Texas appeared as "A Look Back at College" in *McCall's* for January, 1967. The same issue contained a piece by Margaret Truman Daniels on ex-President Truman as a grandfather.

In 1961 the McCall Corporation added *The Saturday Review* to its many properties and seated its editor, Norman Cousins, on its board. In 1968 Cousins as its editorial director began striving to bring a younger and yet livelier look to *McCall's.* The magazine revamped its contents page. It introduced editorials for the first time. It began to integrate scattered departmental features into one central piece, as in a lead article on Mexico in June, 1968, which incorporated travel, beauty, home furnishings and equipment, and food into its treatment of a geographical subject. It contracted with Senator Margaret Chase Smith to contribute regularly and with Claire Booth Luce to resume her monthly column. Cousins was editorial director of *McCall's* for one year.

Vigorously edited and aggressively promoted, *McCall's* is but one property of the McCall Corporation, which owns and publishes other magazines, including the successful *Redbook,* makes and sells dress patterns, publishes magazine-type books and operates a huge contract printing company. Profits of the McCall Corporation were little over $1,000,000 when Herbert Mayes took over the editorship of *McCall's* in 1958; by 1967 they had reached nearly $7,500,000. This inclusive figure does not necessarily reflect much if any profit by *McCall's* magazine. Its advertising revenue was over $43,000,000 for 1967 and about the same for 1968, up 4 per cent for the first half of 1969, but its editorial and particularly its production costs are high. Many of the other popular and otherwise successful mass magazines are beset by this same situation. This is one reason, in general perhaps the controlling reason, for the disappearance of some consumer magazines, the decline of others, and the subsidiary position which many now occupy in large corporations dependent for their profits on other activities.

Large in itself, the McCall Corporation became in 1968 merely a part of one still larger. Norton Simon had been its principal stockholder. Norton Simon, Inc., was formed in July, 1968, to combine Hunt Foods & Industries, Inc., the Canada Dry Corporation, and the McCall Corporation. Since that time it has acquired other properties, including a motion picture and television producing organization. *McCall's* now is one of the possessions, and rather far down the line of a corporate complex that dispenses ginger ale and tomato catsup—which is not too far from where the women's magazines started in the 1880's.

Through their general contents, but especially through the campaigns and crusades they have sponsored, these women's magazines of large circulation have in the past influenced the homes and communities of the nation, and influenced them generally for the better. In February, 1949, for example, *McCall's* ran the first of four full-length articles and five smaller items on its "Yardville Plan." This was a plan by which city dwellers in congested urban areas would bring themselves some of the pleasure and recreation of the suburbs and open country by merging their two-by-four back yards into communal open spaces of grass, trees, and flowers. It was a plan for civic improvement which took hold immediately. Some 355 cities in the United States wrote in asking for plans and suggestions. Civic groups adopted the project wholeheartedly. Inquiries came from Hawaii and Puerto Rico, from eleven cities in Canada, and from two in England. Children took up the plan and pushed it. Minneapolis, Schenectady, Detroit, Chicago, Atlanta, Seattle, Washington, Jacksonville, Indianapolis, Denver, Wilmington, and Fresno were among the American cities participating in this plan for better city living, sponsored and promoted by *McCall's*.

Similarly, the articles and fiction in these magazines affected the minds and imagination of millions of individual readers.

Fiction has always served purposes other than diversion, and the women's magazines, since their inception and publication on a large scale to huge circulations, have published fiction of many kinds, some of it excellent.

It would be hard for any literate individual to decide which of his beliefs, opinions, sentiments, and ideas, and even how much of his general knowledge, have been formed or affected by the fiction he has read. If the analysis were possible, many individuals would find that fiction has provided much of their basic knowledge of people and some of their ethics and has generally affected their approach to human relationships. Very likely, the proportion would be higher among the educated, the imaginative, and the sensitive than among the ignorant and uninterested.

Undoubtedly much of the fiction in the women's magazines, like much mass-magazine fiction in general, has made a specious sentimental appeal, provided an illusory never-never land of incredible slickness and glamor, inhabited only by impossibly beautiful girls and incredibly handsome men. Much other women's-magazine fiction has been the noteworthy work of writers ranking high among the novelists and short story writers of the day. The *Woman's Home Companion* under Gertrude Battles Lane developed and printed the work of such popular women writers as Dorothy Canfield Fisher, Zona Gale, Willa Cather, and Edna Ferber. Edith Wharton, Mrs. Humphrey Ward, and Kate Douglas Wiggin appeared in the *Ladies' Home Journal.* Well-known names are a characteristic of the fiction of women's magazines. At various times they have included Anne Douglas Sedgwick, Cora Harris, Grace Richmond, Hamlin Garland, Ernest Thompson Seton, Mary Johnston, S. Weir Mitchell, Sarah Orne Jewett, Joseph Lincoln, Bret Harte, Zane Grey, Booth Tarkington, William Dean Howells, Robert Hichens, J. P. Marquand, Franz Werfel, Lord Dunsany, Mignon G. Eberhart, and I. A. R. Wylie. The list could be made far longer.

In all the women's magazines autobiographical and biographical materials, usually of the inspirational type, have capitalized on the perennial human interest in other people. The thoughts and ideas of famous people—presidents and ex-presidents, actors, singers, social workers, churchmen, and generals—have been published in articles which they have signed and sometimes written.

The basic subject of most of the editorial content is sex in domesticated guise—how to get, train, and keep a husband; why this marriage failed and this one succeeded; how to bring up your children; what to ask the doctor; and all the rest. The basic approach is that of flattery. The great success of women's magazines in this country seems to have been due in large part to the acumen of publishers and editors in realizing that they can more profitably address women as women rather than women as people. Men like Edward Bok were shrewd enough to realize that the mass of women applaud rather than resent the distinction, and his successors have wisely followed the same policy.

Women's magazines are likewise a valuable advertising medium. Editorial and advertising pages naturally complement each other. Love is the subject of a romantic short story; the accessories of love are for sale in the advertising pages. A glamorous heroine walks the stage of a short story, and her counterpart—dressed in trade-marked girdle, shoes, brassiere, stockings, dress, suit, coat, and cosmetics—parades through the advertising. The beautifully furnished home interior shown in color photography in an article is matched by the beautifully furnished home interior in an equally colorful advertisement.

The mass woman's magazines have been consistently in favor of motherhood, and generally of God. Dutifully they support "freedom," civil rights, and all popular generalizations, but their crusading days seem to be over. Possibly all of the ideal ends for which they could campaign have been achieved. Certainly social reforms can now be accomplished at least equally well by other means and sometimes by other communications media. Whatever the reason, the crusade seems to have disappeared, at least temporarily, from their pages. This is not completely accurate. The big women's magazines are now vehemently crusading for their own survival.

A distinct group of women's magazines have intensively and extensively influenced, and even directed, American women in one of their deepest interests. These are the fashion magazines, typified by *Harper's Bazaar* and *Vogue,* the élite among such periodicals.

Harper's Bazar was founded in 1867 after Fletcher Harper had seen and admired a German fashion magazine called *Der Bazar.* Already the publisher of two very successful magazines, a weekly and a monthly, he resolved to produce an equally good magazine which would be a "repository of fashion, pleasure, and instruction" for American women. The new magazine, promptly dubbed "the ladies' *Harper's Weekly,*" which first appeared in November, 1867, was immediately successful under the editorship of Mary L. Booth. A sixteen-page weekly, it used cuts shipped from *Der Bazar* in Berlin to bring American women news of the latest continental fashions almost as soon as European women knew of them.

Always profusely illustrated with half- and full-page engravings and many smaller ones, *Harper's Bazar,* in the last century, carried editorials, serial fiction, columns of "Sayings and Doings" and "Personals," but was seriously dedicated to women's fashions. Gowns and bonnets, jackets, ornate slippers, cloaks, and directions for embroidery work filled its columns. Patterns for the gowns and coats illustrated in its pages were offered for sale for twenty-five cents. In April, 1878, for example, the *Bazar* featured cut paper patterns of an elegant French Coat, Pleated Over-Skirt, and Demi-trained Skirt, and also a new and useful set of Lady's Princesse Lingerie, consisting of Princesse Petticoat, Princesse Chemise, Combination Chemise (with Drawers), and Long Sacque Night-Dress. After the turn of the century the magazine declined. It climbed back into popularity and influence when it was purchased for $10,000 by Hearst Magazines, Inc., in 1913. The spelling of the key word in its title was changed from *Bazar* to *Bazaar* in 1929.

Edited under Hearst ownership to display greater sophistication as "the mirror of fashion," *Harper's Bazaar* achieved elegance and social repute. It also achieved a 40 per cent increase in newsstand sales when in January, 1962, it published a full-page photograph of an Italian contessa nude from the top of her delicately coiffured head to a discreet inch or two below her navel. The *Bazaar* celebrated its 100th anniversary in 1967 by starting a *Men's Bazaar*. It was not exclusively for men but for both men and women.

Vogue, established in 1892, absorbed *Vanity Fair* in 1936. "A weekly show of political, social, literary, and financial wares," *Vanity Fair,* which had been founded in 1868, was a sophisticated review edited for a time by Frank Harris and for a much longer time by Frank Crowninshield, who had been an assistant editor of *Munsey's Magazine* and art editor of the *Century*. Published by Condé Nast, *Vogue,* whose masthead reads "*Vogue,* incorporating *Vanity Fair,*" has retained some of the *Vanity Fair* flavor and sophistication, carrying articles on the arts and social graces; but it is preeminently a fashion magazine. Its lead position as such is credited to Edna Woolman Chase, who joined its staff in the 1890's, became the magazine's editor in 1914, and did not give up day-to-day editing until 1952. "For almost sixty years," she said in her autobiography, which was published in 1954, "my job has been the true love and focus of my life." [1]

Both *Vogue* and *Harper's Bazaar* are heavy, many-paged periodicals, opulent in appearance, colorful, luxurious. Throughout, they are sacred to fashion. Advertisements and editorial contents alike depict, with all the allure that handsome models handsomely posed can give their pages, the newest, most exquisite, and usually most expensive in women's fashions. Some attention is given to people and ideas, usually

[1] Edna Woolman Chase and Ilka Chase, *Always In Vogue* (New York: Doubleday, 1954). A reviewer of the book wrote in the *Saturday Review,* October 30, 1954: "Mrs. Chase's judgment, taste, uncompromising standards of perfection were the real heart of *Vogue's* success. She stood up to advertisers with the courage of a small, ferocious lion, flatly refused to give editorial mention to any merchandise she thought in bad taste . . ."

the wealthy and the social life of the wealthy, women in their roles as dowagers, matrons, debutantes or subdebutantes, but the emphasis is all on clothes and beauty modes. Advertisements in these magazines are for gowns, cosmetics, lingerie, fabrics, jewelry, deodorants, yarns, fashionable resorts, and the more decorative household items. Often it is difficult at first glance to distinguish a page of advertising from an editorial page, so much skill is exercised in color, composition, and sensuous appeal of the advertising.

The influence of *Harper's Bazaar* and *Vogue* is as strong as women's desire to know what is *de rigueur* in the newest fashions and to do something about it. The consequent influence of these magazines in the market place is powerful. Women decide after carefully scrutinizing their pages—for fashion magazines are studied and intensively considered, not merely read —what they will buy and where they will buy it. Even those women who cannot afford clothes and beauty preparations designed obviously for the well-to-do which they see in these magazines are affected in their choice of cheaper substitutes. The fashion magazines and the fashion departments of the women's general magazines strongly influence the clothes, activities, and the thoughts about clothes and social activities of American women. They began to do this when women's skirts swept the grass or the grimy sidewalks. They continue to do it when women wear microskirts which do not.

Heavy, lush, and with many pictures in color as well as in black and white, *Harper's Bazaar* for September, 1968, covered fashion, beauty, regular features, special features, and fiction. There were 370 pages in the issue with its $1 cover price. For the same date at the same price *Vogue* had 426 pages of fashion, beauty, regular departments, and feature articles—one of them about Conchita Cintron, "The Greatest Woman Bullfighter of All Time." Every issue of these magazines is the last word in fashion until the next word is spoken.

Currently edited by the author of *Sex and the Single Girl*, *Cosmopolitan* is scarcely the magazine it was under John Brisben Walker. It was bought by Hearst in 1905 and converted from a literary and muckraking monthly into a non-controversial magazine of popular entertainment. In the words of its present editor it is now directed to girls as from "a sophisticated older sister." In February, 1961, *Cosmopolitan* ran Winston Churchill, Somerset Maugham, Ernest Hemingway, and an article in praise of advertising in its 75th anniversary issue. In a move since imitated more dramatically, *Cosmopolitan* deliberately cut its circulation in 1953 by lessening subscription solicitation, lowered its advertising rates, and thus attracted more advertising and increased its profits.

The women's magazines have served useful and laudable social ends in their time. They are still a busty column firm in support of the American matriarchy. Within the limits set by their pattern and their editors they still perform an economic service through stimulating consumption of the multifarious goods and products multitudinously mass-produced for their millions of readers.

Chapter 13

Social Consciousness of Magazines: The Muckrakers

Public reaction against the machinations of the Robber Barons in the period after the Civil War, touched off by such magazine articles as Charles Francis Adams' exposé of political and financial manipulation in "Chapters of Erie" and by his castigation of the Tweed Ring in *The North American Review* in the 1870's, and by the *Harper's Weekly* campaign against political criminality in New York, mounted strongly in the 1880's. People learned of the ruthless methods by which a small group of capitalists obtained control of great natural resources, whole railway systems, and great industries, and then manipulated these so as to amass large fortunes for themselves rather than for the public good. What started as indignation and resentment toward some of the most flagrantly unjust monopolies became suspicious of all trusts and "interests." Corporate business was soon under attack from many quarters.

Edward Bellamy of Chicopee, Massachusetts, editor and founder of the *Springfield Daily News*, published his immensely popular *Looking Backward* in 1888. His predictions in this romance of a new social and economic order stimulated the growth of the proletarian movement. The Sherman Anti-Trust Act was passed in 1890. Henry D. Lloyd's *Wealth Against the Commonwealth* was published in 1894. A year before that Samuel Sidney McClure had founded his famous magazine. The name of *McClure's Magazine* is almost synonymous with "muckraking." McClure and his editors made it the chief periodical weapon in the spectacular fight for business, social, and political reform in American life which took place between 1900 and 1910.

Irish immigrant and graduate of Knox College, S. S. McClure had founded the first newspaper syndicate in the United States. With John S. Phillips, another Knox graduate, he had bought novels from such writers as Kipling, Howells, Hardy, Stevenson, and Frank Stockton, and then peddled them to newspapers for simultaneous publication across the country. Short, blond with blue eyes and a wire voice, a human dynamo as William Allen White described him, McClure was already a successful businessman when he founded his magazine and installed John S. Phillips as managing editor. It was to be an extension of his other profitable publishing activities. From traveling this country and Europe in search of authors and ideas, McClure knew that a large audience existed in the Middle West, especially in the country districts and small villages, for a magazine that would tell them something of world affairs, of matters beyond the confines of their own communities, and he decide to exploit that market.

McClure's Magazine began to bring these readers the fiction McClure syndicated, the work of Hardy, Stevenson, and Kipling and of George W. Cable, F. Marion Crawford, Joel Chandler Harris, and other American writers. Between 1902 and 1906 it also brought them, and a much larger audience than even the energetic and enthusiastic McClure had visualized, Ida M. Tarbell's *History of the Standard Oil Company,* Ray Stannard Baker's *The Railroads On Trial,* Lincoln Steffens' *The Shame of the Cities* and *Enemies of the Public,* and Burton J. Hendrick's *The Story of Life Insurance.* These were not the kind of articles McClure had first intended. They were even better, and McClure was quick to recognize their value both as prestige and circulation builders for his magazine and as social documents.

Ten years after *McClure's Magazine* was founded its influence was such that William Allen White accounted S. S. Mc-

Clure among the ten most important men in the United States.[1]

It was in Paris that McClure found Ida Tarbell studying and writing. She had already produced biographies of Napoleon and Lincoln for his magazine. McClure hired her for the staff of the monthly. He assigned to her the writing of a series of articles on the operations of the Standard Oil Company, intending to use the most famous of the trusts as an example of the achievements of business in production and efficient distribution. Ida Tarbell worked in cooperation with Standard Oil executives who gave her assistance and full access to the records of the company. Her investigation was long and thorough, her report objective and complete. Ida Tarbell, a scholar and idealist, spent five years in preparing and writing fifteen *McClure's* articles on the Standard Oil Company, articles which it has been estimated cost the magazine about $4,000 each. The articles showed that Standard Oil was magnificently organized, that it functioned superbly, but that the methods by which the corporation had been built included bribery, fraud, violence, the corruption of public officials and railroads, and the wrecking of competitors by fair means and foul. What had started out to be a study of a great business became, by virtue of the facts uncovered, an exposé of big business as sometimes practiced.

The History of the Standard Oil Company, clear, truthful, and vividly written, not only provided *McClure's* with material that was exactly in keeping with the anti-trust sentiments of the public, but also fixed the pattern for the other exposés which *McClure's* published in rapid succession. Ida Tarbell was soon joined on the magazine by two other muckrakers, who became, with her and McClure, the leaders in the magazine exposure of criminality and corruption in American business and government.

Lincoln Steffens was the second of the muckrakers. Hired by McClure as an editor, Steffens was sent to the Middle West

[1] When McClure died, March 21, 1949, at the age of 92, the press paid little attention. The magazines, except *Publishers' Weekly,* which gave him a one-paragraph obituary, paid no attention at all.

McClure's Magazine

VOL. XX *NOVEMBER, 1902* NO. 1

THE HISTORY OF THE STANDARD OIL COMPANY

BY IDA M. TARBELL

Author of "The Life of Lincoln"

CHAPTER I—THE BIRTH OF AN INDUSTRY

ONE of the busiest corners of the globe at the opening of the year 1872 was a strip of Northwestern Pennsylvania, not over fifty miles long, known the world over as the Oil Regions. Twelve years before, this strip of land had been but little better than a wilderness its only inhabitants the lumbermen, who every season cut great swaths of primeval pine and hemlock from its hills, and in the spring floated them down the Allegheny River to Pittsburg. The great tides of Western emigration had shunned the spot for years as too rugged and unfriendly for settlement, and yet in twelve years this region avoided by men had been transformed into a bustling trade center, where towns elbowed each other for place, into which the three great trunk railroads had built branches, and every foot of whose soil was fought for by capitalists. It was the discovery and development of a new raw product, petroleum, which had made this change from wilderness to market-place. This product in twelve years had not only peopled a waste place of the earth, it had revolutionized the world's methods of illumination and added millions upon millions of dollars to the wealth of the United States.

GEORGE H. BISSELL

The man to whom more than any other is due the credit of what is called the "discovery" of oil; for it was he who first took steps to find its value and to organize a company to produce it. It was he, too, who suggested the means of getting oil which proved practical. After the oil company which he organized obtained oil in the Drake well, he aided in establishing the needed industries and institutions in the new country.

Petroleum as a curiosity was no new thing. For more than two hundred years it had been described in the journals of Western explorers. For decades it had been dipped up from the surface of springs, soaked up by blankets from running streams, found in quantities when salt wells were bored, bottled and sold as a cure-all—"Seneca Oil" or "Rock Oil," it was called. One man had even distilled it in a crude way and sold it as an illuminant. Scientists had described it, and travelers from the West often carried bottles to their scientific friends in the East. It was such a bottleful, brought as a gift

3

One of the most famous magazine exposés of the muckraking period, Ida M. Tarbell's "History of the Standard Oil Company," began in *McClure's Magazine* in November, 1902.

to gather material. His first story was an interview with the prosecuting attorney of St. Louis, who had been gathering evidences of graft and had come to the conclusion that business was corrupting city officials, that for the sake of good business citizens were glad to support bad city governments. Steffens began the investigations that resulted in another series of *McClure's* exposés. In *The Shame of the Cities* and *The Struggle for Self Government,* Steffens, who talked frankly with financiers, philanthropists, and ward heelers, with all those against whom he had gathered damning evidence, showed that American cities, whatever the form of their government on paper, were actually ruled by political bosses supported by reputable businessmen who needed the accommodations they could obtain from corrupt politicians.

Ray Stannard Baker, a Chicago newspaperman, was the third of the trio of crusading muckrakers. He was invited to join the magazine by John Phillips, who had been impressed by his stories in *The Century* and *The Youth's Companion.* Baker became associate editor of *McClure's* and manager of the McClure syndicate. Like Tarbell and Steffens, Baker was given a free hand in the preparation and writing of his exposure articles. He was assigned the management of American railroads and labor-capital relations as his special province, and the facts he uncovered were as damning as those found by the others in their investigations. Baker's articles in *McClure's* described labor racketeering, abuses both by organized labor and by associations of employers. He found all the conditions familiar today, unions preventing non-union men from getting jobs, employers boycotting workers, and all the rest of it, rife in the first decade of the twentieth century. He found, too, that whichever group, capital or labor, was in control, worked according to pattern with machine politicians and with the criminal element. His investigations of American railroads provided *McClure's* with more startling articles.

These *McClure's* muckrakers were capable and honest investigators, of great journalistic ability, who had the gift of making dramatic and damning the material they uncovered and wrote into their brilliant exposés. Strictly truthful in their reporting, they were indignant and outraged at what they saw, and so skillful in arranging and proportioning their facts as to make flagrant abuses manifest. A reformer's zeal motivated and fired their work.

McClure, who knew the value of establishing a reputation for honesty and fearlessness for his magazine, published their sensational articles with gratifying results. *McClure's Magazine* thrived. Instead of being deterred by the attacks on business, advertisers were attracted to a medium which was achieving great circulation and great attention. Appearance in its advertising pages must have seemed almost a guarantee of the honesty of their business. While *McClure's* was running *The World of Graft,* Josiah Flynt's exposures of the league existing among criminals, the police, and politicians, the June, 1901, issue carried 104 pages of advertising. In more *McClure's* articles, which in book form were entitled *The Powers That Prey,* Flynt reported on the underworld's contribution to politics and business.

The *McClure's* exposures of graft and corruption in city government, of fraud and dishonesty in business and finance, of the vicious practices of corporations and labor unions alike, led not only to popular disapproval of the conditions, but also to reform, to legislative action, and to improvement in politics and the conduct of business. The magazine's influence on public opinion was enormous. Its circulation skyrocketed. Copies were difficult to obtain at the newsstands, which sold out their supplies quickly. Leaders in American public life responded enthusiastically. Theodore Roosevelt sent for the *McClure's* writers and discussed with them the conditions they described. Carl Schurz, German-born liberal thinker, statesman, and journalist, invited Baker to come to Wisconsin for a discussion of fundamental labor-capital questions.

The general public, stirred to indignation and aroused to anxiety for the future, devoured the long, serious dissertations, which is really what many of the *McClure's* articles were, and demanded more of the same. Ray Stannard Baker, writing of the popular reception of the exposure articles in his *American Chronicle,* expressed his belief that the articles took such a hold on the public mind because the magazine reporters had looked squarely at the facts and stated them as they were. Their accounts verified suspicions of corruption and privilege which had previously been heard only in the oratory of politicians. At the time, the disclosures of the muckraking reporters had the additional force of being new, of being news. The *McClure's* crusade for better government and for the destruction of the worst practices of business continued. McClure, who like other editors knew the value of names and personalities in the pages of his magazine, had William Allen White do a series of sketches of political leaders—Cleveland, Bryan, Theodore Roosevelt, and others. When Senator Thomas Platt, "Boss Platt" of New York, who was largely responsible for making Theodore Roosevelt governor of New York and then for shunting him into the vice presidency when he proved difficult to manage, threatened a libel suit after the story about him appeared, the editors of *McClure's* let it be known that they had unpublished material about him still more damning, and Boss Platt reconsidered.

President Roosevelt, progressive, announced foe of boss rule, and "trust buster," took prompt action upon many of the evils exposed by the muckrakers. In another series of political articles which he wrote at this time for *The Saturday Evening Post,* William Allen White praised Roosevelt for launching anti-trust suits against monopolies, and described him as an attorney for the people who was leading the fight against the domination of the country by financiers. In a *Post* article, published in October, 1902, for the crusading fervor of *McClure's* had infected other magazines, White wrote: "There are well known bands or gangs of nomadic financial marauders strolling over the American stock markets with no more moral sense than pirates. They are drunk with the power that crass wealth gives them over American civilization. . . . New laws are required to bring these brutes to the halter."

State governments as well as the federal government were forced to take action on facts published by *McClure's* and the other muckraking magazines. For *McClure's* Burton J. Hendrick wrote *The Story of Life Insurance.* In July, 1904, in *Everybody's Magazine,* Thomas W. Lawson, a Boston financier who knew the unsavory story from the inside, began publication of *Frenzied Finance.* In this series of articles, Lawson condemned the investment syndicates used by some of the larger insurance companies, the huge profits made by top insurance executives and the means by which they made them, the expensive sales methods used to sell insurance, and the heavy loss, through lapses, to policyholders.

As a result of these two exposés the New York legislature instituted the Armstrong Investigation in 1905. Charles Evans Hughes, acting as counsel for the legislative committee, proved the truth of many of the accusations brought by Hendrick, Lawson, and Louis D. Brandeis. The result was an overhauling of the entire life insurance business for the greater protection of the policyholder. New York passed stringent new laws governing the activities of the insurance companies, and other states quickly followed. The investigation proved that a number of the large companies had been deliberately influencing insurance legislation through lobbying and methods involving virtual bribery of legislators, and that wealthy executives had drawn exorbitant salaries and swollen these by manipulating profits earned through investment of company funds. Through this investigation Charles Evans Hughes acquired a national reputation.

McClure's Magazine, originator of muckraking and the leader in exposing evils and urging reform movements, was at this time the leading magazine in the country in terms of the social and economic force exerted and succesfully applied to the structure of American life. Tarbell, Steffens, Baker, and their peers were firm believers in the democratic system of government, in free American industrial and business enterprise. They desired not to change the system but to see that the system functioned cleanly and fairly. They demanded destruction of evils and abuses, not fundamental change. Reform writers in the other magazines held like convictions and expressed them in forceful writing.

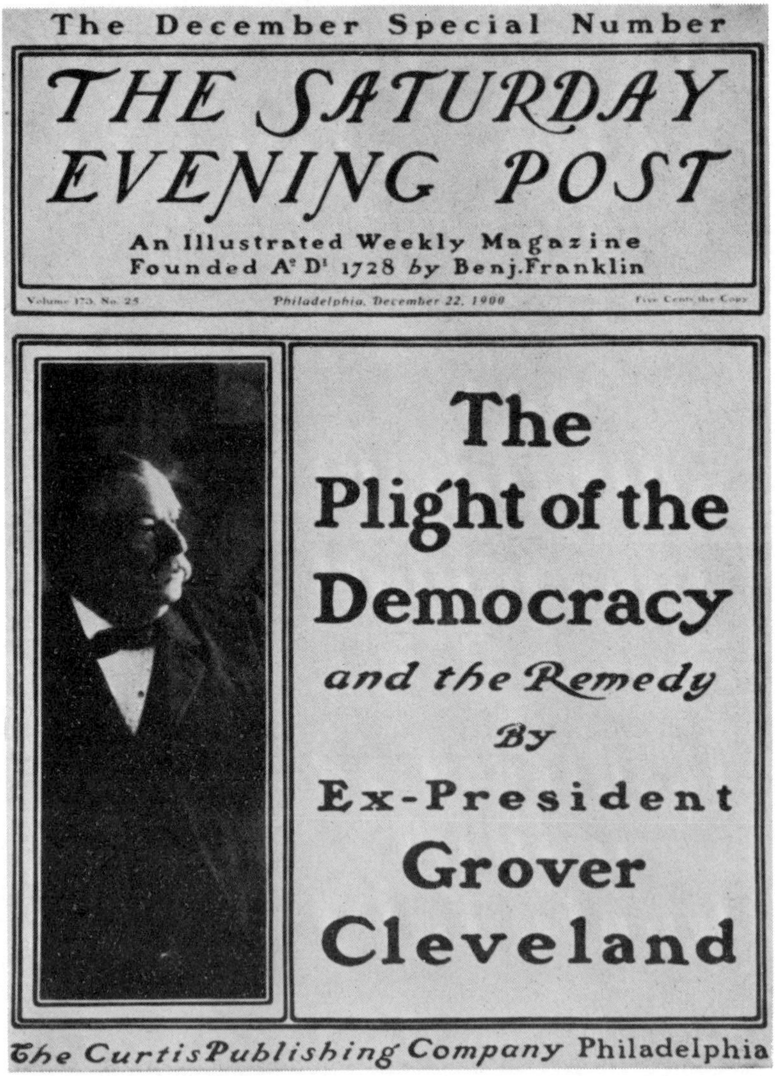

The December Special Number

THE SATURDAY EVENING POST

An Illustrated Weekly Magazine
Founded A° D¹ 1728 by Benj. Franklin

Philadelphia, December 22, 1900 — Five Cents the Copy

The Plight of the Democracy and the Remedy

By Ex-President Grover Cleveland

The Curtis Publishing Company Philadelphia

Public men before and after Grover Cleveland have used the pages of nationally circulated magazines as an effective means of broadcasting their political ideas. (Reprinted by special permission of *The Saturday Evening Post*. Copyright 1900 by The Curtis Publishing Company.)

Cosmopolitan was founded near Rochester, New York, in 1886 as a family magazine. It did not do well. In 1889 it was purchased from Joseph N. Hallock by John Brisben Walker, West Pointer and Pittsburgh and Washington newspaperman who had made a fortune in reclaimed land and alfalfa in Colorado. Owner, publisher, and editor, Walker moved the magazine to New York, turned it into a vigorous popular monthly after the manner of *McClure's* and *Munsey's*, dropped its cover price to ten cents when they dropped theirs, and in five years' time raised *Cosmopolitan*'s circulation from 16,000 to 400,000. Its contributors included Mark Twain, Conan Doyle, Henry James, and William Dean Howells. After he left Boston and the *Atlantic* for New York and *Harper's*, Howells even edited *Cosmopolitan* under Walker for six months during 1891 and 1892.[2]

In December, 1900, *Cosmopolitan* was a magazine of 107 editorial pages and almost as many packed with advertising. The issue carried fiction by Grant Allen, H. G. Wells, Kipling; articles on "Life in Warsaw" and "The County Fair"; and a feature on feminine beauty (with pictures of Maxine Elliott, Sarah Bernhardt, Mary Anderson, and Julia Marlowe) by Harry Thurston Peck, a Columbia professor whose penchant for feminine pulchritude led to his tragic death.

Five years later *Cosmopolitan* was no mean magazine. It was publishing Booth Tarkington, W. W. Jacobs, Ambrose Bierce, James L. Ford, and Edwin Markham. You can hardly do better than that. Its issue for October, 1905, contained the confessions of a New York detective, a lead piece on a Nebraska captain of industry, "Paul Morton—Human Dynamo" by Edwin LeFevre, and an article on the vanishing bison by Major Gordon W. Lillie ("Pawnee Bill"). The issue boasted 100 illustrations and had all the advertising that mattered, pages and pages of it for Grape-Nuts, Anheuser-Busch, Cream of Wheat, Packer's Tar Soap, and all the patent medicines,

[2] As a magazine editor Howells may have been prejudiced, but as America's leading novelist and critic he was in position to know. In *Literature and Life*, 1902, he wrote, "Most of the best literature now sees the light in the magazines, and most of the second-best in book form."

cures for blindness, deafness, pelvic weakness, the opium habit, asthma, poverty—even for being short in stature—that the times could conjure up.

Pears' Soap quoted Bacon: "Cleanliness of body was ever esteemed to proceed from a due reverence to God, to society and to ourselves." You could buy a Cadillac Runabout for $750 but would have to pay $1,200 for a Rambler with a chain drive and a Surrey top. Two of the hundreds of advertisements were for other magazines.

The Youth's Companion of Boston overwhelmed the hesitant with statistics. Every year its 52 issues contained 7 book-length serials, 50 leading articles, 150 special contributions, 250 good short stories, 1,000 brief notes, and 2,000 anecdotes, poems, and humorous sketches. It offered FREE with every new subscription nine additional issues, its double Thanksgiving, Christmas, and New Year's numbers, and a calendar in 12 colors and gold.

McCall's, which even then claimed "more subscribers than any other magazine in the United States" and a total circulation of over 850,000 copies a month, did almost as well. It offered a year's subscription of 12 monthly issues for fifty cents and gave every lucky new subscriber one new dress pattern FREE.

Cosmopolitan joined in the muckraking with "The Treason of the Senate" by David Graham Phillips. Phillips, seated in the press gallery of the Senate, came to believe that these representatives of the people were not representatives of the people at all, but of the special interests, which had placed them in the Senate seats. This was the thesis of his *Cosmopolitan* story. It is said to have been Phillips' writing which caused Theodore Roosevelt, a phrasemaker as well as a politician, to dub the investigations and reports of the magazine writers with the term "muckraking." Though he was in sympathy with the ideals of the reformers and was himself a leader of the reform movement, he complained that the muckrakers were beginning to see only the bad and none of the good in the activities they scrutinized and reported.

David Graham Phillips went on with his muckraking in *The Cost* (1904) and *The Deluge* (1905), both dealing with undercover financial manipulations in Wall Street through which the few profited and the many suffered. In *The Light-Fingered Gentry* (1906) he used material disclosed in the Armstrong Insurance Investigation. Charles Edward Russell was another muckraking journalist, who, in *The Greatest Trust in the World,* exposed the conspiracy between the meat packers and the railroads to keep meat prices high to the consumer while meat producers were kept poor and in debt.

Upton Sinclair, who died in 1968 at the age of 90, was commissioned by a socialist magazine to go to Chicago to write a novel about the deplorable conditions under which packing-house employees worked. The result was *The Jungle,* which disclosed not only economic and social injustices and the same evidences of political corruption which Tarbell and Baker had found in other industries, but also the foul conditions under which meat products were produced. Sinclair's novel created a great stir. As Lloyd Morris points out in *Postscript to Yesterday,* a few pages of gruesome detail in *The Jungle* accomplished more in arousing public indignation than some of the factual and carefully documented reports of the other muckrakers.

In 1906 a split between S. S. McClure and his managing editor, John S. Phillips, resulted in the most famous group of all the muckraking writers leaving *McClure's Magazine.* Phillips, Ida Tarbell, Lincoln Steffens, Ray Stannard Baker, and Albert Boyden purchased *Frank Leslie's Popular Monthly,* changed its name to the *American Magazine,* and began to publish, edit, and write it as a magazine of progressive democracy. With them as associate editors went William Allen White and Finley Peter Dunne. White, a milder, more easygoing reformer, advised the others to go more slowly, to be less the "thin red line of heroes" with do-or-die determination written in their grim faces. Possibly as a result of his advice, probably through the wish to make their magazine a financial success, certainly because Finley Peter Dunne was on the staff, the

American tempered the severity of its muckraking with material dealing with the homely affairs of average people.

Finley Peter Dunne, another Chicagoan, worked first as a newspaperman in that city, becoming editor of the *Evening Journal.* In 1900 he went to New York as editor of the *Morning Telegraph* for William C. Whitney, who practically adopted him. When he became associate editor and part owner of the *American,* Dunne took over a department of the magazine called "In the Interpreter's House," and in it continued the kind of humor for which his Mr. Dooley stories had made him famous. Dunne had invented Mr. Dooley, the Irish saloonkeeper, in the early 1890's, some years before he left Chicago, and Mr. Dooley, who first appeared in the *Chicago Times-Herald,* had made his creator famous as a humorist and social satirist. Using Irish dialect and conversations between the skeptical Mr. Dooley and his friend Hennessey, Finley Peter Dunne not only convulsed a generation of readers who appreciated the shrewd humor of the stories, but also was able to express his hatred of social injustice, of stupidity, pomposity, and the pretensions of politicians in a way that was as effective as it was readable. *Mr. Dooley in War and Peace, Mr. Dooley in the Hearts of His Countrymen, What Dooley Says, Mr. Dooley's Philosophy, Mr. Dooley Says,* were characteristic volumes in the long series that ended in 1919 with *Mr. Dooley on Making a Will.* Mr. Dooley, who became one of the most popular characters in the United States of his day, was informed by the the same spirit which moved the muckrakers of the magazines.

The touch of Finley Peter Dunne lightened the *American Magazine.* The partial metamorphosis of another of the magazine's owners and editors further softened the sternness of its continued muckraking activities. Soon after the group had taken over the *American* Ray Stannard Baker, as "David Grayson," began to write for the magazine the long series of narrative essays, cheerful, humorous, filled with platitudes and homely philosophy, which, published as *Adventures in Con-*

tentment, Adventures in Friendship, Adventures in Solitude, Adventures in Understanding, etc., attained great popularity. Baker's literary career was one of surprising contrasts. Originally, like Dunne, a Chicago newspaperman, he became one of the most incisive of the muckrakers. With his "David Grayson" writings he turned sentimental essayist. Meeting Woodrow Wilson first in 1910 when Wilson was governor of New Jersey, he served as press director at the Versailles Conference, and after Wilson's death was made editor of his posthumous papers. As such he became Wilson's biographer, winning the Pulitzer Price in 1940 for the eight volumes, 1927–39, of *Woodrow Wilson: Life and Letters.*

Other magazines performed notable public service during this muckraking period. *The Outlook,* of which Theodore Roosevelt became an associate editor in 1909, campaigned under Lyman Abbott, against the vicious admixture of politics and business. *World's Work,* founded in 1900 by Walter Hines Page, who became ambassador to England during World War I, was devoted primarily to discussing American participation in international affairs, but it campaigned against those senators who opposed railroad reform. *The Century* attacked slum conditions and turned its efforts to arousing public interest in improved sanitation. *Collier's Weekly,* in a campaign that was synchronized with Edward Bok's efforts in the *Ladies' Home Journal,* published *The Great American Fraud,* attacks on the "poison trust" by Samuel Hopkins Adams, a former *McClure's* writer.

Collier's was founded in 1888 by Peter Fenelon Collier to promote the subscription book business he started two years after coming to this country to study for the priesthood. The magazine's original title, *Once A Week,* was changed in 1896 to *Collier's Weekly,* and Robert Collier became its strong publisher. Collier immediately set about transforming the magazine into "the national weekly" and adopted this subtitle. Like the publishers of other mass magazines, he tried to obtain big-name writers and artists to build up *Collier's.* One of the first serials he published was Henry James' *The Turn of the Screw*. He hired Frederick Remington to do his highly colored paintings of Southwestern scenes and Maxfield Parrish for his delicately colored fantasies. He got Charles Dana Gibson from *Life* by paying $1,000 a drawing. He paid Richard Harding Davis $1,000 a week to cover the Russo-Japanese War.

On the advice of Finley Peter Dunne, Robert Collier hired as editor Norman Hapgood, a scholarly writer who had forsaken law for literature. Hapgood became one of the leaders among the magazine editors who were crusading for social reforms. When Mark Sullivan, working in New York, ostensibly as an independent lawyer but actually as an investigator and writer for Edward Bok in his crusade against the patent-medicine industry, produced an article too long for the *Ladies' Home Journal* to use, Bok took it to Robert Collier and Norman Hapgood. *Collier's* bought and published Sullivan's "The Patent Medicine Conspiracy Against the Freedom of the Press," and in 1906 hired him as a staff writer. Led by Robert Collier and featuring Hapgood's forceful editorials, and Mark Sullivan's political articles, *Collier's* fought for the income tax, the direct election of senators, votes for women, railroad rate legislation, pure food laws, the abolition of slums, workmen's compensation laws, and the limitation of the hours of women in industry.

Theodore Roosevelt singled out *Collier's* for special praise when, as an editor of the *Outlook,* he wrote on "Applied Ethics in Journalism." The newspapers, Roosevelt wrote in the *Outlook* in April, 1911, continued to print objectionable advertisements of a kind that the better magazines, both weekly and monthly had thrown out. *Collier's* had not only refused such advertising but had also publicized the false claims to medicinal properties of a patent breakfast food and had ably defended itself in suits brought against it as a result of its attacks. "We are bound," wrote the ex-President, who had been so strongly supported by the magazines in his reform activities, "to pay a tribute of deserved respect to a paper like *Collier's* when in a matter so vital to the public well being it wages so fearless, aggressive, and efficient a fight for honesty and decency."

By 1908 the muckraking movement had spent its force. Its best writers were turning to material of a different kind, leaving the work they had started and performed well to be carried on by lesser talents. Many of those who followed lacked the skill of the original McClure group, and often presented their materials with more regard for its sensationalism than its accuracy. Writers who wished merely to exploit the popular revolt against the plutocracy wrought some damage with indiscriminate adverse criticism of business and government which did not much slacken until the start of World War I; but they could not undo the good which had been accomplished.

McClure's Magazine, Everybody's, the *Cosmopolitan,* and the others, but especially *McClure's,* let light into situations which had long needed light and air. They instilled a sense of responsibility into the wide public which read them, for the muckrakers made clear their belief that, in the last analysis, the complacent public which allowed and even supported the abuses by business and political bosses was to blame for the appalling conditions they exposed.

These magazines, and again the major credit must be assigned *McClure's,* accomplished one other definite change. Magazines wrested from the daily newspapers the influencing of public opinion by the direct discussion of public affairs, and they have retained the pre-eminence in actuality and in the public view since that time. What had been the chief muckraking magazines degenerated into purveyors of light fiction, but the precedent had been established. All the important general weeklies and monthlies began to give more coverage and more thorough discussion to public matters and thus to exert a greater influence on the minds of their readers.

The group which had spearheaded the muckraking on *McClure's* ran the *American Magazine* until 1911 when it was purchased from John S. Phillips by Joseph Palmer Knapp and made one of the Crowell publications. Ida Tarbell, Lincoln

Steffens, Ray Stannard Baker, and the others moved with the magazine to the Crowell Company, but soon left, and the *American Magazine* began to specialize in inspirational biographies of well-known men. With S. S. McClure these writers had made sensationalism respectable in magazines and, incidentally, accomplished some reforms.

Chapter 14

Magazine Reflection of a Nation: *The Saturday Evening Post*

Though it printed the articles of William Allen White and backed the reforms of Theodore Roosevelt's administration, *The Saturday Evening Post* did not join in the hue and cry of the muckrakers. It was a proponent of business, which both its publisher and editor regarded as the most characteristic expression of American energy. It was less concerned with emphasizing the mistakes of business than with publicizing and romanticizing its leading figures and advertising its dramatic accomplishments. It found most things good in a good, materialistic American world.

In 1848 *The Saturday Evening Post,* one of the most important weeklies of the time, was a four-page periodical printed on large royal sheets. It ran serials, news, poetry, "selected" articles, financial news, and fashion notes. The first page of the issue for January 8, 1848, carried a "Romance of Reality"; "Notes of the Dead Sea," clipped from the *Living Age;* two poems "written for *The Saturday Evening Post*"; and one, by Martin Tupper, clipped from the *Literary World.* The inside pages had a department called "Postscript," but unlike "Postscripts" in the later *Post* it contained shipping news. Editorials dealt with "Peace Prospects" (the Mexican War was not yet officially over), "The Origin of Railroads," "Temperance," "Eye-Glasses," and "Leap Year."

In a two-column box on page three the proprietors of *The Saturday Evening Post* returned their thanks to the "friends of morality and pure literature" for their liberal support during 1847. They did better than that. They announced a "great increase of circulation" and made a new and liberal offer:

> The Post Office of any town in the Union, from which we shall receive the greatest number of subscribers between the 1st of November, 1847, and the 1st of November, 1848 . . . shall be entitled to a continuance of the whole number of subscriptions *gratuitously* for one year after the expiration date for which their subscriptions shall have been paid.

A footnote in four-point type with a pointing-finger cut added further inducement: "Editors copying the above will be entitled to an exchange." On page three appeared, "Fun and Frolic," a "Tale of the Mexican War," and a biography of John C. Calhoun, plus the perennial essay on the "Employment of Leisure Hours." Advertisements were scattered through all but the front page. A filler at the bottom of the page informed the world that "the Pittsfield *Eagle* says that the negro girl, who was put into a mesmeric sleep in that town, has awakened after a nap of forty hours." The 1840's were much interested in mesmerism.

The *Post* was a strong and thriving weekly in 1848. Charles Dickens had been a contributor the year before. Bayard Taylor, Grace Greenwood, T. S. Arthur, Ned Buntline, and Nathaniel Hawthorne were 1848 writers. A January editorial congratulated *Blackwoods* for *not* comparing Emerson, who was then traveling in England, with Carlyle. Henry Clay and Mrs. Myra Clark Gaines, according to a February account, were the lion and lioness of Washington. On March 4, a two-column editorial under the great seal of the United States and a draped flag told of the death of John Quincy Adams in the House of Congress. A feature throughout the year was "Our Portrait Gallery," which displayed engravings of eminent English and American statesmen and writers.

The 1858 *Saturday Evening Post* was a strong and vital paper. Even today it reads with a certain freshness, but by 1865 the *Post* was beginning a long period of decline. Eight pages, of smaller size, still on newsprint, it boasted a more florid logotype, more "literary" content, more advertisements, more dignity, and a pervading dullness. Pages two and three of the April 22, 1865, issue were bordered in heavy black. The lead news story, "Assassination of the President," was subheaded "Probable Murder of Mr. Seward," and stated that "J. Wilkes Booth, the alleged murderer of the President, has thus far succeeded in eluding pursuit." Like *The Atlantic Monthly,* the *Post* had paid little attention to the Civil War.

This was a poor magazine which grew yet worse. By 1874 it was solidly subliterate serials. The entire front page of one issue, and half the second page, was *Davy Crockett on the Track; or, The Cave of the Counterfeiters* by Frank Carroll. Where Crockett stopped, Chapter XLVI of *Claudia's Triumph* by Clementine Montagu began. The issue's only illustration was a four-column engraving of the fabulous Crockett winning an incredible rifle match. The rest of the magazine was more of the same. Perhaps the best serial, certainly the best known, which the *Post* ran in this period was *East Lynne; or, The Elopement* by Mrs. Henry Wood, which began in February, 1874. By 1889 the magazine had doubled its number of pages to sixteen, but in content it was much what it had been in the previous decade.

In January and February of 1895 the *Post* switched over to twenty-four pages of smaller size but returned two months later to the sixteen-page format. The issue of August 21, 1897, was delayed. A notice stated:

> The sudden death of Mr. A. E. Smyth, late publisher of the *Post,* and the legal formalities consequent on the settlement of his estate constitute the cause of, and our apology for, the delay in issue of the paper. We ask your indulgence for a few days, as we expect to be regularly on time commencing with the issue of the 28th.

The simple fact was that the *Post* had no more money. An appeal was made to Cyrus H. K. Curtis who bought the magazine for a thousand dollars. The next week's issue was thrown together so as to save the title rights by continuous publication, and the imprint of The Curtis Publishing Company, which had been established in 1890, was placed on it. Most of the 2,000 subscribers objected to the new material in the issue. They had been used to reprints clipped and pasted up by a reporter on the *Philadelphia Times* who earned ten dollars a week by editing the *Post* in his spare time. They canceled their subscriptions. So Curtis started with an established magazine title and a tradition, but practically no subscribers and no advertising.

It was the nearly unanimous opinion of other publishers and of the editors of the time that this time Cyrus Curtis had made a bad mistake. The weekly magazine, they said, was a dying form. *Printers' Ink,* journal of the trade, prophesied early failure for the venture.

In large type across the top of its front page *The Saturday Evening Post* of 1875 boasted itself: "The Oldest Literary and Family Paper in the United States—Founded August 4, A.D., 1821." Four years later the claim had been slightly modified but the founding date remained unchanged. The *Post* described itself as "The Great Pioneer Family Paper of America —Founded A.D., 1821."

Soon after the magazine became the property of The Curtis Publishing Company in 1897 a box in six- or eight-point bold type was inserted near the top of the front page.

In 1729 this paper was purchased by Benjamin Franklin and published by him as "The Pennsylvania Gazette" until 1765, when it passed into other hands. On August 4, 1821, the present title was adopted, and the office of publication was the one occupied by Benjamin Franklin in the rear of 53 Market Street, Philadelphia.

After this revelation had been run for a few issues it was replaced by a simple one-line statement: "*The Saturday Evening Post*—Founded A.D., 1728." At the same time the volume number was changed from 77 to 170. A year later the *Post* picked up its founder. It became: "An Illustrated Weekly Magazine Founded A.D., 1728 by Benj. Franklin." Ever afterward, at various times on the cover, at the top of the first editorial page or on its contents page, the *Post* carried a small head profile of Franklin, a facsimile signature, and "*The Saturday Evening Post* founded in 1728 by Benj. Franklin." A white marble bust of Franklin long adorned the lobby of the Curtis building on Independence Square in Philadelphia. In 1928 The Curtis Publishing Company struck off heavy bronze medallions bearing a bust of Franklin on one side and a representation of the huge Curtis building on the other in commemoration of the 200th anniversary of *The Saturday Evening Post*'s founding by Benjamin Franklin. The ancestral relationship of Franklin to the *Post* was thus cut in stone and engraved on metal as well as stated weekly in print.

For nearly a year this discovery and announcement of *The Saturday Evening Post*'s proud heritage, unsuspected by its previous owners, was about the only significant change Curtis made. The paper remained much what it had been. Curtis decided to obtain as its editor Arthur Sherburne Hardy of *Cosmopolitan,* but hired as a stop-gap incumbent George Horace Lorimer, a young reporter on the *Boston Post,* who had applied for the job. Before Curtis could keep an appointment with Hardy, then abroad in the diplomatic service, Lorimer had published four issues of the *Post,* and Curtis realized that he already had the editor he wanted.

The Saturday Evening Post which made itself a representative part of the American scene for generations of readers during the first half of the 20th century, its script logotype and cover pictures as familiar as oatmeal for breakfast or mosquitoes in summer, sprang from the shrewd commercial mind of Cyrus Curtis and the shrewd editorial and promotive mind of George Horace Lorimer. *Harper's Weekly, Frank Leslie's,* and *Collier's* were the popular weeklies in 1899. Each was sold at ten cents. Each was concerned almost wholly with the news, news pictures, and politics in competition with the newspapers. The *Post* halved their price and made no attempt to compete with these magazines or with the newspapers as a spot-news medium.

The basic conception of *The Saturday Evening Post* in 1899, when Lorimer took on his active editorship, was that Americans would read and like a certain type of story, certain types of articles, a kind of soothingly competent reporting that it can almost be said to have originated, a certain type of humor, and a distinctive editorial approach. It would make its primary appeal to the intelligent businessman. To do this, it eschewed both the sensational and the intellectual.

In the *Post* of 1899 the businessman and his family were given action stories, romances, stories of business; the life stories of successful men of action; articles on economic and political subjects so dramatized that they were at once informing and entertaining; comment on current events; and a modicum of the serious and sentimental poetry countenanced by businessmen of this period. The issue of September 30, the "Fall Fiction Number," was the first recognizable modern *Saturday Evening Post*. Of the same general dimension as the magazine remained, it wore its first color cover, and carried its first full-page advertisement in color. Every article and every story was illustrated. The issue ran to thirty-two pages and contained thirty-two columns of paid advertising. The cover, under what was to be the familiar *Post* logotype for more than thirty years, showed action aboard a pirate ship. The lead story was "The Sergeant's Private Madhouse" by Stephen Crane; a story by Cyrus Townsend Brady followed. There were "Blaine's Life Tragedy" by John H. Ingalls, and "Under the Eaves" by Bret Harte. The life of Portus B. Weare, a pioneer trader, was dramatized in a "Men of Action" series. Julian Ralph wrote on "The Making of a Journalist." There were also a poem by Bliss Carman, a current events department, "Publick Occurrences," and book reviews. In his editorial, "A Retrospect and a Prospect," Lorimer wrote:

> With this issue, The Saturday Evening Post is permanently enlarged from sixteen to twenty-four pages, with monthly special numbers of thirty-two pages. As soon as the necessary machinery can be

installed—and work upon it is being pushed with all possible speed —The Saturday Evening Post will contain thirty-two pages every week. . . .

There is nothing worthy or permanent in life that is not clean, and in its plans and purposes the new Saturday Evening Post preaches and practices the gospel of cleanliness. It appeals to the great mass of intelligent people who make homes and love them, who choose good lives and live them, who seek friends and cherish them, who select the best recreations and enjoy them.

Lorimer had definite editorial ideas, and definite plans for realizing them. His ambitious master plan was to interpret America to itself. To accomplish this he started quickly to forge his weapons.

To revitalize the ancient weekly he deliberately sought, as Bok had done for the *Ladies' Home Journal,* contributors who were already well-known writers. In 1899 and 1900 he had Stephen Crane, Robert W. Chambers, Rupert Hughes, Jerome K. Jerome, Bret Harte, Joseph Lincoln, and Richard Harding Davis. In 1901 and 1902 came Emerson Hough, Owen Wister, and William Allen White. In addition to these professional writers, he had public men as contributors in those early days: Senator Albert J. Beveridge was one, Speaker Tom Reed and Champ Clark were among the others. In *Post* pages, Beveridge predicted, two years before it occurred, where and how the Russo-Japanese war would break out and its results.

Lorimer introduced business fiction into *The Saturday Evening Post.* Years before in Portland, Cyrus Curtis had read and been impressed by Richard B. Kimball's stories about business. "I want business stories like Kimball's," he said when he bought the *Post.* Lorimer wrote and serialized two books of his own, *Letters of a Self-Made Merchant to His Son,* which presented shrewd business advice in colloquial language, and *Old Gorgon Graham,* a similar tale. Harold Frederic's *The Market Place,* a business tale, as its title indicates, was the *Post's* first serial of the new type under Lorimer. Soon came Frank Norris' great novel, *The Pit.*

Lorimer had another idea, that of a magazine written chiefly by a group of contributors who were identified with the magazine and would give it its peculiar tone and slant. Members of the group changed from time to time, and one group replaced another, but this scheme of editorial production was characteristic of the *Post* all during Lorimer's long editorship and later.

In 1905, six years after his first novel, *The Gentleman from Indiana*, was published, Booth Tarkington appeared in the *Post*. Almost all his best work during a long and productive literary career was published in the magazine. "Mr. Rumbin's Blessed Misfortunes" appeared in the issue of May 19, 1945, exactly one year before Tarkington's death. James Branch Cabell, Wallace Irwin, George Barr McCutcheon, Jack London, Zona Gale, Harry Leon Wilson, and Ring Lardner were others who contributed notable novels and short stories to Lorimer's early *Post*.

By 1900, because of writers of this stature, Lorimer's editorial direction, and the determined efforts of Cyrus Curtis to see through a venture that at one time showed a deficit of $1,250,000 the reborn weekly had a circulation of a half-million. It reached 700,000 in the spring of 1904; 1,000,000 in 1908. By this time the list of *Post* contributors read like a roster of the popular writers of the time whose books are still read. Joseph Conrad, O. Henry, Stewart Edward White, Corra Harris, Robert Chambers, Jack London, Montague Glass, Owen Johnson, Gouverneur Morris, George Pattullo, and Melville Davisson are merely the best-known names among a famous list. By 1909 the *Post* had assumed the pattern and the character that would long identify it.

The Saturday Evening Post became, as Lorimer had promised it would, "the largest weekly magazine in the world." Its circulation rose from less than 2,000 in 1899 to more than 3,000,000 at Lorimer's retirement in January, 1937. For years it was virtually without a competitor as the largest weekly and, if such can be said to have existed at all, the most typical of American magazines. The historian Arthur M. Schlesinger in 1941 described it as "the dinosaur among the periodicals." It was seen and read everywhere. People came to know it as they knew their own names. Its influence was pervasive and immeasurable, spreading simultaneously in many directions. The magazine was continually improved. Its influence mounted continually; but the fundamental Curtis-Lorimer attitudes and ideas on which it was based did not change.

The *Post* operated from the first to reinforce the conservatism, the middle-class sanity, of the economically and morally controlling class in the American community. To do this, it avoided the esoteric, the sensational, and, usually, the adversely critical. It stressed American nationalism, American business, material success, the economic viewpoint; assumed accepted morals and mores without question and built from there. It provided information on every subject of conceivable interest to its readers, information obtained and capably presented by unexcelled reporters. It printed inspirational biographies and the best entertainment fiction of its kind, broadening the horizons of its readers' experience and at the same time providing the factual reports and sensible interpretations which enabled them to form their judgments on subjects of national concern.

The contents of the whole magazine were written for, often by, and editorially directed to, the intelligent, middle-of-the-road, but neither overly intellectual nor overly imaginative American. The *Post* upheld free enterprise and competition, the right of the individual to work for a profit. It saw monopolistic control, whether by business, labor, or government, as dangerous and undemocratic. As a weekly magazine of this kind, informative, entertaining, clear, and direct, its influence permeated the population, from its leaders down through the mass of their literate followers. The *Post* became both a powerful and continuing social force and almost a sign and symbol of the country itself. As Curtis and Lorimer intended, the *Post,* with an accuracy that many have tried to describe and analyze, reflected the United States of the first half of the 20th century to itself—its brilliance and its mediocrity, its materialism and its ideals, its energy, confusion, complacency, its weaknesses, and its strength.

One of the most intelligent estimates and analyses of *The Saturday Evening Post* as it had been even then for almost twenty years, was made by Leon Whipple in 1928. Whipple described the *Post* as a five-sided enterprise. It was at once, he said, a giant, money-making business; a miracle of technical publishing; a purveyor of entertaining fiction and articles; a supersalesman through advertising and thus a main cog in the mass distribution of the products of American industry; and "an engine for propaganda in favor of American nationalism and the present economic system." Whipple, adopting rather than inventing his figure wrote:

> This is a magic mirror; it not only reflects, it creates us. What the SatEvePost is we are. Its advertising helps standardize our physical life; its text stencils patterns on our minds. It is a main factor in raising the luxury-level by teaching us new wants. . . . But it does more than whet our thing-hunger; by blunt or subtle devices it molds our ideas on crime, prohibition, Russia, oil, preparedness, immigration, the World Court. Finally it does queer things to our psychology by printing tales that deceive us with a surface realism but are too often a tissue of illusions. This bulky nickel's worth of print and pictures is a kind of social and emotional common denominator of American life.
>
> Who reads the Post? Who looks in the mirror? Everybody—highbrow, low-brow, and mezzanine; the hard-boiled business man and the soft-boiled leisure woman; the intelligenzia, often as a secret vice. . . . You read it—and I. . . . In 1926 it was figured that if from our population of 105,710,620 you subtracted the children under fourteen, illiterates, foreign language readers, the criminal, insane and paupers, the residual possible market for publications in English was 60,872,577 . . . 20,674,346 families. More than one in ten of these took the Post.[1]

Whipple pointed out what he considered the limitations of the *Post* as well as its virtues. He noted its conservatism, its tendency to support the *status quo,* its ardent nationalism, but he also pointed out: "The Post may neglect new forces, but the forces it understands are very old and very human." Of the cumulative force of the magazine he was describing, Whipple could make no real estimate. He could only exclaim.

[1] Leon Whipple, "SatEvePost, Mirror of These States," *Survey,* March 1, 1928.

Other assayers have experienced the same difficulty. A spot-check analysis of just one year of the *Post* during the period about which Whipple wrote may explain their failure to grasp all that the *Post* represented and accomplished.

In 1924 *The Saturday Evening Post* contained 21 serials, 11 novelettes, 339 short stories, and 413 articles. The articles, among other subjects, dealt with the American merchant marine, the agricultural situation, taxes and tax reduction, immigration, Prohibition, the presidential campaign, war and preparedness, foreign policy, the narcotic trade, the tariff, aviation, and conservation. In addition to sixteen general articles on foreign countries, there were eleven dealing exclusively with Great Britain, seven with Russia, five with Germany, three with Italy, three with Mexico, two with India, two with Turkey, and individual articles about Arabia, Poland, South America, South Africa, China, Canada, Norway, and Holland. Other 1924 articles treated of animals, antiques, auctions, automobiles, building and real estate, general business, crime and law, education, finance, health, food, labor, mining, entertainment, music, the outdoors, patents and inventions, radio, railroads, ships and salvage, travel, and subjects of especial interest to women.

Leading article writers during the year were Kenneth Roberts, Isaac Marcosson, Cosmo Hamilton, Philip Gibbs, Meade Minnigerode, Garet Garrett, Roger Babson, David Lawrence, Samuel G. Blythe, Richard Washburn Child, Henry H. Curran, and Albert W. Atwood.[2] Public men who wrote for the 1924 *Post* included Herbert Hoover, who was then Secretary of Commerce; Joseph Cannon, colorful Speaker of the House; Hubert Work, Secretary of the Interior; Senator George W. Norris; and Brigadier General William (Billy) Mitchell, the famed military air pioneer, who was condemned for beliefs and statements which were vindicated by the events of World War II. *Post* fiction writers during this typical year of the

[2] Atwood said at this time: "The evidences which come to me of the extent to which my articles are read, and the quarters in which they are read, often oppress and frighten me with a sense of the responsibility under which a writer for the *Post* labors." Quoted by Whipple, *op. cit.*

mid-1920's included Ben Ames Williams, I. A. R. Wylie, Roland Pertwee, J. P. Marquand, Earl Derr Biggers, Harry Leon Wilson, Joseph Hergesheimer, and P. G. Wodehouse.

Scores of widely read books resulted from fiction and articles first published in the 1924 *Post*. A few of them were:

Bill the Conqueror by P. G. Wodehouse
Professor, How Could You? by Harry Leon Wilson
The Black Cargo by J. P. Marquand
A South Sea Bubble by Roland Pertwee
Manhandled by Arthur Stringer
Unwritten History by Cosmo Hamilton
The Danger of Europe by Philip Gibbs
After Lenin—What? by Isaac Marcosson
The Fabulous Forties by Meade Minnigerode
The Diary of a Dude Wrangler by Struthers Burt
Racial Realities by Lothrop Stoddard
The Roar of the Crowd by James J. Corbett
Letters from Theodore Roosevelt by Anna Roosevelt Cowles
Balisand by Joseph Hergesheimer
The Rational Hind by Ben Ames Williams

Fifty-seven illustrators and eighteen cover artists saw their work appear in the *Post* in 1924, and in a *Vanity Fair* article on American illustrators, Frank Crowninshield wrote: "*Vanity Fair* here takes the opportunity of pointing out that *The Saturday Evening Post* has done more for American illustration than any other periodical in the history of our country—with the possible exception of *Punch*, in England, more than any periodical in any country. It has brought a discriminating art to the attention of millions of weekly readers—good art—art removed from sentimentality and fraud."

George Horace Lorimer was undeniably a prejudiced witness, but there was truth in his own description of the magazine. "In every number," he wrote, "stories unite with the *Post's* editorials and articles to portray American life—its ideals, its struggles, its defeats, and its successes, in a way that has made it recognized as the dominant and representative American publication not only at home but in every country abroad."

During the first score of years Lorimer, intent on moulding his magazine, refrained from strong expression of editorial opinion. In 1919, after it became apparent that World War I, instead of solving world problems, had only intensified those that existed and added new ones, Lorimer began in his *Post* editorials to attack some of the problems in positive fashion. He began the fight for restricted immigration. Lorimer argued that further immigration had to be limited in volume and that the possibilities and desirabilities of different races had to be analyzed. Risking the displeasure of the industrial class among his advertisers who demanded an unlimited labor supply, he maintained that arguments for unrestricted immigration always went back to some selfish reason, never to the greatest good of the country. Henry H. Curran and Kenneth Roberts presented the subject in a series of *Post* articles. According to W. W. Husband, then Commissioner General of Immigration, the articles by Roberts were responsible for the passage of the restrictive Immigration Act of 1924. Curran became Commissioner of Immigration at the Port of New York.

Lorimer struck at cancellation of World War I debts, pointed out the weaknesses of the Treaty of Paris, which he said "carries the seed of future wars in its text," supported honest overtures for disarmament, and condemned excessive taxation and unrestrained government spending. He wrote and published editorials which required of the reader a serious and intelligent concern in his government and society at large. He warned against bureaucracy: "The simple and amply proven fact is that government ownership does not make men, and rarely makes money. It makes weaklings, dependents, grafters, bureaucrats, autocrats, and deficits. It is the first lesson in Socialism. . . ." Editorially the *Post* argued throughout the 1920's for the kind of nationalism it had always supported.

If the *Post* mirrored the United States to itself during the 1920's some explanation may be found in the mere names of some of its contributors. It reflected the words and ideas, the life stories, the thoughts and actions of Americans of all kinds, presidents, prize fighters, coaches, statesmen, poets, detective story writers, teachers, humorists, new writers, old writers—Jack Dempsey, Scott Fitzgerald, Will Rogers, Emerson Hough, Calvin Coolidge, Katharine Brush, Sophie Kerr, Guy Gilpatric, Dr. A. S. W. Rosenbach, Bugs Baer, Alexander Woollcott, General J. G. Harbord, Alonzo Stagg, Al Smith, Sinclair Lewis, Roy Chapman Andrews, Mark Sullivan, Bernard Baruch, Irving Thalberg, Helen Wills. Like the *Post* the full list would be as diversified and as many-faceted as American life.

The influence of *The Saturday Evening Post* of this period was probably the strongest of any weekly magazine, but it was a permeating and stabilizing influence, not a force making for social or economic change. When the United States was enjoying Coolidge prosperity, it was this prosperity and national self-satisfaction that the *Post* mirrored. Liberal movements were afoot. Social, economic, and literary changes, changes in morals and mores, had begun or were imminent. They were not reflected in *The Saturday Evening Post.*

George Horace Lorimer resigned as an editor of *The Saturday Evening Post* and president of The Curtis Publishing Company in 1936, and died in 1937. *Post* editorship went to Lorimer-trained Wesley Winans Stout, who put out a magazine hardly distinguishable from Lorimer's. Fiction predominated; articles were prolix but thin. America for Americans, big business, isolationism, the Republican Party were *Post* policy and one no longer in accord with prevailing public opinion. The *Post* had begun to lose circulation, advertising revenue, and its long-established hold on popular favor. Stout resigned in 1942 and was succeeded by Ben Hibbs, Kansas newspaperman who had been for a year editor of the Curtis-owned *Country Gentleman.*

The new editor stated his principles immediately. "I believe firmly in the American system—freedom of living—freedom of enterprise. Above all, I believe it is the patriotic duty of the *Post* to help keep alive in the minds of the people that free enterprise literally has made America—that it is the only system under which we can prosper and enjoy the fruits of democracy."

This was familiar *Saturday Evening Post* doctrine. In its essential economic Americanism the magazine would be unchanged. But the new editor had other plans and ideas.

The Lorimer *Post* was primarily a magazine of fiction. The Hibbs *Post* became primarily a magazine of feature articles—shorter, sharper articles. The long-familiar script logotype of the magazine was dropped and replaced by POST in large block capitals with the words "The Saturday Evening" in letters less than one-fifth the size.[3] Layout and style of illustrations were changed throughout the magazine. More vivid titling was adopted and teasing subtitles were introduced. More cartoons and short humorous bits enlivened "the back of the book." A greater variety of subjects in shorter form took the place of fewer subjects and more extensive treatment.

An ordinary issue of *The Saturday Evening Post* under Hibbs contained eight articles, four short stories, and two serial installments. In a year's time the *Post* used about four hundred articles and two hundred short stories. The "typical" *Post* had a humorous and sentimental cover painting in full color by Norman Rockwell or by one of a group of *Post* artists who painted in the Rockwell manner. It carried part of a serial narrative by Clarence Buddington Kelland, Erle Stanley Gardner, or their literary equivalents. These were the recognizable and long-standard *Post* pieces.

More characteristic of the newer *Post* were the highly promotable biographies and autobiographies of entertainers, politicians, military or naval heroes, and other public figures. Usually these were strongly featured in cover publicity and by editorial position and display and carried in six to eight installments. They began in 1952 with "I Was the Witness," in which Whittaker Chambers told in prose-poetry the story of his confessed Communist activities and his part in the trial of Alger Hiss. Then came a series of autobiographies in which popular actors and entertainers, a *Post* editor doing the actual

[3] Many magazines followed suit, dropping or diminishing words in their titles to emphasize a key monosyllable easily spoken and heard at the newsstand. *Time, Life, Fortune* held this advantage from the beginning.

writing, told their life stories in *Post* pages. Bing Crosby's "Call Me Lucky" was followed by Bob Hope's "This Is On Me." The life of Groucho Marx by his son was succeeded by the autobiography of Ethel Merman, "That's the Kind of Dame I Am," then by Arthur Godfrey's "This Is My Story." The life stories of other movie actors followed.

During this same period the *Post* published in weekly installments biographies or autobiographies of Winston Churchill, Alben Barkley, Charles A. Lindbergh, General William F. Dean, and "Murder on His Conscience," the life in prison of Nathan Leopold. These major pieces were offered in the *Post* against a background of articles on diversified subjects: national and international affairs, politics, invention, medicine and health, race relations, light short stories, and the *Post*'s long-continued series of articles on the "Cities of America" which ran later as "Cities of the World."

In 1955 *The Saturday Evening Post* underwent further physical changes. With the issue of October 1 it began use of a different body type, changed its title displays, adopted different layouts for both small and large features, widened the vertical space between columns, and made greater use of white space throughout the publication. The *Post,* which used photographic illustrations for articles, art work for fiction, had already introduced more new editorial features. Chief of these was a two-page spread in each issue, bleed color photograph and sentimental-rhetorical text describing "The Face of America." All of these changes served to make the magazine look more like its competitors, which depend heavily on illustration and layout for their allure.

Bedevilled, like all the mass consumer magazines, by television, outstripped in circulation by the newer and more popular magazines to which it was losing both readers and advertisers, the *Post* suddenly discovered that it was no longer king of the hill. It was puzzled and affronted by this incredible circumstance. Curtis executives had had no real experience of adversity. They resented it and considered it rather unfair of the world in general. For some time they tried to ignore the unpleasantness. Then they tried to research and promote it away.

It did not go. The *Post* was the most important Curtis magazine. For years it had been its unfailingly profitable property. New measures had to be found.

Once widely imitated, the *Post* began slowly then desperately to imitate its chief competitors, inevitably losing some of its recognizable identity in this usually foolish and sometimes fatal process. It did not help that the imitative changes were mostly physical. The *Post* remained middle-of-the-road conservative. It still smacked of the middle western "Americanism" of a decade or two before. It strove to maintain its traditional balance of information and entertainment, kept its articles alert and brightly written, but avoided controversy. Material of the kind which had satisfied a large public under Lorimer began to seem increasingly commonplace, and even ordinary article after article on glamorous Hollywood figures did not make it seem more significant or lighten the tone of the magazine. Without the *Post*'s noticing, the world had slipped from under it. When it did notice, it seemed unable to stop the treacherous abdication.

The *Post* had long pointed with moral pride to the fact that it did not accept advertising for liquor. Its editor announced that if it ever did he would quit. After long soul-searching *The Saturday Evening Post* announced that it would print liquor advertising. The editor did not quit. A few prohibitionists and teetotalers cancelled their subscriptions. A trickle of liquor advertising came in but not enough of it or of any other kind to do much good.

The Curtis company consistently refused to diversify by entering into any other forms of communications, even disdaining the offer of one of the major radio and television networks at a bargain price. It said proudly that it was a magazine publisher. It felt that it was *the* magazine publisher. Alarmed now, it weakly tried a few short-lived ventures into imitative periodicals. *TV Week* was one. Yet one more publication aimed at the bridal market was another. In 1961 it took a drastic step. It announced, then announced again, then announced more loudly and more often the appearance of a still newer "New Post." So much of such dazzling impact was promised that no magazine could have lived up to the gushing advance notices.

The "New Post" appeared September 16, 1961. It carried advertising throughout the issue instead of having the advertising pages grouped before and after the editorial content. The sentimental–narrative–humorous covers by Norman Rockwell and his school—long admired, looked for, and relished by the public which knew them as the familiar lineaments of the *Post*—were dropped. In their place came color photographs and nondescript type designs.

Inside the magazine, story illustrations gave way to what the new *Post* editors (Hibbs had resigned though he remained on the staff) described as "iconography." It was really the substitution of symbols for representations of the actual. Instead of showing a beachcomber digging up buried pirate treasure, crossed spades, a mound of earth, and a skull conveyed the wealth and excitement—or was supposed to. The inspiration for the design and appearance of the "New Post" was said to have been phonograph record albums. It looked to be boxtops and supermarket packaging generally.

The "New Post" fell flat on its iconography. Advertisers and agencies for whom the magazine had been redesigned were not impressed. Faithful *Post* readers, and the *Post* had an enviable group of them, were offended and affronted when they were not horrified. They did not appreciate the bold and brassy "New Post" with its dyed hair and false eyelashes. The new young audience at which the *Post* had aimed its belated attempt at rejuvenation never even noticed the change. It had not bothered with the old *Saturday Evening Post.* It did not bother with the new one.

Once again the changes in the *Post* had been mostly on the surface. The same writers continued with much the same kind of articles and fiction. No one seemed to find the "New Post" vital and forceful. No one seemed to feel it was now the perfect medium for reaching any market. The "New Post" failed to create a new image or to shore up the old. The only thing it accomplished was to blur further *The Saturday Evening Post*'s once clear individuality. The "New Post" was not *Life*. It was not *Look*. It was not *The Reader's Digest*. It was not even television, and it certainly did not seem to be *The Saturday Evening Post*.

New Curtis management came in. New editors took over the *Post*. Insuring further damage to the image carefully created for over 60 years by its Independence Square address and nearness to the grave of Benjamin Franklin, the *Post* was moved to New York. The hope seems to have been that proximity to the advertising agencies might bring in more business or that success might come by contagion from the network studios and the thriving New York-based magazines.

It did not. To cut production and distribution costs the magazine went bi-weekly in 1962 and became the every other *Saturday Evening Post*. Cutting itself in half did not work either. The magazine continued to lose more money each year. In August, 1968, declaring that it would cease to be a mass magazine and become a class magazine with a select audience, it did more cutting. Curtis announced that, using preferred residential addresses as a measure, it would discard those subscribers who were too old, too poor, or too ill-educated to deserve access to the class *Post* and retain only those subscribers of unimpeachable quality who could appreciate the magazine and guarantee its advertisers a select clientele. Those expelled were given *Life*, which thereon passed *Look* in circulation.

It was a melodramatic gesture with comic results that delighted both press and public. If the advertised method of selection and rejection was actually used, the computers were out of line or someone's judgment was faulty. Men of wealth and position were informed by being dropped that they did not qualify for the *Post*. People who had read and valued it for years and put up with its recent eccentricities as one puts up with the oddities of a friend who is growing old were angered and hurt.

For many years *The Saturday Evening Post* could do no wrong. Now it seemed unable to do anything right.

Chapter 15

The Farm Magazines

In 1938 *Scribner's Magazine* ran a series of eight articles entitled "Magazines That Sell." Rather caustic articles with more than a touch of the exposé about them, they analyzed some of the more spectacular modern magazines in an attempt to discover the reasons for their popular and commercial success. The last article in the series discussed a group of magazines, many of them founded in the pre-Civil War period, which have exerted and still exert a powerful social and economic force on one vital department of American life. "Farm Magazines," in the issue of October, 1938, was different in tone from preceding articles in this series. Harland Manchester, its author, found much to praise in farm magazines.[1]

The first agricultural paper in the United States, as Manchester pointed out, was founded by Luther Tucker. Success with the *Rochester Daily Advertiser*, a newspaper which he had established in 1826, led Tucker to bring out the *Genesee Farmer* in 1831. It was the *Genesee Farmer* which became the

[1] The other articles in the *Scribner's* series were "Geography, Inc." by Ishbel Ross; "The Love Pulps" by Thomas H. Uzzell; "One Every Minute; The Picture Magazines" by Jackson Edwards; "High Hat; The Luxury Magazines" by Henry F. Pringle; "Romantic Business; Fortune Magazine" by William A. Lydgate; "True Stories; The Confession Magazines" by Harland Manchester; and "Sex, Esq." by Henry F. Pringle.

Country Gentleman.[2] The first issue of *Country Gentleman,* "A journal for the farm, the garden, and the fireside," appeared in 1853. It was "devoted to improvement in agriculture, horticulture, and rural taste; to elevation in mental, moral, and social character, and the spread of useful knowledge and current news." Luther Tucker explained the title and purpose of *Country Gentleman* in the first editorial column:

> Wherever the honest, earnest feeling of the heart finds utterance—wherever the deed of generous sympathy is performed—wherever the life is ruled by the principles of honor and religion, do we find the gentleman. . . .
>
> Country life is particularly adapted to inspire character of this sort, and the *Country Gentleman* is therefore in truest exponent of those characteristics which should prevail in the American. There is then a propriety in styling a paper for country circulation, and devoted to the interests and pursuits of farmers, the *Country Gentleman.*
>
> In answer to a very natural inquiry as to some one individual to whom the term, as we use it, would properly apply, we have placed a portrait of Washington in our vignette. The independence and magnanimity of his character, the energy and decision of his actions, the excellence and simplicity of his whole life; his love of rural pursuits, and his devotion to his country, make a fit type of the American country gentleman.

In the very first issue Tucker made *Country Gentleman* a practical agricultural paper. There was a sensible article on the professional education of farmers and other informative articles on subjects of basic interest to the farmer: "Farm Economy," "Farm Profits," "The Culture of the Hop," "What Shall We Do for Fodder This Winter?" In addition to departments headed "The Grazier," "Horticultural Department," and "The Fireside," there were a "Record of the Times," which gave domestic, foreign, Congressional, and California news, and a

[2] The *Genesee Farmer* was merged in 1839 with *The Cultivator,* which had been established at Albany in 1834 by the New York Agricultural Society. The *Country Gentleman* began as a weekly edition of *The Cultivator.* By 1858, it reached a circulation of a quarter of a million. In 1866, the offspring having outstripped the parent magazine in popularity and circulation, they were merged, becoming *The Cultivator & Country Gentleman.* Luther Tucker also established the *Horticulturist* in 1846 and edited it until 1852.

The Country Gentleman.

A Journal for the Farm, the Garden, and the Fireside.

Vol. I. ALBANY, N. Y., JANUARY 6, 1853. No. I.

Our Title and Purpose.

THE term Gentleman, like most expressive ones, has been from time immemorial subject to animadversion and misconstruction. It has been made to apply to persons of widely different conditions of life, of radically opposite characters, and diverse pursuits. In its best and proper signification, the word is defined to mean a man of cultivated mind, of refined manners, of genuine kindness of heart, and consequent purity of life. The fashionable acceptation of the term, that obtains in cities and watering places, and its meaning as applied to residents in the country, are essentially different. In the first case, it stands for men of means and leisure, in distinction from those of business; in the latter, it properly embraces all those whose characters recommend them to the respect and confidence of their fellows. In cities it stands more for outward show; in the country, for the possession of sterling virtues. Still the true gentleman is the same in essence, in all situations, in all circumstances, and to all men. The coxcomb and dandy are beings of another order, while the real gentleman is, in all ages, the type of genuine humanity. Politeness, which is considered the evidence of gentlemanliness, though often judged of by formal rules of etiquette, exists in opposition to them, and even in spite of them. Wherever the honest, earnest feeling of the heart finds utterance—wherever the deed of generous sympathy is performed—wherever the life is ruled by the principles of honor and religion, do we find the gentleman. His acts are unconsciously polite, his bearing has on it the stamp of nature's nobility, and his whole character is imbued with those qualities of mind and heart, which endear and dignify man.

Country life is peculiarly adapted to inspire character of this sort, and the COUNTRY GENTLEMAN is therefore the truest exponent of those characteristics which should predominate in the American. There is, then, a propriety in styling a paper for country circulation, and devoted to the interests and pursuits of farmers, THE COUNTRY GENTLEMAN.

In answer to a very natural inquiry, as to some one individual to whom the term, as we use it, would properly apply, we have placed a portrait of WASHINGTON in our vignette. The independence and magnanimity of his character, the energy and decision of his actions, the excellence and simplicity of his whole life; his love of rural pursuits, and his devotion to his country, make him a fit type of the American country gentleman. In his public career, in his social relations, in his efforts for the highest individual and common good, he stands as a model for all time. Placed by Providence and his own superior wisdom, at the head of our nation, before it was rent by political faction and private interest, there has never been a time when the entire population of the United States have not been ready to rally with his name for a watch-word. We place his likeness, then, with confidence at the head of our sheet, and write his name as Father of his Country, and the true representative of a gentleman, without fear of contradiction. Let no one object to our title, who is not prepared to falsify the claim of WASHINGTON to the name of Country Gentleman, or willing to allow that he is not emulous of a similar character, and does not respect his virtues.

It is a fixed fact, that the progress of our rural population demands a journal, independent in its character, and safe and reliable in its teachings, as an advocate and representative of the great agricultural interests of the country. Improvement begets a desire for farther advancement, and so fast as *high* culture takes the place of *low* culture on our farms, so rapidly will a taste for literature, for home embellishment, and true refinement, succeed to the surprising apathy on these subjects which has so long prevailed. It is a truth worthy of remark, that the highest forms of eloquence, the purest diction, the most beautiful works of art, the sweetest music, have always been appreciated by the masses of the people. We hold it an axiom, that the love of the really beautiful, admiration of noble and manly qualities, and respect for genuine virtue and excellence, are instinctive in the heart. The sickly taste for light and vapid reading, is not natural. It has been formed as the taste for sweetmeats is in children,—by feeding sugar plums when they cried for food. But allowing that there are a large class of readers, whose vitiated appetite must be pandered to by a literature as degraded, we deny that our farmers or their families form, to any considerable extent, this class.

We propose, then to make THE COUNTRY GENTLEMAN the repository of such Agricultural and Horticultural matter, such thoughts and principles, such information and current news, as in our judgment will most safely and surely promote the best interests of all country residents. Our readers must bear in mind that our subscribers are scattered over a great part of the Union, and that what may seem of little moment to one, may be of the most vital importance to another. We have so arranged the matter under topics, that one can turn, without inconvenience, to the several departments, and this system will be carefully pursued.

The general arrangement and typographical execution of THE COUNTRY GENTLEMAN, have been studied with a view to combine uniformity and good taste; and it is our intention to make its external appearance a true index to its contents.

With this exposition of our purpose, we invite the attention of every one into whose hands this sheet may fall, to a careful perusal of its entire contents, with the request that if they find it adapted to their wants, they will become permanent subscribers, and use their influence and exertions in its behalf.

Farm Economy.

"I am not *rich enough* to be economical," said a young friend of ours, when we strongly recommended to him the profits of a certain improvement. "The want of means compels me to work constantly to a disadvantage, and I cannot enjoy the privileges and profits of my richer neighbors." This is a difficulty in which many intelligent farmers have found themselves placed, and from which they would most gladly be extricated. Innumerable instances are occurring in their daily practice, where they could secure golden results, had they only the lever of capital placed in their hands; but as they are now situated, they seem to themselves like the man who is digging the earth with his unassisted hands, or the one who is compelled to carry water in an egg-shell, while their more fortunate neighbors are turning up the deep soil with the most perfect instruments, or sending streams of refreshment and fertility through easy channels over their entire farms. Now, we are not about to plan a "royal road" of escape from this difficulty; it must be met and conquered. If the attack is rightly made, the conquest will be comparatively easy; if wrongly, it will be the discouraging and formidable task of a life time.

The eager inquiry is now made, What is the easiest mode of conquest? We answer, the first and great leading means, is a large fund of thorough and practical *knowledge*. The man who, by a close observation of results in his own practice and in the experience of others, in connection with the immense amount of useful *suggestions*, (to say nothing of distinct practical directions) contained in the best publications of the day, possesses, even with a very short purse, a vast advantage over the short-sighted, ignorant, and unobservant capitalist. He will turn to advantage, even with his very limited means, a thousand resources which others would allow to sleep unemployed forever.

We once had occasion to observe the contrast in the condition of two young farmers, one of whom had a four-hundred acre farm "left" to him; the other had but fifty acres, which he had paid for in part, by previously laboring on a farm for some years by the month in summer, and teaching a district school in winter. The one had the capital of money which his own hands had never earned; the other possessed the more valuable capital of knowledge and indomitable perseverance. The young heir was more interested in

The first issue of *The Country Gentleman,* January 6, 1853, carried a picture of George Washington in its vignette as the very type of the country gentleman.

"Farm Products Market," giving Albany and New York prices on cattle, wood, flour, grain, hogs, and whisky. Illustrations in this issue showed Trump, a prize Hereford bull belonging to Mr. Allen Ayrult of Geneseo, New York, and dwarf or pompon chrysanthemums in full blossom.

During the next year *Country Gentleman* advocated the first test plots for corn and announced the seedling grape which was developed by E. W. Bull of Concord, Massachusetts, and was to become known as the "Concord." In 1857 Luther Tucker visited the Middle West and, in a *Country Gentleman* article, pointed out that "one of the advantages the prairie farmer possesses over his eastern brethren is the peculiar adaptation of his land to the use of labor-saving machinery."

It was largely through Tucker's interest in the Middle West, where he appointed correspondents, that *Country Gentleman* became the first truly national farm magazine, reaching just the next year a phenomenal 250,000 circulation. As Mott has reported, the files of *Country Gentleman* during these years mirror the development of the western ranges, the improvement of farm stock, the coming of ensilage and silos, and the growth of the Grange and the Farmers' Alliance.

Country Gentleman did more than record. It interpreted and often led the changing developments in American agriculture. As far back as the 1850's it declared that a milking machine was the most needed improvement in dairying. It urged farmers to prepare for the readjustments that would inevitably follow the close of the Civil War. In 1884 it described the economic advantages of what is now called "baby beef." It recognized, well in advance of the fact, the effect that refrigeration would have on markets for agricultural products. It prophesied with remarkable accuracy: "Florida is to become, at no distant day, the winter garden of the Northern cities."

By the 1890's magazine advertising had become a primary means of distributing farm goods and equipment. To be effective this advertising required a large circulation, which *Country Gentleman* in Albany did not have the facilities to achieve.

Competition in the 1880's and the 1890's from an increasing number of regional farm papers resulted in a decline in *Country Gentleman's* circulation and forced it into editorial coverage more regional in nature than that which had characterized the magazine earlier. In 1911 Gilbert Tucker sold the weekly to Cyrus H. K. Curtis.

The first number of *Country Gentleman* issued from Philadelphia over the imprint of The Curtis Publishing Company appeared in July, 1911. The magazine, made a weekly for nation-wide circulation, concentrated on farm and country life. Power farming, road building, and taxation and freight problems were stressed, but attention also was paid to the rural woman's interests, and popular fiction of the outdoor type was published. Circulation began to rise almost immediately. It reached 300,000 in 1916, and about half a million in the next five years. Circulation was 800,000 in September, 1925, and twice that by 1930, the largest circulation ever achieved to that time by a farm magazine.

Many of the objectives at which Luther Tucker had aimed in the early *Country Gentleman* were reached. By the time that Curtis took over the magazine there were agricultural colleges, agricultural experiment stations, new services, inventions, and agencies to help the farmer. The farmer needed less instruction from magazines on how to do things, now that he had available the professional aid of institutions which magazines had helped to build. Recognizing this, its editors provided a rural magazine of different type with broader aims and interests.

In 1925 the change was made from weekly to monthly publication. Full-color covers, superior makeup on good white stock, illustrations in color, and contents of a quality equal to that provided metropolitan audiences by the general weeklies and monthlies made it a modern farm magazine for a rural America modernized by the automobile, the radio, and power equipment. Fiction was made important in the *Country Gentleman* of the 1920's, when such popular writers as Ben Ames

Williams, Joseph C. Lincoln, Zane Grey, Courtney Riley Cooper, and others appeared in its pages.

Country Gentleman began in the 1920's to stress the value of scientific research to agriculture. In five years' time it ran 300 articles on grass breeding. Largely through *Country Gentleman's* efforts, Congress in 1935 passed the Jones-Bankhead Act, under which twelve regular grass-breeding stations were set up in the United States. Soil conservation and erosion prevention were emphasized in a series of articles by Hugh H. Bennett and by other authorities who contributed to *Country Gentleman* for a five-year period. The soil conservation programs inaugurated by the federal government in the 1930's resulted. Bennett, who was made director of the Soil Conservation Service, said: "*Country Gentleman* may have pride in its consistent editorial 'fight' for practical, workable soil conservation." Lespedeza, a nitrogen-fixing legume, was discovered by J. Sidney Cates of *Country Gentleman's* staff. Grown now on millions of acres throughout the country, it serves both to rebuild worn soil and to provide a useful silage and roughage crop. Other agricultural ideas initiated or backed by *Country Gentleman* have produced action with far-reaching social and economic consequences. American farmers first learned about hybrid corn from *Country Gentleman* in 1924.

Country Gentleman first publicized in its pages how plant hormones could be used to retard blooming of fruit trees until late spring frost had passed, to speed root growth in transplanted cuttings, and to kill weeds. In 1937 it described how phenothiazine could destroy livestock parasites.

Country Gentleman was credited by *Scribner's* with having discovered Paul de Kruif, for many years a regular contributor to *The Reader's Digest* and author of most of its spectacular pieces on medical discoveries, as a writer on health and medical subjects. In 1936 it published portions of his *Microbe Hunters,* and subsequently many of his crusading medical articles. For a dozen years *Country Gentleman* focused attention upon tuberculosis, infantile paralysis, malaria, and other diseases in campaigns for the improvement of public health. It even dared discussion of syphilis. Thus, said Harland Manchester, "the home magazine *Country Gentleman* pioneered in smashing the great taboo."

Luther Tucker had a department called "The Fireside" in the first issue of *Country Gentleman,* and he consistently ran material of interest to the entire family. The farm magazines as a group have devoted intelligently used space to the farm home as well as to the field. They have acted as a definite force in the betterment of farm living as well as in the advance of farming.

In February, 1954, *Country Gentleman,* in financial difficulties and severely pressed by competition, cut its page size. In January, 1955, the name of the magazine was changed to *Better Farming.* Advertising losses continued. In June of the same year The Curtis Publishing Company announced sale of the magazine to the competitor which had outstripped it in both circulation and advertising revenue.[3] *Country Gentleman* was merged with *Farm Journal.*

The September, 1955, issue of *Farm Journal,* the first after the merger, was a magazine of 226 pages, *Time*-sized, modern in appearance, illustrated in full color, replete with advertising, and heavy with a varied editorial offering. It bore little resemblance to the eight small pages of newsprint first issued from Philadelphia in March, 1877. Now the largest and most important national farm magazine with a circulation exceeding 3,400,000 and copies going monthly to half the farm families in the United States, *Farm Journal* had been founded by Wilmer Atkinson as a paper for farmers in the agricultural area about Philadelphia. Atkinson's approach was terse, direct, and homey. He stated his principles in his first editorial.

> There will be 25,000 copies of the first issue of *The Farm Journal* printed and mailed to farmers and other rural residents within a day's ride of Philadelphia. . . . The publisher will insert advertisements of

[3] The purchaser discarded the name *Better Farming* and referred in his announcements and advertising to the merging of *Country Gentleman* with *Farm Journal.*

an unobjectionable character, at 40 cents a line. No lottery swindles, cheap jewelry announcements, quack medical advertisements, nor Wall Street speculator's cards, can find admittance at any price. . . . The publisher does not intend to fill much space with puffs of *The Farm Journal* leaving it for the intelligence of the reader to discern merit, if any exist. Enough said; send along the 25 cents [for a year's subscription].

Wilmer Atkinson, who tells the full story of the founding and the early years of his magazine in a charming autobiography, posthumously published in 1920, wrote a pithy prose and wanted his contributors to do the same.[4]

"After the manuscript is prepared," he told them in his magazine, "strike out the bottom and the top and condense the middle." Direct, economical reporting had characterized *Farm Journal* from the beginning. Atkinson prided himself that:

> *Farm Journal* says a thing and stops after it has said it. It prints no long-winded tiresome essays, and it knows what to leave out as well as what to put in.
>
> It is cheerful and hopeful and wants everybody to have a good time.
>
> It is full of snap and ginger, and hits the nail squarely on the head. . . .
>
> It thinks the humans on the farm are the best stock on it.

Direct, economical reporting and a friendly attitude toward "our folks," as Atkinson called his readers, has characterized *Farm Journal* from the beginning. Early, Atkinson gave practical proof of the responsibility he felt toward the farm families he wrote to. In 1880 he guaranteed to make good any loss readers sustained by "trusting advertisers who proved to be deliberate swindlers. Rogues shall not ply their trade at the expense of our readers." His action made *Farm Journal* the first magazine to guarantee its readers repayment of money lost because of fraudulent advertising in its pages.

That same guarantee, somewhat preciously worded, appears in every issue of the *Farm Journal* still: "To prove our faith by

[4] Wilmer Atkinson, *An Autobiography* (Philadelphia, Pa.: Wilmer Atkinson Co., 1920).

A NATION'S GREATNESS DEPENDS ON THE VIRTUE AND INTELLIGENCE OF ITS FARMERS.

Vol. 1. PHILADELPHIA, MARCH, 1877. No. 1.

PUBLISHED MONTHLY AT
NO. 726 SANSOM STREET,
SATURDAY EVENING POST BUILDING,
At 25 Cents a Year.

WILMER ATKINSON, - - - *Publisher.*

Publisher to Reader.

THE FARM JOURNAL offers no terms to clubs, and no premiums to subscribers. The price of THE FARM JOURNAL is 25 cents a year.

There will be 25.000 copies of the first number of THE FARM JOURNAL printed and mailed to farmers and other rural residents, within a day's ride of Philadelphia. Subscriptions should be mailed direct to the Publisher, or they may be handed to Postmaster to forward. The Publisher will insert advertisements of an unobjectionable character, at 40 cents a line. No lottery swindles, cheap jewelry announcements, quack medical advertisements, nor Wall Street speculator's cards, can find admittance at any price.

The postage on THE FARM JOURNAL will be paid by the Publisher.

The Publisher does not intend to occupy much space with puffs of THE FARM JOURNAL, leaving it for the intelligence of the reader to discern merit, if any exist.

Enough said; send along the 25 cents.

Go West!

Yes, go to Kansas. If the grasshoppers do not overrun your farm, the prairie soil will yield a good crop; then you can send it to market and pocket the proceeds. You can get for butter—choice, 16 to 18 cents per pound; butter, medium, 12 to 14 cents; eggs, per dozen, 18 to 20 cents; corn, per bushel, 25 cents; oats, 17 to 20 cents; wheat, $1.05 to $1.25; rye, 50 cents; sweet potatoes, 50 cents; hay, per ton, $3.50 to $4.50; chickens, per dozen, $2 to 2.25; chickens, dressed, 4 to 5 cents per pound; turkeys, per pound, 8 to 8½ cents per pound; cabbage, per head, 10 cents; cheese, per pound, 12 to 15 cents; wood, per cord, $4 50 to $5.

Go West, young man, go West!

Strawberries—Essex Beauty.

BY WILLIAM PARRY.

As the time approaches for setting out strawberries, it may be well to consider what kinds to plant. In the early stages of strawberry culture, when it was difficult to raise enough to supply the demand, the main question was What kind will yield the most bushels, and bear transportation best to market? quality not claiming much consideration, as any strawberry that looked well, was considered good enough to sell. Then the general sentiment was in favor of Wilson's Albany, which was very productive, turning red before it was ripe and palatable, could be carried a greater distance to market than other more delicious berries, which did not color up well until they were ripe enough to eat without sugar. Now we have many varieties, large and excellent, and if they are not so generally adapted to all soils and climates as the Wilson, some of them can be found to thrive well wherever the Wilson does, and are of much better quality; among which may be named: Charles Downing, Colonel Cheney, Captain Jack, Cumberland, Triumph, Great American, Jucunda, Kentucky, Monarch of the West, Seth Boyden, Triomphe d'Gand, and others—large, luscious, and sufficiently productive to supply the demand; and sometimes, when the markets are overstocked with berries, the Wilsons are left unsold for the want of purchasers.

The accompanying engraving is intended to represent a medium-cized berry of a new variety, recently introduced, called

ESSEX BEAUTY,

being four and a half inches in circumference. It might be called large, compared with the berries most commonly seen in market; yet we have measured berries of the same variety six and a half to seven inches in circumference. It was raised from seed by E. W. Durand, who also originated the Great American, and is second in size only to that wonderful strawberry, single specimens of which have measured nine inches in circumference and weighed from 2⅛ to 2¼ ounces each. When exhibited at the U. S. Centennial Exhibition last summer, the International Judges of the Pomological Department were of the opinion that the flavor of the Essex Beauty was superior to that of the Great American. Ripening earlier than the Great American, and of superior flavor, it possesses in a high degree two good qualities, much sought after by producers and consumers. Both varieties are of a beautiful, bright, crimson color, excellent qualities, firm and very productive, yielding from thirty to one hundred berries to a single plant, and frequently more than a quart to a hill.

They are both desirable to cultivate, and should be grown in preference to the small, sour Wilsons, which have been grown in such quantities as to overstock our markets. A neighbor of ours last year sent to market in one day four wagon-loads of Wilson strawberries (120 crates), which sold at 12½ cents per quart. Another person sent to the same stall, on the same day, one load (30 crates) of large, sweet strawberries, which brought 50 cents per quart, yielding as much money as the four wagon-loads of Wilsons, with only one-fourth the expense for picking and hauling to market.

CINNAMINSON, N. J.

Sheep on the Farm.

BY EASTBURN REEDER.

In successful sheep husbandry at least three conditions are essential

First. Location and adaptation of the farm for the business.

Second. Adaptation of the breed to accomplish the object sought—mutton, wool, or both combined.

Third. Care and skill in their management.

There are very few farms but what are well adapted to keeping sheep. If the surface of the ground is not too wet, sheep will do well almost anywhere. There are many farms that will perhaps pay a better return for the investment if devoted to dairying or general agriculture. It is upon those farms which are unsuited to the purposes of grain raising or dairying that I would urge the claims of sheep husbandry. Steep hillsides, broken and new land, rocky and stony places, will often make excellent sheep pastures, and cannot profitably be devoted to anything else. There is much land of this kind which is now producing nothing but briars and weeds, which, if stocked with sheep, would contribute much to the owner's income. The value of sheep as aids to the farmer in subduing weeds and briars is not sufficiently understood or appreciated. But while it is true that sheep can be kept profitably upon land that cannot be well be devoted to anything else, it is still equally true that upon good land, with care and skill in their management, they will pay as well as any other kind of stock, and with less labor to secure it.

As the principal object sought to be produced, mutton or wool, so should the farmer be governed accordingly in selecting his stock of sheep. Where land is high, and hay and grain bring good prices, it will not pay to keep sheep for the purposes of wool-growing alone. On such land and in such locations the value of the carcass must be combined with that of the fleece to make the business remunerative. The average amount received for the wool of a single sheep ranges from one to two dollars at present prices. On land worth $100 an acre it will not pay to keep sheep for wool-growing when hay is $20 a ton, or corn 60 cents per bushel. The relative gross receipts per acre would stand in something like this proportion:

1 acre of land, cutting 2 tons of hay, worth $40.
1 acre of land, yielding 50 bushels of corn, worth $30.
1 acre of land, pasturing 10 sheep, yielding wool, worth $20.

But if these 10 ewes each produce a lamb worth four or five dollars, then the gross receipts per acre will be swelled above that received from either hay or corn. It is no uncommon thing for the farmer to purchase say 20 ewes for $5 apiece, making $100 for the lot, and before the expiration of a year to sell $25 worth of wool, and lambs amounting to $80 or $100, making over 100 per cent. on the investment, and have the original stock on hand, worth as much or more than at the time of starting. Of course this is not all to be set down as profit. Neither is the whole amount received for a crop of hay or grain to be considered as profit. In determining the actual profit on any crop there are many items of debit and credit to be counted before the true result is reached. In sheep husbandry the credits come in under the heads of wool, lambs, mutton, manure, improvement of the farm, etc. while the principal charges are for provender consumed and labor in their care.

Founded in 1877, *Farm Journal,* which absorbed *Country Gentleman* in 1955, is remaining general national farm magazine.

works, we will make good to actual subscribers any loss sustained by trusting advertisers who prove to be deliberate swindlers. Just as we cannot guarantee a pig's tail to curl in any particular direction, so we shall not attempt to adjust disputes between subscribers and honorable business men, nor pay the debts of honest bankrupts."

Wilmer Atkinson published and edited *Farm Journal* for forty years, making it an agricultural magazine of national prominence and importance. He had been joined in 1883 by a young nephew, Charles F. Jenkins, who became the magazine's business manager. Arthur H. Jenkins, a brother, took over the editorship in 1921, after his uncle's death. He did not retire from active participation in the business until thirty-four years later in 1955.

Atkinson's *Farm Journal* flourished. Its circulation grew far beyond the bounds the founding editor had first set for himself. It exerted a strong influence on the agricultural community through the simple and basic magazine function of keeping its readers informed. A noteworthy accomplishment was recognized when in 1926 the then Secretary of Agriculture gave the magazine a large share of the credit for effort that resulted in the establishment of the Rural Free Delivery postal system.

As *Farm Journal* had flourished, it declined. It lost circulation and influence. Financially, it was near failure. Just as the magazine, a victim of the great depression, was about to be sold at public auction in 1935, it was purchased by Graham Patterson, publisher of the *Christian Herald*. Wheeler McMillen, who had been editor of *Country Home* was made editor-in-chief in 1939. The development of the modern *Farm Journal* began at this time. The change of owner, publisher, and editor was followed by a refurbishing and revitalizing of *Farm Journal*. The format was changed (it has since changed again) to resemble that of *Time*. Stress was placed on the speedy publication of agricultural news. Strongly anti-New Deal during the administrations of Franklin D. Roosevelt, it criticized, as well as reported fully, actions and trends in Washington which affected the farmer and farm life. Printing was shifted to high-speed presses in Chicago. Another important move was made in 1939. *Farm Journal,* with a circulation then of 1,400,000 absorbed *The Farmer's Wife,* published in St. Paul, whose circulation was about 1,200,000. The first issue of the merged magazines appeared in May, 1939, and proudly announced a circulation of more than 2,400,000, "the largest circulation in farm magazine history." The title *Farm Journal and The Farmer's Wife* was used from 1939 to 1945. "The Farmer's Wife" was retained as a separate section of *Farm Journal,* a magazine within a magazine, starting, behind its own full-color cover, about midway in each issue. Firm business and editorial concepts lay behind these changes made to establish *Farm Journal* as "the news magazine of agriculture."

During World War I a shortage of men for farm labor coupled with a world-wide demand for food forced an increase in farm efficiency. The first changes took place in farm practice, in horticulture, and in animal husbandry. The tractor and the tools that it pulled, the automobile, and the farm truck marked the beginning of farm mechanization. Broad social changes reached the farm with the advent of better roads brought by the automobile. At the same time, the teaching of vocational agriculture in rural schools, the development of the Agricultural Extension Service of the Department of Agriculture, and the establishment of 4H clubs all augmented the drive toward better education and created a demand for channels of rural information. This the farm magazines supplied, keeping pace with the rather slow evolution taking place on the farm.

The rate of rural change was speeded by several factors. Beginning in the 1930's the influence of the federal government on agriculture increased rapidly. Adjustment to swift-changing farm programs and legislation put a premium on the farmer's keeping well and quickly informed. Fast, current, accurate information became a requisite for the advantageous marketing of his products. *Farm Journal* established a full-time editor in Washington. In 1944 it began to build a staff of field editors to obtain maximum coverage nationally of farm news. Increasingly *Farm Journal* was planned and edited to translate available speed of printing and transmission into terms of editorial function.

The need for this was reinforced, in the opinion of *Farm Journal* editors, by the fact that agricultural research since World War II shifted from agricultural methods to farm products. Insect and disease control by chemical means opened up entirely new growing methods. New insecticides, herbicides, and antibiotics were made available for general use and farm application. The agricultural process was speeded and improved. *Farm Journal* kept pace, emphasizing its practice of getting usable, profitable information quickly to the farm. Brief, fast-paced articles, their contents immediately applicable, kept the farmer informed. The last pages of an issue of *Farm Journal,* which is printed on the same presses as *Time,* go to the printer's just four days before the magazine is received by the subscriber.

At the same time the magazine manages to keep something of the warm, homey touch that had been Wilmer Atkinson's. The language is direct, the approach colloquial. The editorial ideal is that *Farm Journal* reach the farm family in the guise of a well-informed and friendly neighbor. The tone of the magazine is particularly apparent in *The Farmer's Wife.* The increasing urbanization of the farm family is recognized through slick paper, smart text, and modern illustrations. Fashion, food, home decoration are treated as glamorously as in the popular women's magazines. There is no condescension. In fact there is flattery in recognition of a real difference in its readers. The farm woman may be as well dressed, as well informed, and have many of the same family interests and problems as the city women, but she occupies a more central position in her household. As one *Farm Journal* editor commented, she may also "hold a flashlight while her husband acts as midwife at the delivery of a stubborn calf." The farm woman is the cultural and moral leader of her family and a partner in her husband's enterprise; there is usually one checking account for the business of the farm and for household expenses.

Farm Journal publishes practical advice on gardening, hog raising, apple storage, dairying, and scores of other farm subjects. It runs innocent jokes and has colloquially written humorous departments. Two-thirds of each issue is devoted to farm news, production, markets; one-third to farm women. All this is fairly typical of most of the farm magazines. The distinctive feature of *Farm Journal* is its coverage of the news, in news magazine style, which is of interest to the farm and the farm family. Factual information and fast reporting are what it believes make it "The Most Influential Farm Magazine" and "The Magazine of American Agriculture." Page inserts written and presented in terse, telegraphic style present: "Last-minute news straight from Washington"; Farm Business; Today; "News to help you save time, make money."

In 1958 *Farm Journal* acted to cut its circulation and reduced its national circulation guarantee with a corresponding decrease in its advertising rates. The object was to limit circulation to readers who had an active interest in farming. The magazine, which is not sold on newsstands, now limits subscriptions to those engaged in farming or other agricultural vocations. In 1956 *Farm Journal* was published in three regional editions, East Central, Western, and Southern. In 1968 with a circulation of over 3,000,000 it was published in 29 editions. In August 1969 *Farm Journal* inaugurated a "Top Operator" edition. Mailed separately but treated as part of their regular subscription for those who meet the economic requirement, it goes only to farmers grossing $20,000 or more annually.

For the 102 years of its existence *Country Gentleman* was an important and influential national farm magazine. *Farm Journal* has been leaving its imprint on farm life since 1877. In actuality it is the one remaining general, national farm magazine. Others are listed as national in coverage, but most of them are national magazines devoted to specific agricultural subjects, cattle breeding, the raising of particular crops, separate interests. The other two large-circulation farm magazines —there were three while *Capper's Farmer* was still being published in the late 1950's—are *The Progressive Farmer* and *Successful Farming,* both basically regional.

The Progressive Farmer, which circulates from Birmingham, covers the South in five regional editions. These are published for Virginia and the Carolinas; Alabama and Florida; Mississippi, Arkansas, and Louisiana; Kentucky and Tennessee; and Texas and Oklahoma. The combined circulations of these editions run to well over 1,250,000. Large-sized, well-printed, with a slick color cover, *Progressive* treats subjects pertinent to the farm and the farm home in issues running to about 170 well-filled pages. Practical farm facts and agricultural advice are a mainstay of the magazine, but it covers national affairs in special departments and general articles, devotes generous amounts of space to the farm home, and keeps its readers informed of the latest developments in agriculture and agricultural implements.

Successful Farming, published by the giant Meredith Corporation, which also publishes *Better Homes and Gardens,* circulates out of Des Moines to over 1,300,000 subscribers to all editions. Like its competitors it does not neglect the farm wife and home (a section is titled "Successful Homemaking"), and its editorial offering is diversified, but *Successful* focuses on farm management. Published in twelve regional and state editions and in other special editions for advertisers, the magazine stresses its "in-depth" reporting and experts' counsel on agricultural specialties. It runs multipage farm management guides in various issues, each on a specific subject, as on animal health, farm machinery, weed and insect control. The attractive looking magazine is designed throughout to provide farm management guidance to those in the business of farming.

Farm Journal, The Progressive Farmer, and *Successful Farming* are important farm magazines, but they hardly stand alone. Since the founding of the *Genesee Farmer* in 1831, hundreds of farm magazines, some of them still extant and effective, have been printed and circulated. Founded in 1842 and national in scope for most of its many years, the *American Agriculturist* was stressing the scientific as well as the practical approach to farm problems in the 1860's. Orange Judd, an agricultural chemist, was its most famous editor. Men of the stature of the botanist Asa Gray were among its contributors in the last century. The magazine combatted frauds, encouraged experimental farming, and conducted crop contests. The *American Agriculturist,* which at one time had a very large circulation, has absorbed many competitive farm publications, including the respected *Rural New Yorker,* founded in 1849, which had a circulation of over 221,000 when it was still an independent publication in the 1950's. At one time a thriving property of the Phelps Publishing Company of Springfield, Mass., known for many years as the world's largest publisher of pulp magazines, the *American Agriculturist* is now published in Ithaca, New York, "for the Northeast Farmer." It features treatment of crops and soils, dairy and livestock, farm management, and cracker-barrel humor under the cracker-barrel head, "Shuckin's."

Another Phelps property, *Farm and Home,* was nationally circulated to a wide audience between 1880 and 1925. In 1950 one of the oldest of the regional farm magazines, the *Southern Agriculturist,* was consolidated with *Farm and Ranch.* No longer listed, the combined magazines had a circulation of over 1,300,000 out of Nashville. The *Southern Planter* of Richmond, founded in 1841, still has a circulation of about 200,000. Today's *Prairie Farmer* was founded in Chicago in 1840 as the *Union Agriculturist* for the first year of its long life.

Many have gone and there are few giants left, but there are still hundreds of farm magazines classified by *Standard Rate and Data* as national, regional, and sectional publications. Chicago has the *Big Farmer,* which describes itself as "the national farm magazine for farm executives who manage, own, and/or operate large food factories or family farms." A quarterly which specializes in farm management, economics, and sociology, it has a give-away circulation of not quite 300,000. In St. Paul the Webb Publishing Company directs *The Farmer* to the crop and livestock farmers of Minnesota and the Dakotas.

Every state seems to have its farm paper—the *Ohio Farmer, Nebraska Farmer, Tennessee Farmer, Michigan Farmer, New England Farmer, Maine Farmer and Homemaker*. . . . Some of them are Farm Bureau publications. Necessarily, these farm papers are down to earth and homey.

There are nationally circulated periodicals for fruit growers, dairy farmers, bee culturists, and poultrymen. There are handsome magazines, usually published by associations, for seemingly almost every breed of cattle: the *Jersey Journal*, the *Milking Shorthorn Journal*, the *Aberdeen-Angus Journal*, the *Guernsey Breeders' Journal*, the *Ayrshire Digest*, the *Holstein-Friesian World*. Heavy with advertising and notices of stock sales, some of them running to issues of over 200 pages, these farm magazines are in reality professional trade journals—as is the *Dairy Goat*. They survive and many of them thrive because of their special-interest content.

The general farm magazines, particularly those of national appeal, have had a much harder time, and many of them have lapsed. When it was edited by Herbert Myrick and published by Phelps, *Farm and Home* had a very large circulation. It was sold to the strong *Farm and Fireside*. It too has disappeared.

Like publishing of any kind, farm magazine publishing is subject to the ordinary vicissitudes of profit-making business. Editors get old and die or their skills decline. Owners die, too, or decide to relinquish their interests. A farm magazine may simply succumb to superior competition or be swallowed up in a merger. Farm magazines have also had to face difficulties peculiar to their field.

Once upon a time the great part of the United States population was engaged in farming and lived on farms. Though it is no longer *de rigueur* for a Presidential candidate to be born in a log cabin, until quite recently it was unwise of him to be born and brought up anywhere but on a farm. Failure to do this constituted an admission that he was different and probably considered himself superior to most of the voting population, and that population distrusted city slickers. Most 20th century Americans live in cities or suburbs and many of them cannot tell a horse from a cow or an ox from an ass through any actual experience with any of these animals. They can distinguish between tomatoes and potatoes because the one is usually cellophane-wrapped on supermarket counters while the other is bagged on the floor.

The number of U. S. farms is continually falling. There were 6,361,502 in 1910. In 1967 there were about half that number, 3,176,000. Farm population has declined from 31,974,000 in 1920, when the population of the entire country was 106,000,000, to less than 11,000,000 out of a 200,000,000 population in 1967. At the same time, average farm acreage has risen, from 147 acres in 1920 to 359 acres in 1967.

There is a continually shrinking audience potential for the farm magazines. The characteristics of that audience have changed as farm operations have expanded and intensified. There are few subsistence farms now, few fringe farms. Farming has become a business, often big business.

The once-marked distinctions between rural and urban and suburban families have been virtually erased. There are few Hicksvilles or comic country cousins. The farm family is as well educated, as well equipped with all the conveniences of modern living as the town and city family. Often it is more prosperous. In Nebraska, for instance, average annual farm income was about $21,000 in 1967. Nebraska farm families bought more cars, appliances, and other durables and semi-durables than urban families in the Omaha market.

These circumstances have dictated editorial changes in the farm magazines for changed farm readers. They have also necessitated definition of the markets which the farm magazines could offer their advertisers.

Most of the farm magazines have had to make a choice. They could change their basic content and appeal in an effort to reach and retain a growing number of readers with rural addresses but nonagricultural occupations and interests—or they could concentrate on the smaller but profitable farm market. The choice was really between becoming "shelter books" devoted to suburban gardening, entertainment, and gossip, with light coverage of rural interests; or they could intensify their efforts as farm magazines reaching actual farmers and farm families.

The big national advertisers of agricultural goods and services are not interested in the exurbanite, the exsuburbanite, or even the ex-farm families who still live in rural localities. The city worker who yearns to live in a sylvan dell or a cottage by the side of the road does not constitute a market for reapers, threshers, tractors, seeds, fertilizers, and all the other equipment and working necessities of the corporate, family, or individually owned and operated farm. Advertisers have small interest in what used to be called gentleman farmers who tilled or cut hay as a pastime or found it useful for tax purposes to describe themselves as farmers. It was for this reason that *Country Gentleman* hopefully changed its name to *Better Farming* and *Farm Journal* limited its circulation to those actually living and working on farms or engaged in farm-connected occupations. *Successful* and *Progressive* remained completely farm magazines and emphasize their practical usefulness to the farmer and the farm family.

In this way the leading farm magazines have retained their hold on their readers and on their advertisers. Every year the manufacturers and distributors of farm trucks and tractors, tires, mechanized equipment, chemical fertilizers, and other necessities of modern farming—International Harvester, Ford, Eli Lilly, White Motor, General Motors, J. I. Case, Deere, Standard Oil, Goodyear, and a few other comparable organizations—lead the list of advertisers in farm publications.

National farm magazines long struggled with one difficulty inherent in their subject. Farmers growing truck in southern New Jersey do not have the same agricultural interests as tree farmers in Washington or tobacco growers in the Connecticut Valley. The disparate working interests of farmers in different parts of the country did not matter so much while the United

States still had a fairly homogeneous farm population and farm families in Illinois felt a kinship with those in Connecticut. This fellow feeling which came of closeness to the soil and common social and political interests largely vanished, as did the common market for advertisers which farmers and farm families represented.

The publication of regional, sectional, local, and other special editions has been the device adopted, with apparent success, by the larger farm magazines. Some chose to go the other way, become more general, and appeal to suburban and rural population center interests.

In 1943 *Farm Journal* purchased *Pathfinder,* which had been founded in 1894 as a Washington fact sheet. It changed the name to *Town Journal* and published the magazine monthly as "the family magazine of home-town America." It expanded circulation to nearly 2,000,000 in 1955 when it added the unexpired subscriptions of *Country Gentleman* subscribers with rural nonfarm addresses. *Farm Journal* then offered advertisers a "countryside unit" through purchase of space in both *Farm Journal* and *Town Journal.* Home and garden hints, small-town chatter, health, travel, recreation, and personalities were the basic editorial offering. The experiment did not work and publication of *Town Journal* was suspended.

The shift to close emphasis on a strictly agricultural market has not always worked for a farm magazine. Founded in 1855, *New England Homestead* was published for many years by the Phelps Company in Springfield. *Farm and Home* was actually an offshoot of the *Homestead,* which itself achieved a large circulation. This dwindled when the magazine passed to other owners, but it was still over 200,000 when *New England Homestead* decided to limit subscriptions to regional farm families who had annual farm incomes of $10,000 or over. No subscription renewal appeals were made. Circulation promptly dropped to about 27,000.

In 1967 *New England Homestead* was purchased by the *Inquirer and Mirror* of Nantucket, a weekly newspaper founded in 1821, and the direction of the farm magazine was reversed.

Page size was reduced, format changed, layout redesigned, and the whole appearance of the magazine brightened. The new publisher announced that while the *Homestead* would continue to print agricultural content of interest to New England farm families, it would broaden its editorial coverage to include treatment of the historical, cultural, leisure, travel, and recreational aspects of New England.

New England Homestead now carries a calendar of regional events in each issue. It has departments on entertainment and the arts, antiques, gardening, interior decorating, articles of antiquarian interest, recipes, and fashions. Essentially it has become a regional magazine after the manner of the very successful *Sunset* in California and the equally successful *Yankee* out of Dublin, New Hampshire. In a year's time this new policy has resulted in substantially increased circulation, and, once a farm magazine, *New England Homestead* seems on its way to reestablishing itself as a regional magazine.

Originally the farm magazines were founded in the nineteenth century to give farmers practical, rule-of-thumb advice about their jobs. They were a means of sharing, through periodical communication, the successful farm experiences of one farmer with his interested fellows. From this, the farm magazines progressed to explanations of scientific agricultural procedures as these were discovered in the laboratory and tested in the field. Their reiterated approval of the newer methods was largely influential in overcoming the natural reluctance of the farmer to try and then adopt the newer, more efficient, and more productive methods advocated.

The farm magazines enlarged their activities. Besides disseminating practical farm knowledge and explaining the new scientific methods, they led in the fight for rural improvements and for the establishment of government agricultural agencies and schools of agriculture. Then, through their articles and their advertising, they brought the farmer news and facts about the farm implements and labor-saving devices, as these were developed and perfected, which have improved farming and made farm life more comfortable.

To these basic functions the national farm magazines, the regional farm magazines, and, to a lesser extent, the state farm papers of comparatively local circulation have added increasingly the social and economically important function of informing the entire rural community about national and international affairs. Through the medium of the farm magazines the farmer and the farm family are now brought significant news and thoughtful comment as fully, as accurately, as quickly—and as attractively—as the general magazines bring them to a largely urban audience.

The number of farms and of people engaged in farming will probably dwindle further as mechanization, agricultural chemistry, and larger capital investment continue to increase farm productivity on the intensively utilized acreage of ever larger farms. Bolstered by governmental subsidies, farm incomes are high. Standards of living on the farm, educational advantages, opportunities for recreation are at least equal to those of town and city dwellers. For some of this the farm magazines can justly claim a share of the credit.

The important farm magazines recognize the changes that have taken place on the farm and have made corresponding changes in their adjustment to the situation and to the demands of their advertisers. The largest of the national farm magazines, *Farm Journal, The Progressive Farmer,* and *Successful Farming,* have gone into many different regional and advertising editions. On a smaller scale they have faced some of the same difficulties that face the larger consumer magazines of general appeal and have attempted to solve them by offering advertisers greater flexibility as a medium through specialized regional and local circulation coverage, in the same way that the larger magazines are doing.

Some of the smaller farm magazines, *New England Homestead* a case in point, have taken the alternative, transformed themselves into periodicals of regional interest and strive to reach a wider reading public with changed editorial offerings and appeal. Here again, some farm magazines, stung by necessity, are doing—perhaps anticipating—what changed conditions of one kind and another are forcing some of the large general magazines to do as they sideslip from "mass" to "class" publications, trying to change their appeals, thus their readership and the market they offer to advertisers.

As a group the major farm magazines posted substantial percentage losses in both numbers of advertising pages and in advertising revenue in 1969.

Chapter 16

Liberalism and Iconoclasm in the Magazines

When *McClure's*, the *American*, and the other muckraking magazines ceased to be organs of reform and liberal thought, while the mass weeklies, like *The Saturday Evening Post* and *Collier's* after the days of Norman Hapgood, stayed conservative or neutral in their discussion of business, social questions, and public affairs, another group of magazines—in some respects far more radical than the more powerful muckraking monthlies—upheld the liberal tradition in the twentieth century.

The Nation was founded in 1865 by E. L. Godkin, a twenty-five-year-old Irish immigrant. Designed as a liberal weekly, it has consistently remained what it was intended to be: a magazine which would discuss current affairs, uphold what it considered truly democratic principles, and work for the elevation of labor as a class and for the improvement of the Negro's lot. Godkin edited *The Nation* until 1881 when he merged it with the *New York Evening Post*. Under Godkin, *The Nation* fought for social improvement, for greater good for all, not only for the economically fortunate few.

Henry and Charles Francis Adams, Henry James, Sr., Henry James, Jr., William James, Francis Parkman, and other scholars and writers were all contributors to Godkin's *Nation*, which struck at political corruption and advocated both tariff and civil service reforms. Under later editors, particularly under Paul Elmer More, classicist and humanist, author of the many volumes of *Shelburne Essays,* it continued its liberal attitude and interpretation of events, but stressed literary criticism. Its literary standards have always been high. Carl, Irita, and Mark Van Doren were all *Nation* literary editors during the editorship of Oswald Garrison Villard, who ran the magazine from 1918 to 1933. Villard retained the magazine's liberal viewpoint, opposed ratification of the Versailles Treaty, adopted a sympathetic attitude toward Soviet Russia, and had *The Nation* pay especial attention to foreign affairs.

Leading liberals of the time were on the editorial staff of *The Nation* or appeared frequently as contributors. Heywood Broun, H. L. Mencken, Norman Thomas, Max Lerner, George Seldes, have all been on its editorial board. Its contributors have been and are a mixture of professors, intellectuals, and journalists; Allen Tate, Dorothy Thompson, John Haynes Holmes, Raymond Clapper, Stuart Chase, Louis Adamic, and Reinhold Niebuhr have been some of them. Heywood Broun, consistent opponent of social injustice, ran a page in *The Nation,* variously entitled "It Seems to Heywood Broun" and "Broun's Page," for many years in the 1920's and the 1930's.

The Nation has long been prolabor, a foe of all racial discrimination, collectivist in its leanings, and critical of the free enterprise system. It retained, perhaps intensified, its general characteristics after Freda Kirchwey, who was long associated with the magazine, became its editor and publisher, in 1933. The new editor believed in collective security as the only defense against the rising tide of fascism in Europe, and *The Nation* advocated it editorially. It advocated lifting the embargo on arms to help the Loyalist government during the Spanish Civil War, and favored collective action to check Japanese aggression against China. During World War II, it criticized the American entente with Vichy France and the appeasement of Franco in Spain. *The Nation* after the war advocated world government and the sharing of atomic information.

Always subsidized but long in financial difficulty and unable to raise sufficient funds through continued campaigns, *The Na-*

tion was in still other difficulties by 1951. A former *Nation* art critic accused the magazine of closely following the Communist line in its comments on American foreign policy. *The Nation,* a foe of censorship and shrill in protest at the banning of any of its issues when they contained unpopular opinions, refused the critic a hearing in its pages. When the accusations were published in the *New Leader,* Freda Kirchwey promptly sued both writer and magazine.

In protest Reinhold Niebuhr resigned from *The Nation's* editorial staff. A political writer who had once been the magazine's managing editor also resigned. People who thought of themselves as liberals were shocked at what seemed illiberal intolerance. Granville Hicks, writing in the *Commentary,* said: "One looks back with regret to the time when *The Nation* spoke for all liberals. . . . *The Nation* has preserved what was weakest and blindest in the old liberalism and has carried over attitudes that once were irresponsible but now are dangerous." [1]

There were other signs of unrest at *The Nation.* Its long-time literary editor left in 1953. In September, 1955, Freda Kirchwey relinquished her dual position as editor and publisher. Editorship of *The Nation* went to Carey McWilliams, who had been editorial director. In assuming the office of publisher to which he brought needed new capital, George G. Kirstein reiterated *Nation* policy in the issue of September 17, 1955. "This magazine has been and will continue to be frankly partisan. Our hearts and our columns are on the side of the worker, of the minority group, of the underprivileged generally. We side with the intellectual and political nonconformist in his clear constitutional right to refuse to conform." In 1968 *The Nation* had a circulation of only a little more than 119,000.

Far younger than *The Nation,* for it was founded in 1914, less austere but roughly resembling it physically and in general intent, *The New Republic* is a companion liberal magazine as sharply critical of the social and political scene. *The New*

[1] Quoted in *Time,* April 19, 1951.

Republic also has been the friend of labor, the foe of fascism or anything it sees as fascistic in tendency, the enemy of economic privilege, and a strong proponent and defender of civil liberties.

Herbert Croly was the founding liberal editor of *The New Republic.* He called it "a journal of opinion," and the magazine still uses this phrase to describe itself. *The New Republic* was intended to be antidogmatic. Croly and his associates, as he wrote later, wanted to arouse in readers "little insurrections in the realm of their opinions." The magazine was to "prick and even goad public opinion into being more vigilant and hospitable, into considering its convictions more carefully." Under Herbert Croly and then Bruce Bliven, such writers as Walter Lippmann, Edmund Wilson, Malcolm Cowley, Robert Morss Lovett, Stark Young, and John Dewey made *The New Republic* a sharp-spoken and distinguished weekly. Consistently critical in its attack, it has been more discursive than *The Nation,* and though sometimes shrill, often more tolerant, and at least as sharply perceptive. Social philosophy and prophecy, science, education, morals, economics, and politics have been its chief concerns, as they have been the concerns of *The Nation.* Both *The Nation* and *The New Republic* stress literary, theatrical, and musical criticism. Both magazines devote considerable space to letters from readers. These letters are regular features, designed to encourage further expression of opinion on subjects of social and political interest. They are not filler material, as they often appear to be in some of the larger magazines which have adopted the ancient device.

With the issue of December 16, 1946, *The New Republic* changed its page size, going into a smaller-sized page. It changed its format generally, and changed its editor. In this issue Henry Wallace, ex-Secretary of Commerce and ex-Vice-President, was announced as editor, Michael Straight as publisher, and Bruce Bliven was moved up to be editorial director. During his year and a half as *New Republic* editor, before he resigned to head a third party in the presidential election of 1948, Wallace's extreme liberalism was reflected in the magazine. A weekly page carried his opinions on national and international affairs.

These changes were designed to make *The New Republic,* which is published in Washington, D.C., look more like a news weekly. Cartoons, caricatures, graphs, and simplified charts appeared as illustrations for articles bearing catchy titles and subtitles. New departments—"Farm," "Labor," "Washington Wire," and the like—made their appearance; and the masthead, showing the influence of the Luce publications, paraded a long list of "senior editors," "associate editors," and "researchers." With Bruce Bliven remaining as editorial director and Michael Straight, son of the magazine's founding family, as editor, the appearance of *The New Republic* changed again, returning to something more nearly akin to its earlier conservative format, but the attempt to popularize the magazine was still evident.

In March, 1953, *The New Republic* suffered a severe blow. Financial support derived from a trust fund set up from the Whitney fortune was withdrawn. Michael Straight and the magazine's new publisher, Gilbert Harrison, were faced with a difficult situation. Publication was continued despite a formidable weekly deficit which they had somehow to make up. The magazine still tried, as it said in various editorials during this time while it was appealing desperately for funds, to be nonconformist, original, challenging, militant, and controversial. *The New Republic* was saved when in the spring of 1954 the publisher's wife fell heir to a few millions of McCormick reaper money. There is some irony in the fact that both *The New Republic* and *The Nation* depend for their existence on funds from capitalistic system private enterprise, a system they accept but do not publicly admire.

On November 22, 1954, *The New Republic* published an impressive 40th anniversary issue of 126 pages. Its glossy cover listed the names of forty-one eminent contributors of the past, among them Shaw, Wells, Yeats, Santayana, Joyce, D. H. Lawrence, Hemingway, Dreiser, Faulkner, T. S. Eliot. Their original contributions were reprinted in the issue and Bruce Bliven reviewed the magazine's forty years. *The New Republic,* he said, had consistently represented minority, unpopular opinion. It had been, he admitted, left of center in the 1930's. "Most of the ideas of the New Deal," he claimed, "first saw the light in its pages."

A visitor from the world of the popular magazine (and *The New Republic* has certainly never been loud in its praises of that world), Henry Luce, was the guest speaker at an anniversary dinner in Washington. "Forty years after its formation," Michael Straight said on the occasion, "the place remains for a liberal journal of opinion. So does our ambition to fill that place." Readers have not been that enthusiastic. The magazine's circulation is a little over 29,000.

Both *The Nation* and *The New Republic* have been outspoken in their adverse criticism of generally accepted political and social institutions. *The Nation,* touched with the formal academic manner, has been on the whole more restrained; *The New Republic* the more aggressive in its support of minority groups, minority opinion, and advanced thought generally. Neither magazine, until *The New Republic* in its most recent phases, has made any attempt to be popular or to entertain. Both of them have served as useful gadflies, and as antidotes to complacency, materialism, and intrenched conservatism.

The influence of these liberal weeklies has been circumscribed by several factors. They have always had comparatively slight circulations, standing now at about 30,000 for each of them. Serious and unrelentingly earnest in their efforts, they have not attracted a large enough audience to circulate their ideas widely. Directed largely to the intelligentsia, they have mainly reached readers already sympathetic to the liberal views they express, and have failed to reach a wider audience whose interest might be aroused and which might be converted to the application of greater mental effort in the consideration of problems beyond their immediate personal sphere. Neither *The New Republic* nor *The Nation* attracts much advertising. Published on a heavy-grade newsprint, sparsely illustrated, they lack the physical attractiveness of the mass magazines. Because of all these limitations, they have remained periodicals for those who see themselves as the elect and select.

All such magazines, of course, have a stronger effect than their limited circulations indicate. A very high proportion of their readers are intellectuals, educated people, many of them university and college teachers who disseminate in their classrooms and in their professional associations the ideas obtained from the magazines they read. Neither directly nor indirectly does this magazine liberalism touch forcefully on men and women engaged in practical business or industry, as the liberalism of the profitable and widely circulated muckraking magazines very definitely did.

Another insurgent magazine became one of the social and literary phenomena, as well as a social and literary force, of the 1920's. This was *The American Mercury*. The movement (if so formal a word can describe anything as difficult to classify as the vigorous and untrammeled reform efforts and the startling effects which this magazine obtained issue after issue) had started, long before the *Mercury's* founding in 1924, in another magazine which was turned widely from its original course.

The Smart Set was founded in 1890 by William D'Alton Mann as a journal for New York "society." At first it was written and read mostly by members of this self-consciously exclusive group. Arthur Griscom and Charles Hanson Towne, when they became its editors, transformed *The Smart Set* into a witty literary journal, a kind of dilettante's delight, which they had no hesitation in describing on the front cover as "A Magazine of Cleverness." Nor were they casting pearls before swine. *The Smart Set* was edited, on its own declaration, "to provide lively entertainment for minds that are not primitive." Despite this pose of snobbish discrimination, despite a certain preciosity, *The Smart Set* published notable work. It accepted O. Henry's first short story. It began, after its purchase in 1900 by John Adams Thayer, to publish such writers as Gertrude Atherton, James Branch Cabell, Richard Le Gallienne, and other writers of the more aesthetic persuasion.

In October, 1902, its cover—the familiar *Smart Set* cover with a gentleman in tails bowing to a curtsying lady in evening costume, a cupid with drawn bow in the lower right-hand corner, a masked satyr in the upper left, and the red logotype lettered in flowing capitals—opened on prose and verse by Hildegarde Hawthorne, Arthur Symons, Bliss Carman, Ridgley Torrence, Madison Cawein, Ella Wheeler Wilcox, Arthur Macy, and a score of lesser-known writers. James Branch Cabell was already represented with a romantic story in the genteel mode of the day, its author barely recognizable as the more daring romanticist he was to become in the 1920's. The issue was all fiction and verse. There were no articles. The love stories were of a most sentimental kind, and the jokes, of which there were many scattered as filler, were of such appalling insipidity that it is hard for a modern reader to visualize the kind of man or woman who could ever have found them amusing. There was already, at both the front and back of the issue, a plenitude of advertising for more plebeian articles than those touched on in the editorial pages.

The editor of *The Smart Set* from 1912 to 1914 was Willard Huntington Wright, aesthete and sophisticate, who was later to achieve a different fame as a writer of detective fiction. His *Canary Murder Case*, written under the pseudonym of S. S. Van Dine, and run in *Scribner's Magazine* in 1927, broke all publishing records for the sale of detective fiction. He had set the pattern for a series of Van Dine thrillers with *The Benson Murder Case* the year before. Wright was the first American editor to print James Joyce, George Moore, D. H. Lawrence, and other writers of advanced literary and moral ideas whose work was not acceptable to the mass magazines.

The change in *The Smart Set* in ten years' time was marked. Contributors to the issue of May, 1913, included John Hall Wheelock, Louis Untermeyer, Owen Hatteras, Sara Teasdale, Wright and—certainly a sport in this galley—Irvin Cobb. Most significant, George Jean Nathan and H. L. Mencken, besides conducting, respectively, the departments of theatrical and literary criticism, were each represented by an article. Mencken, who wrote on "Good Old Baltimore," a subject on which he became an established sage, opened his lead book review with this line: "Morality, like culture, belongs to what the psychiatrists call the circular insanities, at least in these states." This reads like a portent of the later Mencken.

There was a further portent in an advertisement in the issue of June, 1913. The advertisement stressed the first of a series of satirical sketches called "The American" by H. L. Mencken. "These articles," ran the blurb, "are to deal with all phases of the native male product of this country—his religion, his ideas of beauty, his politics, his habits, and his social life. The essays will represent the most solid work that Mr. Mencken has ever done. The fact that they deal with the American dispassionately and satirically will make them at once unique and interesting."

The 1913 *Smart Set* was a much stronger, more advanced, more daring magazine than it had been a decade earlier. One lead story, "Daughters of Joy" by Barry Benefield, described the funeral of a New York prostitute, dead of tuberculosis, at her place of business, with her employer and business associates acting as mourners. Editorially the magazine pointed out: "Sex itself is not indecent. It is the innuendoes that make it so." Another editorial deplored the low state into which humor had fallen: "Puritanism and conventionalism have limited our jokesters thematically, and our funny men find their best jokes unsalable. The average American is unable to laugh at himself; he is unable to appreciate sarcasm and cynicism if the ridicule touches any of his pet beliefs." In these editorials it is easy to perceive the hand of Mencken, to read what were to become the familiar Mencken themes. In 1914, Nathan and Mencken became coeditors of *The Smart Set.* World War I hindered them a little, but after its close the new editors went to work with a will on their vigorous campaign to change the prejudices of Americans, to demolish their conceptions of themselves, to rout puritanism and the genteel, to champion realism and naturalism in writing, to shock everyone out of his complacency, to smash every idol within reach, and to tremble all the others off their pedestals by the reverberations of their raucous derision.

What Mencken began in *The Smart Set* he continued from 1924 to 1933 in *The American Mercury*. The new magazine was edited during its first year by both Nathan and Mencken, but after that by Mencken alone. He boomed Theodore Dreiser and Sinclair Lewis; published Eugene O'Neill, Thomas Beer, Lewis Mumford, and F. Scott Fitzgerald. Strident, racy, irreverent, Mencken, by sheer force, was making a place for the newer kinds of writing, throwing out the dainty and delicate, yammering for more realism and stronger naturalism, for literature of the actual, not literature of the ideal. He published Sherwood Anderson, Joseph Hergesheimer, Carl Van Vechten, the naturalists, the aesthetes, the realists, the "new" writers. Meanwhile, in "Americana," a department of clippings selected from newspapers to show the appalling stupidity of the American mass mind, Mencken was berating the American public, and the public loved it. *The American Mercury* struck out in every direction. Irony, satire, burlesque, and outright bludgeoning were its weapons.

The American Mercury of the 1920's was not, any more than *The Smart Set* had been, a muckraking magazine after the pattern of *McClure's*. Neither did it resemble the liberal *Nation* and *New Republic*. It was out, not to reform government or business or social conditions, but to unmake the character of the individual American, to upset the pattern of his conventionalized ethics and his ways of looking at things. It had no positive philosophy to offer. It did not wish to remake the individual in any other mould, except possibly that of a milder Mencken; it intended to disturb, to shock, to arouse, to make people question. Like most magazines which take a discernible stand on any issue, it preferred its own prejudices to those of anybody else. It wanted people to be unconventional, but not so unconventional as not to recognize how daring they were. It was all loud and boisterous, vital and amusing.

It was also effective. What was then newer naturalism in literature, partly as a result of the *Mercury's* insistence, was recognized as worthy of critical consideration as well as reading. The loud boisterousness of Mencken and his magazine offended the fastidious and displeased many academic critics, but Mencken won. Stuart Sherman, Illinois professor, conservative critic in the style of Matthew Arnold, whose biography he wrote, humanist after Irving Babbitt and Paul Elmer More, kept up a long running fight with Mencken. Sherman defended puritanism and the literary values of the student and the scholar, defended the ethical standards and moral codes which *The American Mercury* seemed to be trying to demolish. Mencken won the battle when Sherman, after he became the editor of the book section of the *New York Herald Tribune,* modified his literary opinions and changed to a liberal viewpoint nearer Mencken's. Mencken had already overcome easier opponents.

The American Mercury became the college undergraduate's bible of cynicism and wickedness in the 1920's. The young intelligentsia of an excited decade, who felt that all their standards of value had been upset by World War I, scarcely knew what to think on artistic, literary, aesthetic, and moral questions—especially on moral questions—until the next issue of the *Mercury* came out. Not to know and admire the magazine was to prove oneself an uncouth barbarian, a member in good standing of the "booboisie" which Mencken attacked with such contempt and savagery. The beauty of the *Mercury* was that, looking as sedate in its green cover as *Harper's* or the *Atlantic,* looking like a scholarly monthly thick and rich with advertising, it yet attacked everything—and everything, believed its audience of the 1920's who looked on the *Mercury* as a religion rather than a magazine, needed to be attacked.

In 1927, when *The American Mercury* was at the height of its spectacular career and its influence on at least a part of the literate population was amazing, the November number carried an article on genetics; a study of Tom Heflin; a sketch entitled "A German Grandfather" by Ruth Suckow; a gruesome description of the brutal treatment of convicts on a Texas chain gang, written by Ernest Booth, then an inmate of a California prison where he was serving a life sentence for robbery; and "Days of Wickedness," a story by Herbert Asbury of the gangs in New York's infamous Fourth Ward. In "Clinical Notes" George Jean Nathan commented caustically on the debasing of fine liquors by American drinking habits, and concluded that the American people, acting in this instance as boorishly as they usually acted, deserved the visitation upon them of the Eighteenth Amendment. The issue contained a curious piece entitled "Body's Breviary" by Joseph Warren Beach, critic, literary historian, and university teacher, and a sharply written article on the rise, through dubious means, of the tabloid press in New York. Nathan, of course, reviewed the current plays, and Mencken the new books. Discussing *The Natural History of Revolutions* by Lyford P. Edwards, Mencken concluded that there were (in 1927) many signs of a possible revolution in the United States. He noted a widespread sense of oppression, not coordinated, not voiced, but real. "The peaceable citizen feels a heavier weight of government every day; the army of professional regulators and oppressors grows at a dizzy pace." One of the advertisements—there were nearly one hundred pages of advertisements in this issue—near the back of the magazine was for Mencken's *Prejudices: Sixth Series.*

Mencken's *American Mercury* created a magnificent stir in its day. It did more than that. It permanently affected American fiction and American literary criticism. It changed the attitude toward the conventions and affected the tastes of an entire generation. *The American Mercury* was one of the loudest voices whose noise combined to make the Roaring Twenties roar.

Magazine criticism of the social order and magazine iconoclasm declined during the decade or dozen or so years immediately following World War II. The United States was busy satisfying the voracious appetite for new cars and appliances and all the other goodies unavailable during the conflict. It was intent on reestablishing its industries for a peacetime which never really came. It was enthralled by television, prosperous, and a little tired.

Most of the old idols had been smashed, and the clay feet of newer ones had not yet been identified. Approval of communism, possible and often applauded before the war in intellectual circles, became dangerous, then impossible. With the inspired help of Senator Joseph McCarthy it became, if not criminally liable, professionally and personally suicidal. Most of the immediate social gains seemed to have been gained, and newer causes had not been invented or formulated distinctly enough for journalistic clamor.

The surcease was temporary and misleading. In the 1960's came the deluge. Politically as well as socially motivated and supported by a series of far-reaching Supreme Court decisions, reform measures, most of them regarding the civil rights of the Negro, have brought changes. An upheaval rather than a movement or an evolutionary process, it is being celebrated by riots, murder, arson, mounting and continually fomented racial hatreds, accusations, and counter accusations—all flaming toward an as yet unresolved conclusion.

All of this is taking place to the loud applause of the news media, print or electronic. The sensational aspects of violent expressions of dissatisfaction are manna from the streets. There is also the manifest desire to be known as advanced, sympathetic, and to back the winner. A large segment of the popular magazine press now expresses sentiments once peculiar to a minority of magazines and espouses what were once considered their "leftish" causes. Derision of accepted institutions or values and adulation of every new cause is commonplace as editors faithfully reflect the times they describe and discuss and vie with each other for public favor.

The possible revolution which H. L. Mencken foresaw in 1927 seems to have materialized beyond his dreams or forebodings. The economically overprivileged class has been abolished through confiscatory income taxes, and the newer one created by organized labor and government support is not yet assailable. Mencken's "booboisie" has either been stamped out or immeasurably aggrandized. If he complained of the heavy weight of government on the ordinary citizen in 1927, he would be appalled with the present in which the government of a socialized state directs and controls all profit-making enterprise through regulations and taxation and has largely abolished the privacy of the private individual. Mencken's "army of professional regulators and oppressors" was little more than a cadre when he wrote. It has become a permanent occupation force continually growing in numbers and in power.

The American Mercury of H. L. Mencken exerted its influence. A casual glance at many of the present large-circulation news and pictorial magazines will show what and how strong that influence was.

Chapter 17

Magazines as National Newspapers

Early in the twentieth century *The Independent,* at the time a powerful weekly, could say editorially: "Modern American magazines have to a large extent fallen heir to the power formerly exerted by pulpit, by crowds, parliamentary debates and daily newspapers in the molding of public opinion, the development of new issues, and dissemination of information bearing on current questions." [1]

Colonel George Harvey,[2] later ambassador to Great Britain, long editor of *The North American Review* and *Harper's Weekly,* and when he spoke, president of Harper & Brothers, also emphasized the mounting importance of the new mass magazines in influencing public opinion. Addressing the Sphinx Club in New York, on March 8, 1910, he said that the

[1] October 1, 1908. *The Independent* editorial writer expanded his argument by specific illustrations: "The magazine represents intellectual activity in its terminal buds. Its function is to work over old plots into new stories; to rewrite biography and history in accordance with the taste of the time, to resurrect forgotten truths, to make sound information palatable, to convert abstract science into applied science, to throw a searchlight into dark corners of the earth and some spots of our civilization, to start new movements and to guide old ones, to wake up people who are asleep by sounding the burglar alarm, to twist around the heads of those who are looking backward over their shoulders; in short, to inspire, to instruct, to interest."

[2] Colonel Harvey also enjoyed the title "President-Maker." It was his hotel suite at the Blackstone Hotel in Chicago which became the famous "smoke-filled room" of the Republican Convention of 1920. A conference of party leaders there resulted in the nomination of Warren G. Harding for President.

chief appeal of the low-priced magazines "is to interest in public affairs, and their *motif* is timeless." He continued:

> How admirably they have performed their functions and how accurately they have gauged the public's requirements and inclinations may be judged from their obvious popularity.
>
> The alert new periodicals have been called national newspapers, and to this extent the term is warranted: They do deal largely with vital topics of immediate interest, they do take sides, they do aim to guide as well as interpret public opinion, and their field is the whole country. They are public journals. . . . As such they have done much good and no little harm, but that the good they have done greatly outweighs the harm seems to be evidenced by the apparent fact that their power is increasing.

Colonel Harvey could scarcely have foreseen the extent to which the power of the mass magazines would reach. Four years later, in 1914, the average circulation for one issue of the 54 magazines then checked by the Audit Bureau of Circulation was less than 18,000,000 copies. Now the per issue circulation of the general and farm magazines checked by A. B. C. is well over 236,000,000.

One of the powerful magazines performing the functions which both the *Independent* editorial and Colonel George Harvey described is no longer in existence. Others had not yet been established.

The *Literary Digest,* founded in 1890, became an influential weekly journal of current events, reaching a circulation of almost two million in the 1920's. Never "literary" and scarcely a "digest," the magazine was written almost entirely with the scissors. Every week its editors pasted up, side by side, clippings from the country's newspapers and magazines on current questions. They did not digest, rewrite, or interpret. They simply presented news and editorial comment, including cartoons. Where the interpretations of political events, world happenings, and developments in art, literature, science, and religion differed, they presented both sides of the question and showed the source making the original comments. Regular features of the *Digest* during the days of its greatest success were Topics of the Day, Foreign Comment, Science and Invention, Letters and Art, Religion and Social Service, Current Poetry, Personal Glimpses, Investments and Finance, Current Events, Spice of Life, Radio, and the Lexicographer's Easy Chair.

The virtues of the *Literary Digest* were its careful winnowing of the newspaper and periodical press, and its presentation of information in such a way that the reader could make up his own mind on the basis of all the published facts. It provided the data from which public opinion could be formed, but did not attempt to hand out that opinion ready-made. Such an editorial policy sometimes made for dull reading and always required more active and intelligent participation than some readers could or would give, but, as an accurate and unbiased vehicle of current information, the *Literary Digest* maintained a high standard. Recognition of its complete and unprejudiced reporting caused its wide adoption throughout the American public school system, particularly in the high schools, for classes in English, public speaking, debating, civics, and history. This, added to its general acceptance by the magazine-reading public, made it one of the potent magazines, of the strictly informational type, in the first quarter of the twentieth century.

During the 1920's the *Literary Digest* originated the device of straw polls for measuring public opinion on important questions. It is popularly supposed that the magazine's ultimate failure was caused by its mistake in prophesying, on the basis of a reader poll, the outcome of the presidential election of 1936. This was undoubtedly a contributing factor, but only a factor. If the failure of such polls necessitates collapse of the sponsoring publications and organizations, the ground should have been littered with wrecks of magazines, newspapers, and professional oracles after the debacle of election forecasting in 1948, when the polls were virtually unanimous in picking the losing candidate as the certain victor in the presidential election. There are probably technical and less technical explanations for their loud and concerted failure. Discussion of these would be impertinent here. It is pertinent to note that the

Digest, by its consistent and successful use of the poll technique and the accuracy of many of its earlier survey results, demonstrated the usefulness of sampling public opinion. Opinion polls, with improved sampling and interviewing techniques, are now widely used to gauge public reaction to important social and economic questions, and their results are useful where a greater margin of error can be tolerated than in the forecasting of closely contested elections. In 1938 the waning *Literary Digest* was purchased by the publisher of a much younger competitor which is now the best-known weekly news magazine in the United States.

The man who bought the *Literary Digest* was by 1938 one of the most powerful magazine publishers and editors in the United States. His influence on magazines and, through his magazines, on contemporary American civilization is comparable to that of Curtis, Lorimer, Bok, and McClure a few years earlier. Henry Luce, born in China where his father was a missionary, first went to school in England, then prepared at Hotchkiss for Yale, from which he was graduated in 1920. At Hotchkiss, Henry Luce met Briton Hadden, and it was while they were still preparatory school students that they first had the idea for an informative weekly news magazine. The idea developed further while they were together as undergraduates at Yale, where, significantly, Luce made a tabloid of the Yale *Daily News,* which he edited.

In 1923 Luce and Hadden founded *Time.* The two young men had very definite ideas about the kind of magazine they wished to publish and very definite purposes in mind. Both were dissatisfied with existing journalism. They found that the newspapers were diffuse and disorderly in their presentation of the news, and that most of the magazines gave what they considered inadequate coverage to world events. Their earnest purpose, didactic from the start, was to shape and circulate a magazine which would do what they felt both newspapers and magazines failed to do. In the prospectus for the "weekly newsmagazine," a descriptive phrase which they coined and *Time* continues to use, Luce and Hadden stated flatly: "People

The first *Time* cover, in black and white, pictured Uncle Joe Cannon, Speaker of the House, who was retiring at the age of eighty-six after serving twenty-three terms in Congress. (Courtesy of *Time,* copyright Time, Inc., 1923.)

in America are, for the most part, poorly informed." Americans, they said, were uninformed because "no publication has adapted itself to the time which busy men are able to spend on simply keeping informed." This deplorable condition they intended to correct.

Their proposed magazine would organize the week's news in a pattern of departments, give the news in narrative form, and describe the people who made the news. *Time* would select the facts, tell what the facts meant, and state or strongly suggest what the reader should think or feel about them. The new magazine was to be "curt, clear, complete," so written and arranged that each issue would be an orderly and coherent account of the preceding week's news.

Its determined founders had difficulty in obtaining financial backing for their venture. It was five years before *Time* was soundly established. By 1928, with Hadden as editor and Luce as business manager, it had attained a circulation of 200,000. Long since, *Time* "the weekly newsmagazine," has been firmly fixed in the American scene.

Unlike the *Literary Digest,* the powerful predecessor and at one time strong competitor which eventually it absorbed, *Time* did not limit itself to clippings and quotations. It could not and fulfill its self-imposed mission of instructing the populace. It presented each news story crisply and smartly in what it is charitable understatement to describe as *Time*'s distinctive style, a style which has since been happily modified. It spoke from the beginning with complete assurance, *ex cathedra* authority, and metallic certainty. Hadden and Luce had introduced a new kind of magazine.

They put new practices to work in publishing it. One was the use of library research to make each news story not an isolated occurrence but part of a continuous historical stream of events. Another was the technique of writing and editing by which reporters, writers, researchers, and editors pooled their knowledge and skills to produce the copy published anonymously in each *Time* issue. In its early years *Time* proudly used the phrase "group journalism" to describe this operation.

It has since gone on record as regretting invention and use of the term. "Its Editor and Managing Editor, like those of any other publication, are and always have been responsible editors. Every other *Time* staff member is responsible for whatever he or she contributes (or omits to contribute) to the week's work." [3]

The pattern of departments which the founding editors adopted has varied very little to the present time. Currently it is: Arts, Books, Business, Cinema, Education, Law, Letters, Milestones (marriages, deaths, anniversaries), Modern Living, Nation, People, Press, Religion, Science, Sport, Television, Theatre, World. These are large subjects. *Time* coverage is wide and its intent is the largest possible. Subscribing readily to the hero theory of history, *Time*'s ambitious founders said in their 1923 prospectus that people make the news, so *Time* would tell about these people. It still does. Usually there is a picture of a man or a woman on the cover of each *Time* issue. Inside the magazine, a featured cover story tells about the person's life, thoughts, ideas, and accomplishment—and always, as with every subject, how *Time* views them.[4]

The first issue of *Time,* March 3, 1923, was written, edited, and published in New York by a small group of young men, most of them but a few years out of college. A large central office staff of writers, editors, and research assistants puts out the magazine now. Besides using the facilities of the standard news-gathering services, *Time* has its own bureaus in United States and Canadian cities, a large Washington force, and bureaus in important news centers abroad. All of these and field correspondents report to the editors in New York. Unlike most newspapermen and magazine article writers, *Time* reporters do not write directly for publication. They gather facts and opinions for transmittal to the New York editorial group who write, shape, and polish the material for publication in the issues which appear every Thursday. Besides the domestic, there are international editions of *Time,* all in English. *Time*

[3] *The Story of an Experiment* (New York: Time, Inc., 1948).

[4] It is of passing interest that Whittaker Chambers, then a senior editor of *Time,* wrote the cover stories on Marian Anderson, Arnold Toynbee, Rebecca West, and Reinhold Niebuhr.

Pacific is printed in Tokyo and Honolulu; *Time Atlantic* in Paris. They are identical in content with the domestic edition. *Time Canadian* and *Time Latin American* carry additional pages of editorial material on the areas in which they circulate, and, of course, different advertising. In 1923 the brash idea of two idealistic and intensely ambitious recent Yale undergraduates, *Time* has long since ticked its way into contemporary history.[5]

Time is prepared for and directed to a hypothetical man who is assumed to have no other source of information on current events. *Time's* purpose is to provide him with all the important news of the week, background enough to make the news intelligible, and enough comment to direct his opinion. Its intent is to enlighten by presenting information as complete as possible, and by interpreting the information provided. Each issue is prepared much as a newspaper is prepared and sent to press. Everything in each issue is checked and approved by one man on *Time's* staff, its managing editor. Henry Luce himself approved the *Time* jargon, the inverted sentences, slick epithets, the air of brassy omniscience which *Time* intentionally displayed in its earlier years.

What came to be known, admiringly or derisively, as "*Time* Style"—Luce would have called it "Timestyle"—was highly mannered and preciously affected. The magazine tagged people as "tycoons," "pundits," or with less flattering epithets. It smothered them under hyphenated adjectives. It concocted compound words, as "cinemactor" for a motion picture star. Hoping to attract attention, to create surface distinction, or just to indulge its own cleverness, it inverted its sentences so that they seemed to have been spoken by a child, a foreigner, or someone so knowing he was not constricted by the commonplace usages of ordinary English. Perhaps the most famous example came not from *Time* itself but from a parody by Wolcott Gibbs in *The New Yorker*, November 28, 1936: "Backward ran sentences until reeled the mind."

[5] Briton Hadden's chief ambition was to make a million dollars by the time he was 30. When he died in 1929 at the age of 31, his *Time* stock was worth over $1,100,000.

Time's cleverness was as unbridled as the earnestness and missionary zeal of Henry Luce who said in the prospectus already quoted: "*TIME* is interested—not in how much it includes between its covers—but in HOW MUCH IT GETS OFF ITS PAGES INTO THE MINDS OF ITS READERS." Luce applied his philosophy without hindrance to *Time* and the other magazines he founded or purchased from 1929 until his death in 1967. He was convinced that the world needed information and that it needed it presented according to definite Luce concepts; facts aligned, joined, related, explained, and built toward an opinion ready-made for his patients.

Time's first editorial employee—he became its managing editor, later its chief foreign correspondent—once described the ideal *Time* story. "The basis of good *Time* writing is narrative, and the basis of good narrative is to tell events, 1) in the order in which they occur; 2) in the form in which an observer might have seen them—so that readers can imagine themselves on the scene. A *Time* story must be completely organized from beginning to end; it must go from nowhere to somewhere and sit down when it arrives."

This calm and pleasantly worded description of an intense performance omits one important ingredient, the editorializing which is an essential part of most *Time* stories. Far from hiding the attempt, *Time* boasts of it. From the beginning it said it would give both sides of a story but clearly indicate which side it believed to have the strongest position. Its editors have reiterated their conviction that it is the duty of the press to evaluate as well as to report. *Time* has never claimed to be objective. If fact, it derides objectivity as impossible, which probably it is. The very selection of facts to report implies the action of some interpreting and, per se, prejudiced mind. *Time* goes further. It puts its selected facts into selected concepts. Inevitably there is distortion in its effort to make the isolated news event part of a significant body of coherent thought—or a coherent body of significant thought. This does, though, make it easy for *Time*'s mythical one-man reader to feel that he has both got all the news and placed it in context and perspective.

Once brash, *Time* has long since modified its approach. It has been around now for a long time and has the respectability which comes with age and consistent achievement. Substantial and widely quoted, it has the public guarantee of approval—unassailable in the magazine world—of a circulation of over 3,900,000.

Time's masthead is packed with the names of editors, researchers, reporters, and correspondents in many parts of the world. Its neatly ruled columns are packed with mingled news and comment. *Time* is informative, and it is timely. Robert F. Kennedy was assassinated in California, June 6, 1968. *Time* carried RFK on its June 14 cover and his career story inside the issue. With all of its articles anonymous, *Time* reflects the contemporary scene swiftly and adequately. Various 1968 issues featured Charles de Gaulle, "The Gun in America," "The Police in the Ghetto," the quiet Republican national convention in Miami Beach, and the much noisier and more sensational Democratic convention in Chicago. All of the news magazines cover much the same material from the same sources with comparable personnel and facilities. They live on current events, and the modern world supplies them in continuous profusion. Distinction has to lie in how completely and accurately a given news weekly does its job. *Time* is distinct, and it is always *Time* that does the work and makes the statements. It has no by-lined departments. Even the "Time Essays" on various subjects in the news are unsigned.

Before Hadden's death, Luce had conceived the idea for another magazine. Like *Time*, this magazine would educate its readers. Again the Luce purpose was didactic. *Fortune* would describe and explain American business. A *Time* editor provided the inspiration when he discovered "the vast, lurid, and exciting bibliography of balance sheets." Like Curtis and Lorimer, in this instance at least, Luce felt that business was the basic expression of the American spirit. He proposed to establish a magazine which would "reflect industrial life as faithfully in ink and paper and word as the finest skyscraper reflects it in stone, steel, and architecture."

The prospectus of *Fortune* promised that the magazine would do for business what other periodicals had long been doing for sports, society, fashion, travel, the arts, and the country estate. It would be handsome, and it would be seriously executed. A declaration of principles and intent listed things it would not do.

1. It will avoid generalities such as "cooperation between Capital and Labor."
2. It will have no "inspirational" matter.
3. It will contain no advice on how to run your business.
4. No tipstering.
5. No puffing of individuals.
6. No "defending" of Business.
7. No propaganda.
8. No ghost-written banalities by Big Names.
9. It *will* have literary standards of the highest—and if Babbitt doesn't like literature he doesn't have to read it.
10. It *will* be beautiful.

This was a large promise. Unlike many supplicants for public favor, *Fortune* has kept its word.

The first issue of *Fortune,* an expensive, beautifully dressed monthly, went to 30,000 subscribers in January, 1930. Started shortly after the 1929 stock market crash, by 1933, in the middle of the depression, *Fortune* was earning money. The magazine, physically magnificent, handsomely printed and illustrated on quality stock, was addressed not to the masses but to business owners and executives. Business alone was the subject of articles during the first years. As government became increasingly important in business and to the business community in the 1930's, *Fortune* branched out into governmental and social subjects. The pages of a current issue of *Fortune* may include the biography of an eminent industrialist, an article concerned primarily with economics, or a complete description of the organization and operation of one great business house —an oil company, a baking company, an advertising agency.

Like *Time, Fortune* is staff-written. Articles are the product of thorough and extensive research. A staff of women researchers does an exhaustive job of file research. Staff writers or their assistants interview anyone and everyone who can give them the facts they need to know in order to present a full and accurate picture. *Fortune* articles, in their length and thoroughness, and in the completeness of the research done in preparing them have been compared to the full-bodied studies done by the muckrakers for *McClure's*. They are hardly comparable otherwise. Once there was more than a touch of iconoclasm about many *Fortune* articles. There is none now. *Fortune*'s purpose is not to expose but to explain. Though facts are given as they are found, the effect of the articles in *Fortune* is to make glamorous the industry or business described. Luce originally wanted to find and describe "the technological significance of industry." Actually, *Fortune,* though it took a stand for the Wagner Labor Relations Act when it was under attack by business generally, and has never modified its conclusion to suit the prejudices of overconservative businessmen, presents, handsome issue by handsome issue, the facts and the romance of American business as they are.

Fortune believes and says that its editorial role is to analyze and illuminate American business enterprise and the things that affect it. Each issue contains a 30-day business roundup and departments on specific aspects of the business news. Current departments are: "Fortune's Wheel," "Businessmen in the News," "Personal Investing," "Books and Ideas," "Editor's Desk," "Introduction to an Issue," "Anomalies and Paradoxes." Heart of an issue is always the full-length articles on various corporations, individual business executives, and on science and technology or economic situations affecting business. Some of these articles are signed; others are by *Fortune* writers speaking for the magazine. Integral part of an issue is always the many pages of rich corporate advertising. *Fortune*'s circulation is under a half-million, but 85 per cent of its readers are business executives of the kind that advertising is designed to reach.

With a cover price of $1.50 a copy and a subscription price of $14, *Fortune* in 1968 is a monthly magazine but publishes 14 issues a year. In mid-June it releases its annual directory of the 500 largest United States industrial corporations, breaking the list into banks, life-insurance, merchandising, and transportation companies and utilities, and ranking them by assets, earnings, number of employees, and other statistical descriptions. Such an issue may run to 350 pages or more. In mid-September it publishes a directory of the 200 largest industrial corporations outside the United States. *Fortune* is published in seven advertising editions.

Yet *Fortune* does not limit its coverage to business. Its January, 1968, issue, published later in book form as *Business and the Urban Crisis,* was devoted to the Negro and the city. In May it carried both a colorfully illustrated article on oriental rugs and a thoughtful piece on "The Strange Death of Liberal Education" by Irving Kristol. Usually two or three books on social or economic subjects emerge each year from *Fortune* articles. Some of these, like *The Exploding Metropolis* are "by the Editors of *Fortune*"; others are signed by individual authors. *The Organization Man* by William H. Whyte, Jr., was prepared partially on *Fortune* assignment, parts of it first appearing in the magazine.

In two magazines, *Time* and *Fortune,* Henry Luce had undertaken and practiced the education of the American public. In 1936 he purchased a name made deservedly famous as that of the best of American humor magazines [6] and borrowed the pictorial weekly idea originated by Frank Leslie and practiced

[6] *Life,* founded in 1883, was a magazine devoted to delicate social satire, a little more subtle than its contemporaries *Puck* and *Judge.* Charles Dana Gibson created his "Gibson girl" for the earlier *Life.* All three magazines have now ceased publication in anything like their original form. Most of the college humor magazines which imitated them have also disappeared. *The New Yorker,* satirical, sophisticated, an institution in its own right since its 1925 founding, is the sole important survivor of the type.

Luce paid $85,000 for the old *Life.* According to Margaret Case Harriman in a two-installment *New Yorker* "profile" of Clare Boothe Luce, entitled "The Candor Kid," the idea had been forwarded three years earlier. Henry Luce married Clare Boothe, playwright and later Congresswoman, former Ambassador to Italy, in 1935. When he told her of his purchase of *Life,* she brought out a memorandum she had written in 1933, when she was managing editor of *Vanity Fair.* The memorandum suggested that Condé Nast purchase *Life* for $20,000, at which price it was said to be purchasable in 1933, and turn it into a picture magazine.

so successfully by *Harper's Weekly* until it ceased publication in 1916. Despite gloomy prophecies by trade observers who based their predictions largely on the comparative failure of *The New York Times' Mid-Week Pictorial,* Henry Luce combined title and old idea to produce one of today's most popular weekly magazines.

Success of the venture was astounding from the start. There were 230,000 subscribers even before the new magazine, which had had dry runs as *Dummy* and *Rehearsal,* had a name. The first print order was for 466,000 copies. A month later it was for 533,000; four months later for 1,080,000.

In purple rhetoric *Life* announced its purpose in its original prospectus:

> To see life; to see the world; to eyewitness great events; to watch the faces of the poor and the gestures of the proud; to see strange things—machines, armies, multitudes, shadows in the jungle and on the moon; to see man's work—his paintings, towers, and discoveries; to see things thousands of miles away, things hidden behind walls and within rooms, things dangerous to come to; the women men love and many children; to see and take pleasure in seeing; to see and be amazed; to see and be instructed.

The educational intent of *Life* has been basic from the beginning. The magazine was formulated to instruct as well as to attract, entertain, and amuse. As evident was *Life*'s early journalistic formula: lavish use of sex pictures and of gruesome pictures displaying slaughter, executions, strewn corpses; deliberate appeal, through publicizing their activities in glamorous photographs, to the "smart set," the sporting group, the college and preparatory school crowd, and every group susceptible to the flattery—as what group or individual is not?—of attention and favorable display in a national magazine.

Life covers the news pictorially. It shows in photographs the dramatic and spectacular events that will strike the reader with greatest force. Its picturing of sex, glamor, violence, crime, and disaster is effective. These are subjects of intense and lasting interest to everyone, from the vulgar to the fastidious. It shows public figures in action, gangsters and prime ministers, actors and presidents. People, places, and events are spread before the reader in their authentic actuality. *Life*'s picture reporting made World War II more vivid than any words could have made it. Timely, informative, entertaining journalism is a part of *Life*'s function.

Life has other functions. By pictures, diagrams, and charts, it explains scientific and medical facts, facts about the world's food supply, facts about color, about electronics. World affairs, industry, labor problems are explained in pictures, charts, and text. Seemingly no subject is too large for the magazine whose field is limited only by its all-encompassing name. Its full-color reproductions have acquainted millions with classical and modern masterpieces of painting. It has not only reproduced the work of Titian, El Greco, Grant Wood, Van Gogh, and scores of other painters from the Italian Renaissance to the contemporary American, but has also commissioned modern artists for particular work and published their interpretations of what they saw. During World War II it took over the contracts of a group of artists whom the War Department had commissioned, sent them to paint and draw scenes at the battle fronts, and later published their work.

Besides recording contemporary history, *Life* has devoted whole issues to such historical periods as the Renaissance and the Middle Ages. Almost completely a pictorial magazine when it was established, *Life* has increasingly admitted more and more text to its pages. It publishes feature articles in almost every issue, some of them staff written, some of them contributions by outside authorities on the subjects of which they write. In signed articles historians have written of history, statesmen of world affairs, and critics of the arts they patronize. Most of the text, however, as in all Luce magazines, is anonymous. Like a number of its magazine competitors, *Life* performs its stated function of balancing the attractive and entertaining with the educational and informative in still another way—by publishing condensations or abstracts from books, some merely journalistic successes of the day.

Life has changed as it has grown older. There is less cheesecake in the editorial, more homey Americana. In both pictures and text there is less news; there are more essays. It has published noteworthy issues: its tenth anniversary issue, November 25, 1946, surveyed a decade that had seen a major war and much social change. It reprinted historical events it had depicted and had Mark Sullivan do an *Our Times* of 1936–1946. It spoke proudly of controversies the magazine had stirred up, particularly when after printing pictures of actual childbirth in "The Birth of a Baby," April 11, 1938, the magazine was banned in various cities, and its publishers were arrested.

January 2, 1950, *Life* printed its mid-century issue, making it a pictorial history of "American Life and Times, 1900–1950." A Gibson Girl cover, pages of vital statistics, Prohibition, the Hall-Mills murder case, early magazine advertisements; all came in for attention. There were pictures of Ford, Edison, Burroughs, and Firestone, of Lindbergh and Grover Whalen, of Red Grange, Clara Bow, Jack Dempsey, Gilda Gray, Herbert Hoover, each allied to his own specialty. *Life* goes in for nostalgia often, as well as for entertainment and easy education.

Life has always its more pretentious projects—Winston Churchill's war memoirs, the autobiography of the Duke of Windsor, its successive outlines of history from the beginning to the end of time, "MacArthur's Rendezvous with History," its impressive series on "The World We Live In." It ran its special series on America's arts and sciences, closed its series on great religions by a thick special Christmas issue in 1955 which told the story of Christianity. But *Life* has its other points and pleasures. August 11, 1941, it printed a picture of Rita Hayworth in attractive *deshabille.* It reprinted the same picture in its tenth anniversary issue, saying, "When they first saw it, *Life*'s editors thought it the best girl picture ever taken. They have never changed their mind." The picture was printed for the third time some years later in the *Life* department called "What's In a Picture." This time the text divulged more of *Life*'s philosophy: "Pretty girls are as much a part of today's life as the irrational bloodiness of war, the unrealities of some contemporary art, and the devious channels of international politics."

All of these things, sentiment and sensation, cuddly things and stark things, war, archeology, religion, physics, and fashions, *Life* covers. It can make drama of them all—insanity, storms, jail riots or Kant—and it does.

The exploits and achievements of *Life* photographers on battlefields and in dangerous situations in remote parts of the earth have been celebrated in handsome hard-cover volumes, *Life*-sized, prepared by Time, Inc.[7] Margaret Bourke-White, Robert and Cornell Capa, Carl Mydans and many others contributed essentially to the success of *Life* and its characteristic appearance. The excellence of *Life* photography is well established.

For many years of its existence pictures came first with *Life*, and it can boast with reason of its "photo-journalism." In the 1960's *Life* covered American space probes and exploration—the astronauts, blast-offs, capsule exteriors and interiors, and recoveries of the space craft—with brilliant pictures and enough text to carry them. It has documented Project Mercury from the first manned flight of Commander Alan Shepherd in May, 1961. Year-end photography issues (one issue is used to cover two weeks of December) are devoted to coverage of special subjects such as the city, photography itself, and "the wild world" of jungle, desert, and arctic wastes. *Life* is tied to the news but not limited by it. During a year it seems to cover more topics, some of them very briefly, than its competitors. Results of a survey showed that in 1963 *Life* ran 719 articles against 581 for its nearest rival among the top ten magazines in circulation.[8]

[7] *How Life Gets the Story*. New York: Doubleday & Co., Inc., 1955; and *Life Photographers, Their Careers and Favorite Pictures*. New York: Doubleday & Co., Inc., 1957.

[8] Root, Robert H., "The Contents of the Ten Largest Magazines," Magazine Publishers Association and Magazine Department, School of Journalism, Newhouse Communications Center, Syracuse University, 1965.

With its issue for June 2, 1961, *Life* modified its format. Using the same page size, it appeared with a new typeface, a simplified index, and a new block arrangement of advertising and editorial content which allowed uninterrupted text. The familiar logotype with LIFE in white against a red block was retained, but the red band was eliminated from the bottom of the cover. Other physical changes have been made since that time, in general giving the magazine a more sober appearance and emphasizing text at the expense of pictures.

It combines both in most of its stories, but many of the stories are longer. The June 14, 1968, issue carried both pictures and a piece by Theodore H. White on the assassination of Robert Kennedy and a round-up piece by Paul O'Neil on the tragedies in the Kennedy family. Taken from the book by Hunter Davies, it ran 26 pages, mostly text, of the first of a two-parter, "The Days in the Lives of the Beatles." Next to it, pictures predominating, were five pages on Denny McLain, organist-pitcher of the Detroit Lions.

A "Special Life Section," August 30, 1968, devoted forty pages, with advertising interspersed, on "The Mob," mostly text but with pictures of some of the murders and murderers. There was a nostalgic essay in 1968 on "The Passing of the Long Trains" illustrated with pictures, but pictures in color told more of the story than the descriptive text in the coverage of a heart transplant operation in Houston. *Life* does it either way now and expands or contracts the length of its articles, uses more signed essays, but maintains its breadth and variety of coverage.

Millions of people, those who receive the magazine through subscription or buy it on the newsstands, and those who see it after it has been passed along by the first reader, read each single issue of *Life*. Other millions read *Fortune* and *Time*. This huge audience not only demonstrates the success of the three magazines established and published by Henry Luce, and designed to his editorial concepts, but serves also to demonstrate the widespread force in the twentieth century of magazines of these kinds. Obviously Henry Luce was correct in his original belief that the busy twentieth-century American hungered for adequate, easily assimilated news of his increasingly complex world. Everybody who ever decided or guessed that pictures attract more people, and attract people more readily, was also correct.

Time and *Life,* in a primary sense, are complementary. One gives the news crisply in words and briskly explains it. The other gives the news in pictures, dramatizes it. Together they give the impression of confidence, speed, and alertness. Together they make what is, in effect, a national tabloid weekly newspaper. Together they show the magazine taking over what had been almost solely the central function of the newspaper—dissemination of the news, of the week if not the day, as it happens throughout the world.

It is hardly surprising that the *Time–Life* concept of instructing its readers should provoke severe criticism from those who believe in the right of the individual to look over the facts, weigh the opinions, and make up his mind for himself. The Luce publications have often been adversely criticized for the very concept of their journalistic responsibility in which they take most published pride.

Oversimplification of complex subjects is one point on which they are attacked. An Emersonian disregard for consistency is another. Marked shifts in editorial position is still another. In the opinion of one sharply spoken observer, *Time–Life* thought jumps from Jeffersonian materialism to Neo-Toryism by way of Niebuhrism or sometimes Roman Catholic humanism. "What it amounts to is a complete lack of any kind of principle at all." [9]

Others have pointed out ambiguities in the thought apparent behind *Time* or *Life* stories or editorials, shifting viewpoints, changes in position. *Life* upheld General Douglas MacArthur as commander in the Far East early in the Korean War. It cooled toward MacArthur after his recall by President Truman. Later, with marked approval, it ran his life story by

[9] Anthony West, "The Mind and Muscle in Luce's Empire," *Saturday Night* (Toronto, Canada), March 20, 1954.

General Courtney Whitney. It wavered in its attitude toward American foreign policy much as American public opinion—which it helped form—wavered. "Luce's theory of history and human destiny is simply too superficial . . . Luce and his school seem to be trapped by the very American blandness which is his real enemy—immaturity, provincialism, and love of surrogate excitement."[10]

Even the superficial reader cannot help being impressed by the studied omniscience of both *Time* and *Life*. An opening editorial in *Life*, more homey and colloquial in tone than it would have been a few years earlier, cheerfully recognized public awareness of this. "Each issue of *Life*," it admitted, February 9, 1953, "contains a lot of pretty positive statements, and we have been asked, not always jokingly, 'Do you guys ever admit you just don't know something?' "

Few readers of *Time* or *Life* care one way or the other. Why should they? The magazines are modern, bright, and alert. They are infallibly informative and too vital to be indifferent. They are diverting. They give pleasure; they instill confidence. They make life both more exciting and more intelligible. That is a major accomplishment, and if the intelligibility they offer is an illusion, it is at least a comfortable one to have.

After long struggle and more than a year of trade rumor, most of it pessimistic, Time, Inc., ventured into what for it was a comparatively small and specialized arena. The first issue of the weekly *Sports Illustrated* appeared August 12, 1954. Observers were still dubious. Participants and enthusiasts in one sport were not necessarily interested in other sports. Bowling fans are not usually tennis buffs, and professional football followers may care little about soccer, but again the prospectus was colorful. The goal of the new magazine would be "to cover all sports; to turn to the world of sports the talents of the best writers and the best photographers; to find in every sport not only the enduring essentials of human achievement,

[10] John P. Mallan, "Luce's Hot-and-Cold War," *New Republic*, September 28, 1953. A further Mallan comment: ". . . they accept their own righteousness before the Lord too comfortably to be successful apostles."

but the exuberance, color, and quiet pleasure of sports; above all to be authoritative."

Certainly during its first year of publication *Sports Illustrated* competed successfully with its program. It covered 95 sports. It talked pleasantly and expertly of matters of import at Wimbledon, Forest Hills, Churchill Downs, Belmont Park, Yankee Stadium, Indianapolis, Saratoga, and all the other hallowed spots. In text and sharp pictures it gave over 600,000 readers the dope on fights, football, tennis, soccer, chess, baseball, track, golf, swimming, and all the other 86 diversions. Nobel and Pulitzer prize winning authors wrote for it—William Faulkner, John Steinbeck, J. P. Marquand—as well as writers more closely connected with sports, like Paul Gallico, Herman Hickman, and Red Smith.

Sports fans want to know the score and who won. They are as avid of statistics as an actuary or the U. S. Census. All this they can obtain from their daily newspapers or from radio or television. With a guarantee to advertisers of a net paid circulation of 1,500,000 in 1968, *Sports Illustrated* has proved that they want much more if they can get it in accurate and entertaining form.

Marbles, top spinning, baseball, football, and all the rest follow each other around the year with the exactitude of the stars in their courses and to greater interest and applause. From the nature of its subject *Sports Illustrated* can depend on a wealth of material pertinent to seasonal excitements and a rabid demand for all the inside dope. Afficionados of a given sport want the expert advice and comment of experts—and few experts are as expert as sports experts. *Sports Illustrated* gives it to them in quantity and quality. It goes out on many tangled limbs with forecasts, predictions, and prognostications. In the 136-page issue of September 16, 1968, for instance, under "Pro Football 1968," it devoted 36 pages to describing and appraising every NFL and AFL team, analyzing its strengths and weaknesses, and picking the winners in each division.

Sports Illustrated does the usual things and does them very well. For a magazine with its basic subject it also does some unusual things.

All of the popular magazines exploit personalities; in general, politicians and entertainers. Sports figures fall in the second category. The world of sports is always rich with characters, and the public slavers for the inside story of great personal triumphs and the inside stories of Christy Mathewson, John L. Sullivan, Jim Thorpe, and their professional-athlete descendants. *Sports Illustrated* uses not only well-known writers for these articles, but also those whose occupations and positions gives them intimate and sometimes novel viewpoints.

It used the trainer Angelo Dundee for a three-part series on Muhammad Ali and Floyd Patterson; and Mark McCormack, his manager, for a four-part series on Arnold Palmer. It had Fran Tarkenton, quarterback of the New York Giants, analyze the Green Bay Packers. The magazine has taken an active part in sports discussions and controversies. It urged marked changes in the structure of professional football, changes in methods of draft choices, trading of player personnel, selection of superbowl teams, and the setting of training camp deadlines. In the summer of 1967, naming names and techniques, it discussed baseball's controversial spitball, the pitch and its results achieved by the application of saliva, hair oil, vaseline, slippery elm, coal tar, sea moss, and other exotic substances to the ball.

Sports Illustrated fights the good fight for conservation of the natural resources of the United States. It has advocated Congressional establishment of a national council of ecological advisers, the establishment of state councils, and enlargement of the Department of the Interior to give it greater powers. Among other recommendations it asked in December, 1967, for an end to the tyranny of the engineer. "Putting an engineer in charge of a resource such as a river basin is no smarter than hiring a lumberjack to design a fountain," Robert Boyle wrote. "They have technical competence, but often a limited outlook as well."

Each year *Sports Illustrated* chooses its "Sportsman of the Year" and presents him with a reproduction of a Grecian amphora of about 510 B.C., the decoration of which shows discus and javelin throwers, a sprinter, and a trainer. In 1954 the award went to Roger Bannister for the first four-minute mile; in 1967 it went to Carl Yastrzemski of the Boston Red Sox. The magazine has received awards itself, some of them, surprisingly, for its use of fine arts.

In search of what its publisher describes as "an element which eludes mechanical reporting" through the use of photography and text, it has commissioned many artists to execute

Annually *Sports Illustrated* awards a reproduction of this Grecian amphora of 510 B.C. to the "Sportsman of the Year." Roger Bannister won the first for his four-minute mile.

sports events and figures in oil or acrylic paintings or in water color, published reproductions in its pages, then held traveling exhibitions of the artwork. Out of one of its editorial features, *Sports Illustrated* developed a "Design for Sports" exhibition which, with the National Sporting Goods Association, it conducted at the Museum of Modern Art in New York. Because of the close relationship of aesthetics to function, the exhibit drew admiring attention, even from the competitive and discriminating *New Yorker*. Some 115 items, ranging from the crossbow, the kite, and the discus to racing cars, hydroplanes, and the armor of football players were shown, the museum's director commenting that the design of sports implements "are characterized by intensely developed forms which directly contribute to proper use." They may be largely promotional in purpose, but activities of these kinds have added to the stature and repute which *Sports Illustrated* has developed through its print and photographs.

Other magazines have been established on the general *Time–Life* pattern and function in much the same way. The vigorously promoted and very successful *Look,* when it was founded as a pictorial magazine in the *Life* manner, appeared for the first time in January, 1937, just two months after *Life* began publication. Though it has long since moved to New York, it was founded in Des Moines by Gardner Cowles and John Cowles, the venture growing out of their experience with the Des Moines *Register and Tribune* and early studies by Dr. George H. Gallup which showed that a national market existed for a picture magazine.

"*Look* gives you a thousand eyes to see round the world," the first issue stated. The magazine promised to bring "current events, science, sports, beauty, education, all in interesting pictures, to both the Colonel's Lady and Mrs. O'Grady (and their respective husbands and children) to make them better informed on what's happening in the world."

Started as a monthly, *Look* changed to bi-weekly publication after the first four issues. It resembled *Life* in format but lacked *Life*'s smartness of appearance and crispness of presentation. It looked as if it was more for Mrs. O'Grady and her family than for the colonel and his wife. It differed also from *Life* in that it did not report the news. Instead it relied on Sunday newspaper-type feature articles, mostly in pictures, to form pieces which were mostly about people. *Look* has always exploited personalities.

The early *Look* went in for a sensationalism which moderated as the magazine strove to develop family appeal. It calls itself the "family magazine" now. Like *Life, Look* covers the national and international scene, but its approach is more popular and the published product less polished. When she was a *Look* associate editor, Fleur Cowles said, "*Life* is an example of glittering objective reporting. Ours is—we hope—the warmest form of subjective reporting." [11] To give its readers this kind of reporting (and some marked variations from it) *Look* has used such big-name contributors as Adlai Stevenson, Thomas Dewey, Earl Warren, William O. Douglas, John Gunther, Walter Lippmann, Robert Sherwood, and even Bertrand Russell. Ernest Hemingway did some of his last work and writing, "Safari" and "The Christmas Gift," for *Look,* but most of the magazine is written by *Look's* own senior editors.

In recent years *Look* has changed sharply in some ways and developed rapidly. Like *Life,* it has ceased to be primarily a picture book. Text predominates. The magazine has shot up in circulation and the public acceptance which circulation indicates. Well designed and superbly printed and produced, it is splendid physically, often flashy. In basic approach *Look* has changed little. It still exploits glamorous personalities. It parades beauteous models across its pages in the latest fashions. It delights in theatrical starlets and in enduring movie stars. It purveys the latest on sex and pot on the college campus. It thrills to expensive leisure in expensive and photogenic resorts.

Beautiful women, sports, Julian Huxley on "All About Love," and for some time "Norman Vincent Peale Answers Your Questions," yet *Look* also runs earnest articles on health

[11] "Cowles Empire—A Magazine Phenomenon," *Business Week,* October 8, 1949.

and education, human relations, religion, safety, civic responsibility. A 1954 promotion piece opened with this statement: "Any general magazine which draws to its pages millions of people across the country, issue after issue, is . . . a powerful social force. And, as such, it has certain obligations and responsibilities, not only to its readers but to the nation at large. One of these responsibilities is to encourage better citizenship —to quicken people's latent desire for improved standards of health, education, safety, government, and tolerance." Evidently in pursuance of this high purpose, *Look* has run substantial articles on communist Cuba, "Revolution in the Pentagon" by Theodore H. White, promotable pieces on the Kennedys, Harlem, birth control, changes in the Catholic church, and before the country as a whole was aware of the region and its problems, "Appalachia, U. S. A." in its December 4, 1962, issue.

Look may not be tied to the news, but it does not neglect the journalistic possibilities which the news affords. May 19, 1964, *Look* ran "Behind the Plot to Assassinate Robert Kennedy." The Justice Department had been informed of such a plot by a Teamster boss in 1962 when the activities of James Hoffa were under investigation. A few weeks after the slaying of Senator Kennedy in Los Angeles in 1968, Cowles Communications, Inc., of which *Look* is a part, was on the stands with a hard-cover "quickie" of 272 pages and 96 photographs, *Assassination, Robert F. Kennedy, 1925–1968.*

In two June issues of 1964 *Look* ran "CIA: The Invisible Government," reporting the world-wide activities of the Central Intelligence Agency with its 200,000 employees and its huge budget. It was thus a surprise when in 1967 *Look* editorially defended CIA payments to traveling students, a maneuver just uncovered and the subject of controversy. This was the more surprising because, in general, *Look* is markedly "liberal" in its viewpoints and the opinions stated or indicated in its articles.

About 85 per cent of *Look* is written by its own staff writers, while much of the 15 per cent procured from the outside consists of serialization of best-selling books or abstracts from them. In order to convince advertisers that they reach the youth and "young married" market, most of the large consumer magazines are careful to run subject matter which their editors believe will reach young readers and to treat it in such a way as to gain their approval. *Look* seems more obvious than some of its magazine competitors in trying to reach and please this audience and market. This has to be, in part, at least, editorial policy, but *Look* prefers to ascribe it to the "personal journalism" which the magazine supports and to the fact that its staff "write it as they see it." These are useful clichés of the trade.

For the last six months of 1967 *Look* achieved a circulation which ranked it fourth among all U. S. magazines. Currently it guarantees advertisers an average net paid circulation of 7,750,000. Following millions of dollars worth of free publicity after Mrs. Jacqueline Kennedy filed suit to stop *Look* serialization and Harper & Row book publication of William Manchester's *The Death of a President, Look* obtained circulations of over 8,000,000 for its 1967 issues containing the story.

Originally both *Look* and *Life* were picture magazines, a description both now disavow. They looked alike. Except when they are making circulation claims against each other, *Life* and *Look* do not encourage comparison, but it is almost inevitable. For many years *Look* appeared the clumsier of the two, the more provincial in tone and manner, the less well written. It seemed to appeal to the less well educated reader. Differences between the two magazines are no longer as marked. *Look* looks bright and smart. In general it seems less restrained than *Life,* sounds a little noisier. Often it is more superficial. It may lack the hard finish of *Life and Life*'s polished competence, but it has its own homelier virtues. Despite fine reproduction on quality stock, it seems still to betray its newspaper origin and approach. The popularity of the magazine makes it clear that this is not a practical handicap.

The success of *Look* led early to other Cowles magazine enterprises. *Quick,* condensations strangled to capsule size, was started in 1949. Though it attained a circulation of 1,300,000, it was dropped as unprofitable in 1953. The title was purchased by Walter Annenberg, publisher then of the Philadelphia *Inquirer* and other newspapers and magazines. Republished for nine months by its new owner, *Quick* was abandoned again in 1954. Cowles Communications, Inc., now publishes many magazines and newspapers. One of them, *Venture*—"The Traveler's World," was founded in 1964 to circulate only to subscribers holding American Express Company credit cards. A class magazine with a comparatively small circulation, *Venture* is a plush bi-monthly with a high cover and subscription price which goes now to any subscribers who wish it.

Newsweek was founded by an English newspaperman, Thomas John Cardel Martyn, as *News-Week* in 1933. In 1937 it was combined with *Today* which, founded by Vincent Astor and W. Averill Harriman, was edited by the renowned New Dealer, Raymond Moley. The name was dehyphenated to *Newsweek* and Moley remained as editor. He continued to contribute a weekly column until January, 1967.

Originally, *Newsweek* differed fundamentally from *Time*, which it resembled in format, coverage, and editorial departmentalization. It insisted upon its objective presentation of reporting events of the day and the people prominent in them. This gave the newer magazine a talking point in competition with its established rival. Instead of the anonymity enforced by the *Time* concept of group journalism, *Newsweek* also emphasized signed opinion in departments conducted by assigned specialists. *Newsweek* was clear, adequate, a little colorless.

The masthead of the current *Newsweek*—packed in miniscule type with the names of editors, departments, and bureaus in key United States cities and abroad—carries "Associated with the Washington Post Company" under the magazine's title. It is a little more than an association. Although published in New York, the magazine is the property of the *Post* which purchased controlling interest from the Vincent Astor estate in 1961. This change of ownership infused *Newsweek* with large amounts of money and expanded editorial resources. It injected new vitality and a marked competitiveness into the periodical.

Newsweek covers its worldwide beat in the fairly standard departments: National Affairs, International, Medicine, Science and Space, Business and Finance, Education, Sports, Life and Leisure, Religion, Press, and at the end of the issue carries about ten pages of signed book reviews, theatrical, art, and motion picture criticism. The War in Vietnam is also a department by itself, indicating that it is a fixed subject which like national affairs or education will stay around for a long time.

In addition *Newsweek* has its distinctive features. Established as far back as 1937, "The Periscope" is two pages of briefs on miscellaneous items in the news. "Top of the Week" on the index page leads into the principal articles in an issue. "Where Are They Now?" is asked of names that were in the news in the past, a feature rather like the standard newspaper bit on 10, 25, or 50 years ago today. Personality gossip comes under "Newsmakers." Obituaries, birth and divorce notices, sometimes an anniversary such as Maurice Chevalier's 80th birthday, are listed under the considered head, "Transition."

Columnists have always been a *Newsweek* feature. Walter Lippmann, Kenneth Crawford, Stewart Alsop, Milton Friedman, Henry C. Wallich, and others inform and comment on their particular if often overlapping interests.

Newsweek's covers carry in full color portraits of the great and near great. In the election year of 1968 supplicants for party nominations, then after the conventions those chosen as candidates for the Presidential election, virtually monopolized the *Newsweek* cover, though Charles de Gaulle made it. Like the other news magazines, *Newsweek* gave full coverage to the assassination of Robert Kennedy. His picture appeared on its June 17, 1968, issue, and inside, headed "Once Again . . . . . Once Again" across a double spread, 26 pages were devoted to the story of his campaigning for the Democratic nomination, his murder, and a roundup story on the Kennedy family.

Each issue of *Newsweek* has a dominant subject treated on the cover and in a principal piece. These are substantial articles, carefully prepared and presented. Subjects are large: Vietnam, the Czech crisis, prospects for peace, the Negro in America, the school crisis, heart surgery, the crisis in education, the "French Revolution, 1968."

Politicians do not always get *Newsweek*'s cover. When the issue's principal subject was "the beauty business," the cover was a closeup of a woman's face with false eyelashes and eye shadow highlighted. When "Bringing Up Baby" was the chief article, September 23, 1968, the cover showed a toddler in baby blue nightclothes. A simulated yellow sticker in a diagonal slash across the upper right hand corner of the cover—a standard *Newsweek* attention-getter—asked, "Is Dr. Spock to Blame?"

Newsweek used this same cover slash for its "Battle of Chicago" issue, September 9, 1968, and put plenty of blood and police violence into the color pictures that illustrated the story inside. A photographer with a generous splash of blood streaking his face and caking his neck was the showpiece.

The original *Newsweek* was rather staid. Its slogan was "A well-informed public is America's greatest security." Kenneth Crawford, manager of *Newsweek*'s Washington Bureau, when he spoke at an editor–educator conference, May 11, 1955, was a little apologetic that the news magazines had to entertain as well as inform. "We can't be more substantial than our audience will let us be. We print pictures of Marilyn Monroe along with articles trying to explain why Albert Einstein was the great man of our time; anatomical studies along with intellectual exercise." None of the news media apologize now for the sensationalism and over-dramatization, the emphasis on conflict and violence of which they are increasingly accused. The usual response is that they reflect the times. Some of their adverse critics think they help create what they eagerly single out for scare-head reporting.

Newsweek is vigorous, competent, packed with information, bright with photographs in strong colors, and sharp with the comments of its columnists. Most of the large magazines make a serious business of lobbying for awards. Their public relations departments are expected to be alert in discovering and capturing them. As in most other competitive activities, these awards exist in profusion, but they are valuable to the winners for promotional purposes. Almost any magazine can boast of the awards it has gathered in. *Newsweek* has received its share, and the recognition seems deserved.

The once vaunted objectivity of *Newsweek* is no longer apparent. Opinion is the province of the columnist and superiority becomes the critic, but *Newsweek*'s reporting itself leaves little doubt where its writers stand, thus, in unsigned pieces, where the magazine stands. What used to be called editorial comment is generally obvious in *Newsweek*'s news stories which are imaginatively and brightly written, their opening enticements often more in the manner of the novelist than of the reporter. Sometimes there is an evident straining after humorous, dramatic, or ironic effects.

The subhead of a *Newsweek* story about the hippies encamped on Boston Common was "Is Nothing Sacred?" There were, of course, references in the lead paragraph to "proper Bostonians" and "the sacrosanct Somerset Club." The subhead of an item headed "Chicago" asked "Safe for Democracy?" Puns abound in *Newsweek* heads. A paragraph report that a princess of Thailand had entered Concord (Massachusetts) Academy was headlined, "She Stoops to Concord." Often *Newsweek* seems to be imitating the discarded *Time* style of the 1920's and early 1930's, even to the concoction of multisyllabic epithets. A 1968 article referred to the publisher of *Playboy* as "Sexploitationist Hugh Hefner."

The newer *Newsweek* is thriving. Its circulation, over 2,300,000 in 1968, climbs steadily, as does its advertising revenue.

The syndicated columnist David Lawrence was editor and president of *U. S. News* 1933 to 1948. He founded *World Report* in 1946, and in 1948 became editor of the two magazines combined as *U. S. News & World Report.* His back page editorial is a familiar feature of the informative and conservative news weekly.

Unlike *Time* and *Newsweek, U. S. News & World Report* does not categorize the news into a score of specific containers. Instead it has loose departments called March of the News, People of the Week, Washington Whispers, U. S. Companies Abroad, Labor Week, Plus and Minus, and Finance Week. The bulk of the magazine is made up of a series of newspaper-like articles and special one- or two-page inserts in telegraphic style and typewriter type suggesting instant transmission of important last-minute facts.

There are a number of these tersely informative inserts: "Worldgram" ("International Week—From the Capitals of the World . . ."); "Newsgram" ("Tomorrow from the Nation's Capital"); "Business Around the World"; "News Lines"; "News YOU Can Use in your Personal Planning."

U. S. News & World Report carries no cover pictures. It uses its cover to list in poster style the titles of major articles within an issue. These articles, unsigned, are replete with headlines, subheads, bold-face breaklines, and often printer's ornaments at paragraph openings to act as fingers pointing to facts emphasized.

The magazine does not have the surface shine of the other news weeklies. In keeping with its utilitarian purpose its appearance is sober. Pictures, when there are any, are in black and white. Color is limited to the advertising pages, though color stock is used for some of the various staccato inserts; and some of the many charts and graphs used in the presentation of economic and financial data, much of it from government sources, are tinted.

Typical articles indicate the magazine's position on social and political issues. In June, 1968, *U. S. News & World Report* forecast a middle-class revolt by hard-working, tax-paying "forgotten men" who do not make the headlines as strikers, looters, rioters, and draft-card burners. Consistently for law and order, the magazine had one 1968 article titled "More Power for Police, Less for Criminals?"; another, "Is the Big City Problem Hopeless?" A Newsgram saw people turning away from permissiveness toward insistence that laws be enforced and violence stopped. The magazine expressed its belief —a consummation devoutly to be wished—that the country is fed up with lawlessness.

As consistently, *U. S. News & World Report* is against inflation and riotous government spending. It attacks them often in such articles as "What's Back of Your Dollar Now?"; "Inflation Treadmill—Why You Need More Income to Break Even"; "Bigger Taxes, Higher Prices, but Spending Spree." The magazine is for established moral and social values, common sense, and human decency. Besides transmitting economic facts to its readers it has an observable didactic purpose. "Where Socialists Cut Welfare," "Who Really Picks a President," "Surge of Christianity in New Lands" characterize aspects of its attitude and offering.

U. S. News & World Report shows courage along with its competence. It risks prophecy, sometimes dares display a touch of naiveté.

Early in June, 1968, it decided that despite spending millions of dollars, exerting all the pressures at the command of his family, and winning a few primaries, Senator Robert F. Kennedy could not win the Democratic nomination for President. July 22, 1968, it gave the "real reasons" in an article titled "Why LBJ Is Quitting." Presented mostly in quotes from White House intimates, the article listed Johnson's fear of divisiveness ahead for the nation, the attacks on him and his policies by intellectuals, his difficulties with the press, and his being hit by social, racial, and student revolts. An additional reason given by the presumably informed insiders was that Johnson yearned for private life and return to Texas. This hardly carried conviction, and the entire article hardly justified the now-it-can-be-told air with which it was presented.

U. S. News & World Report, its circulation over 1,700,000 is serious, functional, concerned, and a foil to the contrasting beliefs and attitudes of its news magazine contemporaries.

Founded in 1949 as "A Fortnightly of Facts and Ideas," *The Reporter* was originated and edited by Max Ascoli, an Italian-born antifascist and political scientist. Staffed by ex-newspapermen and using name writers, *The Reporter* claimed to give the whole picture of the news, to give its readers the kind of information about national and international affairs to which ordinarily only specialists have access. Ironically, *Newsweek*, April 18, 1949, could discover no real distinctions made between "facts and ideas" and "news and opinions" in *The Reporter's* reporting.

Of modest format, old-fashioned in appearance through its profuse use of pen and ink illustrations and printer's ornaments between pieces, the magazine showed a nice diversity in editorial coverage. Its articles, well written and sensible, commanded the respect of professionals. *The Reporter*, which won numerous journalistic awards, ceased publication in 1968.

The magazines of news and comment on or dramatic photographs of passing events and people are really newspapers with the local news and color, the want ads and the comics omitted. The newspaper is a rich jumble; the news or news-oriented magazine is a coldly ordered array. By departmentalizing the confusion of current events or selecting for blowup into features, they distinguish and define. They explain as they relate. There is something neat and sanitary about these magazines. They are like vitamin pills. They are nourishing and sometimes stimulating but generally not succulent.

Their omniscience and assurance can be very hard to take. All of them cover much the same subjects. Distinction has to lie in the manner of treatment, which may account in part for the forced sprightliness of some and the sobriety, when it is not the stodginess, of others. For some years "personal journalism" seemed to be submerged. It has returned sharply in these magazines—which is fine when the person making the journalism personal has a personality worth projecting and is at the same time honest, intelligent, and professionally competent. Usually he is. Sometimes he is not. The laws of chance operate impersonally. When you buy one of these magazines, you pay your money and you take your chance. Infallibility in fact and opinion has always been hard to come by and, despite their authoritative appearance and manner, these magazines have no more of it than other media and most people.

What is printed in black ink on white paper or on the inserted pages in other colors used to convey the impression of being up to the minute or a few seconds ahead is apt to seem more significant and convincing than the same information transmitted on newsprint or by transistor. When the once influential *Literary Digest* clipped a column or a paragraph from a metropolitan daily or a country weekly and reprinted it, the material seemed more important than when it originally appeared. It was better reproduced on better stock, and the reader felt that it had been selected for its virtues by informed and experienced editors. It became of value *per se*. People are apt to read the magazines basically concerned with current events and personalities and stare at the compelling full-color, full-page, full-bleed photographs with something of the same respect. Sometimes they deserve it.

Chapter 18

Common Denominator: *The Reader's Digest*

The original *Harper's Monthly,* the *Literary Digest,* and other eclectic periodicals had profitably clipped, pasted, and reprinted. In 1922 new ingredients were added to an old idea. These were the condensing or digesting of articles from other magazines and their reprinting in a pocket-sized monthly periodical. The result was *The Reader's Digest.*

When the idea was first suggested to many of them in 1920, no established publisher would seriously consider it. In February, 1922, the man who had conceived the idea and experimented with the form published the first issue of *The Reader's Digest.* This issue of 5,000 copies was edited and distributed from a basement room under a speakeasy in New York's Greenwich Village. DeWitt Wallace, founder, editor, and, with his wife, Lila Acheson Wallace, co-owner and co-chairman of the magazine, did not expect to reach a large audience. He felt that serious material digested from serious publications would not command the attention of a multitude of readers. He was wrong. The operation soon outgrew its basement room. It was moved to a room over a garage, which was also the home of its owners and editors, and an adjacent pony shed in Pleasantville, New York.

In May, 1970, *The Reader's Digest* had a circulation in the United States of over 17,000,000 copies a month. It has a world circulation of over 29,000,000. Published in French, German, Spanish, Portuguese, Japanese, Dutch, Italian, Finnish, Danish, Norwegian, Italian, Chinese, and Arabic, it is read every month by 100,000,000 people. A fact of American life since the first years of its publication, *The Reader's Digest* has become an incontrovertible American fact of international life. Ubiquitous, recognizable everywhere, *The Reader's Digest* is the world's one international magazine, its influence incalculable.

The "little magazine" has become the world's largest, but size alone cannot account for its achievement and repute. Its multi-millions of faithful readers look upon the *Digest* almost as Holy Writ. They read it, believe it, quote it, in some ways live by it. They hardly think of it as a magazine at all. It is the *Digest* and unique. The magazine's phenomenal success has likewise provoked awed admiration, inarticulate dismay, rhetorical wonder, envy, scorn, bitter derision, and, time after time, unsuccessful imitation.

Son of a Presbyterian preacher, DeWitt Wallace attended Macalester College in St. Paul, of which his father was president, then (repeating the same two undergraduate years) the University of California in Berkeley. He worked in an uncle's bank in Colorado, for a publisher of books and farm magazines in St. Paul, then for a firm of calendar printers. He sold real estate and wholesale groceries for a time. While working for the farm publications firm, he had the idea of listing and condensing bulletins of the U. S. Department of Agriculture. The idea developed into that of a small magazine which would condense and reprint material from other magazines in handy, pocket-sized format. While hospitalized in France after being severely wounded in World War I, he practiced digesting magazine articles.

When he returned to St. Paul, he did not seek a job. Instead he haunted the Minneapolis Public Library seeking article material that he considered "of lasting interest" in the current and back numbers of the magazines. Early in 1920 he printed several hundred copies of a dummy magazine. It was:

THE

READER's Digest

31 articles each month from leading magazines,
each article of enduring value and interest,
in condensed and permanent form

January, 1920

Published monthly by The Reader's Digest Association,
Globe Bldg., St. Paul, Minnesota, DeWitt Wallace, Editor
25 cents a copy; $3.00 a year

All of the essential ingredients of *The Reader's Digest* were in this dummy: title, condensed articles, blurbs for articles in forthcoming issues, even the cover and subscription prices as they were to remain for many years.

Wallace submitted copies to all of the leading magazine publishers. He would have given the idea to any one of them who would establish the magazine with him as editor. None of them wanted either him or his projected periodical. Wallace took a job in a publicity department of the Westinghouse Electric and Manufacturing Company of Pittsburgh. Six months later, during the depression of 1921, he was fired. Wallace returned to his room and began to write mail order solicitations for provisional subscribers to his projected magazine. He sent his circulars to lists of teachers and nurses. He called on women's clubs and women's professional groups to make his pitch. In New York, October 15, 1921, he married Lila Bell Acheson, daughter of a Presbyterian missionary family. Together, with a borrowed $1,300 and $5,000 brought in from Wallace's Pittsburgh mailings they placed an order with a Pittsburgh printer for 5,000 copies of volume 1, number 1 of *The Reader's Digest.*[1]

A monthly periodical, pocket-sized, thin, unillustrated, the new *Digest* had a serious and economical look. Clearly printed on poor paper stock, it offered deftly cut-down versions of ar-

[1] Wood, James Playsted. *Of Lasting Interest.* New York: Doubleday & Co., Inc., 1967.

ticles—no fiction—which had been previously printed in other magazines. The material came from magazines like *Harper's*, the *Atlantic, The Forum, World's Work, The Outlook, Scribner's, The North American Review* as well as from the more popular general and women's magazines. Wallace had originally made his circulation appeals to college and university men and women, particularly women. In all his mail-order promotion he stressed the *Digest* as a time-saving and informative service to its readers. For these reasons *The Reader's Digest*

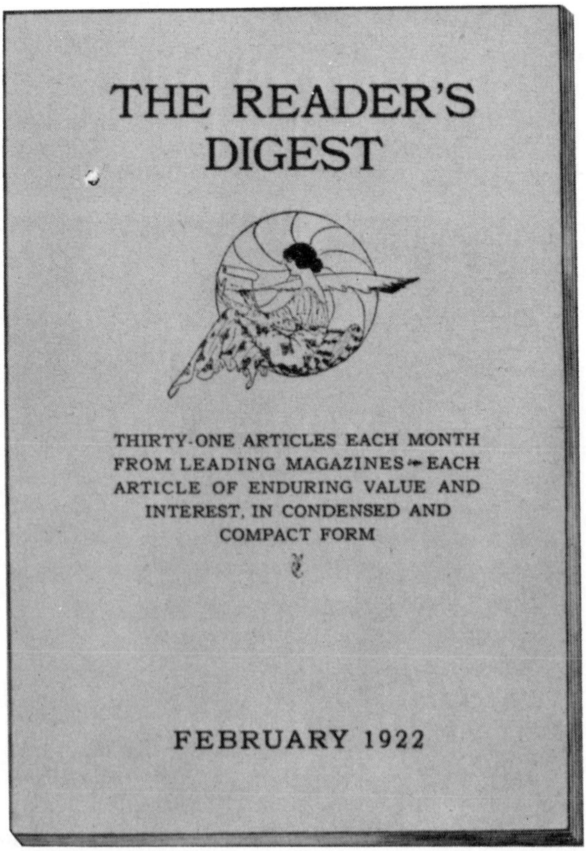

Solely eclectic when it started, now largely original, *The Reader's Digest* has the largest circulation of any magazine in the world.

was originally considered an intellectual venture for an intellectual audience. Now the most mass of all the "mass magazines," it was at first considered distinctly a "class" publication.

In the early years of the *Digest's* existence other editors were glad to give DeWitt Wallace permission to reprint without charge articles from their publications. They had already used the material. Its condensation, with credit, in the *Digest* looked like good free publicity. As the *Digest* grew in circulation and importance—and it grew rapidly—Wallace began to pay an annual fee to other magazines for the right to digest and reprint articles he selected. This arrangement was superseded by one where the *Digest* pays both the magazine from which it extracts material and the author for specific articles used.

Wallace promoted his magazine unrelentingly, but he was as surprised as anyone else at the extent and rapidity of the *Digest's* growth. He widened his sights and his appeal. He said that the intent of his magazine was to print "articles of lasting interest which will appeal to a large audience, articles that come within the range of interests, experience, and conversation of the average person. The over-all emphasis . . . a more or less conscious effort to promote a Better America, with capital letters, with a fuller life for all, and with a place for the United States of increasing influence and respect in world affairs." [2]

In practice, *The Reader's Digest* has presented digested material with unfailing mass appeal. Stories of human kindness, of successful community experiments, of new inventions and devices, popularized medical articles, biographical sketches of entertaining characters, and anecdotes of simple human goodness triumphing over inimical forces are its stock in trade.

[2] DeWitt Wallace came out of evangelical Presbyterianism in the northern middle west. Henry Luce was the son of a Presbyterian minister and missionary in China. The father of George Horace Lorimer was a famed Baptist evangelist. Joseph Palmer Knapp's mother was the daughter of a Methodist evangelist and the composer of music for hymns. The Protestant evangelical strain is strong in the heredity of some of the most influential editors and publishers and in their magazines. It is particularly manifest in *The Reader's Digest.*

Articles on the art of living, on health, and medical topics are *Digest* staples. Issue after issue has described, sometimes almost rhapsodically, new and quick cures for new and old diseases. Homey success stories, stories showing how ambition, thrift, and kindness paid high rewards, sometimes material as well as spiritual, but always spiritual, usually to lovable little people in small towns or in the country, are unfailing in the *Digest.* There is inspirational material in most American mass magazines. The proportion in *The Reader's Digest* is high. There is emphasis on sex in *The Reader's Digest,* not the blatant cheesecake of some of the picture magazines, but sex in simple and soothing guise. Articles on married life, on childbirth and child-rearing, on what men think of women and women think of men, on the mating of animals, and the like, appear and reappear in *Digest* pages.

The *Digest* specializes in striking titles followed by entertaining but often superficial accounts of diverse subjects. It disliked the New Deal and the Fair Deal and has consistently attacked the extravagance and overexpansion of bureaucratic government. Aware of the widespread human liking for accumulating unusual facts, it specializes in providing odd bits of factual information. Complicated analyses of facts, figures, and theories it avoids. These are not easily adapted to the condensed form in easy words, nor are they within "the range of interests, experience, and conversation of the average person" at whom the *Digest* is directed.

In 1933, *The Reader's Digest* began to produce a limited number of original articles. It instituted special departments, "My Most Unforgettable Character," "Drama in Everyday Life," "Life in These United States." By this time a number of well-known magazines on which Wallace drew had ceased publication. The *Digest,* to keep itself supplied with sufficient good copy, was almost forced into some original production. By this time Wallace also had devised another method of keeping his magazine supplied with the kind of folksy, humorous, inspirational, sometimes journalistically provocative material to which his audience had become accustomed. *Digest* originals, articles assigned to staff or free-lance writers, were also prepared in more extended form and placed for first publication in other magazines. After initial publication, they were reprinted in digest form in *The Reader's Digest,* with credit given the cooperating outside publication. Some of the best material appearing in the *Digest* has been developed in this fashion. A study of the *Digest*'s content from 1939 through 1943 showed that 42 per cent of the articles appearing during that period were straight reprints. The remaining 58 per cent were originals, some appearing for the first time in *Digest* pages, some prepared cooperatively with other magazines. Similar percentages were found in 1944 and 1945. Thus, well over half the articles in *The Reader's Digest* were prepared directly for the magazine. Presently sixty per cent—in some issues considerably more—is written for the *Digest* and published in it as original or first placed elsewhere, then reprinted. Sometimes publication in the credited periodical source and *Digest* publication is simultaneous.

Carl Sandburg once said that the *Digest* was "often as solemn as death and now and then funny as a barrel of monkeys." Human interest anecdotes abound in such departments as "Life in the United States" and "The Most Unforgettable Character I've Met." These and other departments which appear regularly or occasionally supply a considerable part of the sentimental humor characterizing *The Reader's Digest.* The jokes strewn profusely through each issue as an integral part of the editorial offering rather than as filler are sharp and often surprisingly risqué. They must account for part of the *Digest*'s hold on its readers, who often run through an issue searching for them, relishing them, and repeating them.

If world-wide circulation and diffusion of its subject matter through many populations and social and educational levels are measures of the influence of a magazine, no magazine exerts a wider influence than *The Reader's Digest,* and few editors have been more influential than DeWitt Wallace.

That influence operates less in the political and economic spheres than in the social. Its message is to the individual. Its strongest influence is on the reader's personal life. The *Digest* operates to make the individual feel more secure, more successful in his human contacts, better satisfied with his lot in life. It assures him month by month that he is a member in good standing of a country-wide or world-wide group of people much like himself. They are decent, good people. He likes them, and they like him. The *Digest,* and this is the magazine's triumph, makes the world seem understandable and warmer.

Despite scientific advance, socialism acknowledged or merely practiced, a near-Utopia of material prosperity, television, and computers, the human spirit has not ceased to want hope and comfort. The optimism, the moral precepts, the gentle parables of *The Reader's Digest* supply to millions some of the same sustenance they once imbibed from prayer meeting and Sunday school. The magazine gives simplicity to a world gone frighteningly complex, offers spiritual help and moral guidance to many who have few other sources from which to obtain them. This is a fundamental part of its hold on its readers and a fundamental part of the magazine's accomplishment.

We have lost little of our taste for miracles, and *Reader's Digest* is continually announcing miracles, miracles of science, education, medicine, personality, and human accomplishment. It offers that satisfaction, too.

An earlier generation took a lively interest in patent medicine. It read the advertisements for a thousand nostrums and cure-alls with avidity, and generally was most convinced when the claims forwarded were most incredible. Men and women tried each new pill or liquid as it came along, in no way deterred because the last one tried had failed to work the wonders expected. The recurring medical articles in the *Digest,* many excellent of their kind, are hardly comparable to the ads for now discredited patent medicines. What are comparable are the psychological needs to which both the articles and the patent-medicine advertisements appeal. Understandably, most people wish to make their bodies last as long as possible and to have them perform as efficiently as they can be made to perform. The diseases to which the flesh is heir, the most common and the most obscure, and the ways in which they can be avoided or cured, are of perennial interest to everyone. It is not an interest which the *Digest* slights.

Toward the end of the nineteenth century the new magazines drew on an audience untouched by the literary monthlies. *The Reader's Digest* has drawn largely on an audience whose wants were not fully satisfied by the popular weeklies and monthlies founded or resuscitated in the 1880's and the 1890's. There are readers of the *Digest* who read no other magazines. In this way, it has vastly widened the total magazine-reading population. Its digested articles and condensed versions of current books bring to the attention of millions subject matter which, if published only in its original form and vehicle, these millions would never see at all.

From its garage room and pony shed, *The Reader's Digest* burgeoned during the 1930's into all the available office space in Pleasantville. Stores, lofts, offices, and garages bulged with *Digest* workers and activities. Between 1933 and 1937 its circulation, during bitter depression years, went from less than 500,000 to almost two and a half million. In 1939 the magazine was moved into a $1,500,000 towered Georgian headquarters which, with many additions built since, sprawls over spacious and pleasantly landscaped grounds at Chappaqua,[3] a few miles north of Pleasantville. There, though the post office address of Pleasantville has been retained, the *Digest* is edited and published.

During World War II, when all mass magazines registered large circulation gains, *Digest* circulation rose from under four million to more than nine million. For many years *Digest* profits were high. The income from its vast circulation and sale was sufficient for expenditures that would seem extravagant to the editors and publishers of less successful periodicals. This halcyon situation ended abruptly in 1954 when, reportedly,

[3] Horace Greeley, ridiculed as "the woodcutter of Chappaqua" in the uneven Presidential contest of 1872 and no mean journalist himself, would be amazed at circulation figures achieved by the *Digest* and the physical evidences of journalistic success in his town today.

the astonished *Digest* found itself faced with a deficit of about one million dollars for the year.

Paper, printing, and other production costs, together with increased postal rates, had mounted greatly during the years, and *The Reader's Digest* was still selling at its original 1922 price of twenty-five cents a copy or a year's subscription for $3. For thirty-three years, though it took advertising in its foreign editions, the *Digest* had thrived without the advertising revenue on which all the other large-circulation magazines depend for the bulk of their profit. A decision had to be reached on whether to accept advertising or to raise the newsstand and subscription price of the magazine. DeWitt Wallace took the question to his readers and awaited their answer before reaching a decision.

A New York research agency was retained to find out through personal interviews whether *Digest* readers preferred to pay an increased price for their copies or to have the *Digest* print advertising. Eighty-one per cent of the respondents, forming a cross section of the magazine's readers, declared in favor of advertising. Late in 1954 *Reader's Digest* announced that it would accept 32 pages of advertising for the first time in its April, 1955, issue. It would accept no liquor, tobacco, or medical remedy advertising. Its editorial policy would remain unchanged.

The *Digest* had many times attacked the abuses of advertising in its columns. Motivated by a crusading zeal that is often a concomitant of its kind of idealism, it had never hesitated to attack what it disapproved. Its anticigarette articles had provoked a furor, actually affected the manufacture and sale of cigarettes in this country. It had forthrightly printed exposés of government inefficiency, of labor abuses, of fraudulent dealings with the public. Its exposés of the bilking of the public by unscrupulous garages, watch repairers, radio experts, and purveyors of eyeglasses were well known. It had brought other abuses of public trust to public attention.

On the other hand, the *Digest* had often singled out branded devices and products for praise in such a fashion that its manufacturers profited hugely. It brought a preparation for waterproofing cellars to favorable notice. It praised a comparatively unknown adhesive. It lauded a rug cleaner. An enthusiastic report on a meat tenderizer resulted in its manufacturer's expanding from one to six factories but finding himself still unable to keep up with the demand caused by the magazine's article. Many advertisers built entire testimonial campaigns around *Reader's Digest* consumer articles which expressed or seemed to express approval of given brands of dentifrices, cigarettes, paper filters, and the like. Some of them quoted praise out of context or in other ways misrepresented facts and opinions. The advertising fraternity was well aware of all of this.

With this record, what would be the result of the *Digest*'s announcement that it would accept advertising? Also, would the publishers of other magazines continue to extend the *Digest* reprint permission now that it was to become a competitor as an advertising medium?

Answers were soon known. Requests for space—at $31,000 for a full-color page, the largest price of any magazine—poured in. There were over one hundred in a matter of hours, Within two weeks after the *Digest* announced its decision to take advertising, orders were received for 1,107 pages, more than three times the number that could be accepted for the entire first year. Before any issue of the *Digest* containing advertising had appeared, $11 million had been placed. The *Digest* found itself in the difficult, if pleasant, position of having to decide which advertisers it would admit to its pages.

The April, 1955, issue, when it appeared, contained 216 pages instead of the previous 168. Full-color advertisements on glossy stock made it a thicker and more colorful book. The list of advertisers read like a bluebook of American industry: American Telephone & Telegraph, Eastman Kodak, Union Carbide and Carbon, Ford, Proctor & Gamble, General Electric, General Mills, Borden, Chrysler, Goodyear, and the others. Advertisers and media buyers in advertising agencies had no hesitation. The astronomical *Digest* circulation provided a market potential for products of all kinds. The unusual faith that *Digest* devotees seem to have in their magazine, a faith attested to by a subscription renewal rate of about 80 per cent, might easily extend to the new advertising pages.

No magazine withdrew from the *Digest* its permission to condense and reprint selected pieces. Many welcomed the *Digest's* move as an aid in achieving magazine solidarity against the competing media of television and radio. The business community and its periodical peers were merely affirming their belief in the influence of the *Digest* that had been discernible for a long time. In April, 1956, the *Digest* began to accept additional advertising up to 20 per cent of the total pages in an issue.

Digest influence is pervasive, seems ubiquitous. The magazine is read, admired, and quoted by people of almost every age and profession, by high school students and teachers, clergymen, public officials, housewives, mechanics, and circus performers. Its first foreign edition was in Spanish. It was published because Latin American readers asked for it. Editions published in Iceland, in Italy, and in Egypt came into being at the direct request of officials in those countries. In 1935 the *Digest* published what is probably the most successful magazine article ever printed in this country: "—And Sudden Death" by J. C. Furnas. Its realistic description of bloody highway maimings and fatalities at a time when automobile accidents were killing thirteen people for every 10,000 cars in use shocked the American public. The *Digest* article has been more widely reprinted than any magazine article before or since. About five million copies have been distributed.

Other *Digest* articles have had an almost equally wide dissemination. *Digest* pieces have provoked social reforms, legislative changes, and wrought emotional and spiritual changes in the lives of countless individuals. Readers in their letters to the editors have insisted that *Digest* pieces have saved their health, their marriage, or even their lives. A young Venezuelan, who seemed doomed to spend his life in a wheel chair, read "Where What's Left Works Wonders," scraped up passage to New York, and learned to walk again at Dr. Howard Rusk's rehabilitation clinic. A young mother read a *Digest* excerpt describing an antidote. She made up a batch, administered it promptly after her small son ate some poisonous food, credited the *Digest* with saving his life. *Digest* pieces are quoted in conversation, recommended from the pulpit, read to traffic offenders from the judicial bench; and its jokes are repeated with guffaws in dimly lit bars.

How is it all done? There are numerous partial answers. The *Digest*'s editorial purposes are clear. The magazine is expertly edited. Its large staff of senior and roving editors scour the field for ideas. These editors are well paid. Writers are very well paid for anything the *Digest* accepts. *Reader's Digest* editorial costs are high.

The digesting itself is done with meticulous care. A reading and cutting staff examines all the other magazines of any importance for its purposes, about 300 of them. The staff recommends articles for *Digest* use, and makes the original cutting. An editor goes over the cut article. The managing editor goes over it. One of the executive editors goes over it. If the condensed article has survived the scrutiny and editing of all of these, another editor goes over it. He may restore portions of the original text deleted along the line or make further cuts. This excising of selected and adapted material is a continual process.

The selection of a subject for original *Digest* treatment and its assignment to a writer for preparation are done with the same care. The idea may originate with Wallace, with one of the top staff editors, with a roving editor, or reach the magazine as a suggestion from an outside writer. There is no direct chain of command. If the idea is adopted and the article is written, it gets the same scrutiny and editing to which an already published and adapted piece is subjected. It may emerge, like some famous *Digest* pieces, with little resemblance to the original article.

Beyond all this, there is something else underlying the success of *The Reader's Digest* less easy to define. There is a kind

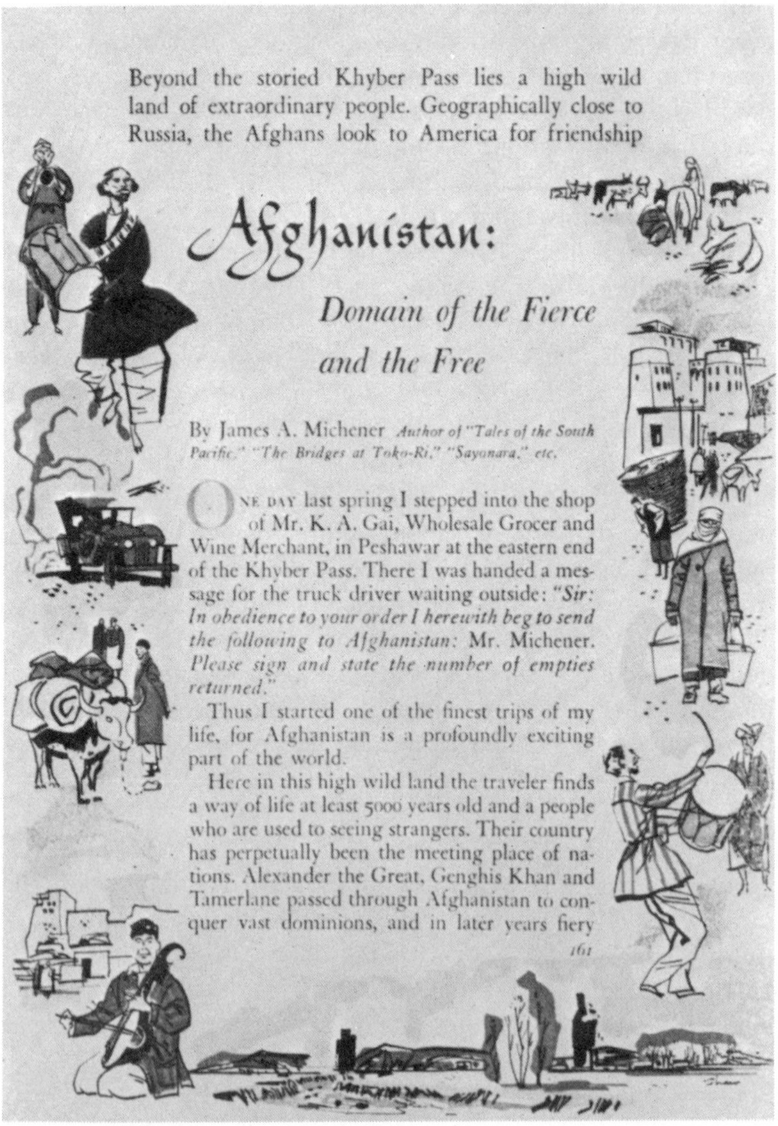

Beyond the storied Khyber Pass lies a high wild land of extraordinary people. Geographically close to Russia, the Afghans look to America for friendship

Afghanistan:

Domain of the Fierce and the Free

By James A. Michener *Author of "Tales of the South Pacific," "The Bridges at Toko-Ri," "Sayonara," etc.*

ONE DAY last spring I stepped into the shop of Mr. K. A. Gai, Wholesale Grocer and Wine Merchant, in Peshawar at the eastern end of the Khyber Pass. There I was handed a message for the truck driver waiting outside: *"Sir: In obedience to your order I herewith beg to send the following to Afghanistan:* Mr. Michener. *Please sign and state the number of empties returned."*

Thus I started one of the finest trips of my life, for Afghanistan is a profoundly exciting part of the world.

Here in this high wild land the traveler finds a way of life at least 5000 years old and a people who are used to seeing strangers. Their country has perpetually been the meeting place of nations. Alexander the Great, Genghis Khan and Tamerlane passed through Afghanistan to conquer vast dominions, and in later years fiery

161

Originally unillustrated, *The Reader's Digest* now uses artwork in color on front and back covers and colored line drawings, often in lighter vein, on editorial pages. Advertising adds more color to the magazine.

of mysticism and magic at Chappaquà. No one has yet proved that these are bad things, and at the *Digest* they are allied to great journalistic skill and shrewdness. DeWitt Wallace's editorial associates are men long experienced and skilled in magazine editing and publishing. Several were editors of magazines from which, in the early days of the *Digest,* Wallace obtained permission to extract articles. Most of the well-known early editors and writers on the *Digest* have died or retired. Fifteen or a score of familiar names disappeared from the magazine's masthead in 1968. Nearly all of its present top editors have been *Digest*-trained, and a number of them never worked elsewhere. These men are where they are and doing what they do because they share or reflect Wallace's attitudes and beliefs. They like the kind of thing he likes.

DeWitt Wallace likes inspirational pieces. He likes writing that proffers hope, that tells of courage, that exemplifies kindness, that shows simple human goodness triumphant. The *Digest*'s editor and his staff can make stories of this kind read so simply that reading is almost as painless as watching television. There is no pain in the act of reading, no pain in what you read. There is a better, simpler, happier world in *The Reader's Digest,* and it does not go away. It returns once a month forever. The reader is reassured. Life is better than it was before the new *Digest* came in the mail. There are miracles still, and there always will be—and in between the miracles are the earthy jokes, the best humor, probably, in any modern mass magazine.

Heroes and heroines in *Digest* pieces are people like the reader. Villains are the big things, the government, criminals, cigarettes, those who try to mislead or defraud, things the reader already detests or knows he should. Every line justifies him in what he wants to believe and feel. The *Digest* is an anodyne, a palliative, and a stimulant. It is easy, it is comforting, it is exciting—and "Did you hear this one?"

Digest editors select articles from other periodicals for digesting because they like them. They assign original subjects which appeal to them. They state that they do this, and there can be little doubt that what they say is true. A more cynical approach could not, consistently, produce the product, ensphered in its own sincerity, that the *Digest* is. The *Digest* is edited by men who dislike the abuses of power whether by big government or by big labor, who dislike seeing people pushed around, who have a crusading spirit about some things, who believe in faith, hope, charity, and the ability of man to rise above adverse circumstances. As one of them said, they concentrate on the human in the animal, rather than on the animal in the human. They believe that goodness is a good thing, and say so.

If there is a secret underlying the whole, the secret is simply DeWitt Wallace. He had an idea. He has carried it out. It is his idea, his taste, his editorial judgment that govern the whole. He has been described as Everyman—with everyman's hopes and desires, everyman's beliefs and grievances, everyman's sense of humor. In trying to explain their motivation and their magazine accomplishment, the *Digest's* circulation, and its hold on its readers, one of the magazine's editors a few years ago could say only "If D. W. likes it, automatically twelve million other people will like it. It's like that."

Though he suggests and directs some features DeWitt Wallace no longer selects and condenses already published articles or books for *The Reader's Digest*. Relinquishing little of his authority, he has delegated editorial judgment and functioning and the business operation of his magazine to others, leaving himself free to devote his time and energy to his philanthropic and educational interests. In 1961 the Wallaces quietly began to appoint certain of their leading editors and executives to vice presidencies. Just after Christmas, 1964, Wallace announced almost casually that he and Lila Acheson Wallace had decided to create the office of president of the *Digest* and had chosen Hobart D. Lewis, who joined the Digest in 1942, as president and executive editor. When A. L. Cole, long head of the business operation, became chairman of the executive committee of The Reader's Digest Association in 1966, Paul W. Thompson, youngest ground forces brigadier general in

World War II who joined the Digest at the end of the war, was made executive vice president. In the fall of 1969 Lewis was also made "editor-in-chief," a title not previously used at the *Digest*.

The Reader's Digest has its manifest shortcomings. It does not essay what it is not equipped to accomplish. It cannot please the discerning and discriminating intellectual. Its huge circulation does not permit inclusion of subjects or treatment of any subject in ways that only a few can appreciate. It is edited and published for the average man and woman concerned with their average day-to-day affairs. It is edited for everyman and directed to everyman here and abroad, and it reaches him. What the *Digest* tries to do it does with great competence.

Every piece of writing, article or book, that goes into an issue is condensed—digested. Even pieces written on *Digest* assignment are cut down, perhaps to half or a quarter the length of the writer's manuscript. The *Digest* gives the nub of the matter, not the details; the facts and opinions, not the flourishes. This can displease the perfectionist, but even the redoubtable H. L. Mencken, no easy critic, said, "I have yet to encounter an article that was seriously damaged by the condensation. And I can recall dozens that were palpably improved." Much depends, of course, on the kinds of articles or books selected for digesting. Obviously there are subjects and treatments, short or book-length, which do not lend themselves readily to the process. These cannot be digested or, if the attempt is made, digested well. For this reason and because it must appeal to an ever mounting circulation, the *Digest* studiously avoids what the trade calls a "think piece."

In a viciously competitive industry one periodical seldom goes out of its way to praise a rival, particularly an awesomely successful rival. Yet, in "The Common Touch," *Time* wrote, December 10, 1951, "No one can measure the influence the *Digest* has had on its readers, but it has certainly been considerable. It has also had a marked influence on other U. S. magazines—and through them on U. S. education. . . . Wallace has lured many people to read about serious topics and, in this sense, has helped raise the reading level of America." In this same article *Time* commented that the *Digest*'s articles in its international editions "have probably done more than all the government propagandists combined to allay the fear, prejudices, and misconceptions of the United States in other lands." [4]

DeWitt Wallace formed and shaped *The Reader's Digest.* The contemporary *Digest* with its issues of 250 to over 300 pages and thick with colorful advertising bears his imprint throughout, for as closely as they can his editors strive to make it coincide with the pattern he fixed and proved successful. Sometimes in their eagerness to balance humor, art of living advice, sentiment, self-help pieces, inspiration, and indignation—or the innocuous with the informative and stimulating —they seem to make an issue more DeWitt Wallace than Wallace ever was. In the opinion of those who should know they also accomplish something else. David Ogilvy wrote (in a *Digest* testimonial advertisement in 1965): "Digest editors have a profound influence on people who are free to read what they want. *This magazine exports the best in American life.* In my opinion, it is doing as much as the U. S. Information Agency to win the battle for men's minds."

There can be another way of looking at it. Year after the year before, issue after the issue preceding, *The Reader's Digest* is a reflection of the American people. To phrase it differently, it *is* the American people. It is what they are like or what many of them are like or what many of them in many parts of the country are still like. Not what they are told they should be like, not what they think they are like; not, perhaps, what they would like to be like, but what they are actually like. The *Digest* talks to them under all the surfaces turmoils, the screaming and shouting, the crises and calamities headlined morning and night. It is as if they heard themselves talk-

[4] Despite the *Digest* and many more government propagandists than there were in 1951, understanding of and affection for the United States has not increased at an alarming rate.

ing or as if the *Digest* overheard and put their thoughts and feelings, their fears and their remaining hopes into form and handed them back clarified and perhaps strengthened. What it does for its readers in the United States, the *Digest* does for its millions of readers in other countries and does in their own languages and in universal human terms.

The Reader's Digest seems to be what they are and who they are wherever they are, and they like the feeling.

Chapter 19

Satire and Humor: *The New Yorker*

Understandably the larger magazines find each other subjects of fascinating interest. Especially if a magazine is commercially successful and its editorial content compels attention and respect, competitors are given to anxious probing and peering. Usually they emerge from their investigations with puzzled frowns or surface lugubriously shaking their heads. They seldom approve what they think they have discovered—but occasionally they do.

The New Republic wrote early of the Curtis magazines. After 1960 many magazines worriedly or happily dissected or vivisected that dying giant. *Fortune* wrote enlighteningly of *The Reader's Digest* in 1936 and wrote of what was then the Crowell-Collier magazine group. Writing in the 90th anniversary issue of the *Atlantic* in 1947, Frederick Lewis Allen, then editor of *Harper's*, tried to sum up the peculiar qualities of the various types of American magazines which appeared for the first time after World War I. In 1945 *The New Yorker* had its say, derisively and at great length in a serialized book, about *The Reader's Digest*. In 1936 it had passed caustic judgment on *Time*, *Life*, *Fortune*, and Henry Luce.

Fortune, *The Saturday Review*, *Advertising Age*, *Cosmopolitan*, *Newsweek*, *Herald-Tribune Books*, *The New York Times Book Review*, *Newsweek*, and how many other publications—including *Women's Wear Daily*—have all tried to describe and assay *The New Yorker*. Usually they approach their subject with diffidence and even timidity. The disproportion between the magazine's circulation of under a half million and its influence, reputation, and prestige is in itself disturbing. The Bombay *Times* once called *The New Yorker* part of the social history of the United States. The London *Spectator* went considerably farther and further: "*The New Yorker* is an important part not only of American culture but of Western culture generally . . . ." Frederick Lewis Allen called *The New Yorker*'s style "errorless perfection." December 18, 1960, *The New York Times* stated flatly that *The New Yorker* is "the best literary magazine in the English-speaking world, big or little."

Pronouncements like these are a deterrent to rash judgment. Critics squint respectfully through the haze of legend that has surrounded *The New Yorker* almost since its founding in 1925. They looked on Harold Ross, the magazine's founder and until his death in 1951 very much its editor, with awe and with incomprehension in which awe had no part, and came away baffled by the contradiction between his appearance, manner, and editorial methods, and the appearance, manner, and reputation of his magazine. Few editors since Edward Bok received so much publicity. The dramatic contrast between man and magazine, shrill with exclamation points or their equivalent, colored all the articles about them.[1]

Harold Ross, born in Aspen, Colorado, began his journalistic career by leaving his high school course half finished to become a tramp newspaperman in Salt Lake City, Sacramento, San Francisco, New Orleans, and Atlanta. World War I gave him the opportunity he seized. As a private in the railway engineers, he maneuvered himself into the editorship of *Stars and Stripes,* the enlisted man's weekly newspaper of the American Expeditionary Forces, which was published in Paris. With him on *Stars and Stripes* were others who already were, or were to become, literary or journalistic celebrities: Grantland

[1] As might be expected, the *Fortune* article of August, 1934, though parts of it are dated now, is the longest, most thorough, and most detailed. It pulled no punches in describing the rages, the naiveté, the uncouthness, and the temperament of "Roughhouse Ross." It printed a gap-toothed photograph, listed his many phobias, noted his prudishness, and made it clear that he was a great editor. Two years later, *The New Yorker*'s "profile" of Henry Luce was acid.

Rice, Alexander Woollcott, John T. Winterich, George Bye, and Franklin P. Adams. When he returned to civilian life, Harold Ross, after his failure in an attempt to carry on *Stars and Stripes* as *The Home Sector,* became editor of the *American Legion Weekly,* a position he held for five years. The editorship of *Judge* followed. It was shortly after he left *Judge,* angered by a cut in his editorial budget, that he managed to put into operation his idea of a humorous weekly of and for the New York that fascinated him.[2]

Harold Ross founded *The New Yorker* after discussions with the literati who then frequented the Hotel Algonquin in New York, a group to which he was introduced by F.P.A. and Alexander Woollcott. Raoul Fleischmann put up the money with which to start the magazine, some $560,000 before the venture showed signs of success.

Original contributors and advisory board to *The New Yorker* were the Algonquin wits: Woollcott, Robert Benchley, George S. Kaufman, and Dorothy Parker. The first issue of *The New Yorker,* dated February 21, 1925, bore the now famous cover by Rea Irvin of a supercilious early-nineteenth century dandy disdaining a butterfly through his upraised monocle. Eustace Tilley, as this exquisite was named by Corey Ford, reappears on the cover of each anniversary issue and is *The New Yorker's* sign and symbol.

[2] Ross first thought of *The New Yorker* as a humorous magazine modeled after *Punch.* It would carry cartoons and illustrations, but primary emphasis would be on text. Another editor of humorous magazines believed that the future of such weeklies lay in profuse use of cartoons and a playing down of text. Norman Anthony, who had been an editor of both *Life* (the old *Life*) and *Judge,* founded *Ballyhoo* in 1931. Despite the depression, it quickly attained a 2,000,000 circulation. *Ballyhoo* burlesqued advertising: "Keep Kissable with Old Colds," "Avoid Athlete's Brain," "Read a *Fresh* Magazine" (the issue was wrapped in cellophane). *Ballyhoo's* most famous creation was Elmer Zilch, president of the Zilch Corporation, an advertising agency. Elmer was assisted by Langhorne Zilch, Percy Bysshe Zilch, Llewellyn Zilch, and a score more of his relatives, all vice presidents. The magazine disappeared in 1939 after its spectacular short success. An attempt to revive *Ballyhoo* was made in 1948.

The New Yorker did not reach its present position because of dependence on writing, nor did *Ballyhoo* fail because of its extravagant use of cartoons. Quality and appeal determined this, but the contrast in choice between primarily graphic and primarily verbal humor is not without interest.

Rea Irvin's disdainful dandy appeared on the cover of the first *New Yorker*, February 21, 1925. "Eustace Tilley" reappears on the cover of each of its anniversary issues. (By permission. Copyright 1925 The New Yorker Magazine, Inc. Formerly the F-R Pub. Corp.)

In the prospectus for his magazine Ross had said, "*The New Yorker* will be a reflection in word and picture of metropolitan life. It will be human. Its general tenor will be one of gaiety, wit, and satire, but it will be more than a jester. It will not be what is commonly called radical or high-brow. It will be what is commonly called sophisticated. . . . It will hate bunk. . . . Its integrity will be above suspicion."

In its first issue *The New Yorker* said that it would have a serious purpose but would not be too serious in executing it. It hoped to keep up with events and affairs of the day, but it would not deal in scandal for the sake of scandal or in sensation for sensation's sake. It was not out to tap American buying power for its advertisers. *The New Yorker* has lived up to every item in these declarations of its intent save one. It has long since become a strong and unusually successful advertising medium.

The early years of *The New Yorker* are those around which the fog of legend is thickest. Ross hired and fired—or, if he did not fire, managed to suggest the wisdom of resigning—rapidly and frequently. The magazine is supposed to have been published in an atmosphere of querulous profanity, spectacular rages, abrupt and arbitrary decisions, quips and cranks and wanton wiles, and a general loud explosiveness. Writers and editors leaped in and leaped out, usually helped both ways.[3] By April, 1925, *The New Yorker* had only 8,000 readers and was losing $8,000 each week. The decision was reluctantly made to abandon what was clearly a practical failure. This decision was reversed when Raoul Fleischmann was persuaded to reconsider and to risk more capital.

Many accounts testify, wonderingly, that it was an article by Ellin Mackay—Mrs. Irving Berlin since 1926—which started *The New Yorker* on its way to success. Its author, a post-debutante, wrote on "Why We Go to Cabarets." In her

[3] Dale Kramer, in *Ross and The New Yorker* (Garden City, N.Y.: Doubleday & Co., 1951), gives a colorful account of the early years. *The New Yorker,* in a review, found the book conspicuously uninformed if well-intentioned. There is precedent for the attitude. *Reader's Digest* editors were unable to recognize themselves or their magazine in John Bainbridge's "Little Magazine," which *The New Yorker* ran in five installments in 1945.

article, which appeared in the Thanksgiving issue for 1925, she explained that debutantes sought refuge in cabarets from the unpleasant kinds of individuals who frequented private debutante parties. The article caused both shocked and amused comment, and placed the name of *The New Yorker* on the front pages of the newspapers.

At various times Robert Benchley, Ogden Nash, Dorothy Parker, Sally Benson, Ralph Ingersoll, Frank Sullivan, Nunnally Johnson, Lewis Mumford, Clarence Day, Robert Simon, Lois Long, H. L. Mencken, Rebecca West, Edmund Wilson, and how many others have written, as outside contributors, staff writers, or both, for the magazine which Ross edited "not for the old lady in Dubuque." Yet the two writers whose names are still most closely identified with *The New Yorker* are James Thurber and E. B. (Elwyn Brooks) White.

E. B. White, a Cornell graduate who had worked in an advertising agency, joined *The New Yorker* in 1926, ran "The Talk of the Town" for eleven years, and contributed signed verse and prose essays to the weekly. In 1929 he married Katharine Sergeant Angell who, first as the literary editor, then as the efficient managing editor of *The New Yorker,* is usually given much of the credit for establishing the high literary standards and the impeccable good taste of the magazine. James Thurber, who was on the staff of the Paris edition of the *Chicago Tribune* when he first heard of *The New Yorker,* started to submit material to it in 1926 after his return to this country. His first twenty efforts were rejected. The twenty-first, written, at the suggestion of his wife, in little more than forty-five minutes, was accepted. Thurber met White, who introduced him to Harold Ross, and Ross immediately hired him for *The New Yorker* staff. Thurber's experience with his humorous drawings matched that with his writing. For two years Ross consistently rejected them. Then his frustrated men, determined women, and strange big dogs became *New Yorker* familiars.

Thurber's *My Life and Hard Times* ran in *The New Yorker* in 1933. Together he and White produced *Is Sex Necessary?* Thurber and White remained frequent contributors and the two most characteristic *New Yorker* writers. Just as White introduced Thurber to Ross, Thurber later introduced Robert M. Coates, who has been art critic, book critic, short story writer, and prolific general contributor to *The New Yorker.* Wolcott Gibbs, author of the Luce "profile" in 1936, long wielded one of the weekly's sharpest pens.

It is the severe editing and re-editing of the complete text of each issue that makes *New Yorker* prose what it is, and has produced the famed "*New Yorker* style." Harold Ross edited the full contents of each issue with meticulous attention to detail. Factual accuracy and complete clarity are demanded of every writer in every piece. There may be no recondite references, no unanswered questions in the reader's mind, no learned allusions. Slovenly writing, precious writing, "fine writing" stood no chance of survival. Because all the writing in each issue is still made to conform to these standards, all of it seems sometimes to have been written by one man, the same man who wrote last week's issue and will write the next. Perfection, or *The New Yorker*'s idea of perfection, is alone acceptable. Ross applied a microscope to all copy and wrote his sharp complaints, ironic queries, and firm directions on the galleys. It is in the rewriting, in energetically scouring with steel wool and pumice after applying the putty filler—and not too much of this—that *The New Yorker* surface is applied to its prose.

For twenty-six years the same gimlet-eyed scrutiny bored into the art. *The New Yorker* gives far more space to text than graphics. Despite this deliberate preponderance of words over pictures, there are many who think of *The New Yorker* as primarily a cartoon vehicle, and look at it first for the amusement which its cartoons afford. Often they never get beyond the cartoons.

The New Yorker originated the one-line cartoon, and *The New Yorker*'s artists have done at least as much to establish the magazine's reputation as have its writers. Rea Irvin, Gardner Rea, Gluyas Williams, Helen Hokinson, Peter Arno, Whitney Darrow, Jr., and John Held, Jr., R. Taylor, Charles Addams, William Steig, George Price, Steinberg, Kovarsky were as familiar in *New Yorker* pages as White, Thurber, Liebling, Berger, Maloney, Coates, Gibbs, Perelman, and Ogden Nash. The magazine goes far to insure having the kind of graphic humor it wishes. It may, and often does, supply the artist with the idea for a cartoon. It may change the "gag lines" submitted by the artist, or it may buy the cartoon alone and work up its own captions. However they are developed, the cartoons must measure up to specifications as rigid as those set for *New Yorker* prose. They usually say something and say it clearly.

Its cover cartoons in color are one of *The New Yorker's* most successful features. Except in its advertising, this is the only place in the magazine where color is used. Unlike the other well-known magazines, almost all of which are using more and more color both in photographs and in artists' illustrations, *The New Yorker* eschews color in its editorial pages. This complete reliance on black and white results in a physical unity and restraint, literally a distinction, when it is compared with most of the other national magazines. *The New Yorker* runs no enticing blurbs on its covers. Stories and articles have no by-lines under the titles; authors' names appear at the end. There are no subtitles in display type whipping the reader on. Regular departments are listed in a small box on the first page of the weekly calendar of events. The product of all this *Punch*-like restraint, careful selection, and close editing goes each week to a circulation of some 478,000, a circulation which no doubt could be greatly enlarged if *The New Yorker* considered the move profitable. In relation to circulation, its advertising rates are high now.

The New Yorker's distinctiveness is not limited to its chaste format. It is the finest magazine of gentle satire, subtle humor, of shrewd and witty comment on the passing scene which appears in the United States today. Its quiet prose is firm and lucid. It is sane and reasonable, intelligent, urbane, calm, and suave without being fulsome or overly smug. It is also, and basically, informative. "Goings On About Town," at the very front of the magazine, is, as it describes itself, "a conscientious calendar of events of interest" in New York. A section usually of six or seven pages in small type, it is a full, definite, and useful guide to sports, movies, radio programs, plays, concerts, night clubs, hotels, museums, and varied entertainments scheduled for the week. "On and Off the Avenue," farther on in the magazine, is again factual. It is a pleasantly discursive shopper's guide which gives advice and specific information, naming places and things and prices. Like a good newspaper, *The New Yorker* selects its simple, useful facts and reports them accurately. Its sections on books, the theater, and the motion pictures are informative but essentially and usually adversely critical.

Those mentioned are standard *New Yorker* offerings, but it is other long-continued features which are usually considered most characteristic. "The Talk of the Town," the first major editorial piece, with its "Notes and Comment" opening each issue under a cut of Eustace Tilley, supported by an indicative skyscraper and an owl with one eye open and very wise, is the most famous. "The Talk of the Town" seems *The New Yorker* itself. A score of subjects—narrative, anecdote, description, essay, quip—may appear here. Here the tone of *The New Yorker* is set. Whimsey, satire, irony, mockery, comment that is aloof and amused, but never vindictive or crude and seldom cruel, are the distilled ingredients. Some of it is just clever gossip. All of it is perfectly formed into a whole of light, firm texture which, like the texture of the entire magazine, is of superior quality.

Almost as characteristic of the essential *New Yorker* are its "profiles." *The New Yorker* biographies have influenced—the opinion is neither novel nor original—biographical writing in the other magazines and, indeed, biographical writing of our time. Mrs. E. B. White is credited with having set the pattern for them, and certainly Alva Johnston, who wrote a great number of the early *New Yorker* profiles, established the form. These biographical sketches, some of them brief enough to be run in one issue, others appearing in several installments, are frequently assigned to writers outside the regular *New Yorker* staff. The subject may be an industrial leader, a writer, musician, theatrical character, an editor and his magazine, anyone whom *The New Yorker* considers newsworthy and noteworthy.

Characters as diverse as Nicholas Murray Butler, Jake Ruppert, Sir Joseph Duveen, and W. C. Fields have appeared in the long list of *New Yorker* profiles. Wolcott Gibbs, who thrust and slashed and hammered at Henry Luce in one of them, practically demolished Alexander Woollcott, once a patron saint of the magazine, in another entitled "Big Nemo."

These biographies are far different from the admiring and unctuous success stories of great men which used to be popular in many magazines, a kind of biographical writing which stemmed from the uncritical adulation which Victorian writers thought it proper to accord their eminent subjects. They differ markedly, too, from the kind of debunking biographies popularized by Lytton Strachey and his imitators in the 1920's. *New Yorker* profiles are life stories, told as if their writers had looked squarely at a man or woman, without preconceived estimate, and had put down the facts as they saw them. Often the profiles are astringent and sharply ironic, but the facts, the admirable facts if there are any as well as the ridiculous facts, especially the ridiculous facts, are there to be read.

Wisely, Mark Twain once refused Edward Bok permission to publish in the *Ladies' Home Journal* an account of an interview. He wrote Bok, "No, no—it is like most interviews, pure twaddle and valueless. . . . No; spare the reader and spare me; leave the whole interview out; it is rubbish. I wouldn't talk in my sleep if I couldn't talk better than that. . . ." [4]

P. G. Wodehouse remarked somewhere that no man could talk for two hours without making a fool of himself and begged off being profiled. Whether in *The New Yorker* as "profiles" or as question and answer interviews, usually taped, in any periodical, biographical sketches of this kind are often entertaining for just this reason. They allow a subject to make a fool of himself out of his own mouth.

[4] Bok, Edward William. *The Americanization of Edward Bok.* New York: Charles Scribner's Sons, 1920.

The reader may not agree with the judgments implied in a *New Yorker* profile, but he does not doubt the facts. The reader is not apt to doubt any of the facts in *The New Yorker*. He may cavil at some *New Yorker* opinions and attitudes, or detest some of the arrogance, but *The New Yorker* carries on every page conviction of its own kind of integrity. No concessions are made to the supposed tastes of the masses. No concessions are made to anybody or to anything except *New Yorker* editorial decisions. This is the life of New York, thus the life of our times in epitome, as it looked to Harold Ross and looks to his successor.

Horace Greeley called his weekly magazine of literature, politics, and general intelligence the *New-Yorker*, hyphenating the name of the city as was conventional in the 1830's and 1840's, but the real prototype of today's *New Yorker* among Americans was Joseph Dennie's *Port Folio* in the early nineteenth century. There is a strong family likeness between Oliver Oldschool and Eustace Tilley. Joseph Dennie, wit, dandy and satirical essayist after Addison, might well have been the subject of a Rea Irvin caricature in 1925. Discounting its political bias, there is a fundamental similarity between *The Port Folio*, the best magazine of its day, sharp, brilliantly written, ironic, boldly addressed only to men of education, taste, and intelligence, and today's civilized weekly, equally fastidious, occasionally as disdainful, as neatly independent, and even more self-assured.

It is often said that *The New Yorker* has developed the short story into a new kind of perfection. Perhaps it has. Certainly, it has offered from the beginning a kind of story superior to the standardized mass magazine product. *New Yorker* stories are unpretentious narratives in monotone and monochrome. Sometimes they have a beginning. Often there is no discernible end. There is no contriving of plot, no straining after obvious dramatic effects, no rhetorical climax. Characters in the stories underact, understate. Here, the stories seem to say, is a bit of life, formless as life itself. They are unperturbed, unaccented recitals. No moral is stated, seldom is one implied.

The stories are cool. They never shine. They eschew the vulgar with great determination. At their best, *New Yorker* stories can be delightful. At their worst, they show more finish than substance. This is generalization which does not fit "Life with Father," "Pal Joey," "My Sister Eileen," "The Secret Life of Walter Mitty," and other famous *New Yorker* successes and many less well-known *New Yorker* stories.

New Yorker essays are beautifully finished. The facts, as in the reportorial pieces and even in many of the stories, are accurate; yet the essays sometimes seem pallid, a little bloodless. Irony, when it lacks a real target or motivation stronger than mannered habit, can go anemic. *New Yorker* humor, and there is less and less of it, is sometimes simply not funny. The attitude of superiority, which *The New Yorker* assumes in publicizing the errors of its contemporaries, seems as much informed by a schoolteacherish delight in the discovery of flaws as by wit of any discernible kind. Eustace Tilley can be very squeamish.

Discarding the protective armor of its humor, and lowering its guard a little, *The New Yorker* publishes a certain amount of direct social commentary. Its war reports were noticeable. Its London Letter and the letters from Paris, West Berlin, and other foreign centers, which appear occasionally, are informal but serious in tone. It has written almost soberly about world government and the uneasy peace following World War II. It talks down to these larger subjects indulgently. There is a self-consciousness in some of its writing about them, as though it were a little ashamed to be caught taking them and itself seriously; but it does acknowledge them.

The New Yorker ran a series of articles on Oak Ridge, the warborn town in Tennessee where atom bombs are manufactured. In 1945 and 1946 it carried Rebecca West's almost painfully detailed reports of the treason trials in England, together with her mordant descriptions of William Joyce, John Amery, and Norman Baillie-Stewart, and her analysis of the reasons for their behavior. *The New Yorker* made spectacular play, and undoubtedly carried conviction of grim realities and grim possibilities to many readers, by devoting an entire issue to John Hersey's "Hiroshima" in August, 1946. The magazine is no longer solely, or even principally, concerned with the coffeehouses, or their twentieth-century equivalents, of New York City.

In 1949 and 1950 Harold Ross was gleefully and characteristically busy. Enraged by what he considered an invasion of his privacy, he carried on a one-man, one-magazine crusade against music and commercials blasting out of sixty-five amplifiers concealed in Grand Central Terminal. After persistently castigating Grand Central in *The New Yorker* for its maltreatment of a helpless captive audience, he testified ironically at a Public Service Commission hearing (blandly accepting a description of himself as editor of 'an adult comic book'), and the noise which was bringing the railroad a $93,000-a-year revenue was stopped. As bitterly, Ross ridiculed *Flair,* a lush and pretentious new monthly magazine published by Cowles, deriding it in text and cartoons. Doubtless there were other contributing factors, but *Flair* ceased publication.

The New Yorker was so much the projection of this one mind and temperament, so much the product of one man's intensive editing, that it was often doubted the magazine would survive Harold Ross. *Fortune* said in 1943 that *The New Yorker* might well disintegrate without him. The magazine *'48* said *The New Yorker* would probably disappear if Ross retired. Other opinion and comment were much the same. Harold Ross died December 7, 1951, at the age of 59.

Only one article appeared on the first page of *The New Yorker* of December 15, 1951. It was headed simply, "H. W. Ross." It was not the usual prepared obit, not the usual tribute. No attempt was made to disguise the grief of its writer or to hide the sentiment which, thinly veneered, underlies so much *New Yorker* writing. It was no eulogy either. Ross had lacked formal education. He used two books at *The New Yorker:* a Webster's dictionary and a Fowler's *Modern English Usage.* He had been difficult to understand, but ". . . he wanted the magazine to be good, to be funny, and to be fair."

(He had made *The New Yorker* a good magazine, but it was sometimes not funny, and it was often unfair.) "Ross set up a great target and pounded himself to pieces trying to hit it square in the middle."

The ending of the piece was emotional. Ross, it said, had been used to ending his interviews, calm or stormy, with a wave of his hand and, "All right. God bless you." The death notice in the magazine he had created ended: "We cannot convey his manner. But with much love in our heart we say for everybody, 'All right, Ross. God bless you!'" The whole left little doubt that Ross's surviving staff would try to carry on *The New Yorker* in the Ross tradition.

James Thurber's *The Years With Ross* appeared in 1957. Obviously no one else could have written as informative, moving, as well as amusing a book that is both tribute and fond reminiscence.

Six weeks after the death of Harold Ross, William Shawn was made editor of *The New Yorker.* Born in Chicago (his surname originally spelled "Chon") he had become a reporter on the Las Vegas *Optic* after two years at the University of Michigan. He went to New York in 1932 and the next year joined the eight-year old *New Yorker* as a Talk of the Town reporter. He became one of the magazine's long list of usually short-lived managing editors but eventually Ross's own choice as a successor. Ross-trained, he naturally thought when he took over that any changes reflected in the magazine's pages would simply be those that come normally through changing times and writers.[5]

Popular magazines thrive on gossip and the exploitation of personalities. Ironically many of their editors prefer anonymity and try to avoid publicity. George Horace Lorimer (*not* Edward Bok), Henry Luce, DeWitt Wallace, and Harold Ross himself, though he failed at it, are cases in point. William Shawn is even more reticent. Generally he has refused to give interviews or allow himself to be photographed. Obviously he has carried on in the Ross tradition. Just as obviously he is an

[5] *Tide,* February, 1952.

editor of skill and character, for the magazine which was once Harold Ross is now as clearly William Shawn.

Superficially *The New Yorker* seems to have changed little since 1951. It looks the same. The writing is almost as good. Most of the same departments remain. The cartoons are almost as amusing. Most of the Ross writers and cartoonists are gone, dead or out of action, but the younger writers and cartoonists who have taken their place closely approximate the talents of their precursors. The changes are more essential. *The New Yorker* is quieter. It is more serious. It is wordier. Its long stories have grown interminable. *The New Yorker* has kept its imperturbability, but it has lost its ferocity and most of its humor.

Some of this is William Shawn. Harold Ross was a product, if not the prototype, of the exuberant post-World War I United States of the 1920's. He had been in Paris with the victorious AEF. He had seen flappers and knew about cabarets. He talked with New York wits. Shawn struck New York at the dark bottom of the grim depression of the 1930's. Wits did not seem so witty. Near starvation was a reality for many, and the flappers had grown middle-aged. Even Ross saw by 1939 that he could not keep his *New Yorker* as humorous a publication as he wished.

Some of the change in *The New Yorker* is neither Shawn nor Ross. It is the times which, like any other magazine, it reflects. A deadly seriousness of almost religious intensity prevailed in the United States of the 1960's. Among atom bombs, moon flights, unpopular wars, and flourishing violence, humor is as out of place as politeness. There shall be no more cakes and ale. Riotous protest was literally the prevailing mood and the admired form of expression. Planned destruction continued in 1970. The atmosphere is one of fear and bloodthirstiness. Wit is as suspect as civility. *The New Yorker* is still beautifully dressed and mannered, but increasingly it is caviar to the vulgar.

Eustace Tilley still disdains the world through his upraised glass, but, older now, he is serious occasionally—as in James Baldwin's "Letter from a Region in My Mind," Rachel Carson's attack on the indiscriminate use of pesticides in "Silent Spring," and Richard Harris's "If You Love Your Guns." Sometimes now Mr. Tilley sounds more like Oliver Goldsmith than like Horace Walpole. He shows more sentiment, less acerbity. Success is said to be softening, and *The New Yorker* has succeeded in many ways. Harold Ross may never have intended it to be courted as an effective and even distinguished advertising medium, but it is.

Though far down the list in size of circulation, *The New Yorker* heads the list in number of advertising pages. In the peak year of 1966 the magazine—which values its tradename at just one inflated dollar—carried 6,114 pages of advertising from which it derived a revenue of over $23,390,000 and showed a net profit for the year of over $3,000,000. All magazine advertising fell off in 1967 but *The New Yorker* far less than most. It ran 5,653 advertising pages for a return of $22,147,727 and showed a net of nearly $2,775,000. Magazine advertising continued its decline into 1968, but the situation was hardly serious because in 1967, for the tenth consecutive year, it still led all consumer magazines in amount of advertising. Yet *New Yorker* management is cautious. It began regular newspaper advertising promotion for the first time since 1953.

The New Yorker, which has never stooped to circulation promotion, has always advertised itself as an advertising medium, and some of this advertising has been beautiful. It took a full page in the New York newspapers, January 18, 1951, to tweak the noses of its large-circulation competitors for research claims which presented each one of them as somehow the biggest and the best. Then in a bold-face line, all caps, it blazoned its own statistic.

EVERY COPY OF THE NEW YORKER IS READ BY PEOPLE

The New Yorker's advertising promotion is consistently as quiet as the magazine itself. It need not be noisier.

For many years it was in the enviable position of having to turn down many pages of advertising for its Thanksgiving to

Christmas issues in order to maintain issue size (about 250 pages) and to insure the editorial-to-advertising rate which insures magazine second-class mailing rates. Its record is the more remarkable in that the magazine has always been fastidious in its acceptance of advertising.

Writers cannot use four-letter obscenities in writing for *The New Yorker*. The magazine has never permitted sexual suggestiveness in its pages. Its editors insist on conventional good taste. The editorial in *The New Yorker* is impeccable. So by fiat and in practice is the advertising. The relationship between the editorial and advertising departments is just that which Talk of the Town prescribed for *The Reader's Digest*. Business and editorial departments are on different floors. They have different telephone numbers. As one executive of the magazine phrased it recently, "Editorial and business function as separate entities—with barbed wire in between." When A. J. Russell retired as president of *The New Yorker* in May, 1968, he said he had met Harold Ross once a year at the magazine's birthday party and sometimes had seen him in the elevator but could not say "Good morning," as Ross did not like to be talked to in the elevator.

That is only the beginning of *New Yorker* restrictions on advertising. It will allow no exaggeration, superlatives, or innuendoes. It eschews feminine hygiene, bad breath, body odors, and patent medicines. It will picture nothing which is worn beneath a woman's slip. It will permit no expression in advertising of opinion on controversial subjects. Since publication of the Surgeon General's report on the dangers of smoking it has rejected all cigarette advertising. It will admit nothing to its advertising pages which would not make what it considers appropriate dinner table talk. Liquor advertising is strictly limited to 16 per cent of the advertising pages in an issue. Multipage advertisements which would upset the balance of an issue are refused.

Despite all this exclusiveness—perhaps in part because of it—*The New Yorker* is rich every issue with prestige advertising for books, restaurants, hotels, amusements, and with advertising for luxury goods for a class market, particularly advertising from high-priced retail outlets or advertising for high-priced items by department stores. Jewelry, fabric, perfumery, other items running from the sedate to the lush but always suggesting refined taste characterize *New Yorker* advertising. There is always the flattering assumption that expense is no handicap to the discriminating.

The New Yorker audience is composed of people who read, or they would buy instead a different kind of magazine. They will read smartly presented advertising as well as editorial content. They are people of taste, education, and discrimination (or want to be), or they would not like the magazine. That they do like it is attested by the high rate of subscription renewals. Shrewd advertisers of the kind of merchandise that will appeal to such people know this. They know also that *The New Yorker* carries a high carriage-trade prestige.

Besides its regular and critically appreciative readers, there is a class of people, and, fortunately for *The New Yorker,* not a small class, which praises the magazine extravagantly. These men and women, whether or not they understand the more subtle qualities which help to make *The New Yorker* what it is, whether, indeed, they often read the magazine, consider it a mark of "sophistication" to admire it uncritically. College undergraduates continually try to imitate the *New Yorker* manner in their themes for English classes. Usually they fail badly in the attempt. Their straining after spare prose produces poverty-stricken prose. They bungle the aloof irony and amused perception, produce instead a bored disdain or a spindly contempt. Occasionally one does almost as well as his model, which shows the same flaws. Seventy-seven per cent of the circulation of *The New Yorker* is outside the metropolitan area of New York. *The New Yorker* may not be edited for the old lady in Dubuque, but it is to provincial readers that *The New Yorker* seems the essence of the glamor and excitement of the city.

Arrival of a new copy of *The New Yorker* was the high spot of the week for William Shawn when he labored for the Las

Vegas *Optic*. In January, 1963, a stricken but forgiving subscriber in California wrote, ". . . one of your magazines fell through the mail slot landing on the family's pet turtle. We still love you though we miss the turtle." A young reader expressed the intensity of his interest in still another way. His carefully lettered note was to the point. "Dear Sirs, I thought you might be interested to know that I added togeather [sic] all the money figures in your August 20th issue. The total came out to be $1,383,184.44." An impressed *New Yorker* executive replied, "In all the years that I have been at *The New Yorker*, I don't think that anyone has ever done this before and we are terribly appreciative."

There is little else with which to compare apparent *New Yorker* weaknesses than *New Yorker* strength or what is best in other very good magazines. The *London News Review* once said, "Aiming at nothing in particular, *The New Yorker* excels in everything in general."

It excels, but satire—still the recognizable *New Yorker* approach in its criticism, sometimes in its "profiles," and often in its comment—is critical, not creative. It can provide intellectual delight to those capable of intellectual pleasure. The appreciative can enjoy the magazine's mental and emotional honesty, its scrupulous exactness, and its common sense. It loves gossip, coffee-house gossip as Joseph Dennie or before him Joseph Addison and Richard Steele understood it and as Mark Twain loved it. It is no accident that "Shouts and Murmurs," an Alexander Woollcott column of gossip and anecdote was once a characteristic *New Yorker* department.

The New Yorker's mockery of stupidity was always gentle. Its ridicule was consistently against the fraudulent and false. Its sharpest thrusts were meant to pierce pretense and hypocrisy. It loosed keen barbs for sanity which were often more effective than the loud blows of critics of American society who pranced about belaboring it with pigs' bladders or bludgeons. *The New Yorker* is more serious now. It shows social consciousness on occasion and even, as in "If You Love Your

Guns," April 20, 1968, willingness to join in a popular journalistic crusade.

Yet *The New Yorker* is still characteristically aloof and coolly assured. As it always has been, it is amusedly pontifical. It remains, as *The Wall Street Journal* called it March 27, 1968, "a model of urbane unflappability." It still values polished prose and polished manners. Eustace Tilley seems less a Regency buck than a gentleman of the prosperous 1920's which delighted with its own sudden sophistication, could afford to laugh and even, with happy self-mockery look down its nose. Such indulgence is now considered immoral. Elegance is not admired. Restraint and good manners are the quaint and culpable impertinences of a period piece.

Except for a small box directing to its regular departments, *The New Yorker* had never listed its editorial offerings in the front matter of an issue. It did not care to waste space and lead position on unseemly display and could confidently assume that many of its readers were capable of looking for themselves. In March, 1969, it unveiled a formal table of contents. It is small, discreet, and civilized, but it was something of a shock to come upon it in the first page of "Goings On About Town."

The move was not rashly made. William Shawn said it had been under consideration for some thirty years. Readers had asked for a table of contents and it might prove useful to librarians and researchers. Still, it is dangerous practice. Someone could scan it and decide there is nothing at all in an issue that he cares to read. The change can be seen as concession to periodical convention or admission that the public needs direction and usually a smidgen of enticement. It is hoped that this innovation does not portend further drastic change in *The New Yorker*. Probably it does not, and probably this is unnecessary viewing with alarm. Most readers ignore a magazine's table of contents anyway.

E. B. White made no secret of his admiration for Henry Thoreau, and the influence of Thoreau showed in his thought and in his *New Yorker* prose. By his own confession, Thoreau marched to a different drummer. The *New Yorker* marches to a different drummer than many in the contemporary world seem to hear.

In this one instance it is to be hoped that it is the world which is out of step.

Chapter 20

The Quick and the Nude: *Playboy*

The circulation of *Playboy* burst over 5,000,000 with its issues for the early months of 1968 and has stayed there. Its circulation revenue for fiscal 1967 was nearly $25,000,000. Advertising revenue for the same period was $15,358,982. Playboy Clubs International—19 night clubs in the United States, one in Montreal and one in London—recorded sales of over $27,000,000. Sales of Playboy Press reached $1,610,000. Playboy Products sales of men's jewelry and accessories were over $2,675,000. Real estate holdings of the various Playboy enterprises are valued at over $25,000,000. In June, 1967, Playboy ordered a $4,500,000 jet airplane with a private suite, a guest compartment, and a combined living room and conference room to move its busy executives around the world at 550 m.p.h. Net profits of HMH Publishing Company, Inc., and Playboy Clubs International, Inc., were $6,480,347.[1] *Playboy* continues to climb with bacchanalian abandon. It gained another 18 per cent in pages of advertising and 37 per cent in revenue in the first half of 1969. It took in over $21,000,000 for the first nine months of the year.

It is difficult to find a figure describing *Playboy* which is not in the millions. The figures have catapulted upward year by year, and it looks as if they will continue to catapult. Present figures contrast gloriously with those for 1954 when they to-

[1] "Playboy Progress Report" (annual report), 1968; Hefner, Hugh M., "On Passing 5,000,000 circulation," *Playboy* brochure, 1968.

taled zero, or more accurately, a minus $25,000.[2] All of these millions are solidly based on outsized bosoms and bottoms. Sex never paid Casanova, Lothario, or even Kinsey as prolifically.

Born in Chicago in 1926, Hugh Marston Hefner attended Steinmetz High School where he drew cartoons for the school paper and started the multi-volume looseleaf autobiography of cartoons, pictures, and some text which he still keeps. He had a wonderful time at Steinmetz after he felt he became attractive to girls. Six months after his graduation in 1944 he entered the army in which he spent two years as a company clerk in replacement centers in the United States. On his discharge and because Mildred Williams whom he had dated in high school went there, he entered the University of Illinois. There he drew cartoons for an undergraduate magazine and sang at campus spots with a three-piece band. He married Mildred Williams soon after his 1949 graduation and tried for a job on *Esquire*. Even when he was in high school he had decided that was where he would work.

Esquire had no job for him at the time so he took one as personnel man for a Chicago carton manufacturer. He hated it, quit, and did not work for about a year. His wife, who was teaching, supported them until he got a new job at $40 a week as an advertising copywriter for the Loop department store of Carson Pirie Scott. This did not satisfy either. After failing to sell a college comic strip idea, "Fred Frat," Hefner decided to take graduate work so that he could teach psychology at the college level. He lasted one semester at Northwestern University, then joined *Esquire,* which had an opening now, as a $60 a week circulation promotion man.

When *Esquire* moved to New York in 1952, Hefner was offered an incentive increase up to $80 to make the move. He asked for $85. *Esquire* did not think he was worth it. Restless, unhappy, soon to be divorced after three years of marriage and two children, the thin, five-foot-eleven Hefner did circulation work for some small publishing houses in Chicago and planned feverishly.

[2] Whitney, Alan, "The Story of Playboy," *Chicago Magazine,* October, 1955.

He had felt repressed at home and credits a strict upbringing with the sharp dissatisfactions that provoked development of his talents. In the World War II army he had been ordered around. He felt that his marriage had built a restrictive wall around him. He was even dissatisfied with the *Esquire* he had worshipped when he was in high school. Older and very successful, the men's fashion magazine lacked the blatant sexiness which had appealed to him.

Hefner was determined that he would publish his own magazine, a magazine with all the libidinous virtues of the earlier *Esquire*. It would be a magazine of entertainment for men. He did not want a sports magazine, an outdoorsy magazine after the manner of some men's magazines already published, but a magazine devoted to the entertainment and indoor entertainments of knowing young city males like himself. It would be an all-out delectation with primary appeal to the primary appetite.

For $200 Hefner purchased from a calendar printer the two-color plates and one-time reproduction rights of a picture of Marilyn Monroe in the nude. He lined up some large-name reprints, pieces by well-known writers which had previously appeared in out-of-the-way publications. He collected some cartoons and some risqué jokes. He solicited orders for his proposed magazine from magazine distributors about the country and got more orders than he expected. On the basis of these he obtained 45-day credit from a printer. He sold a few hundred dollars worth of stock in his venture to relatives and friends, got a bank loan of $500 on his furniture and another bank loan of $300 on the same furniture. He borrowed on his 1950 Studebaker. In all he raised a little less than $7,000.[3]

Dark-haired, thin, intense, as he still is, Hefner poured all his small resources and all his energy into his scheme. He worked frenziedly. ". . . for the first time in my life I felt free. It was like a mission—to publish a magazine that would thumb its nose at all the restrictions that had bound me." [4]

[3] "The Beginning and the Early Years," Playboy Information Library, n.d.

[4] Quoted by Davidson, Bill, in "Czar of the Bunnies," *The Saturday Evening Post*, April 28, 1962.

Paying him in stock, Hefner got a young art director, Arthur Paul, still art editor of the magazine, to design his first issue. At first they thought of calling the publication *Stag Party*. At the last moment they changed to *Playboy* and because of its reputation for sexual activity chose the rabbit for symbol. Hefner thought that putting it in a tuxedo achieved the sophistication he admired. Undated because there might never be another, the first issue of *Playboy* appeared in December, 1953. It sold a startling 51,191 copies at fifty cents each out of a press run of 70,000.

Hefner was ecstatic, and there has never since been much reason for any diminution of his ecstasy. The first four issues of *Playboy* were published from his Chicago apartment. Then he and his small staff were able to rent modest offices in downtown Chicago. Hefner slept there. By 1955 when he was becoming rich and beginning to be something of a celebrity, he could exclaim happily, "From the time I left high school until the magazine succeeded, I was never a very happy guy. Now it's something like being in high school again, but on a much greater scale." [5]

Five years later that scale was even larger. *Playboy*, which had none during its first year, had an advertising revenue of $2,300,000. It had a circulation of over 1,000,000. Hugh Marston Hefner was a millionaire. The magazine was on its way up and up and up, and the Playboy Clubs had been started. Hefner in his tuxedo with his man-of-distinction pipe, his magazine, his nightclubs, the bunny tails and rabbit ears attached to his bunnies who wear just enough to keep tail and ears in place, the three-page center spreads of not quite nude nudes are established parts of the contemporary American scene.

The Petty pinup girls of *Esquire* were artist's creations. The elongated female figures had grace, charm, seductiveness, and about as much reality as Maxfield Parrish prints. *Playboy* nudes have all the reality of their owners. Though Marilyn Monroe was borrowed, Jayne Mansfield and all the others have been *Playboy*'s own full-color photographic creations

[5] Quoted by Whitney, *op. cit.*

with lavish credit given the originals. These "Playmates of the Month" have another distinction which the pinup girls lacked. They show a manifest pleasure in the exhibition of their charms. The young actresses and models are forthright in the pleasure they take in pushing forward every claim they can make to all the attention they can attract. They appear in a roseate aura of unbounded self-approval. "Hey, look at me!"

To add to the piquancy of its famous feature *Playboy* runs stories of the girls pictured as they appear clothed driving their cars, seated at their desks, preparing gourmet meals in cute kitchens or wearing their Phi Beta Kappa keys as they read Kant or dabble casually in astrophysics. There is hardly a straight line in any of the other photographs, drawings of females or cartoons studded profusely through each *Playboy* issue of some 200 pages of editorial and advertising. They are all revealed in exaggerated curves.

It may all look like glorious abandon and carefree bacchanalian revelry. It is not. It is carefully calculated merchandise displayed for carefully calculated circulation, advertising, and financial ends. *Playboy* is edited and decorated as "The Man's entertainment Magazine." In nudes, hackneyed burlesque hall jokes, and cartoons it is no more coy than its models and bunny girls in going directly to the point. *Playboy* makes parenthetical acknowledgment of recorded music, show business, clothes, cars, and some of the arts, but its subject is, was, and will continue to be sex as entertainment—not its only subject, but its paramount, emphasized, and zealously cultivated subject.

Playboy is edited for the 18 to 34 year old urban male. It tries to appeal specifically to three groups within that age limit: those from 18 to 22; those 22 to 29; those 29 to 34. It hopes to captivate in addition other males under 50, but it concentrates on those most susceptible to its basic interest. The youngest can skip some of the solid and sometimes noteworthy editorial material which *Playboy* offers in increasing amounts.

In his first issues Hefner used reprinted articles and stories by established authors. He began to pay for original manuscripts from well-known writers as soon as he could. At various times *Playboy* has published Hemingway, Dos Passos, Woolcott Gibbs, John Lardner, Ben Hecht, Evelyn Waugh, P. G. Wodehouse, John Steinbeck, Budd Schulberg, Carl Sandburg. It publishes avant-garde fiction, mostly of the kind that used to be set in the boudoir but now can be set in any convenient locale, and uses in it as in its jokes all of the four-letter words *The New Yorker* deletes. It can get very popular or very good authors because it pays well—$3,000 for the lead story in each issue. *Playboy* has achieved real secondary distinction through the prose in both fiction and non-fiction of distinguished writers.

Its editors—and it has a packed masthead though Hugh Hefner continues to set policy, develop ideas, and scrutinize the editorial and advertising in every issue—believe that the 18 to 34 year old urban male has a greater interest in ideas than his counterpart of the early years of the magazine had. This may or may not be so. What definitely is so is that *Playboy* provides social and political commentary by some of the biggest names in the business. It has run sound articles since its early years.

Playboy has been banned off and on and here and there, or earnest and usually self-appointed guardians of public morals have tried to get it banned. Twice it was pilloried in Baltimore when Hefner's brother Keith, who now works for him, was the "Mr. Toby" of a children's television program in that city. It was ruled obscene in Italy and refused the mails, but in September, 1968, Italy's Constitutional Court decided that the ban was unconstitutional. Even in Italy now *Playboy* goes through. Strictures, attacks, and restrictions placed upon it added to the delightful irony when in October, 1957, *Playboy* published the first part of a two-part article, "The Pious Pornographers" by Ivor Williams.[6] An excursion into "sex and sanctimony in the ladies' home jungle," the article merrily,

[6] This was a transparent pseudonym. The author signed the second part of his article, titled "The Pious Pornographers Revisited," and his later "Venus Defiled" about the confession magazines, William Iversen.

mercilessly, and deservedly took popular women's magazines apart for their smug exploitation of sex in stories and under the guise of confidential medical advice about obstetrics, menstruation, and copulation as a service to their enthralled readers. Under the title of the second part of the article the *Playboy* editors said, "a vivisection of the prim ladies' mags reveals that behind the medical advice and case histories, beneath the surface of soap-operatic fiction, there lurks a furtively morbid preoccupation with the seamier, steamier aspects of sex." Naming magazine and story, article or department, Iversen proved the point. *Cosmopolitan* took some punishment for its fiction in the amusingly and shrewdly written piece, but *Ladies' Home Journal* got most of the body blows.[7]

Playboy began editorial pleas for a sane nuclear policy in 1959, its articles drawing letters of praise from university presidents, politicians, editors, Steve Allen, and Lord Bertrand Russell. It has run articles by such of the grave and unimpeachably great as Senator J. William Fulbright, Supreme Court Justice William O. Douglas, J. Paul Getty, and comparable public figures. It publishes in depth question-and-answer interviews. One was with Arthur Schlesinger, Jr.; another with Dr. Martin Luther King, Jr. In June, 1968, it ran 19 full or part *New Yorker*-sized pages of a "candid conversation" with John Kenneth Galbraith, billed as "the protean economist, best-selling author, trenchant social critic, advisor to president kennedy, and former ambassador to india." *Playboy*'s questions were carefully prepared to evoke Galbraith's articulate and lengthy responses on a wide variety of social and political subjects.[8]

Playboy makes no attempt to fuse its cheesecake, banality, and one-subject jokes and cartoons with its thoughtful articles

[7] The young *Journal* editor whose letter approving Iversen's article *Playboy* printed soon ceased to be a young *Journal* editor.

[8] Among others Galbraith made the point that there was no prospect of a third-party movement sparked by George Wallace in the presidential race of 1968. He said that it was against the nature o Americans to countenance a third party and that it would be difficult to get a third party on the ballot in all 50 states.

and interviews. After all, sex and cerebration do not fuse in life. They coexist without, as *Playboy* might see it, cohabiting. People accept adolescence and maturity as conflicting elements in society that somehow manage to survive together

Playboy is mostly variations on a single theme, sex, but it also publishes serious articles on subjects of contemporary interest. (Copyright © 1968 by HMH Pub. Co., Inc., and reprinted with its permission.)

Sometimes they accept both at the same time in individuals they know and even in themselves. *Playboy* readers accept both in the magazine. Some 5,000,000 purchasers and more than 10,000,000 adult males approve the mixture every month.[9] *Playboy* has achieved repute for literary and intellectual achievement as well as reputation for purveying vicarious sexual enjoyment.

The sex is vicarious; titillation not satisfaction. In the magazine it is the striptease in print. In the Playboy Clubs with their hundreds of thousands of card-carrying members, diners and winers may look at the floor shows, night club acts, and the big-bosomed bunnies, but they may not touch. Bunnies, who can make as much as $350 a week in tips, are forbidden to date patrons, and *Playboy* employs its own investigators to make sure its restrictions are observed.

Hefner, who makes frequent television appearances, usually with some of his bunny "Playmates," almost always in his tuxedo and with his pipe, lives in an ornate Victorian mansion, well advertised as the Playboy Mansion, on Chicago's near North Side. Personal and administrative staffs serve him and his many and frequent guests there. In June, 1967, over 900 members of the headquarters Playboy organization moved into the 37-story Playboy Building on North Michigan Avenue. Hefner recognized early that his nightclubs might become even bigger business than his magazine, and the success of the Playboy Clubs has been even greater than he could have visualized. In Lake Geneva, Wisconsin, Playboy Clubs International operates a $9,000,000 complex of 1,000 acres which includes a 300-room hotel, a championship golf course, ski facilities, and a recreational program. Other such installations are planned.

Playboy has to owe large part of its success to the American heritage of puritan conventions and as much to the Victorian morality which reigned in the United States as well as in England for longer than Victoria herself ruled. The rest has to be the shrewdness and energy of Hugh Marston Hefner who once

[9] "PROFILE: THE PLAYBOY READER," Playboy Information Library. (Total audience figures based on Simmons & Brand Rating Index.)

considered himself an unjustly repressed young man and to the development of the magazine by capable editors and executives.

Playboy is a handsome and prosperous magazine which has won many awards for artistic production. *Playboy* is virile expression of complacent American virility. *Playboy* is adolescence whether the adolescent is 18, 34, or 50 going on 100. *Playboy* is literary quality and intelligent curiosity. *Playboy* is a house organ for all the other Playboy enterprises. The total of these various approximations may add to something more than 100 per cent or considerably less, but so does *Playboy.*

Playboy's fortuitous foster father, *Esquire,* was not happy with its offspring. Its president in 1957 made it clear that the two magazines should not be mentioned in the same breath. "Playboy wants to be compared with us, but we don't feel the magazines are in the same league." [10]

Esquire has even denied that it refused Hugh Hefner the additional five dollars weekly he demanded as the price of moving to New York with the magazine in 1952. "We didn't invite him to move." [11]

Esquire itself, founded in 1933, once featured its own rabbit in a tuxedo in its symbolic character of "Esky," the pop-eyed, white-mustached and smartly senile reveler who chased determinedly through the lush pages of the magazine of men's fashions. Esky doesn't live at *Esquire* any more. At $1 a copy, *Esquire* has gone hip, mod, and in. It is iconoclastic and irreverent and like *Playboy* doing very well. With circulation over 1,000,000 and advertising revenue of $10,900,000 in 1968, it has its many admirers, mostly in the 33-year old "young executive" category.[12]

[10] Quoted by J. Howard Rutledge in *The Wall Street Journal,* April 19, 1957.

[11] Quoted by A. Kent MacDougall, *The Wall Street Journal,* May 8, 1968.

[12] *Newsweek* is another admirer. September 23, 1968, it described *Esquire* as "far more than a graduate Lampoon. Despite its pop flippancies and its facile impieties, *Esquire* is one of the brightest and most imaginative forces in journalism."

Chapter 21

All Networks, All Channels: *TV Guide*

Television is a fact of which the mass magazines are bitterly conscious. There were only a few thousand television sets in use in 1944, but there were 3,000,000 by the end of 1948. Twenty years later there were over 68,000,000. Some 94 per cent of United States homes have television. People with television in their homes spend more than five hours a day watching it. From 18 to 27 million homes watch television every evening and other millions during the daytime. The top-rated show reaches 17,000,000 homes and the tenth-rated about 14,000,000. The figures would be higher but, despite great technical advances, it is still uncomfortable to watch more than one program at a time.

When they are watching television, people are not reading magazines. The magazines know this and so do advertisers. Those wishing to reach a mass audience spend most of their advertising money in television. About 50 of the largest advertisers spend $5,000,000 or more annually in television and some of them—who once used magazines extensively—spend from about $50,000,000 to nearly $80,000,000.[1]

Television is immediate. The action is now. Moving, talking people appear on the screen. This is actuality or as nearly actuality as makes little difference to most people. They do not have to exert themselves to read about space flights, street riots, wars, Olympic contests, football games and all the rest

[1] Wood, James Playsted. *This Is Advertising*. New York: Crown Publishers, Inc., 1968.

anywhere from a day to a week after the event. They happen in the living room as you watch. You can wince at a hard tackle, smash out a home run, ogle the overflowing contents of a bikini, or nod in agreement with an omniscient commentator, all without leaving your chair. Politicians no longer need to have magazine articles ghost-written for them in order to promise voters everything and all at once. They can do it in person with all the benefits of smiles, grimaces, earnest voices, skillful lighting, and flattering makeup. Supplicants for every conceivable cause have the same advantages, and the viewer has more advantages than them all. He can choose between a talk show and the blast-off of a rocket from Cape Kennedy or between a detective mystery and a floorshow staged from "the Apollo Room, high above everything" by astronauts orbiting in outer space.

All this has had its many and varied effects on magazine editorial content and on magazine advertising. The magazines affect "spectaculars" in an attempt to match television spectaculars. They make full use of their remaining basic advantages. The television viewer has to be on the spot at the stated time to see and hear a program. He can read or reread a magazine article or story at his leisure; he cannot reread a television program.

If a subject, either editorial or advertising, necessitates detailed information or close argument, television cannot handle it. The magazine can inform at length, explain in detail, persuade at the reader's own speed. Occasionally television can produce and transmit a thoughtful piece, but usually the magazine can do it better. As the magazine industry knows too well, where mass audiences and mass markets are concerned, most of the remaining advantages—even color reproduction, which was once a magazine exclusive—lie with television.

In the face of this formidable and sometimes overpowering competition at least one periodical has proved the validity of the adage which advises joining them if you can't beat them.

Walter H. Annenberg founded *TV Guide* in Philadelphia in April, 1953, as one more of his Triangle Publications, Inc., which then included the Philadelphia *Inquirer,* the Philadelphia *Daily News, Morning Telegraph* and *Daily Racing Form, Seventeen,* and a half dozen radio-television stations scattered from New England to California.

Circulation of *TV Guide* reached 1,500,000 the first year. In 1968, published in 79 regional editions, *TV Guide* had an average weekly circulation of 14,000,000. It has a staff of more than 1,100 in 29 offices in the United States and Canada. In 1957 it moved about 300 people from Philadelphia to newly built offices in Radnor, Pennsylvania, a few miles west of the city on the Main Line. There are now 600 people in the editorial and business headquarters of the magazine in Radnor.

Just five years after its founding, *TV Guide,* which is promoted vigorously, could boast that it had the "Largest Circulation in Weekly Magazine History." [2]

It has become second only to *The Reader's Digest* in size of circulation of all United States magazines. In 1967 it was the sixth largest of all consumer magazines in advertising revenue, which was $45,800,000 for 1,634 pages. Advertising revenue for the magazine, which is spending $23,000,000 to expand its plant and communications systems, was given as $56,000,000 in November, 1969.[3]

Printed in gravure and offset sections, *TV Guide* is a listing, Saturday to Saturday, of all the television programs, times, stations, brief descriptions, where you live. That is the reason for all the regional editions, and there probably will be more of them. All editions carry the same national editorial matter. The day-by-day program details with concomitant advertising are in the center of the book. They are preceded by a yellow page, "TV Teletype," front-of-the-book TV movie criticism by

[2] A full-page promotion in *The New York Times,* August 1, 1957, was headlined: ". . . TV Guide, the most successful magazine . . . started since the war," a quotation from *Time,* July 8, 1957. A full-page advertisement in the *Times,* September 10, 1968, got down to the competitive details: "*TV Guide* beats Life, Look and the Digest in reaching the highest concentration of people married less than two years."

[3] Dougherty, Philip H., "Advertising: 15 Years on the Same Channel," *The New York Times,* March 31, 1968; *TV Guide* advertisement in *The Wall Street Journal,* April 22, 1968; *Newsweek,* Nov. 10, 1969.

Judith Crist, and a brief article or two on television personalities. They are followed by another one or two pieces of the same kind and the back-of-the-book program criticisms of Cleveland Amory.

Published in many editions and embellished with capsules of show business chitchat, *TV Guide* is a weekly program to television listening and viewing. (Reprinted with permission. Copyright © 1968 by Triangle Publications, Inc.)

The stories in each weekly issue of *TV Guide* are about the fabulous private lives, fabulous incomes, and fabulous performances of the fabulous stars. They are the movie magazine staples. Every male star is a loner and every famed movie and TV actress really a homebody, but the stories are not all goo. There is some guff. *TV Guide* gets sharp in its comments at times.

Laurence Olivier, Tiny Tim, Brian Keith, Mary Pickford, Tyrone Power, Clara Bow, Rowan and Martin, Fred MacMurray, Dean Martin, Theda Bara, Bob Hope, Tony Curtis, Greta Garbo, John Bunny, Mike Douglas, Grace Kelly, John Barrymore, Claudette Colbert, Arthur Treacher . . . because old movies are listed and advertised along with the newest romps, the names of all the motion picture and television personalities since the beginning of each medium seem to appear again and again. All of them were always sure-fire copy.

The usefulness of *TV Guide* is obvious. Its publishers like to call it a "magazine of essentiality." There are those who do not consider it a magazine at all. It is the universal theatre program. It gives the names and numbers of all the players. It gives you the inside dope on what's to come. It is the week's timetable of the times that really matter. The editorial content of *TV Guide* could hardly be thinner as it skims the gossip of the television rialto and hands out the behind-the-scenes tidbits that have always fascinated. It doesn't hurt anybody, and it pleases many millions.

About the same height but nearly a half inch narrower and much thinner than *The Reader's Digest, TV Guide* is on sale in display racks at about 350,000 checkout counters in food outlets throughout the United States and Canada. All of the major food chains and many independent markets distribute it. It is easy for the housewife to pick up a fifteen-cent copy and shove it along with the cans and packages for tally at the cash register. *TV Guide* is as much a household staple as salt or cereal.

The publication has had and still has many competitors. Most newspapers list television programs, stations, and times.

Many Sunday newspapers carry full programs for the week. People could easily obtain the information they wish from other sources. That so many prefer to use *TV Guide* is an indication that it serves up its fare in form they like.

TV Guide has had its magazine competitors as well. Annenberg founded it by purchasing program publications in New York, Chicago, and Philadelphia, then adding several more. For a time it even had competition just down the street in Philadelphia. The then still mighty but uneasy Curtis Publishing Company started *TV Week*. It lasted for a few issues in 1955.

Possibly *TV Guide* is less magazine than what it says it is, a guide. Whatever it is, it is devoured. In many homes it is used as much as or more than the telephone book. As television is the most characteristic communications phenomenon of contemporary American civilization, it is equally possible to see *TV Guide* as the country's most characteristic magazine.

Chapter 22

The Supermarket Magazines

The supermarket has become a leader in the single-copy sales of consumer magazines. They distribute virtually all of the large consumer periodicals, the movie and confession magazines, comics, and one-shot paperbound books and periodicals. Long open shelves invite browsing and purchases of all kinds of magazines. Near the checkout counters are *TV Guide, The Reader's Digest* in their special racks, and then one of the women's magazines specifically designed to reach the housewife who is doing her family food shopping. Originally the best-known of these magazines were published and sold by food wholesalers and retailers. Ownership has changed but not the intent and coverage of the magazines which have had their real development since World War II and the growth of self-service shopping-center supermarkets.

Editorially directed to the housewife and used by advertisers to appeal to women as purchasers of food, clothing, appliances, and other household goods, these grocery-distributed magazines resemble the women's general and service magazines which they imitate and physically approximate. They differ in that they were originally published and are still distributed as adjuncts to the food business.

These magazines are not sold by subscription nor in drug stores, hotel lobbies, airplane and railroad stations, and the like. They reach the supermarket operator with his dog biscuits, furniture polish, and myriads of other food and non-food items and are sold with them.

Competition and other forces have been at work. Perhaps a dozen of these magazines were started. In the early 1950's there were four giants. Two of the larger grocery-distributed women's magazines remain; as it happens, they were the earliest founded.

Though standards of editorial selection and mechanical reproduction vary, the store-distributed magazines are attractive. They are thinner and smaller in page size than most of the leaders, but they look like the larger-circulation women's magazines. Cover pictures are pleasant and enticing. In general, the printing, whether by letterpress or gravure, is good. Illustrations are colorful. The contents of the magazine—and they range from thoughtful in the best of the group to flimsy in the least prepossessing—are easy to read, sensible, and realistic in their approach to the interest and problems of the middle- and lower-income-group housewife and her family.

They have been called "primarily 'how to do it' primers,"[1] but they are more than that. There are recipes which are generally inexpensive and practical. There are menus which the housewife in ordinary circumstances can use. There are fashion articles with dress patterns given or made available. There are diet discussions, beauty hints, discussions of child care, safety or other problems in which the family is interested. There is movie news. Public affairs, thoughtful biographies, discussions of international problems, subjects which call for educated tastes and appreciations are generally, and properly, left to the established women's magazines; but the store-distributed magazines provide glamor in their mildly romantic, safely domestic fiction, sometimes in an occasional travel article, and always in their illustrations. The names of well-known writers, though seldom attached to their most seriously considered output, appear frequently in two of the grocery magazines.

During the economic depression of the 1930's stores of The Great Atlantic & Pacific Tea Company throughout the country

[1] "Food Store Magazines Hit the Big Time," *Business Week,* February 9, 1952.

began to publish and distribute gratis to their customers a menu leaflet. The A & P leaflet told the housewife how to get the most for her food dollar, then how to use the food purchased to provide her family with appetizing and nourishing meals. The menu was so well accepted that plans were laid in 1937 to enlarge it into a magazine, and a contest was run to select a name for the proposed publication.

The planned magazine was to be, like the menu, a free service to A & P customers. A circulation of 775,000, the same as that of the menu leaflet, was envisioned. The first issue of *Woman's Day* appeared in 1937. It was of 32 pages, six of them given over to recipes and menus. There was one article on "What To Do About Worry" and another which asked, "Is Football Worthwhile?"

Policy was set in this first issue of October, 1937. This statement appeared in the opening pages.

> Running a home and caring for a family successfully is one of the hardest jobs in the world. You have to be a combination politician, nurse, cook, maid-of-all work, interior decorator, mind-reader, teacher, dressmaker, shopper and bookkeeper. You never have enough money to do all the things you want to do—and the job gets pretty tiresome at times. Maybe we can get together and help make this job easier . . .

Understanding sisterly sympathy and practical advice were the keynote not only of *Woman's Day,* but also of the other store magazines; and woman in just one of her listed onerous occupations was the target, woman as shopper.

Immediate demand sent the circulation of the new magazine up far beyond what had been planned. It was no longer possible to distribute it without charge. After various tests had been run, the price was set at five cents a copy. The magazine sold for five cents until 1951 when, as a result of rising production costs, the price was raised to seven cents. By that time the magazine had grown tremendously in circulation, in size, and in editorial coverage. A year later, 1952, *Woman's Day* could state in its advertising, "More women go out and buy *Woman's Day* than any other magazine in the world." Average sale per issue at that time was given in the magazine's trade advertising as 3,793,000, and the magazine, which is held at a 60–40 editorial-advertising ratio, was carrying more than $6 million annually in advertising.

While it was wholly owned by The Great Atlantic & Pacific Tea Company and distributed only through its stores and supermarkets, *Woman's Day* made itself one of the large and significant women's magazines. Fiction, reputable feature articles, good writing, and excellent art work, color photography, and reproduction made it a formidable competitor of the standard women's magazines, both for readership and advertising revenue.

The main departments in every issue were Articles and Fiction, the largest; Home Workshop and Decorating; Needlework; Fashion; Food. Under other monthly features came News and Gossip, a section which includes notes on the contributors to each issue; Neighbors, comprised of letters from readers; movie critiques; and miscellaneous discursive, essay-type offerings. In the popular trend, *Woman's Day* has run how-to-do-it material since its first issue. Beginning with 1947 it ran a complete how-to section—its subtitle, "How To Make It—How To Do It—How To Fix It."

Woman's Day developed an enviable rapport with the audience it elected to reach. Readers write in, asking how to repair a roof, how to stop the baby's crying, how to build this or cook that, how to control a child or a husband. They are gratifyingly eager to purchase special items offered in the magazine's editorial pages.

The store-distributed magazines do not have the prestige of the big-name women's periodicals, neither the prestige nor the awesomeness of great reputation. Possibly for this reason, they seem more approachable to many of their readers. There is often the simpler reason that women readers like what they see pictured and described in the magazine's pages and want it.

In 1954 *Woman's Day* ran a series of Audubon bird prints so reproduced that they could be cut out and framed. The magazine received requests for an additional 55,436 sets of the prints, and another 45,000 requests for a series of colored flower prints run in the same year. Patterns for sweaters, plans

The *pièce de résistance* is hamburger delectably translated and appetizingly displayed, but this *Woman's Day* cover in 1956 combines the allure of food with baseball, a film star, and educational appeal.

for lawn furniture, directions for building a skiff, all featured in the magazine, drew hundreds of thousands of requests. A *Woman's Day* piece featured a special fabric for use with a housedress pattern. The manufacturer of the cloth reported sales of a million yards as a result of the *Woman's Day* writeup and its promotion.

Entire communities have been stirred to action by *Woman's Day* features. An October, 1953, article, "Teen-Agers Can Be Skilled—Not Killed," told of the success of a road driving program sponsored by the Junior Chamber of Commerce. Over 30,000 requests for posters on the subject, which the magazine offered, poured in from schools, clubs, and police organizations. Within a few weeks after issue date of the magazine, the Junior Chamber of Commerce received 150 inquiries on how to set up similar programs in other communities.

A comparable article on a schoolchildren's bicycle safety campaign in White Plains, New York, brought a comparable response. Requests for posters offered to stimulate interest in bicycle safety came in from all over the country. Florida used its entire state police force to distribute the posters to all its schools.

Many *Woman's Day* articles, such as its pleasant "Old Autos Never Die" in February, 1955, had not the remotest connection with the sale of foods or other supermarket products, but it was its close alliance with the food wholesaling and retailing industry which got the very successful magazine into trouble in 1956. Two Chicago wholesalers and 23 food retailers brought antitrust suits against A & P, *Woman's Day*, General Foods Corp., Hunt Foods, Inc., and Morton Salt Co. They also asked $3,000,000 in damages. Essentially, the complaint was that A & P operated *Woman's Day* as a competitive device to increase store traffic and that it had a captive audience. The food companies sued were heavy advertisers in *Woman's Day*, and the plaintiffs claimed that these companies did not give them comparable advertising advantages.

In 1957 both A & P and *Woman's Day* were cleared in a court decision of the charges against them. In his opinion Federal Judge William C. Campbell, sitting in Chicago, said in part, "Woman's Day is accepted by the public as an excellent magazine and by established advertising agencies as an excellent advertising medium." [2]

Despite this decision in its favor A & P sold *Woman's Day* in 1957 to Fawcett Publications, Inc., which printed the magazine and had taken on its distribution. Fawcett maintained the format and general content of *Woman's Day* but began immediately to expand its distribution in other than A & P outlets. Competition among the grocery-distributed magazines is sharp. Chains sometimes switch from one magazine to another. Circulation expands when new stores of a carrying chain are opened, contracts if a chain closes some of its outlets.

Woman's Day, once an A & P exclusive, is now distributed by 50 food chains. By July, 1967, it was in all Safeway outlets. Safeway had previously been a *Family Living* exclusive. *Woman's Day* is still practical. "How To Make Inexpensive Clothes Look Great," for instance, but it goes a little further than it did with "Secret World of the Newborn Baby" and "The Pill and a Mother's Responsibility" by Pearl Buck—who won the Nobel Prize for literature in 1938 with quite different material. Its 1967 circulation of more than 6,355,000 placed *Woman's Day* tenth in size among all United States magazines. Its advertising revenue of over $8,000,000 for the first six months of 1968 was six per cent higher than that for the same six months of 1967. During the year its circulation rose to over 8,500,000 and its advertising revenue another 10 per cent in the first half of 1969.

Founded in 1939 and distributed originally by one of the largest wholesale grocers, *Everywoman's* was later purchased by the Cuneo Press. Its widespread sale through such supermarkets as Food Fair, National Tea, Gristede Brothers, and other chains began in 1951. Published in four sectional editions, it had a total net paid average circulation of about 1,700,000 in 1956.

Like its larger counterparts, *Everywoman's* carried romantic fiction, feature articles, and fashion and beauty departments. A monthly "Memo" (To: Everywoman; From: The Editor) was

[2] Quoted in *Woman's Day* advertisement, *Advertising Age,* August 12, 1957.

used to establish rapport with the reader. The magazine's title was repeated in many features: "Everywoman Wears Blouses in the Spring"; "Everywoman Is Beautiful thru Pregnancy," "Everywoman's Woman." "That Man is Here" provided whimsical "man talk" as, presumably, the earnest housewife likes to hear it. Often the talk got around to food and drink.

The largest department in *Everywoman's* was "Food and Equipment." Food, drink, menus, recipes, illustrations of pastries, colorful salads, and decorative servings bulked large in the magazine's pages. Full-page or double spread advertisements of food distributors rang changes on the theme with more extravagant illustrations in the advertising pages. The family table was very much the heart of the matter. The commercial intent of *Everywoman's* was hardly disguised. By 1958 the magazine had disappeared into the larger *Family Circle.*

Better Living, which made its initial appearance in May, 1951, was founded jointly by the McCall Corporation and a group of capitalists including Nelson Rockefeller, Clendenin Ryan, and Douglas Dillon. It was published in New York by Mass Markets, Inc., and distributed through stores operated by members of the Super Market Institute. Unlike the three store-distributed magazines already mentioned, *Better Living,* which was printed by *McCall's* and offered as a part of a *McCall's–Better Living* advertising package, was a larger magazine when it started than subsequently it became. Selling at five cents a copy, it began with an issue of 100 pages, 42 of them advertising, and a circulation guarantee of 1,500,000. The magazine's circulation rose to over two and a half million in 1954. It began to lose both circulation and advertising in the first quarter of 1956. In April, 1956, it was announced that publication would cease with the May issue.

In general, though it was thinner in number of pages and in scope and depth of editorial content, *Better Living* carried the same type content as the other store-distributed periodicals. Monthly it published one or two pieces of fiction, features which seem of less general magazine appeal than those in its contemporaries, beauty and fashion departments, and a large section on foods. A department called "Let's Shop" told of new items on sale in supermarkets and where to buy clothes and gadgets mentioned in the editorial matter. Markedly throughout the publication the emphasis was on foods and on the supermarket.

Oldest of the large-circulation, store-distributed women's monthlies, *Family Circle* was established in New York by Family Circle, Inc. and for some years was distributed through a nation-wide chain of stores at seven cents a copy. Though the list is apt to change, it includes or has included First National, Grand Union, Safeway, Stop and Shop, Bohack, American, Acme, Dixie Home, Winn & Lovett, Albers, Kroger, Butt, Red Owl, and now A & P. Like *Woman's Day,* it is published in numerous sectional editions which provide distribution paralleling distribution of the advertiser's product.

Family Circle's largest feature in the 1950's was "All Around the House," which covered food, household equipment, home building, and home furnishings. Under "Your Children and You" were pieces on child care, parent–child relationships, and party suggestions. Movie notices came under "The Reel Dope" and gossip about contributors under "The Personal Touch." Divorce, teen-age problems, sports, travel, and gardening were the usual feature subjects. In April, 1955, Quentin Reynolds was an expert on the problems of adolescence with "Help Over the Teen-Age Hurdle." In September, Herman Hickman explained that "Football Is a Ladies' Game." In May, Art Linkletter told "Why People Are Funny." Richard Armour supplied the humorous verse in many issues.

Family Circle seemed simple and relatively unsophisticated. Very domestic in its approach, it made much of homemade fun, offered quantities of figure and complexion advice, and generally advised its readers on how to enjoy life happily and healthfully.

Now a property of Cowles Communications, Inc., publishers of *Look,* the current *Family Circle,* which emanates from Mount Morris, Illinois, at twenty cents a copy, is a different magazine. Though it carries the usual food, beauty, health, child care, and home decorating departments, it has broadened its coverage to include matter of general interest, and certainly it has changed in appearance. As splendidly produced as *Look* itself, *Family Circle* is a substantial magazine running over 100 pages in most issues and extravagant in its use of color. The magazine is as pretentious as the general women's monthlies, as smartly designed, and as colorful.

Your horoscope by Santha Rama Rau and "On Sex in Marriage" by Ann Landers—you can hardly do better than that either. An interview with Truman Capote on violence in the United States—"Raise Your Child's IQ"—four pages of beautiful girls, *Look*-style close-ups, showing "coast-to-coast hairdos from 10 top stylists." *Family Circle,* which in effect gives Cowles a strongly competitive woman's magazine in a profitable market, is modern, fast-paced, and aggressive, but it does not neglect any of the tried and true devices which give the grocery-distributed magazines their mass audience and their value as advertising media.

The November, 1968, issue—the November issue of any monthly is, of course, a key issue for holiday advertising—was packed with "Gifts to make while you watch TV" (a neat trick), calenders to make, plenty of recipes calling for plentiful consumption of food store products, pages of shopping hints. Center of the book was given to four handsome pages of living room interiors with a jump to the advertising pages in the back of the issue where a list of stores and locations showed where all the furniture, paintings, draperies, and all the rest displayed could be purchased.

The *Everywoman* name survives in "Everywoman's Shopping Circle." In this issue it was nine pages of small-space advertisements for a welter of skirt hangers, magnifying reading glasses, sweaters for tall or big men, animal traps, "Identical Forms" for wear after breast surgery, playhouses for pets, ship models, and even "Brothers United," one photograph showing John F. Kennedy and Robert Kennedy together in profile. This issue of *Family Circle* had six more pages of small-space advertisements in vivid color and bound in among them the multi-page catalogue of inexpensive gifts, all shown in bright colors, of a mail-order house. It was all advertising but it was practical, useful advertising for the housewife Christmas shopping for family and friends. Any one of them might need a U. S. Medical Corps stethoscope or a patented fire escape ladder.

Under Cowles, *Family Circle* reached seventh place in circulation among all United States magazines, but its circulation dropped 12 per cent in 1968. In England where it is published in cooperation with a London publisher, *Family Circle* is the largest selling British monthly for women. In Germany, *Family Circle* is *Ich und meine Familie.* Though average circulation guarantee was dropped from 7,500,000 to 7,000,000 in 1967, the domestic *Family Circle* took in over $10,000,000 in advertising during the first six months of 1969.

Editorial and advertising sections are even more frankly complementary in the grocery-distributed magazines than in the general women's magazines. Aimed at a specific mass market, these periodicals are rife with advertising for products that the housewife buys or can be persuaded to buy. All of these magazines are strongly promoted for their usefulness as advertising media of this kind.

Often it appears that recipes and menus blown up in the pages of one or another of these periodicals are intended specifically to promote the sale of slow-moving or seasonal grocery items. Many of them call for specialties rather than for staples. Prepared mixes get great play in the culinary concoctions featured, and new items being marketed by canners or processors of frozen foods are not neglected. The impression is unavoidable that the left hand is shrewdly aware of what the right hand is doing—and rather hopes it will soon be shoveling a few million mouthfuls of high-profit-margin food into the great consuming maw.

Chapter 23

Magazine Advertising

Advertising supported and fattened the literary and intellectual magazines of the United States—*Harper's,* the *Atlantic,* the *Century,* and the others—in the second half of the 19th century and the first decades of the 20th. It made possible the popular weeklies and monthlies founded in the 1880's and 1890's when astute businessmen saw the profit possibilities in the second-class postal act of 1879.

All of today's leading magazines depend on advertising for the greater part of their revenue. If their incomes were limited to the prices paid for subscriptions and for single copies bought at newsstands, most would show impressive deficits at the end of the year. As business, communications, and entertainment are organized in the United States it is advertising which pays for the spread of public information through the press, both newspaper and magazine, over the radio, and on television. National advertising began in magazines which until the commercial advent of radio in the late 1920's were the sole means of taking an advertising message simultaneously to all parts of the country, and for many years magazines constituted the leading vehicle for the transmission of national advertising.

In this way magazines played a leading role in originating modern methods in the distribution of manufactured goods and products, and national advertising in magazines has been one of the chief supports of this system of distribution. By mass selling through their advertising magazines helped make mass production possible.

By enticing with the delights of automobiles, appliances, packaged foods, liquor, tobacco, travel, jewelry, clothing—all the necessities and luxuries industry could produce—magazine advertising changed the tastes and habits of the greater part of the population. There is not too much exaggeration in the often-repeated claim that magazine advertising was a primary force in raising the vaunted American material standard of living to what its admirers like to think it is.

There has been magazine advertising since magazines have existed. Addison's comments in 1710 on the advertising in *The Tatler* were noted earlier. In 1758 Dr. Samuel Johnson wrote: "The trade of advertising is now so near perfection that it is not easy to propose any improvement." In this instance, Dr. Johnson proved his fallibility. Advertising has not yet attained perfection.

The first advertisement in an American periodical is said to have been run in Andrew Bradford's *Weekly Mercury*, a Philadelphia newspaper. In its issue for December 29, 1719, a Phillip Ludwell of Green Spring, Virginia, advertised for a runaway slave. The next year the *Mercury* carried its first product advertisement, one for a patent medicine manufactured by one Frank Knowles. Early magazine advertisements were mostly announcements and notices of various kinds together with the claims of various specifics, listings of books and magazines, and a few outright advertisements for such articles as anthracite ornaments, cheap coffins, India rubber shoes, and patent straw cutters.

In those magazines which carried them at all, the advertisements appeared in columns where notices of the removal of a business from one location to another, marriages, births, deaths, offers of fifty-cent rewards for "indented" apprentices who had run off, notices of public sales, and the claims of compound syrup of sarsaparilla for the cure of scrofula, white swellings, pains in the bones, scaly eruptions, and "all disorders arising from an impure state of the blood" were all run in together. The advertisements were short, an inch or two, three or four at the most, in eye-tearing type. A few were decorated with printer's ornaments or small engravings.

Many of the early magazines completely eschewed advertising. It gained entrance gradually into the stronger periodicals during the second half of the nineteenth century. *The Atlantic*

$5 Reward.

RAN away, on the 15th of 8th month, from the subscriber, living in Willistown, Chester county, an indented apprentice to the farming business, named WM. HART, aged about 18 years, of a light complexion and hair, of a forward, talkative disposition. Said boy had on and took with him a blue cloth coat, red striped and blue cotton pantaloons, figured waistcoat, fur hat, and sundry other clothing. All persons are forbid harbouring or employing said boy at the peril of the law. Whoever takes up said boy and lodges him in jail in Chester, Delaware, or Philadelphia county or city, so that I receive information of him, shall receive the above reward.

aug 23—3t* MORDECAI THOMAS.

Five Dollars Reward.

RAN away on the 10th of August, from the subscriber, living in Blockley township, Philadelphia county, near Haddingtonville, an apprentice boy, by name JAMES ROBERTS, eighteen years of age, and large of his age, dark complexion, brown hair, grey eyes, and marked J. R. on one arm. Had on striped pantaloons, white roundabout, Marseilles waistcoat, and fur hat. Came back on night of same day, broke open the house, and stole a green cloth coatee, waistcoat, boots, and sundry other articles. Whoever brings back the said boy, or will lodge him in jail, so that I can get him again, shall receive the above reward.

aug 23—3t* WM. CARTER, Farmer.

A Teacher wants a Situation.

A YOUNG man who has had some experience in teaching, and who is well acquainted with the various branches of a polite English education (including Natural Philosophy and Chemistry,) who is also qualified to teach the higher branches of mathematics, desires a situation in a good school, or private family. Satisfactory testimonials of character and qualifications will be given. A few lines addressed to H. Q. W. (post paid) Jefferson College, Canonsburg, Pa., will meet with immediate attention.

P. S. The applicant would have no objections to teach a class of Latin scholars. aug 23—3t*

Early advertisements often were simply notices. Runaway apprentices and a job-hunting teacher occupied paid space in *The Saturday Evening Post*, September 6, 1834.

Monthly, which carried none of it during its first three years, began to accept advertising in 1860. By May, 1866, its entire back cover was given over to the advertising of photographic materials, albums, stereoscopes, photographic cards, and a "Complete Photographic History of the Great Union Contest." The inside front cover advertised the Florence Lock-Stitch Sewing Machine (Best in the World! Great Simplicity! Great Capacity!); and Steinway & Son's Grand, Square, and Upright PIANOFORTES. Small-space advertisements for steel pens, tonics, nursing bottles, shoe dressings, life insurance, carpet sweepers, and window shades filled the back pages of the issue. In 1868 the *Atlantic* carried advertising for Tiffany and Company, Clark's Cotton, The Great Atlantic & Pacific Tea Company, the electro-plated flatware of the Gorham Manufacturing Company, and New Grecian Style Billiard Tables.

Those were the more respectable of the advertisements. Cosmetics and patent medicines were more in evidence: Turner's Tic Doulereux or Universal Neuralgia Pill, "the Undoubted Cure for All Excruciating Ills Known as Neuralgia or Nervous Ache"; Dr. Babcock's Hair Dressing, its purity guaranteed by S. Dana Hayes, State Assayer for Massachusetts ("Scientific, Rational, Safe"): Russian Salve, "a pure vegetable ointment"; and Dr. J. W. Poland's Humor Doctor, "An Invaluable Medicine for Purefying the Blood." With brassy fanfare the *Atlantic* ballyhooed itself as unique in American literature and—as it had the proud right—listed Dickens, Emerson, Harriet Beecher Stowe, Grace Greenwood, Hawthorne, Whittier, Lowell, and Owen Meredith as contributors.[1]

For some years *Harper's* spurned all advertising except for books published by the house. In the early 1870's Fletcher Harper indignantly refused an offer of $18,000 a year for use of the last page by the Howe Sewing Machine Company, but twenty years later *Harper's* led all the other magazines in advertising volume.

Even the most literary and conservative of them all, *The North American Review,* which had such dignitaries as Ed-

[1] Wood, James Playsted. *The Story of Advertising.* New York: The Ronald Press Co., 1958.

ward Everett, Jared Sparks, James Russell Lowell, Henry Adams, and later Henry Cabot Lodge as editors, succumbed. It continued with its belletristic and historical approach but compromised its Boston and Harvard austerity by deigning to accept fifty pages of profitable assorted advertising in every issue.

Scribner's Monthly took some advertising from the start in 1870. When in 1881 Roswell Smith turned it into the *Century Illustrated Monthly Magazine,* he began the outright solicitation of advertising, took the lead in advertising volume and held it until 1890 when the worried *Harper's* began a comparable drive. *Harper's* soon far outstripped its rivals. By November, 1899, it carried 135 pages of advertising to 163 of editorial.

The dignified periodicals of literary and intellectual pretentions waxed prosperous and powerful on pages and pages of questionable advertising for questionable products—cures for the morphine habit, painless cures for hernia and rupture, all kinds of patent medicines, financial and real estate speculations as well as other advertisements for horseless carriages, soaps, schools, baby foods, shirts, watches. . . . A *North American* advertisement for Waterbury Watches in September, 1893, read like a track and stud farm notice: "Well-bred watches *result from noble ancestry,* early association, discipline, and natural selection."

Once they had opened their chaste pages to the suspect and at least mundane, the publishers of the literary monthlies considered an advertisement an advertisement. It occupied paid space. It brought in gold, and *caveat emptor* was both classical Latin and sound advice. Advertising reforms were a generation away, and the new nickel and dime magazines for the vulgar were yapping at the heels of the respectably established magazines.

The first to recognize the possibilities of national magazine advertising, Cyrus H. K. Curtis founded the *Ladies' Home Journal* in Philadelphia primarily as an advertising medium, not, as the older magazines had been founded, as a vehicle for editorial expression and communication. He was exploiting advertising to the full in the *Journal* and in 1897 used it to reestablish the moribund *Saturday Evening Post,* again as an instrument for transmitting advertising rather than primarily as a magazine for readers to read.

Business was quick to recognize the power of the force intensified and expanded by the popular magazines. In 1892 the astute Chauncey M. Depew, then president of the New York Central and Hudson River Railroad, said: "Every enterprise, every business, and I might add every institution, must be advertised in order to be a success. Talk in any other strain would be madness."[2] In the same year Pennsylvania Railroad spent $230,000 in advertising, and the Union Pacific almost as much.

In 1888 George Eastman invented the portable camera which he named "Kodak." He spent $25,000 in advertising the new device that first year. By 1895 magazine advertising had made "Kodak" and camera almost synonymous. Ivory Soap was being advertised by Proctor & Gamble in the magazines of the early 1880's as "$99^{44}/_{100}$% pure." Its advertisement in *The Independent,* November 12, 1885, read: "Did it ever occur to you how much cleaner and nicer it is to wash the Napkins Towels, Handkerchiefs, Table Linen, etc., by themselves with soap *not* made of putrid fats or questionable grease? Do it with Ivory Soap . . . made of vegetable oil, and use them confident that they are clean and not tainted." The Ivory Soap slogan has been in use ever since. It is perhaps one of the best examples of continuity and consistency in advertising. It staggers the imagination to contemplate how many billions of cakes of Ivory Soap that continued repetition of its time-honored slogan has sold.

The same 1885 issue of *The Independent* carried advertisements for Esterbrook's Pens, Royal Baking Powder, Columbia Bicycles, LePage's Glue, R. H. Macy & Co., Connecticut Mutual Life Insurance Company, Massachusetts Mutual, the Travelers, Chicago and North-Western Railway, and Weber Pianos, as well as for a dozen more insurance companies and advertisements for Congress boots (with a patent adjustable

[2] Quoted in *Printers' Ink, Fifty Years.*

lace), corrugated picket fences, a scientific system of protection from lightning, reversible collars and cuffs, curtain grates, cures for deafness, and the Grand Union Hotel at Saratoga Springs.

By 1890 more advertisers had joined Kodak and Ivory Soap and those already mentioned in making their company names and the names of their products more widely known. A few were Rambler Bicycles, Rogers & Brother, Remington Standard Typewriter (and Densmore, Williams, Caligraph and No. 4 Yost), Hires Root Beer, Rubifoam for the Teeth, Ed Pinaud's, Packer's Tar Soap, Scott's Emulsion, Pyle's Pearline, Mellin's Food, Walter Baker Cocoa, W. L. Douglas Shoes, Castoria, Buffalo Lithia Water, and Sapolio. In an 1894 advertisement Mt. Holyoke College, opening for its fifty-eighth year, was advertising board and tuition for $250.

By 1900 the names which magazine advertising was making familiar to everyone included these and many more: Ivory Soap, Sapolio, Royal, Postum, Lea & Perrin's Sauce, Pettijohn's Flaked Breakfast Food, Welch's Grape Juice (for "Young and Old"), Cream of Wheat, Van Camp's Concentrated Soups, Knox's Gelatine, Hires, 1847 Rogers Bros., Cable Pianos, American Radiator Co., Smith & Wesson ("A Smith & Wesson Revolver is the choice of the Japanese Navy"), Hart, Schaffner & Marx (Varsity Summer Suits at $10, $12, and $14), Wheatena, Johnson's Prepared Wax, Globe-Wernicke, Standard Sanitary Manufacturing Co., Anita Cream, Cascarets, Woodbury's Facial Soap, Cuticura, Boston Garters, President Suspenders, Stein-Bloch Clothes, Lowney's Chocolates, Regal Shoes, Armour & Co., Boston & Maine Railroad (and all the other railroads).

The *pièce de résistance* in the June, 1901, issue of *McClure's Magazine* was an inset full-page advertisement in full color on cardboard, obviously lithographed and beautifully reproduced, for products of the National Biscuit Company. One side of the inset page showed a girl in Dutch costume holding a package of Uneeda Biscuits. The legend, lettered across her wide white skirt, read: "Do You Know You Needa Biscuit?" The reverse of the sheet pictured Ramona sugar wafers appetizingly dis-

Magazine advertising popularized Pears Soap. Pears ceased advertising and disappeared. Its copy in *McClure's*, June, 1901, quoted Winston Churchill, "English war correspondent."

played on delicately colored china, and Athena wafers tumbling out of an upset cookie jar.

This advertising not only made the names of these companies and these products known in households all over the country, but it changed fundamentally the sales methods of manufacturers and the buying habits of consumers. Magazine advertising brought about the sale of goods and products nationally and accustomed purchasers to buy not the articles made and sold locally, but those made and sold on the larger market.

It created new desires in the minds of readers, desires that grew into needs and resulted in purchases. By increasing consumer demands and arousing new ones, the advertisers stimulated the processes of invention. Manufacturers who had previously made their products only on the comparatively small orders, and often to the specifications, of jobbers catering to the retail trade in a few localities, found themselves working for a far larger and very different market. To meet the greatly increased demand from the ultimate consumers of their products in every section of the country reached through magazine advertising, manufacturers were forced into product improvements and into mass production. Mass production for this newly created mass market necessitated improved and more economical methods of manufacture. This resulted in lower prices which, in turn, made the product available to more and more people. Articles once luxuries, obtainable only by the affluent, became available to the average man and woman.

Advertising increased the competition among manufacturers. Only the manufacturer, large or small, making a good product and succeeding in making that product well and favorably known, could retain his share of the market. Those making inferior merchandise and failing to advertise usually failed. Advertising brought the consumer not only a cheaper, but also an improved article.

The whole process of distribution has had to be enlarged and improved as a result of the huge new markets which advertising has created. Faster, more efficient, and less wasteful methods have had to be instituted to get more and more goods to a continually enlarged market. In all of these and other ways advertising has operated to change the living habits of the American people. It has provided them with those products which science and industry have devised to lessen drudgery in the home and in the office or factory, thus aiding the health and increasing the leisure of the housewife and the worker. It has educated people to demand material and mechanical conveniences unknown to earlier generations, stimulated the production of these conveniences to meet their demands. Magazine advertising has, as its proponents point out, been a causative factor in bringing more and better material things to more people at a lower cost.

As new products have been invented, developed, and perfected, they have been brought to the attention of the public through magazine advertising. The automobile industry, for instance, was quick to capitalize on the selling force of national advertising in magazines, and this advertising was largely responsible for the wide and rapid acceptance of the new vehicle by the American public. Through creating the popular demand that made mass production imperative and economically possible, it helped bring the price (pre-World War II) down to where a car could be purchased by the average family. Other mechanical conveniences—the electric refrigerator, the washing machine, the other household appliances—reached the people who use them largely through the same channel.

The use of advertising of this kind is closely tied to the whole conception of brand merchandise. Magazine advertising on a large scale and the growth of small industries and business organizations to the stature of manufacturers and distributors of nationally known and purchased brands of specific merchandise were coeval. Most consumer advertising in magazines is intended to support the distributor and retailer and to establish and maintain a company or brand name favorably in the public mind.

Trade-marks were originally imposed upon the craft guilds of the Middle Ages as a protection for the public. They were intended as a means of identifying the maker of an article so as to fix responsibility for inferior materials or poor workmanship. The compulsion made the use of good materials and the application of good workmanship a necessity for guild members who took pride in their product, wished to avoid censure and punishment, and likewise wished approval for the articles they made. As a result the trade-mark became a prized asset and, later, a recognized mark of public confidence in a given brand.

It is these trade-marks or brands which are advertised nationally. The purchaser is taught to buy a given make of car, rather than another; to ask for soap or soup of a certain name, rather than for just soap or just soup. Advertising makes this name known; satisfactory use of the advertised product makes that advertising believable. The brand name comes to serve as a guarantee of the good faith and competence of the seller and the reliability of his product.

Advertising of this kind, which names a particular article and fixes responsibility for its manufacture, serves as a guide to the purchaser. It enables the purchaser to identify the article he prefers—and to avoid that brand of a product which he has learned does not meet his requirements. Without the identification made possible by the trade-mark which he has learned to recognize through magazine advertising, the consumer could discover only through repeated trial and error, an expensive process, which make of a given product will meet his needs and which will fail to do so. In this sense, brand advertising is a device for the mutual guidance of maker and buyer.

The consumer, who cannot know the intricacies of an automobile or a washing machine, or the technical specifications which must be met by materials of a stated quality, comes to know an advertised trade-mark, and to look for it or avoid it when he has need to make a new purchase. It is a reliable short cut which the consumer can use in making his purchase decisions; a device, in such a community as ours, of distinct social usefulness.

The owners of trade-marks, which they have established through the manufacture and sale of sound merchandise and through advertising their brands so well that people think of them as almost synonymous with the objects these brand names describe, place a high value on them. As long ago as 1915 it was said that the Royal Baking Powder Company, one of the first national magazine advertisers, considered its trademark worth just $1,600,000 a letter. In 1928 it was estimated that when the Postum Company paid $43,000,000 for Maxwell House Coffee, not less than $30,000,000 of that amount was for goodwill, for the advertised name. In 1935 Adolph Zukor was quoted as valuing the name "Paramount" at $15,000,000.

Actually, advertised brand names, assuming that the public has had satisfactory experience with the brand advertised, are invaluable. How large a part advertising plays in erecting and upholding their value can be seen from the experience of brands, once well and favorably known through magazine advertising, when they ceased to be advertised. Rubifoam and Sozodont dentifrices, once widely known and sold, disappeared from the market when their advertising ceased. Force and Egg-O-See breakfast foods went the same way. Pears Soap is a classic example. Pears placed its first national magazine advertising in 1901 and continued aggressive advertising for twenty years, spending more than a million dollars annually. The company, considering its brand well established, decided suddenly to cease advertising. Sales dropped $1,500,000 the first year, more the second. An attempt to regain lost ground through the resumption of magazine advertising after several years of falling sales was unsuccessful. Its market completely lost, the company was sold to a competitor.

Some of the effects of modern magazine advertising have been indicated. It went hand in hand with "big business" in consumer goods. Without it, it is doubtful that large companies and corporations, large manufacturing in many industries, would have developed or could exist. It seems hardly necessary to point out that this same advertising had the opposite effect of causing the virtual disappearance of smaller manufacturers and distributors in many lines. Just as magazines, through both their editorial and advertising contents, seem sometimes to have made everyone look and act alike on monotonously uniform Main Streets across the country, national advertising has helped to make successful local enterprise more difficult. It has made for economy and standardization, not for individual craftsmanship, not for art.

The importance of one economic function of advertising has become increasingly apparent since World War II. As C. H. Sandage has pointed out, American industry is now organized to produce goods and services far in excess of the basic requirements of consumers. To keep capital and the labor force adequately employed, we must consume more than we actually need. "A luxury or surplus economy," Sandage wrote, "cannot be built upon the physical needs of society. It is dependent primarily upon the psychological needs and wants of consumers. If capital, labor, and natural resources are to be combined to produce non-necessities, . . . the consuming public must be informed of their existence, educated as to their want-satisfying qualities, and persuaded to buy them. It is here that advertising plays an important role." [3]

There are many definitions and descriptions of advertising, each with its own refinements, but analysis of them is beside the subject here. Fundamentally advertising is information. It states where an article is for sale and obtainable, what the article is like, its uses, its quality, and usually its price. The article is described in terms which will make it appear attractive and desirable, and which will influence the reader to purchase it. Like every other tool, magazine advertising can be and has been misused. Especially in the early days of its modern development, advertising was marred by extravagant and fraudulent claims. Inferior merchandise was described as superior; injurious products were sold as healthful, and cure-nothings were described as cure-alls.

If only as a means of self-protection, magazines, were quick to recognize the need for control of the force of advertising. Both the public and the legitimate advertiser had to be protected from the quack and the advertiser who misrepresented

[3] C. H. Sandage, "The Role of Advertising in Modern Society," *Journalism Quarterly*, Winter, 1951, p. 32.

his product. In 1880 *Farm Journal* announced that it would refund to subscribers any loss sustained "by trusting advertisers who prove to be deliberate swindlers." The Curtis Publishing Company in 1892, when the *Ladies' Home Journal* still needed all the financial support it could obtain, firmly ruled out all patent medicine advertising. This was the real beginning of the move toward establishing standards in advertising.[4]

A second very influential move was made when the Curtis Advertising Code of 1910 was set up and adopted. This code stated that neither the *Ladies' Home Journal* nor *The Saturday Evening Post* would accept advertising meant to deceive or defraud. They would not accept medical or "curative" advertising, advertising which attacked the products of a competitor, advertisements for liquor, advertising from mail-order houses, blind advertising, any advertising of an immoral or suggestive nature, or any advertisements for installment buying. The *Journal,* in addition, would not accept financial, tobacco, or playing-card advertising. The *Post,* though it would accept advertising for reputable bonds, would accept no financial advertising of a highly speculative nature. Cigar or pipe but not cigarette advertising was acceptable for the *Post* of 1910. All advertising must meet stringent standards of responsibility before it can be published today in any of the reputable magazines.

Advertising is a method of selling, of making a product known, of obtaining the widest possible distribution for it. To create the desires that will lead to sales, it uses appeals of many kinds. It appeals to the mind with argument, to taste with artistic display, to fear, to ambition, to envy. It uses every possible device to convince the prospective buyer that he should purchase what the advertiser has for sale. Applied

[4] Ralph M. Hower says in *The History of an Advertising Agency, N. W. Ayer & Son at Work, 1869–1939* (Cambridge, Mass.: Harvard University Press, 1939), p. 449: "The main reform [in advertising] waited for the crusading efforts of Edward W. Bok of the Ladies' Home Journal, ably backed by his employer Cyrus H. K. Curtis. This reform began in 1892 with The Curtis Publishing Company's refusal to handle any patent-medicine advertising, and it reached its climax between 1904 and 1906 when the agitation for pure food and drug laws became nation-wide."

psychology is nowhere more cunningly used than in advertising.

Intent calculations and many skills are utilized in forming the presentation that the public finally sees in the pages of its magazines. The advertiser or his agency considers the kind of circulation as well as the extent of the circulation of a given magazine. He wants to know into what income brackets readers fall, where they live, what education they have, what their jobs or professions are. These facts the publisher makes known to him, and the approach of the advertisement is planned on the basis of these and other known factors. They determine, in part, whether the advertisement will inform, coax, wheedle, threaten, or simply announce; whether the display will be violent or delicately restrained. The methods and the emphasis will vary with the nature of the product, the magazine used as a medium, the potential purchasers the advertiser is trying to reach, whether the product is a necessity or a luxury, and whether the advertisement is designed primarily to create immediate sales, to build good will for a brand, or to make the reader receptive to the approach of a salesman.

The contention of those critics who consider advertising unfavorably is not that it is ineffective but that, socially, it is too effective. The prose descriptions and graphic displays of the advertiser have an insidious plausibility which makes expertly presented articles look larger than life and entirely too captivating. Advertising they see as the siren which lures men to their destruction by awakening cupidity and greed, and fastening their attention on the desire for material things. Their objections are based on moral and aesthetic grounds, and certainly there are kinds of advertising, though little of it is magazine advertising, which afford just grounds for complaint.

A point worth noting here was made by a group of Harvard professors who acted as advisory committee for a study of advertising and its effects. Their sharp coment was: "Advertising is sometimes criticized on the ground that as part of the capitalistic system of free enterprise it leads consumers to buy the wrong things and spend too much for them, whereas consumers would be better off if they bought different things and spent their money in different ways. When this criticism implies, as it often does, that someone in authority might better decide what things should be bought and how consumers should spend their money, then the essential clash is between rival ideologies of individualism and authoritarianism; and the basic argument is not really about advertising at all." [5]

The complaint is often made that advertising costs too much. Actually, advertising adds so small an amount to the cost of a product that it makes no appreciable difference in the price paid by the consumer, a price that would be many times higher if advertising did not provide the mass consumption which allows of the economies and efficiencies of mass production. The cost of advertising is said to average out at less than three cents of the consumer dollar. The cost of advertising of one brand of nationally advertised soups has long been estimated by its producer at seventeen hundredths of a cent per can. A manufacturer of national advertised biscuits reports his advertising expenditure at less than one tenth of a cent for a ten-cent package. On a passenger car the advertising amounts to about as much as the extra cost of white-wall tires.

Another frequently repeated charge is that advertising only urges people to buy this instead of that brand of the same commodity or to switch brands, with no net gain to consumption. Cigarette and soap manufacturers are among the heaviest and most competitive consumer advertisers. Advertising, as well as addiction to a minor vice of which the government no longer approves and a fever for cleanliness, must assume some of the responsibility for these increases. It must take an equal

[5] "A Statement of the Advisory Committee" prefaced to *The Economic Effects of Advertising* by Neil H. Borden (Chicago: Richard D. Irwin, Inc., 1942), p. xviii. The statement of the advisory committee was signed by Theodore H. Brown, Edmund P. Learned, Howard T. Lewis, Malcolm P. McNair, and Harry R. Tosdal.

responsibility for today's congested highways. Advertising, as well as the desire to go somewhere, anywhere, and most of the time, gave the United States to the automobile.

To the basic charge that advertising makes for vulgarization there can be no defense. It does. The whole process of democratization is one of leveling to a classless mean. Advertising, as one of the most vociferously operative agencies in that process, helps do just that. It makes products which were once the possessions of the privileged available to the masses. It stirs desire, dissatisfaction, and material ambition. It invades privacy. Often it violates good taste. The tendency of our society and our time is to do these things. Advertising is in the van of the forces destroying older values.

Whether its existence and use in magazines is good or bad, Americans are deeply conditioned to advertising. It is virtually inescapable. We see and hear it everywhere. We would feel somewhat uneasy without it.[6] Because we have little choice, we have learned to take advertising nearly as naturally as we breathe. We react to it almost by reflex. If a product is not advertised, we do not know it; if it ceases to be advertised, we forget it. We are apt to suspect the nonadvertised article when we come on it in a shop. Something must be wrong with it.

Magazine advertising, fortunately for the readers of periodicals, provides certain satisfactions in itself. For familiar, long-advertised products, it seems friendly and reassuring. The Fisk "Time To Re-tire" boy, the Campbell Soup kids, Aunt Jemima, the fox terrier listening to His Master's Voice were old friends. They have their modern counterparts. De Beer's diamond advertisements and Weyerhaueser woodland scene paintings are in themselves pleasant things to regard. There is a vicarious satisfaction to be gained from looking at the illustrations and reading the descriptions of luxury items most people could not possibly buy: unique creations in jewelry, costing into the

[6] During World War II, men in the armed services overseas received editions of popular magazines without the normal advertising contents. . . . The absence or decrease of advertising was keenly felt by the readers." Darrell Blaine Lucas and Steuart Henderson Britt, *Advertising Psychology and Research* (New York: McGraw-Hill Book Co., Inc., 1950) p. 657.

thousands of dollars, in *The New Yorker,* exotic furs in *Vogue.* It is warming to think you might look like the attenuated model in the ravishing Dior frock or the distinguished explorer-sportsman-epicure dining in the smart restaurant pictured in a *Holiday* travel advertisement. If you can't buy "The Best Car in the World," you can at least look at the picture of a Rolls Royce in an English magazine. Few can buy a Lincoln Continental, but there is pleasure for the many in looking at it in a fold-over advertisement in a magazine. Magazine advertising of this kind makes the reader feel a little larger than life, a little better than well. It offers a few moments of escape from pressing anxieties. It demands no thought. It presents dreams of a lovely world, and the reader is grateful. The pages of less splendid advertisements can give the same kind of pleasure as looking at a Sears, Roebuck catalogue on a rainy day in the country or looking at an L. L. Bean catalogue at any time. *Vogue* and *Harper's Bazaar* are read as much for their advertisements as for their editorial content. One suspects that the advertising in many magazines sometimes gives more satisfaction than the articles. Publishers like to think, and their promotion managers often claim, that some of the confidence readers have in an established magazine's editorial content, some of the warmth aroused in the reader by the humor, human interest, and sturdy thinking, is transferred to the advertising pages. The reverse action can and does take place. There has been advertising ever since a man claimed that something he had for sale or to barter was of superior quality, and certainly better than the comparable article which someone else had to sell or barter; but modern magazines have been largely responsible for the growth and development of advertising and for its marked effects on our economic and social life.

In other ways the advertising and commercial side of the national magazine has made its influence felt in the conduct of American business. The advertising agency as it exists and operates today was established and developed largely through the efforts of the publishers of national magazines. These publishers worked with the advertising agencies during their early struggles toward a sound operating basis and, by their encouragement and support, aided in bringing about recognition of the advertising agency as an integral part of the American business structure.

The agency method of handling national advertising began a little over one hundred years ago when the first advertising agents were actually employed by the newspaper in which they sold space. Twenty years later, these agents had become brokers who bought and sold space in newspapers and magazines. Publishers had no established rates. Agents bought advertising space in publications at as low a price as possible, then sold it at the highest price obtainable.

In the 1870's publishers again began to employ their own special agents to sell space, and these men operated in competition with the wholesale agents. A step toward more efficient and regular methods was made when, in 1872, N. W. Ayer & Son in Philadelphia established their open contract under which the Ayer advertising agency agreed to buy space to the best of its ability, and then to bill the advertiser at the net rate plus an agreed percentage. George Batten developed a similar idea in New York.

It was in the 1880's, when magazine publishers had begun to stabilize their rates, that advertising agencies, in competing for the business of advertisers, first began to prepare copy for them. The publishers realized that this meant more effective and intelligent use of advertising space. The service agency also had a distinct value for them in the development of new advertisers, and dealing with responsible agencies lessened their own credit risk. As a matter of enlightened self-interest magazine publishers took steps to protect the agency in its efforts to sell advertising.

Standards of advertising agency recognition were discussed by the board of directors of The Curtis Publishing Company in January, 1898. In May, 1901, at a time when 45 per cent of its advertising came directly from advertisers, Curtis adopted and put into immediate effect the first Curtis contract. This contract provided that the advertising agency would maintain, and charge its clients, the full rate for advertising space set by the publisher in *The Saturday Evening Post* and the *Ladies' Home Journal.* In return Curtis would allow the advertising agency a commission of 10 per cent on the cost of the advertising space, plus a discount of 5 per cent for cash payment. It also agreed to accept no advertising, either directly or through any of its agents, at less than the published rates. This contract was far-reaching in its effects. It established the idea among publishers and advertisers that the advertising agency by its presentation of ideas and preparation of copy, art work, and typographic layout, performed a service for the advertiser which ordinarily he could not perform himself and which the publisher was not equipped to perform. It made rate-cutting by either agency or publishers illegal. It recognized the value of the service agency to both periodical and advertiser.

Other publishers followed the Curtis lead, and the position of the advertising agency as a business institution was greatly strengthened. In the conclusion to his thorough study of advertising agencies James Webb Young pointed out [7] that the support of publishers hastened the development of the adver-of agency compensation. The standard advertising-agency in the development of new advertisers. They encouraged advertising agencies to expand their services and set standards of agency compensation. The standard advertising-agency commission has long been 15 per cent plus a 2 per cent cash discount.

What the agency and the advertiser demand of magazines is markets. They are not interested in the possible social or economic significances of their advertising. Like the magazines themselves, they are solely interested in profits. They select the magazine, or list of magazines, which, all considerations weighed, they believe the most effective medium or media for the sales message they wish to transmit. It follows that advertiser and agency want an audience, circulation, usually the

[7] *Advertising Agency Compensation* (Chicago: University of Chicago Press, 1933).

bigger the better; but it must be the kind of circulation which they think parallels the market for their product. It is of small use advertising industrial machinery or hearing aids in *Jack and Jill* or cosmetics in *Business Week.*

Magazine advertising, bought and sold by the page or page fraction, is usually estimated in terms of cost per page per thousand, i.e., the cost of reaching a thousand readers with a page advertisement. This is generally figured on the basis of the black and white page. Space rates for two- and four-color pages, for center spreads, and for back and inside covers are substantially higher than those for black and white and make the cost of reaching a thousand readers through these units correspondingly more expensive.

The magazine publishing industry likes to boast that it has survived powerful onslaughts on the time and attention of readers. It survived the bicycle, the automobile, motion pictures, radio, and television. It has even expanded since the advent of these counter-attractions. At the same time magazine publishing has had to make many concessions and modifications to withstand the competition. The others, even radio, it took in stride, but not television. If there is one central and pervading fact about magazine advertising in the second half of the 20th century, that fact is television.

The magazines have had to make editorial changes to meet the drowning competition from television as a stream of capsuled information and seas of popular entertainment. They have been forced into many more changes in their efforts to combat television as an advertising medium.

Television is, *par excellence,* the mass medium. The performance is continuous. Everybody stops, looks, and listens. Big advertisers were quick to realize all the manifest advantages of television advertising and acted quickly on their realization. Television fascinated them as it fascinated the layman. They deserted other media, and most of the largest moved into television as soon as network time was available. Others followed. Advertisers of cigarettes, beer, detergents, cosmetics, food products, automobiles, appliances—of most convenience goods, durables, and semi-durables—moved *en masse* to the new medium. Since the early 1950's most of the "blue chip" accounts have been spending by far the greater part of their advertising appropriations in television, magazines getting some of the remainder of the budget where the advertisers continued in magazines at all.

The change in a sixteen year period will serve to indicate quickly what happened quickly. In 1950 advertising expenditures in magazines were $515,000,000, nine per cent of all advertising investment, as against $171,000,000, three per cent of the total, in television. By 1966 magazine advertising had more than doubled to $1,295,000,000 but dropped to 7.8 per cent of the total, while television advertising had multiplied to an expenditure of $2,765,000,000, 16.7 per cent of all the money spent in advertising in that year.[8]

To compete, the magazines charged wildly after larger and still larger circulations. Despite the swollen figures they obtained they could hardly make a dent in the size of the television audience. Individual magazines did make headway against their competition by badly damaging each other in the frantic circulation race.

The magazines hastily developed spectacular mechanical innovations: bleed, inserts, foldovers, gatefold, new space units. They did much more than this. In effect, the magazines abandoned their once proud position as national media. It is a poor magazine now that is not published in regional, sectional, local, and a variety of other special advertising editions. All editions carry the same editorial, but an advertiser can buy space only in those copies of an issue which circulate in a specified region, state or metropolitan area, or in any combination of them which he wishes.

The Reader's Digest, for instance, is published regularly in ten different advertising editions in the United States with other circulation permutations and combinations available. *Newsweek* established regional editions in 1957 and in 1966

[8] *Statistical Abstract of the United States,* 88th edition. Washington: U. S. Department of Commerce, 1967.

began to offer "Sectional Central Market" editions based on postal sectional centers. It has nine of these sectional editions in addition to its six regional ones. *Look* went into regional editions in 1959. Currently it offers 75 different advertising editions based on geographic limits. In February, 1968, *Look* inaugurated a "Geodemic Edition," an advertising edition going only to subscribers in postal zip codes where there is a concentration of high median incomes.

The December 8, 1967, issue of *Life* was published in 225 different advertising editions: 26 regional, 20 "Spot Life," 48 state, nine test markets, nine combinations of them, and all of these doubled for newsstand circulation. The 225th edition was Life Canada.

It seems almost possible for an advertiser to buy any part of a magazine's total circulation he wishes. He can use a region, a state, a city and the area surrounding it, or an income group. Presumably, with the help of the computer and willing sellers, he may in time be able to buy space in issues going only to schoolteachers or blacksmiths or even to the one prospect in all the world he hopes to reach with his pitch. The advertiser can buy split runs (different copy for the same products in different advertising editions) on a geographical basis or use different copy in subscriber and newwstand copies. Where magazines are concerned, he wallows in a buyer's market.

The magazines see all these innovations as giving them greater flexibility. What the changes really mean is that the mass magazines have retreated into being "class" magazines which offer selective rather than mass markets. This brings them into competition with the local newspaper, radio, and spot television and avoids head-on collision with network television.

Until recent years magazine rate cards were advertising rate cards. Now they are generally booklets giving different rate schedules for various advertising editions and combinations of editions. They offer complicated discount schedules for frequency and continuity of insertion, sometimes rates for combination advertising in other magazines under the same ownership. An advertising agency can make almost any kind of buy it wishes for an approving client. Some magazines offer different rates to different classes of advertisers. *The New Yorker*, with a general rate of $6,600 for a four-color inside page and $8,175 for its back cover to its full circulation of a guaranteed net paid 430,000, in 1968 had different rate cards with varying charges for real estate, hotel, museum and art gallery, restaurant, retail store, and book advertising.

Roughly, a full-color page in one of the magazines with a multi-million circulation costs about as much, around $45,000 one insertion, as one minute of prime commercial time on full network television. In both media there are additional costs; composition and plate charges in magazine advertising and production costs, much higher, in television. The agency and the advertiser can choose. The magazines—with the high cost of network television one of their assets—are making it as easy as they can for the advertiser to choose them. They are being pressed. Some are being pressed to the wall. A few have been pressed right through it.

Advertisers like the glamor of television, the prestige carried by highly rated programs. Agencies like the high returns from their commissions on costly television advertising. Yet the magazines still possess a few advantages in the struggle with their powerful adversary. The television commercial can excite, but the magazine advertisement has at least a chance to convince. It can tell the reader more than the viewer can grasp and absorb in the sixty, thirty, or fifteen seconds of the usual television commerical. On the screen cars roar up steep and twisting mountain roads, undergo ingenious torture tests to show their impeccable springing or awesome power, or are danced at by a line of chorus girls and chorus boys. The static magazine advertisement, no matter how glamorous the photography, lacks speed and excitement. It may have beauty. There may be a girl behind the wheel or draped over a fender, but most people know by now that the girl does not come with the car. The magazine advertisements offer instead a little more detail. The reader can study the dimensions and specifications of the car. He can count the cylinders, carburetors, doors, and wheels. He looks for and gets in magazine advertising information about the automobile he has admired or disliked when he saw it on the screen or on the road. When there is reason for an advertisement to appear in depth, a magazine may well be the place for it.

The viewer has to be looking at his television receiver and listening to it to be exposed to an advertising message. If the set is not on when the commercial is or the viewer has switched off his attention, no contact is made. A reader can read and reread a magazine advertisement when he wishes where he wishes. He is often reminded by a second, third, fourth, or fifth exposure to a magazine advertisement. Like the newspaper, the magazine can offer coupons, free booklets, catalogues or other inducements. These keyed devices enable the advertiser to test the efficacy of his copy and magazine medium and also provide customer and prospect lists for follow-up mailings or salesmen's calls. It is difficult to clip a coupon from a television commercial.

No matter how mass a mass magazine is, it is by its very nature more selective than television. Magazines go to the literate. A women's magazine goes to women, *Playboy* to adolescents, *The New Yorker* to the sophisticated, a news magazine to those interested in contemporary events. There are these rough distinctions, and individual periodicals can justly claim other reader, audience, and marketing distinctions. Through their editorial content magazines appeal to specific audiences. There may be some duplication, but ordinarily the *Yale Review* and *The Reader's Digest* or *Seventeen* and *Popular Mechanics* appeal to different kinds of readers who are potential customers for different kinds of products and services. Through the planning and weighting of their circulation effort, magazines obtain the kinds of readers they wish in chosen localities. Through media research the magazines refine—and refine and refine and refine—on their subscribers and on their total "audiences," breaking them down by age, sex, education, income, home ownership, and all the other demographic characteristics which define them as consumers.

In terms of both revenue and pages, total magazine advertising fell off in 1967 when revenue was off 0.8 per cent from the previous year; $1,161,599,170 for 1967 against $1,170,517,360 in 1966. [9] Advertising revenue continues to slip badly for a number of the big magazines, though overall gains were reported for the first six months of 1969 when magazine advertising revenue reached nearly $611,000,000.

Once upon a time, say *The Saturday Evening Post* in the 1920's, magazines could be cavalier in their acceptance or rejection of advertising. They picked and chose, often did not deign to solicit. Magazine advertising is no longer in this pleasant position. Many of the surviving large-circulation magazines are noticeably thinner than they were last year or the year before. Yet there is still plenty of advertising, informative, even dignified by comparison with some other forms of advertising, still with the authority and finality of print, in the magazines—more than $1.6 billion of it yearly. It seems in no danger of immediate disappearance.

It is to be hoped that it will not disappear. The advertising is an essential part of a magazine, which is a more satisfactory product with advertising in it. Generally, magazine advertising shows a restraint of which all advertising cannot be accused, and it has reflected in it something of the appeal and perhaps the integrity of the magazine carrying it. A pair of flannels illustrated in severe black and white in *The New Yorker* is imbued with all the wit of the Talk of the Town. Fabrics or gowns advertised in *Vogue* by their very presence there are *haute couture*. A firearm advertised in *Sports Afield* has about it the open-air, thrill-of-the-kill adventure that springs out of hunters' tales in the magazine.

In an odd sense television advertising is mundane reality while magazine advertising is art. Tires squeal as the automobile flashes up the mountain road. You don't buy that dusty, protesting car or even the one displayed in the showroom, but the beautiful and lovely thing pictured in the magazine advertisement with all the promise of romance about it that the

[9] Magazine Advertising Bureau figures based on Publishers' Information Bureau reports, 1968, 1969.

Jordan Playboy once achieved through its famous "Somewhere West of Laramie" series of *Saturday Evening Post* advertisements. People scrub their teeth on television, crunch on potato chips, smear their faces with shaving cream, grimace with pain before they swallow the best aspirin preparations. You can see and hear all that in your own bathroom or kitchen. The packaged product looks better in the magazines. The upright and sterling image of the corporate advertiser seems almost believable. There it is in black ink on a white page. It must be true. Perhaps merely because it has been going on for a long time magazine advertising seems often to carry its own conviction.

Chapter 24

Magazine Research: Circulation

The large-circulation magazines spend considerable to appalling amounts of money in research of several kinds. The mastheads of many periodicals, particularly the news magazines, display long lists of researchers, usually young women, who use standard library references and ask questions of people to obtain useful information for writers and editors. Depending on the organization of the magazine, these same researchers or others use the same and perhaps additional sources to check the accuracy of articles in manuscript or proof. Editorial research of this kind is unpublicized workaday routine which helps essentially in building the editorial product.

There is another kind of editorial research, also largely unpublicized. This is research conducted by question and answer methods with a sample of a magazine's readers to find out what they liked or disliked in a given issue, what they read, how much of it they read, and what they did not read at all. This kind of editorial research is also used to find out what subjects interest readers, what they might like to read in future issues, what kinds of covers and illustrations they prefer, and how they respond generally to editorial departments and treatment.

Dr. George H. Gallup began research of this kind when he developed "A New Technique for Measuring Reader Interest in Newspapers" for his doctoral dissertation at the University of Iowa. He made readership studies for the Des Moines *Register* and *Tribune* and then for such magazines—all now defunct—as the *Literary Digest, Collier's,* and *Liberty.* During fifteen years with a New York advertising agency he continued using his technique to check reader reactions to both the editorial and the advertising content first of the women's magazines, then of the general magazines.

This kind of reader research is conducted on a routine basis, every issue or perhaps every other issue, by the larger publishers. Questionnaires are sent to an indicative sample of readers, usually subscribers. Respondents' answers are tabulated and analyzed. Findings are then made available to editors to show them what items in an issue have been popular, which failed, and to help guide them in the selection of material in preparing future issues. Results of these surveys which show failures as well as successes are generally kept confidential.

One result of this kind of editorial–reader research is to make the magazines more and more alike. One editor knows much what another editor knows about readers and what pleases or displeases them. Nor has this research improved editorial quality. With large circulations the goal, the commonplace and promotable piece is a safer choice than the unusual and even distinctive piece which will not score as well with readers or in the tabulated results by which publishers may judge the performance of their editors.

Two other kinds of magazine research bulk larger, and in contrast to those mentioned, they are publicized and often loudly touted. These are marketing and media research. Marketing research came first. Extensively practiced throughout business and industry, it had its origin in magazine publishing.

In 1911 The Curtis Publishing Company hired Charles Coolidge Parlin, a Wisconsin high school principal, and established a Division of Commercial Research in its advertising department. The idea behind the move was to provide advertisers and prospective advertisers with knowledge of where their markets lay, how they were constituted, and how best to reach them—and, of course, to establish the value of *The Saturday Evening Post* and *Ladies' Home Journal* for reaching and retaining these markets.

The first studies made were comprehensive reports on entire industries. Parlin issued a typed 460-page report on the market for agricultural implements in 1911. He followed with a department store study in several volumes in 1912—actually the first census of distribution ever attempted—and with a pioneer survey of the automotive industry in 1914. Others followed. At the time business had few dependable sources of information. This kind of "commercial research," as Parlin called it, was new and welcomed.

In comparison with those used today, the methods were crude. Parlin and his associates simply went everywhere they could go, talked to everyone who would talk to them, wrote down their answers, then tried to interpret the results. They turned up a lot of information useful to advertisers. Their forecasts ranged from clumsy approximations to inspired guesses.

Marketing research has become a far more ambitious undertaking. There are many vigorous and prosperous marketing research firms. Market analysis has become a recognized profession. Many more sources of statistical information are available, particularly from government which supplies them in profusion and continuously. Publications of the Bureau of the Census loom largest. Marketing analysts mine them for data that can be extracted, realigned, interpreted, and applied to all kinds of marketing situations—"marketing," of course, being but another word for selling.

Techniques have been refined and complicated. Area probability sampling based on random selection has taken the place of the early quota sampling. Questionnaires are devised so that straight answers can be obtained to straight questions. Fearsome computers tabulate and analyze the results. The refinements and complications have been multiplied, but essentially marketing research is just what it was in Parlin's day. Researchers ask people questions and write down their answers.

Surveys are conducted by personal interview, armies of interviewers descending on huge national samples. Other surveys are conducted by mail, by telephone, or by variations and combinations of the three methods. Sometimes a group of individuals or families is selected as a panel whose members record their buying habits, possessions, purchases, preferences, and opinions. Advertising agencies, magazines, newspapers, and other enterprises all do marketing research of this kind, and some of it is impressive. For a major market survey of the European Common Market and Great Britain, for instance, the internationally published *Reader's Digest* made 12,500 personal interviews in seven countries in 1963 and obtained answers regarding 140 marketing items as well as to attitude and opinion questions. In 1966 the *Digest* published an oversized hard-cover book titled *The New Far East.* Its tabulations were obtained through 7,457 personal interviews in Tokyo, Manila, Singapore, Bangkok, Hong Kong, Tapei, and Seoul. The information made available in these two studies had socio-economic as well as merely marketing value. Other examples where marketing research has produced important data could as easily be forwarded.

Magazine media research developed out of marketing research. If a magazine is of any value as an advertising medium, it is different from any other magazine in some respect. Media research attempts to point out what these differences are and to present them as advantages. It tries to do this by attesting through research to the size and composition of the group who read or see a given magazine.

Magazine media research is, in general, statistically reliable. It is honestly conducted by reputable experts using authenticated techniques. Results are published in impressive reports flaunting tables, charts, mathematical symbols, and all the other graphic appurtenances of scientific unimpeachability. In the larger sense, it is not research at all. Research methods are used, but the intent is to reach *a priori* conclusions.

It is promotive, competitive, and lightened by legerdemain. There is not a magazine which cannot prove that it leads all the rest in some important category. If it does not have the most readers, it has the most readers with family incomes over $25,000 a year or the most readers with credit cards or false teeth or children in school or the most readers with beards or without them.

To validate its accuracy and authenticity most of the big magazines have their media research done by outside research organizations. These organizations are usually hired because in soliciting the business they present research plans and ideas which they believe will produce favorable results for the magazine prospect. The magazine becomes a client and pays the research organization in the expectation of finding plus factors for it in the eyes of advertisers. If they do not prove favorable, the results are filed out of sight. If they do prove favorable, they are ballyhooed to the last echo of the last hoo.

Magazine media research is a form of promotion. Virtuously the magazines refuse to accept advertising copy in which one producer or distributor derides the products of a competitor. At the same time the magazines continually advertise against each other and even advertise their own research findings to attack the research of a rival. The newspaper reading public in the larger cities of the United States is treated almost daily to entertainment of this kind in full pages of paid space. It is always amazing that magazine publishers who prate learnedly of audience selectivity do newspaper advertising like this. The waste circulation is awesome. They advertise to huge circulations to reach a few hundred, at most a few thousand, advertisers and agency media buyers who may be interested. Evidently they cast their pearls before so many swine in the devout hope that the porkers they really wish to attract will snuffle them down.

The first magazine media research was simply a circulation figure. A magazine told advertisers and prospects that it has this large or this small and select a circulation. The next step was to break this number down by the individuals and families in a magazine's circulation. Circulation was analyzed by age, sex, income, and the other social and economic characteristics. A magazine tried to show that it had so many people reading, interested, willing, and able to buy the products and services advertised in its pages.

This situation changed in two ways. Circulation figures proved inadequate. Advertisers wanted to know not just how many people purchased a publication but how many actually read an issue. This led to the development of the "total audience" concept, a figure comparable to the total audience figures used first by radio and then by television. With an outside research organization *Life* pioneered here. It produced figures which included not only primary readers, as subscribers and newsstand purchasers were called, but also secondary, tertiary, pass-along—everybody who saw an issue whether at home, in a physician's or dentist's office, at the hairdresser's, or at the barber's. Huge figures competitive with those of the electronic media resulted. *Look* adopted the total audience concept and issued its research reports. Other major magazines followed, and total audience became an accepted measure of the numbers of people reached by a magazine.

Now the established breakdown by age, sex, *et al.* could be applied to tremendous totals. The magazines could delineate proven large readerships in terms of actual and potential buying power and consumer characteristics.

The second major change has come through research which attempts to describe magazine advertising effectiveness in closer and more direct terms. The advertiser is always demanding more and more proof of the value he can hope and expect to receive through purchase and use of magazine space. With the same research organization which had put forward the total audience idea, *The Reader's Digest* began to report on two new measurements. For itself it discovered and revealed how many times an issue of the *Digest* is picked up for reading and re-reading. This concept of "reading days" enabled it to show on how many days an issue containing advertising was exposed and re-exposed to consumers. In "A Study of Seven Publications, their Audiences and Reading Days" it gave this information for itself and for six competing magazines.

The Saturday Evening Post carried this research one step further and through research showed the number of times a *Post* reader was actually exposed to a page of advertising in the magazine. The *Digest* and the *Post* then joined forces to apply this advertising page exposure concept to four magazines: the *Digest*, the *Post*, *Life*, and *Look*.

Needless to say, advertisers and advertising agencies take magazine media research *cum grano*. They check findings carefully, do their own research of a comparable kind, and issue their reports for internal use or use with clients.

It sometimes seems that there are almost as many pages of statistics prepared by research and published by magazine promotion departments as there are editorial pages in the magazines. How much of it is actually used it is impossible to say. Notoriously the space salesmen for whom much of it is prepared ignore it. Sometimes, and they are not alone here, they cannot understand it. Often they find that a well-placed martini or a half dozen do as well or better than media research in selling space.

Advertising managers and media buyers are people too. They study the media research, but perhaps the agency buyer's wife always reads this woman's magazine instead of that or the president's wife plays bridge with the publisher's wife or the space salesman plays golf with an account executive. It may be that the marketing manager's cute little girl prefers to cut pictures from this periodical and cries when her inquisitive father suggests she cut them from a different magazine. It is hard to put a stop to things like this.

Obviously there would be no media research or excuse for it if magazines did not have circulations to dissect and promote. The magazine has three basic departments: editorial, advertising, and circulation. Of the three, circulation is the toughest and most realistic.

Magazines make most of their profits from advertising, but they cannot make it unless sizable circulation of measurable quality is first obtained. There are certain truisms repeated endlessly among magazine circulation men. One is that magazines are not bought; they are sold. A significant part of the population still believes that it is possible to live and even, given television, to live quite well without buying magazines. It has to be persuaded. Another truism is that magazine circulation is a nickel and dime business. It is, but quite a few nickels and dimes are amassed before the circulation men have finished, and they have not finished yet. A third comment is often heard in circulation departments. Virtuously, wryly or cynically, circulation men insist that they sell only the editorial.

They are telling the truth. They may use fair means or foul, gadgets, gimmicks, competitive warfare or blackmail, but they are selling only the editorial quality of the book. It is all they have to sell. If they can be persuaded to buy at all, people buy magazines to read the editorial.

Magazine selling has long been one of the most derided and suspect of business activities, and with reason. Circulation effort has advanced nobly from the days early in this century when strongarm boys rode the newspaper delivery trucks and beat up recalcitrant dealers who insisted on selling a rival newspaper or, in emergencies, bombed their stands, but it has not advanced too far. Though the Central Registry of Magazine Subscription Solicitors sponsored by the Magazine Publishers Association works unremittingly to maintain and enforce ethical stands, it is never without legitimate complaints. Householders are fleeced by door-to-door canvassers who collect money for subscriptions that are never fulfilled. Subscriptions crews descend on a city or community with fraudulent offers or with legitimate offers that are often misrepresented. People are bilked by telephone operatives who offer a "free gift" of a list of magazines. The fortunate donee has only to pay the postage. There is, of course, an agreement to sign. The unwary are generally trapped for $100 or more. They receive the magazines promised but at a price which they did not realize they would have to pay.

Most legitimate circulation agencies register and post bond with the Central Registry. Door-to-door solicitors of these agencies are then supplied with credentials. The field activities of salesmen and sales crews are checked by Better Business Bureaus or chambers of commerce in about 1,000 communities. Complaints are heard and where necessary adjustments made locally or a problem is reported for action to Central Registry. Through this self-regulation the magazine industry does as well as it can to keep its house clean, but not all crews are legitimate and not all operatives of registered agencies adhere to the rules set down.

Basically, magazines are sold in two ways; single copy from newsstands and by subscription. There are well over 100,000 retail outlets to which, through distributors, the magazine circulation companies supply magazines. Biggest are the long-established Curtis Circulation Company, since 1968 as Perfect Circulation no longer a subsidiary of The Curtis Publishing Company, and S-M (Select Magazines). Each of these companies distributes the magazines of many client publishers.

Single-copy circulation is good circulation. It is the best subscription sampling device the magazines have. It is also voluntary circulation. A man or woman picks up a copy at the rack in a supermarket, a drugstore, or at an actual newsstand in a hotel, airport, railroad station and looks at it. He buys it or he puts it down. If he purchases the copy, the likelihood is that he will read it. He will at least be exposed to the advertising.

There are many factors which are difficult to control in magazine circulation, particularly newsstand circulation, from the original draw at the publishers down to the smallest newsstand dealer. The draw—print order—must be based upon some estimate contrived out of past experience, imagined reading appeal of features in a given issue, even seasonal conditions. All of these must be taken into consideration weeks ahead of the on-sale date of an issue. The best-laid circulation plans gang aft agley if there is an epidemic, if a war starts or stops, if there is too much bad weather or too much good weather. Returns, and magazines are 100 per cent returnable to the publisher for price paid, can be affected by attendance at football or baseball games or the fact that a hotel which held a convention of learned societies one week and sold out all its newsstand copies of *Playboy* has a convention of modistes and registered nurses this week and runs out of *McCall's* and *Humpty Dumpty*.

There must always be returns of unsold copies for the publisher to be sure that sufficient copies were on sale to meet the demand. There must not be too many or the additional manufacturing, shipping, and selling costs will wipe out profit from copies actually sold. Most of this profit goes anyway to distributors and dealers. Magazines go to wholesalers at 40 per cent off list price and another five per cent goes to the national distributor. The publisher gets little or no profit from single-copy sales.

Magazine competition at the newsstands is strong and continual. Each magazine demands preferential display for itself and wants little or none for its competitors. A distributor may try to insist that because his lead magazine is a quarter the size of some others it be given four times the shelf display. Some magazines provide and insist on the use of special racks. When a salesman finds that a local distributor has stuffed them with other magazines, he goes righteously indignant. By dealer design or distributor instruction some magazines may be placed under the counter while others are flaunted. Circulation men use various dealer incentives to increase sales, thereby achieving their ends and provoking the ire and counter action of competitors. Single copy accounts for only 10 to 15 per cent of total magazine circulation.

Subscription selling of magazines is more complicated. The more copies of a magazine a publisher manufactures and distributes the higher his costs. Often the more he sells the more he loses. Magazine publishing is an economic anomaly in that real profits come not from sale of the article produced but from the sale of a by-product, advertising space. Yet that cannot be sold unless the carrying vehicle itself is sold. It is to cut these costs that publishers retreat from once a week to biweekly publication, combine two year-end issues into one or deliberately cut circulation. Even when a magazine subscription is sold the publisher has taken on a new liability. He has obtained money in advance for a contract which he must now fulfill by supplying magazines for a year, two years, or whatever the term of the contract. The publisher has assumed a debt which he must pay. Yet subscription circulation is vital to his business.

It is regular and continuing circulation upon which the advertiser whose business has been solicited can depend. It too, is good circulation because by subscribing people have expressed their faith in a magazine and their wish to read it regularly. It enables the publisher to set his base rate of average circulation guarantee to the advertiser.

Magazine subscriptions are sought and obtained in a variety of ways, most of them expensive to the publisher. Subscriptions are sold by full or part-time agents working on commission directly for the publisher, by independent catalogue agencies which canvass for long lists of magazines, by what the trade calls PDS (Paid During Service) agencies, by department stores, by schools, clubs, and civic organizations as a fund-raising activity, and by direct-mail solicitation.

Some publishers make money consistently on subscription circulation, but some make little if any. Ordinarily the subscription agent working for the publisher keeps half the stated subscription price which he collects, remits the other half. Commissions range upward from this fifty per cent, going much higher to many of the independent subscription agencies.

Circulation has to be bought. If a magazine lacks adequate circulation among the newly married aged 24 in and on the outskirts of Seattle or more subscribers, female, aged 50, with income from dividends averaging $50,000 per annum in northern Westchester County, New York, it must buy it. What it costs to get this circulation—and he may have to pay agents up to 80 per cent commissions—matters little to the publisher if a large advertising contract depends upon his strengthening circulation where geographically or demographically it is weak or the advertiser so considers it.

Magazine publishers spend many millions of dollars annually in direct-mail solicitation of subscriptions and obtain about 62 per cent of them in this way. The method is standard, effective, expensive, but can be profitable. Depending upon the mailing lists they use, whether they offer published or bargain rates, they can generally estimate returns with some accuracy. With no commissions to pay, the publisher gets the entire amount remitted, but the costs of preparing and mailing a campaign can be high, high enough sometimes to show a loss. Usually a second mailing to different lists will reduce the loss and perhaps show a considerable profit.

The most profitable kind of subscriptions for the publisher are renewals. They cost little or nothing to obtain, perhaps only an expiration notice in a final copy, a reminder through the mails, perhaps not even that. The publisher receives the full subscription price. He also obtains a promotable advantage. Renewals prove reader—consumer—satisfaetion.

Mass magazine publishers have developed one method of subscription solicitation which works well for them and for the public, providing a rare instance of a business contract profiting both parties to the agreement. This is the selling of magazine subscriptions through the schools. Developed out of the selling of *Country Gentleman,* the Curtis (now the Perfect) School Plan has been in operation since the early 1920's and profitably. Crowell-Collier developed a similar operation. *Look* had its school plan. There are some sectional operations, but the largest and most active nationally are the Perfect School Plan and the Quality School Plan owned jointly by *The Reader's Digest* and Time, Inc. and operated by the *Digest.*

Under these school plans, organized and directed by Curtis (Perfect) or Quality representatives, participating high or junior high schools stage magazine subscription campaigns of anywhere from a day or two to a week. Students solicit subscriptions to long lists of magazines. They receive prizes for various numbers of sales made, but the commissions—usually about one-third of the profits—go to the participating schools. This is unbudgeted money from other than taxpayer sources which school authorities and the students may use to purchase band uniforms, instruments, library books, drinking fountains, a school bell, or new doors—for any desired objects or improvements the school decides upon. Looked upon by some educators as giving students valuable experience in business and salesmanship, these school plans are a fund-raising activity for the schools and provide sound circulation for the magazines. Quality, now the leader, grosses about $17,000,000 annually and leaves some $6,000,000 with nearly 10,000 schools.

Subscriptions expire every day. New ones start. Subscription fulfillment is not a simple operation. People move and do not notify the publisher of address changes. People die. Computers make mistakes, and when they do they usually make big ones. Subscriber complaints are incessant and errors cannot always be easily corrected. Whole staffs of correspondents are employed just to answer subscriber complaints. At least one magazine deals with them effectively. It simply enters a new subscription in his name when someone complains that he is not receiving the copies for which he has paid. This is the easiest and cheapest solution to the problem for that magazine. One disintegrating publishing house with several magazines circulating in the multi-millions used another method in recent years. It let complaints go unacknowledged and mistakes unrectified. It had no staff to answers letters and no money to spend in correcting mistakes.

When a magazine is sold, unexpired subscriptions go with it not as an asset but as a liability. The new owner has to give the subscriber something for his money, either his version of the magazine or a generally unsatisfactory substitute which the subscriber would have ordered in the first place had he wanted it.

There are those in the magazine business, extremists perhaps, but seasoned circulation men, who advocate a completely different way of dealing with magazine subscriptions. They would give magazine subscriptions gratis to selected circulation, then sell lists of subscriber names to other direct-mail solicitors in larger lots and for larger amounts of money than they are sold now. The idea is practical. As most people have occasion to know and as W. S. Gilbert noted in the *Mikado* as long ago as 1885, once you're on a list . . .

Chapter 25

Magazine Impact

If there ever was a time when he could, the individual can no longer live in a world bounded by the range of his five senses and by what information of people and events outside that small realm he can obtain through rumor. The geographical contraction of the world achieved by speeded transport, viciously improved armament, and the feverish tempo of domestic and international activity have emphasized the need for adequate communication. What is happening in Manchuria, Germany, Africa, Tibet, at the North Pole, in science and technology, education, politics, and our embattled cities is now a matter of worried concern to the man or woman in Brooklyn, San Francisco, and everywhere else in the United States. Whether he likes it or not, the citizen of Cincinnati or Waycross, Georgia, is now a citizen of the world. He always was, but he did not always realize it until radio, television, and the press told him so. These communications forces have taught him to be aware of the world and the space around it, have kept him aware of it, and have made the American copiously and confusedly informed.

As rapidly as the news can be obtained, transmitted, and printed the daily newspapers tell him of the alarms on every continent and in his own neighborhood. Spot news is the essential matter of the newspaper press, and 1,754 morning and evening newspapers in the United States with a combined circulation of about 61,400,000 handle it very well. The magazine-like features which the large-city newspapers have incorporated, particularly in their Sunday editions with their 50,000,000 combined circulation, are often entertaining, but secondary to the newspaper's main editorial purpose and performance. Essence of the daily newspaper's service is immediacy and transiency. Proverbially, nothing is as dead as yesterday's newspaper.

Once a miracle and a wonder, radio has been a communications fixture of American life since the 1920's. It gripped the imagination of the country and seized its fascinated attention, reaching peak performance during and immediately after World War II. Radio seemed to bring everybody everything: events as they happened, the voices of figures in the spotlight of public attention, Amos 'n Andy, opera, Bob Hope, the invasion of northern New Jersey and New York by Martians, football, baseball, mystery, comedy, zeppelin disasters, battlefront reports, Dr. I. Q., Henry Aldrich, election returns, earnest discussion by university professors, and Duffy's Tavern.

Radio paved the way for television, which, when it came, seemed simply the addition of video to audio, pictures to words. The vacuum tube, the networks, the singing commercial, the vaudevillians were all there for television to take, and television took them. Radio almost disappeared. Then it made the strongest comeback in the history of modern communications. It discarded its soap operas, comedies, and mysteries along with its major national advertising and let television take over as entertainment. Then radio went local, factual, and musical. It was as simple as that, though the decline and then the rebuilding were not that easy for the people involved.

Radio let Fibber McGee go and concentrated on what it could do best. Its formula became news, weather, chit-chat, recorded music, and local or largely local advertising. Development of the transistor and of frequency modulation broadcasting helped. In 1967 there were 4,121 AM and 1,637 FM radio stations and 262,700,000 radio receivers in use in homes and automobiles.[1] As the industry likes to say, "Radio is a fact of life." It is an indisputable fact. The traveling salesman gets the news and weather as he drives to his next turn-down, high school students rock and roll to its sound, housewives listen to women's programs as they do their ironing, elderly gentleman ice skate in swamps to the music of the transistor radios in their coat pockets.

Since its public advent in about 1946, television has achieved what amounts to national penetration. It nearly destroyed radio. It closed movie houses across the land. It has preempted variety and fiction. You don't go to the movies to see movies; you stay at home and let the movies come to you. You speak to your wife only during the commercials, between the halves of professional football games, or after the baseball game is over. If the wrong side wins, you may not speak to her at all.

Looking at television and listening to it have become a major leisure-time activity of the American family and the chief occupation of some. Television is the best baby sitter in the world, and what respectable traveler would stop at a motel which did not have color television in every room? In an incredibly short time television has become an integral part of the standard mores. Its appeal has proved irresistible both for the time and attention of the public and for major advertising investment.

Television's virtues as a medium of communication are many and obvious. It can bring events in their actuality—Congressional investigations, games, meetings of the United Nations, street riots, political discussions roller-skating derbies—directly to the eyes and ears of people at ease in their own homes. Photography, electronics, and reporters being what they are, it can sometimes enhance the actuality of what it reports for greater drama and effect. Television had been accused of distorted reporting even before its melodramatic coverage of the Democratic National Convention in Chicago

[1] Wood, James Playsted. *This Is Advertising*. New York: Crown Publishers, Inc., 1968.

in the summer of 1968. Given the exaggerations to which the medium lends itself, television's on-the-spot reporting of events is matchless, and many of its other achievements are admirable.

Adverse criticism of television is insidiously inviting. It has become the sport less of intellectuals than of those who wish to appear intellectual and beyond the reach of entertainment for the vulgar, and of those others who have political or professional ends to gain through derision. Yet television's flaws and faults are as apparent as its virtues.

Because it has become or been made by advertisers *the* mass medium, its characteristic programs are directed to what those responsible for its offerings consider the taste and intellectual level of the mass audience. The system of program ratings used makes numbers alone the measure of a program's value. If it does not enthrall a sufficient number of millions of viewers, a program is dropped and one with greater arithmetical appeal substituted. Quantity, not quality in either program or audience, is the hotly pursued goal. Thus television has made entertainment its major objective and conceived of entertainment in terms of endless westerns, crime dramas, soap operas, give-away programs, variety shows, and comedy skits. Much of what is shown on television would be appalling if it were not ridiculous. Perhaps it is appalling anyway.[2]

"What have you done with my child?" Lee De Forest, inventor of the audion tube, cried out at a meeting of National Association of Broadcasters in Chicago. "He was conceived as a potent instrument for culture, fine music, the uplifting of America's mass intelligence." And De Forest went on:

> You have debased this child, you have sent him out on the streets in rags of ragtime, tatters of jive and boogie-woogie, to collect money from all and sundry for hubba hubba and audio jitterbug. You have

[2] After examining television in *The Great Audience* (New York: The Viking Press, 1950), Gilbert Seldes wrote: "At a moment when every report indicates that television stands a good chance of destroying the habit of reading altogether, the intelligent popular magazine may be the last fortress of those who believe that we cannot survive unless we preserve our capacity to think."

> made of him a laughing stock of intelligence, surely a stench in the nostrils of the gods of the ionosphere . . . This child of mine, now thirty years in age, has been resolutely kept to the average intelligence of thirteen years. Its national intelligence is maintained moronic, as though you and your sponsors believe the majority of listeners have only moron minds . . .[3]

Perhaps because television fascinates, because it becomes insidious and makes addicts of its adherents, perhaps because it satisfies to numbness the modern American's insistent demand that he be entertained, it has largely taken over the entertainment function once performed for the mass audience by the newsprint story magazines of the nineteenth century with their endless tales by T. S. Arthur, Mrs. Southworth, or Ned Buntline. Television has so far taken over mass entertainment that many editors, seriously believe popular fiction is no longer a magazine province. They relegate melodrama to television, stress the informative article as the modern magazine staple.

Television has influenced magazine editorial content in several ways. It has forced magazines to improve in the direction of physical attractiveness, with more pictures and better reproduction, with more generous display. Graphic means have been utilized to make magazine pages pleasanter to look at. Pieces have been shortened and sharpened for greater ease of reading. Some magazines, notably the pictorial weeklies, compete with television "spectaculars" with what are obviously typographic spectaculars of their own. Magazine features vie in attempted glamour and in achieved superficiality with their counterparts in television treatment. Other magazines, and it would seem more wisely, emphasize the difference between the competing media by discussion, authoritative treatment of subjects which do not lend themselves to television screening, and by the greater use of what is clearly print rather than television screen material. Either

[3] Quoted in "The Revolt Against Radio," *Fortune*, March, 1947, and in *The Effects of Mass Media* by Joseph T. Klapper (New York: Bureau of Applied Social Research, Columbia University, 1949).

imitiation or accentuation of differences is discernible in periodical after periodical.

That magazine circulations have climbed to new heights during the period of television's expansion and arrival can be taken as proof enough that the appearance and use of the new and powerful medium has far from supplanted the older one. The public seems simply to have added television to newspapers, magazines, and radio, the various media complementing each other. There are even studies which seem to indicate that the people who watch television most are often the same people who spend the most time reading magazines.

Casual observation hardly bears out the contention, and the magazine industry makes a different claim. Using government and Brand Index Rating figures, it contends that television is really the province of the poorly educated while the better educated neglect television and concentrate on reading magazines.[4] The National Industrial Conference Board reports that families in which the family head has graduated from college spend four and one half times as much for magazines as families of low educational level.[5]

The decent and orderly separation of editorial and advertising matter observed in the newspaper and the magazine, blinked at in radio, has been extravagantly abrogated by television. With six or eight commercials, the result of multiple program sponsorship and the uninhibited sale of television spots, inserted in many half-hour programs, the salesman is with the television viewer always. He smirks, cajoles, insinuates, threatens, beseeches, and repeats, repeats, repeats between and in the midst of drama, news, weather, variety, comedy, and crime. The vacuum cleaner salesman has got into the parlor and all the other house-to-house canvassers have burst in too, and they are having a wonderful time. Often the performer takes up the product plea where the professional salesman leaves off. Part of the reason for all this is that the

[4] "The Education Explosion and the Magazine Influence," Magazine Advertising Bureau of Magazine Publishers Association, Inc., 1966.

[5] *Ibid.*

magazine advertiser can purchase and use only white space in a publication; he has no control over the magazine's editorial content or policy. In most cases, the advertiser purchasing television time can use it as he wishes. He can plan and produce the "editorial" content as well as the advertising. He and his advertising agency can exploit it as they will.

There are, though, fewer agency-produced programs than there were. Most are produced by the networks or by independent producers for the networks and the commercial time in them then offered for sale. So expensive is television advertising that only a few of the very largest national advertisers can any longer afford full program sponsorship. Multiple sponsorship is the rule observed by most of the more than 360 national advertisers using network television to advertise some 1,820 branded products.[6]

The four major forces affecting and controlling national public opinion, the magazine, the newspaper, the radio, and television, first created the public opinion they affect. It is axiomatic that no public opinion exists where no materials, no facts, no ideas have been provided. They serve a hunger they themselves have aroused. The newspaper is local in circulation. Its influence ends at the boundaries of its distribution. The day's newspaper is discarded upon being read, replaced by tomorrow's editions. Except where a definite crusade has been undertaken and is pressed in a journal's pages day after day over a period of weeks or months, the approach of the newspaper is fragmentary. Active human memory being what it is, the strongest effects of television and the radio quickly fade. The magazine suffers from these limitations less than the other major media. Ideally, the national magazine, prepared weeks ahead of issue date, need not compress, limit, or oversimplify in the presentation of a subject. There is time to deliberate and prepare a full and thoughtful article. The magazine has retained its original characteristics as a *magazine,* a storehouse of varied material. The offerings in every issue—articles, fiction, illustrations, sports, politics, science, economics,

[6] Wood, James Playsted, *op. cit.* About 2,540 advertisers use spot television for about 4,600 brands.

fashions, art, music, and all the other subjects covered in the modern magazine—allow reader selection and concentration.

The American public spends an appreciable part of its time reading magazines that have been skillfully enough edited and made physically attractive enough to catch and hold its undivided attention. The magazine is usually retained for further reading, for reading by other members of the purchaser's household long after the newspaper has been discarded and the radio program has faded. Reliance is placed on both the editorial and the advertising contents of the magazine in proportion to the repute which the magazine has established and maintains.

All of these contentions have been substantiated by surveys. A Gallup poll of June 14, 1948, asked how many people recognized a famous magazine cartoon character by sight or by association with the place they met her. Some 30,000,000 people correctly identified character and magazine. Another 25,000,000 recognized, by name or by association with a magazine which frequently carries his work, a famous magazine-cover artist. Other surveys discovered that readers spend an average of two hours and twenty-four minutes in actual reading of copies of a famous weekly. Answers to questionnaires placed in 80,000 copies of one periodical showed that current issues of the magazine were kept by the family in places where it would be picked up and reread, and that 66 per cent keep their copies for a month or longer after the issue is published.

Such studies aid in determining something of the social force of a magazine. Postulating a cause-and-effect relationship, the results obtained by a magazine's definite campaign are concrete evidence of its power. Not as easily determined is the sustained force of magazines in moulding and influencing their readers' attitudes toward people and ideas, in conditioning their reactions, in making them, in part, the people that they are.

Lacking this evidence, perhaps the best proof of the ordinary and continued impact of a strong magazine on its readers is the letters to the editor and similar indications of attentive reading that follow on the appearance of each issue. Here it must be remembered that only a small fraction of those who feel tempted to write the editor do write, and that only a small fraction of those moved to strong agreement or disagreement with some statement in an article even consider placing their comments on paper. Examples of this could be multiplied almost at will from the experiences of any of today's reputable and widely circulated periodicals. It is commonplace for a magazine to receive requests for thousands of reprints of a given article.

"—And Sudden Death" by J. C. Furnas, which appeared in *Reader's Digest* in 1935, was probably one of the most widely circulated magazine articles ever published. A highly dramatic story of fatalities from automobile accidents, and a gruesome warning, it was republished again and again in newspapers and in publications other than the *Digest*. *Reader's Digest* distributed thousands and thousands of reprints to civic societies and other organizations alarmed by the growing number of highway fatalities.

Sixty-eight words in the middle of a 1,750-word *Country Gentleman* article on dogwood trees offered seeds to those requesting them. In less than two weeks 15,000 readers wrote the magazine asking for the seeds; almost 25,000 requested them within a short time, virtually exhausting the supply available for distribution.

Occasionally a magazine article provokes marked and even unexpected results directly traceable to its appearance. Mark Sullivan, while still a student at the Harvard Law School, suggested to William Belmont Parker, an associate editor of *The Atlantic Monthly*, that he do an article on the political corruption in Pennsylvania. Parker approved the idea, and Sullivan wrote a strong indictment of Pennsylvania politics. He attacked Senator Matthew S. Quay, Republican boss of the state; he described bribery and vote-buying, the parceling out of political favors, the oppression of those who refused to conform to demands of the machine. Pennsylvania, he said, wallowed in corruption. Sullivan went further. He drew unpleasant comparisons between the contributions of Pennsylvania and Massachusetts to literature and public life. Bliss Perry bought his article for forty dollars but suggested that, as Sullivan was young and unknown, it be published anonymously. The article appeared as "The Ills of Pennsylvania" by "A Pennsylvanian" in the *Atlantic,* October, 1901. It created a furor. Outraged Pennsylvanians wrote indignant letters to the magazine. The anonymous author was excoriated. The most forceful reply was written by Samuel Whitaker Pennypacker, a very learned judge in Philadelphia. His able defense of both Pennsylvania and Senator Quay brought him into such favorable notice that he was made Quay's nominee for the governorship of Pennsylvania and was elected.

In 1934, *The Saturday Evening Post* published "Schoolhouse in the Foothills." These articles by Alvin F. Harlow told the story of a young teacher's struggles in her school at "Shady Cove" in the Tennessee mountains. Though no solicitation was made, gifts of money, clothes, books, and other equipment poured into the *Post* from every part of the country for transmission to the teacher. To handle the enormous correspondence which resulted from the articles, the magazine had to employ an assistant for the article writer and a secretary for the school-teacher. The "Shady Cove" school received everything it needed, and so much more that arrangements were made to direct the continuing flow of gifts to schools in other mountain villages.

It is not always by their expressions of approval that readers demonstrate their reactions to a magazine. When *The Atlantic Monthly* published Harriet Beecher Stowe's "The True Story of Lady Byron" in September, 1869, shocked and horrified subscribers hurriedly canceled their subscriptions, and the magazine was made to feel the sting of popular disapproval. James T. Fields, who succeeded James Russell Lowell as *Atlantic* editor in 1861, may have had this experience in mind when he admitted ruefully: "I could double the merit of the articles in the *Atlantic Monthly* and halve my subscription list at the same time." When Edward Bok dared discussion of sex and venereal disease in the *Ladies' Home Journal* the genteel feminine world of the 1890's declared shrilly for his annihilation, and the *Journal* lost hundreds of indignant subscribers. A few years ago one of the larger magazines published an article which was widely misconstrued as anti-Semitic. Though the magazine received many letters approving the article, it received thousands from others who believed it inaccurate and unjust. So violent was the attack on the magazine that its editor had to explain and apologize in paid space in large city newspapers the intent of his magazine in purchasing and printing the article.

The significance of these last three illustrations is not that magazine audiences disapproved certain editorial items, but that the influence of magazines is strong enough to cause quick and strong expression of opinion. One newspaper in its bitter attack on a magazine for what it considered a biased and intolerant article inadvertently paid unusual tribute to a competitive medium when it said editorially: "Any magazine that reaches 3,000,000 readers is one that is bound to have far-reaching influence on the thinking of the United States."

The potential influence of material appearing in the modern national magazines is not limited to the readers of the magazine and those influenced by the thinking of magazine readers. The vast audience of these magazines is many times multiplied when the same material is later published in book form and when, as often happens with a novel, the book becomes a motion picture. The modern national magazine exerts its power among the experts discussing economic or scientific questions, and affects the adolescent sighing and bubbling bubble gum in a darkened movie house while she lives vicariously the life of her Hollywood heroine.

The magazine pours its stream of facts and ideas into the great well of information and suggestion to which other sources, radio, television, newspapers, speeches, books, also contribute. Given the great number of American magazines, their large circulations, the number and diversity of subjects which they cover, and the important fact that magazines are periodical—that they come out each week or each month, each time with new diversions and new facts, or at least rearrangements of old ones—their contribution to this pool of knowledge and sentiment for the forming of public and private opinion is immeasurable.

According to the Magazine Publishers Association, A.B.C. count of only those general and farm magazines which take advertising shows them to have a combined per issue circulation of 236,948,953. Every time they are published there are about 168 copies of magazines for every 100 adults in the United States. Led by *The Reader's Digest* and *TV Guide,* 50 consumer magazines have circulations exceeding 1,000,000; 77 magazines have average circulation per issue of over 500,000. All of these, of course, claim total audiences in much higher numbers, usually about four times circulation. The *Digest,* internationally, measures over 100,000,000 readers, which is quite a lot. The spread of magazines is wide. Magazine penetration is deep. Magazine pressure on the American mind is considerable.

These readers are directly subject to magazine influence. The same magazine material, or the sustained editorial attitude of some one magazine or a group of them, may reach others through a lecture, a sermon, a serious discussion, or a newspaper account of something a magazine has published. Whether or not they are acknowledged as the source, magazines have certainly provided the material of countless sermons, books, and lectures.

It is probable that in the Presidential election of 1928 many citizens voted for or against Al Smith because of what he said and the way he said it in *The Atlantic Monthly.* Many whose attitude toward the New Deal, and later toward Russia, was determined by what they read in *The Saturday Evening Post* might not have acknowledged, perhaps had ceased to be aware of, the source of their disapproval; just as others, consciously or unconsciously, had their opinions of Prohibition changed when *Collier's* articles showed that it was not working successfully. The hostess who is complimented on the appearance of her dinner table is not apt to credit the illustration in an advertisement in one of the women's magazines as the inspiration she carefully followed. Charles Dana Gibson influenced the dress, manners, and appearance of an earlier generation of American young women by his famous drawings in the old *Life* and then in *Collier's.*

Most individuals find it difficult to isolate the original bases of their opinions, tastes, prejudices, and beliefs. Often they can distinguish no single source. They stem from conversations, from odds and ends remembered of their formal education, from their experience with people and things, sometimes from simple imitativeness. More often than they realize, their conceptions, sometimes their misconceptions, had their ultimate origin in a magazine.

Society lives by ideas and the communication of ideas. It is itself the result of ideas and discussion of ideas, and must depend for its continued sustenance and growth on the circulation of facts, opinions about facts, beliefs developed from these opinions, and decisions reached on the basis of considered judgments. There is today no scarcity of the raw material on which social decisions must be reached and social action taken.

There is a great glut of communication. The individual and the social group are assailed, and sometimes almost overwhelmed, by facts and fiction, by fantasies labeled fantasy, and by other fantasies labeled fact. Truths, partial truths, distortions, mistaken convictions, and deliberate falsehoods confront us everywhere in print and in broadcast speech. The fulsome mouthings of omniscient radio and television commentators, the eternal knowingness of political columnists, freshly agog every day over new and horrendous revelations that they have just divulged and delirious over new alarms that they have originated or helped manufacture, are part of our daily diet. The smirkings of gossip columnists, as they ladle out juicy rumors of marital discord among the glamorous great of the entertainment and sporting world, and post advance notices of obstetrical events among the same group, are as familiar as the syndicated advice of tipsters on romantic love, etiquette, health, and "life." Daily a flood of expertly prepared publicity is released on behalf of corporations, government departments, labor organizations, or anyone willing to pay generously for the purchase of public approval and affection.

With all of this there is the unceasing clamor of pressure groups of every kind, all intent, for purely selfish reasons, on influencing private and public opinion favorably, and the vociferous outcries of injured minorities—all minorities, seemingly, being injured, and all of them shrilly articulate. So many groups are continually engaged in lobbying, jockeying for advantage, strenuously engaged in putting both their best feet forward in print and on the air, that thoughtful segments of the public are sometimes inclined to distrust most of what they read and hear.

The reputable magazines, "class" or "mass," are comparatively free of the worst material of this type. A glance at the contents of a representative group will bear out the truth of this assertion. Though it would be absurd to attribute to all of them ethical impulses which many of them do not share, or claim for them ethical practices which some of them do not perform, magazine standards of editorial responsibility are fairly high. Magazine traditions, professional pride, and the interest in matters of public concern which the magazines have shown since 1741 account in part for this circumstance. There are practical as well as idealistic reasons.

The reputation, hence the acceptance and circulation, of a magazine can be seriously damaged by publication of irresponsible material. One seriously mistaken article, or an article which is merely sensational, can do almost irreparable damage to a magazine's standing. Again, the national magazines, as business enterprises, are directed at people with the money to buy the products which they advertise. These people are apt to be those with enough taste and education to discriminate between reputable and disreputable editorial content, as well as between superior and inferior merchandise. The demands of their audiences operate to keep magazine editorial content at a certain level of intelligence and public usefulness.

The magazines are comparatively free of special pleading, if only for the reason that special pleading will inevitably offend groups of readers whom the magazines wish to retain, readers whom they must retain if they are to keep their circulations at the figures guaranteed to advertisers. The weakness here is that, for the same reason, magazines of wide circulation must be circumspect in their treatment of some controversial issues. Some magazines are so circumspect as to omit treatment of some serious social and political issues altogether, a policy which vitiates their force as instruments of social persuasion. Allied to this avoidance are the superficiality, oversimplification, and glibness which weaken the substance of material of social import communicated in some widely circulated magazines.

The distinctness of individual magazines helps to prevent their publishing some of the kinds of material, running from the vicious to the useless, which are printed or aired today. The magazine which is all things to all men has not yet been developed and will not be. A magazine has to establish its identity in order to be recognized and received. The most successful large magazines—and "successful" is used here to mean financially profitable and widely known, read, and respected—have made themselves as nearly as possible synonymous with specific kinds of editorial attempt and performance.

The character of a magazine limits its audience, and thus, to some extent, the spread of its influence, its educational force, its persuasion to belief, and possibly to individual or social action. A reader, on the basis of his experience with the periodical, knows that he will find certain writers, at least writers of certain recognizable types, in one magazine; and that the magazine will consistently display attitudes which he approves or disapproves. He may read or avoid a particular magazine for this reason. He can, if he wishes, read one magazine as an antidote to another. The diversity of magazines enables him to strike a balance between facts as stated and opinions as offered in one magazine, and treatment of the same subject in another magazine. Despite its partisanships—and most of the stronger magazines are partisan politically and socially—one periodical will often present authorities and arguments on several sides of controversial issues.

Magazines are in competition with each other and with the other media of public communication. This competition provides another safeguard against magazine publication of ill-considered material. Magazines do not willingly invite the adverse criticism which is sure to follow its publication. That same competition, of course, is one insurance the public has that the magazines will try to cover every subject of public concern and will offer various interpretations of such subjects. As an integral part of the free press of a free society, magazines share this privilege and responsibility.

Except in arithmetic texts and tables of scientific formulas, little unbiased writing has ever been published. Everything is written by someone, someone with beliefs, emotions, prejudices, and ignorance of his own. Usually a writer has the desire, and sometimes the skill, to sway his readers to his views, but acceptance of what any writer says in any magazine, as in any newspaper or any book, must depend finally on the education and critical intelligence of the reader. Honest and careful magazine editing can screen out obvious inaccuracies and distortions, but the last and final editing the reader must do for himself. For a long time the better magazines have been providing him with the information and helping to develop in him the critical equipment which will enable him to do this.

Much has been written—little has actually been discovered—about how, how much, and in what ways the mass media of communications affect their vast audience. Research in what has come to be called the field of communications is being done continually by sociologists, psychologists, and political scientists drawn to the study; but up to this time few reliable conclusions have been drawn. Most published studies begin or end with the reiterated lament that too little is known and that more study should be done. Wilbur Schramm, in acknowledging and assaying work done by investigators to the end of 1949, could say only that "The present trend of thinking about the study of communications effects is to recognize the full complexity of the problem, and also to recognize that it cannot be solved by any simple and direct attack, but only by analyzing the whole situation minutely and painstakingly, bringing to bear on it all potential evidence from the different social sciences, and then whittling away at the unknown area by means of carefully controlled experiments."[7] Carl I. Hovland, after reviewing studies available five years later, could only repeat in 1954 that some writers thought mass communications were all-powerful while others minimized their effects.[8]

One difficulty which plagues researchers into communications effects is that people must form the basis of their study. If the proper study of mankind is man, as Alexander Pope insisted, he is also the most difficult subject of study. Usually he cannot answer questions accurately about his beliefs and behavior, simply because he does not know. His observed actions, even when controlled under laboratory conditions, are apt to be disconcerting and of small help in reaching valid generalizations. The student of communications must give much of his time and energy to the establishing of study techniques, borrowed many times from marketing research or the pollsters; and, as often as not, he gets lost in the process.

Little of the communications research done thus far has been done specifically on magazines. Magazine publishers make studies continually on the size and composition by age,

[7] "The Effects of Mass Communications: A Review," *Journalism Quarterly,* XXVI (Dec., 1949), No. 4.

[8] "Effects of the Mass Media of Communications," in *Handbook of Social Psychology,* Vol. II, *Special Fields and Applications* (Cambridge, Mass.: Addison-Wesley Publishing Co., 1954). The chapter contains a useful bibliography, pp. 1100–3. Containing, as it does, some of the work of Paul F. Lazarsfeld, Walter Lippmann, Bernard Berelson, Hadley Cantril, Douglas Waples, and other investigators, *Mass Communications* edited by Wilbur Schramm (Urbana, Ill.: University of Illinois Press) is a good indication of the status of the general study.

sex, income, and other social factors of their reading audiences, but these are usually for the purpose of proving to advertisers and potential advertisers that their magazines reach an interested group of customers and prospects. Such studies are not concerned with the effects of a magazine's editorial content upon its readers. Though they were talking of reading of all kinds of printed media, what Waples, Berelson, and Bradshaw pointed out in 1940 can be applied to magazines. They indicated that people read for information to apply to personal problems, to enhance their self-esteem by reading what praises the group to which they belong, to reinforce positions already taken on controversial issues, and for respite or escape. Their aesthetic experience is usually enriched in some way in the process.[9]

These authors contend, and sensibly, that the effects of reading depend on two forces: the content of the publication and the predispositions of the reader, both of them compounded of many elements, few of which are easily isolated. Joseph T. Klapper in *The Effects of Mass Media* makes the further point that people select material to satisfy already established tastes, and that all the mass media tend to reexpose their audiences to the kind of material which their patrons already like best.

In magazine circles there has been discussion in recent years of "impact." Subjectively, the existence of magazine impact is acknowledged. A given periodical does have distinctive characteristics and does awaken particular responses in its readers. Objectively, impact is difficult to prove, difficult even to describe. Some "impact" is measurable; most of it is not.

We speak of the impact of a man's personality, meaning the effect of his physical presence, the sound of his voice, the color and texture of his clothes and how he wears them, what we know of his past or his present or his possibilities—and meaning also our own prejudices, how what we knew of him previously or suspect of him measures against whatever stand-

[9] D. Waples, B. Berelson, and F. R. Bradshaw, *What Reading Does to People* (Chicago: University of Chicago Press, 1940).

ards and beliefs we have amassed from our own total experience.

Impact is pleasant to the one affected and favorable to the object which provides it, if our previous experience with it has been satisfactory from our own viewpoint. This is true whether the object creating the impact is a man, a circumstance, or a magazine. The impact of a given magazine is a possibility made of a thousand related and diverse impressions. The magazine, in the past, has pleased us by its cover pictures and what it has said about cancer, aspects of St. Paul, Minnesota, the habits of polar bears, the Formosan situation, the Vietnam War, or the "flower children." It has seemed credible and reliable or has jibed with what we wish to believe. The type and layout, the general makeup, were aesthetically pleasing or, at least, did not annoy. The illustrations were romantic or their colors did not jar. It took very little mental effort to understand what was said about cancer, Formosa, polar bears, or the advisability of buying a particular brand of motor oil. We read the magazine after a good dinner. It pleased, and we assume that it will please again. We have been made receptive. Succeeding issues of the magazine will have impact—they will reach us equipped with the possibility of arousing a favorable response.

This can work the other way, and still be "impact." We distrusted and detested what the magazine said about cancer, Formosa, and the motor lubricant. The periodical has established an effect of annoyance and displeasure. We will not believe what it may say of the Aleutians, tuberculosis, or any motor oil of any kind.

The probability, though, is against the second reaction. The magazine has long been a familiar part of the American scene. It has been able to become so because it has impressed millions, even billions, of its total audience favorably for generations. The probability is that the individual reader is enough like those millions that he too will be receptive to the carefully concocted allure of the periodical. The force of every issue which was ever published, of the fact that the magazine has been around all his life, that his father used to read it, perhaps his grandfather, all help.

Because of all these things or things like them, a magazine has impact, the capability to create an effect. The impact of various magazines, because of the reader's experience with them, is different. The sight of one arouses warm, friendly, reassuring feelings; another, the idea of excitement, cleverness; another stirs troubled feelings of unsolved problems and perplexing issues, though there may be a kind of admiration intermingled with the reader's unease. He makes his choice on the basis of his feelings and his mood of the moment.

There may also be an unconscious element of despair in the reader's choice. "The fact is," Nathaniel Hawthorne wrote in his notebook in 1855, when he was American Consul in Liverpool, "the world is accumulating too many materials for knowledge." The confusion which Hawthorne found perplexing more than a hundred years ago has multiplied until modern man finds it and himself many times worse confounded. Experts and specialists in thousands of fields and the boggy corners of these fields have sprung up in increasing numbers because few can cope with, understand, or attempt even to gather the materials for understanding much of the larger social, political, economic, scientific, and what-else world we live in. Most of us cannot form usable judgments on myriads of subjects that touch us because we have not bases on which to form them and cannot hope to accumulate enough of the pertinent facts to provide them. It is part of modern man's dilemma. It is also part of the reason why he seizes avidly on magazine digests and condensations; why he spends so much time seeking escape in entertainment; why he gladly reads a superficial journalistic foray into some subject he knows influences his world and which he would like, if it does not entail too much effort, to know a little about.

Chapter 26

The Magazines and War

The Atlantic Monthly, The Saturday Evening Post, and most magazines of the time could virtually ignore the Civil War, leaving it to *Harper's Weekly* to cover it vividly in text and pictures. Especially since the advent of the news weeklies and what were primarily pictorial magazines, the magazines have welcomed war as a subject and have thrived on its drama, excitement, and reader appeal. In the 20th century, during which wars have flowered from chivalric jousts between small professional armies to cosmic disputes with annihilation of whole peoples possible, American magazines have both reported as observers and served as propagandist participants.

In turn, war, which has become more characteristic of international relations and human behavior than peace—or seems to be because the press, including magazines, has publicized it more zealously—has wrought changes in the magazines. World War I was reported solely by newspapers and magazines with some motion picture newsreel reporting. World War II was reported by newspapers, magazines, motion pictures, and radio. Wars since that time have enjoyed the additional advantage of television coverage.

Because public opinion had come to its decisions well before governmental action was taken, magazines did not wait until the actual entry of the United States into World War I in April, 1917, before offering their resources to the government. Quickly they made themselves powerful engines for publicizing the war in its many phases, for stirring patriotic emotions, and for keeping their audiences informed of wartime activities urged by the authorities. They began, in fact, to apply effectively some of the devices of organized propaganda before that term was in general usage, and long before its still loosely defined principles were generally understood or its force as a weapon was fully recognized.

Public figures appointed to head various programs turned to the magazines to get their messages before the public. Ex-President William Howard Taft used the magazines to publicize the activities of the American Red Cross. Herbert Hoover's plans as Food Administrator were first announced in the magazines. Assistant Secretary of the Navy Franklin D. Roosevelt wrote "What the Navy Can Do for Your Boy" for one of the women's magazines in order to stimulate Navy recruiting. "The Y.M.C.A. in the War" became a monthly magazine feature edited by John R. Mott.

Inspirational stories, articles, and pictures with patriotic themes were rife in the magazines. Patriotism was stressed as a compelling motif in World War I. But there was more factual coverage, too, of the war. The actual progress of the conflict in Europe was reported by such correspondents as Irvin Cobb, Mary Roberts Rinehart, George Pattullo, and Will Irwin. The war news from Washington was reported along with the biographies and comment about the war leaders: Wilson and his cabinet members, Bernard Baruch, R. S. Lovett, Charles Norton, and others who were members of the Advisory Committee of National Defense or were in other ways active in the prosecution of the war on the political and industrial fronts.

The *Literary Digest* practically transformed itself into a war journal in 1917 and 1918. Its pages were crammed with feature articles about the war, with war comment extracted from the newspapers, with war cartoons, and with maps outlining from week to week the progress of the Allies against Germany. A greatly increased number of readers looked to the *Digest*, the only news weekly during World War I, for accurate and authentic war information. *The National Geographic Magazine* issued maps of the western front so that its readers could follow the Allied armies over known terrain and, in issue after issue, concentrated on the geography of the countries at war.

The women's service magazines aided Herbert Hoover's food-saving campaigns by publishing practical explanations and illustrations of how to save flour, how to make bread of whole wheat, bran, Graham flour, and other substitutes for the refined white flour housewives were accustomed to use in their baking. They printed photographs of women in their new wartime occupations as farmerettes, factory workers, street-car operators, and the like, in order to stimulate more women to replace men in occupations which, until the war, had been considered wholly masculine. They told how to knit socks, sweaters, mufflers, mittens, and even "the new aviator's helmets" for men in the armed forces.

Their contents filled with the war news, the general popular weeklies, such as *Collier's* and *The Saturday Evening Post,* carried covers displaying men in uniform, Red Cross girls, aviatrixes, and World War I planes in battle. A few advertisers were reproducing recruiting posters in their paid magazine space.

When the war to end war, as H. G. Wells called it, the war that Woodrow Wilson promised would make the world safe for democracy, and which did not do either one came to a victorious end, the magazines could look back with satisfaction at having done their bit, as the phrase was then. They had supported the war with all the idealistic fervor then expected of every right-thinking American and had reported it thoroughly.

Earnest and effective as they were, the reporting and the propaganda effort of the magazines in World War I seem amateurish by comparison with the expert handling of their job by the magazines, as well as by the other press media, during World War II. This was a larger and a different war. The ideological conflicts behind the national differences were more apparent. The destruction was greater, and it was realized that this destruction could be made complete enough to extinguish whole countries and whole ideas, whole ways of living. There was little inspirational idealism in the air. No one seemed able to state national war aims in understandable terms. It was accepted that not to win was not to survive nationally or politically.

No war in history has been as thoroughly recorded, documented, and covered in news, story, and pictures as World War II. The importance of such complete coverage was understood from the beginning. So was the increased wartime importance of all communications media. The attention of the magazines, the newspapers, and the radio was immediately focused on the war as the one subject of consuming interest; and all of them were immediately utilized for morale purposes and for the dissemination of war doctrine to produce concerted national action. Again, both as reporters and as instruments of psychological and propaganda warfare the magazines performed efficiently.

The position of the magazines in relation to the other media was changed by the time of the second major conflict of the twentieth century from what it had been a quarter century earlier. The radio was available for the rapid transmission of the highlights of the news. The news weeklies and the pictorial magazines founded after the first of the two wars, could supplement and augment the radio and the newspaper by fuller coverage of the war news itself, but the chief magazine coverage, in the new type magazines as well as in the older magazines, was in articles that discussed as well as reported in greater detail than radio and newspapers could report. Scores of magazine correspondents with the armies and naval forces of the United States and with the fighting units of the other United Nations reported battle action from every theater of operation. With no sharp deadlines to meet, these writers could cover their subjects in greater detail than could representatives of radio and the daily press who had to meet the demands for spot news. American magazine readers followed the course of the warfare in Africa, Europe, and the Pacific in the word and photographic reporting of the magazines which at the same time could analyze and discuss the news they offered. *Life*'s photographs, *Time*'s comments, *The New Yorker*'s observations, and thoughtful articles in the general weeklies and monthlies merged to form the magazine picture of the war and to describe its progress.

The propaganda force of the magazines, better understood in World War II than in World War I, was utilized fully by the national government, and skillfully channeled by the magazines themselves. There was no exalted patriotism this second time. As there were fewer military bands, fewer parades, fewer emotional appeals generally, there was less flag-waving and sentimentality in the magazines. Instead there was the effort to present the facts clearly and to interpret what the facts, as they were seen at the time, seemed to mean. The magazines addressed their material to an audience whose war consciousness was not aroused by slogans but, increasingly, and largely through the efforts of the magazines, by an understanding of the conflicting political and social concepts which were largely responsible for the war. In this way, the reportorial and propaganda forces of the magazines were joined.

Articles in American magazines discussed the issues involved in the war, the causes for which the United Nations fought. Other articles described the German and Japanese enemy, analyzing the nature of our adversaries, their political beliefs, social institutions, and the character generally of the Germans and Japanese as individuals and national groups. The governments and the peoples of the various members of the United Nations were explained to American readers in hundreds of magazine articles. Other articles stressed the importance of American industrial production; literally thousands of news stories and articles were devoted to publicizing every aspect of life in the armed forces in training and in action. Within a year after Pearl Harbor national magazines had printed fifteen hundred stories and articles containing war information.

The national magazine became during the war years a forum, attended by the population of the country, for the exposition of the government's wartime policies and programs.

It gave the facts of each problem—industrial, agricultural, social, and sometimes military—that the nation had to meet and solve, explained the significance of the facts, urged on every reader again and again the importance of each element in the complete war picture. Articles explained the need for price control as a war measure, and its functioning. Others gave repeated warnings of the dangers of inflation and showed what inflation would mean; or reported our mammoth plane production or showed to what use Russia put the American war equipment it received. Practical advice on how to live under rationing, how to conserve on tires, or how to get the most out of home-heating when fuel was scarce was run alongside explanations of Lend-Lease and descriptions of operations in Attu, at Kawjalein, in England, over Schweinfurt, on Omaha Beach in Normandy, at Anzio, and at Cassino.

One illustration may serve to indicate the extent to which the American people came to look upon magazines as national newspapers during the war, how far magazines influenced public opinion on war subjects, and how far this situation was recognized. *The Saturday Evening Post* published in two parts, May 13, and May 20, 1945, an article by Forrest Davis entitled "What Really Happened at Teheran." Until its publication almost nothing had been disclosed of what had transpired when Roosevelt, Stalin, and Churchill met for the last time as the leaders of the United States, Russia, and England, to plot the final strategy of the war. It was from the *Post* that the public learned something of the conversations that had been held and the decisions that would affect not only the conduct of the last part of the war but also the world's post-war future. Columnists and commentators were quick to remark the appearance of this information in the *Post* and to comment on the significance of its appearance there. Two stated that the articles were supposed to have been initialed in advance by the President. Another noted that the *Post* "told far more of the President's intentions in the post-war world than had been disclosed to the senators in the course of the discussions." The remarks of a fourth pointed squarely to the stature which the magazine had attained in the eyes of government as an effective medium of nationwide communication. He saw publication in the *Post* of "What Really Happened at Teheran" as a deliberate device used more than once by the President and the State Department; that of letting a magazine of national circulation tell the inside story to the people.

Outright publicity was used by the magazines, as over the radio and in motion picture theaters, to enlist support of the various wartime campaigns conducted among civilians: campaigns to sell War Bonds to increase industrial and agricultural production, campaigns for blood donation, the United Service Organizations, the Red Cross, salvage, food conservation, and all of the other government-sponsored promotions designed to intensify war realization throughout the population and to mobilize all of the country's resources.

Magazine editorial space was devoted to these subjects, but much of this work, significantly, was done through magazine advertising. It was directed by the War Advertising Council, an association formed by advertisers, advertising agencies, and advertising media. By December 7, 1944, three years after Pearl Harbor, nearly a billion dollars' worth of advertising, much of it run in magazines, was thus used for the promotion of such programs.

Advertisers filled their space with the kind of vigorously written copy and forceful art work that would aid in recruiting WACs and nurses, emphasize the necessity for security of information, fight waste, influence people to buy more and more War Bonds and to keep them, combat absenteeism in war plants, get more women to take jobs left by men drafted into the armed services, and support the National War Fund. Magazines and magazine advertisers devoted over $15,000,000 in space to the promotion of War Bond sales alone. Full pages of space in 828 magazines with a combined circulation of 109,000,000 were used from August, 1943, to November, 1945, to warn Americans of the dangers of inflation and to promote conservation.

Wartime activities of these kinds wrought what seem to be permanent changes in American magazines. Wartime factual reporting and discussions of economic, political, and social issues, of scientific advances and possibilities, and of ideas previously handled only in the more pretentious periodicals accustomed popular magazine audiences to more serious treatment of serious subjects. The proportion of factual over fictional material in magazines mounted during the war. Standards and precedents set for themselves by the magazines during the war years were maintained. Generally they contained less froth, more information.

Habits developed by magazine advertisers during the war years carried over into the years immediately subsequent. Magazine advertising was used during the war to convey information, to publicize ideas, and to persuade to social action. Since the war a considerable number of advertisers have continued to use paid magazine space for these same purposes, running copy and displays meant not primarily to sell their wares but to sell ideas that will affect thought and social action. Some of this advertising is basically informational in character; some of it is argument. Other advertisements are designed to influence public opinion favorably toward an industry, to defend a business or business generally, to explain an economic or social situation, and to state the viewpoints of an industrial institution or an organization.

Stories, articles, and reminiscences of World War II have been a magazine staple ever since that war ended. It is a poor general or upper-echelon wartime politician whose memoirs have not been serialized in one or another of the popular magazines. Land, naval, and air campaigns have been refought by observers or participants and intelligence secrets hidden under wartime security divulged in exciting accounts. One issue of *Reader's Digest,* that of November, 1953, ran two such British intelligence thrillers, "The Corpse That Hoaxed the Axis," a condensation of *The Man Who Never Was* by Ewen Edward Samuel Montagu, and a much longer tale, "The Man Who Wouldn't Talk" by Quentin Reynolds. It was the fault neither of the writer nor the magazine that the second story, purported war experience of a Canadian spy captured and brutalized by the Nazis, proved to be the greater hoax of the two.

Magazine circulations zoomed during World War II, and only wartime paper shortage kept them from zooming higher. It was the magazine's pictorial reporting of the war that sent *Life*—only six years old at the time—to the top of the list. When the war ended and paper was again plentifully available, magazine circulations continued to climb. Industry was beating its swords back into plowshares in a race to fill the pent-up demand for cars, tires, nylons, and all the luxuries it had been unable to make and distribute during the war. With television not yet available, business needed the national magazines to get its goods to an unmatched sellers' market.

War and rumors of war have been an actuality in the magazine press since the close of World War II. The unpleasant possibilities of atomic warfare have been explored in article after article, notably in a *Collier's* issue devoted to World War III; and the so-called cold war between Russia and the United States, between world communism and western democracy, was waged hotly and dramatically. Early in 1947 *The Saturday Evening Post* published two articles telling how Russia spied on her wartime allies to obtain atomic secrets. This was before Russia's attitude and purposes were generally recognized. Since that time the *Post, Life, Reader's Digest,* and virtually all of the popular magazines carried both sober appraisals of Russian life and political action and pieces by escaped political prisoners, men released from slave labor in Siberian mines, American correspondents and businessmen imprisoned and mistreated, and other stories illustrating the temper and characteristics of the acknowledged antagonist.

Geared to war coverage, the large-circulation weekly magazines went into action quickly when the Korean War broke in June, 1950. A *Life* photographer was shooting pictures of the fighting two days after the war began. A *Saturday Evening Post* correspondent accompanied United Nations troops to the first fighting, and the *Post* was soon printing his stories of the exploits of Brigadier General, then Lieutenant-Colonel, Mike Michaelis and the Twenty-seventh Division. Harold H. Martin was joined by Nora Waln, Demaree Bess, William L. Worden, and later *Herald Tribune* correspondent Marguerite Higgins in covering the Korean War for the *Post*. Robert Sherrod, made managing editor of the magazine in 1955, served as chief correspondent for the *Post* in the Korean War area. *Life*'s first man on the scene was joined by eleven other photographers and ten correspondents in reporting the Korean War. One *Time-Life* correspondent was killed in ambush early in the conflict, and three others were injured in Korea. During the 157 weeks of its duration *Life* published 454 pages of pictures of the Korean War. In its issue of July 6, 1953, it ran complete *The Bridges at Toko-Ri*, a novel by James Michener based on American naval fighting in Korea.

Time, in its issue of June 26, 1950, the day before the Korean outbreak, had carried nothing on Korea, but it had warned in its June 5th issue: ". . . South Korea can be made a sound political and economic unit. . . . Withdrawal now would leave not only a shattered and broken nation, but a broken moral obligation as well. Failure in Korea would cost America priceless prestige and augur American failure elsewhere in Asia." By July 11th, *Time* carried a cover picture of General Douglas MacArthur ("His Job to Police the Boundaries of Chaos") and a ten-page lead story on "War In Asia." "War In Asia" was retained as a regular department of *Time* until the issue of July 20, 1953. *Newsweek*, which featured Gloria Swanson on its June 26, 1950, cover ("The Great Comeback"), had nothing about Korea under its Foreign Affairs department. Soon, "Korean War," often in the lead position, was an established feature for the duration. *U.S. News and World Report*, given always to blacker and bolder type in startling heads, covered the war with more "exclusives," "inside information," and "reasons behind." In their Korean War coverage magazines not only gave chill reality to a particularly bloody war, conveying thoroughly the bitterness of the conflict, but strove to make clear the war's significance in the larger struggle for world power. The political implications of the whole were recognized in magazine articles as well as the narrative and drama of battle, Truman's abrupt removal of General Douglas

President Harry S Truman and General Douglas MacArthur shake hands at Wake Island before their controversy which resulted in the recall of the Far Eastern commander. *Life* published both their stories.

MacArthur from command, the armistice negotiations which the communists dragged out for two years, prisoner repatriation, and the general aftermath of the war.

Early in 1956 two magazine articles in the general field of war and international affairs, published in the same week, brought renewed and unexpected proof of the vitality and effectiveness of the magazine in public communication. *Life* for January 16 carried an article by James Shepley, chief of the magazine's Washington Bureau, entitled "How Dulles Averted War." The article quoted the Secretary of State as claiming he had three times brought the United States to the brink of war—in Korea in June, 1953, in Indochina in April, 1954, in the Formosa Strait in January, 1955. As the article read, the Secretary defended such action as part of the strategy of foreign policy called for by a tense world situation. He spoke of it as the "necessary art" of risking war to maintain peace.

The article caused an immediate furor. The Secretary of State was berated. The President of the United States found it necessary to comment and explain in press conference. The Secretary of Defense became embroiled. Senators and Congressmen of the opposition party used the article to attack the administration's conduct of foreign affairs. *Life*'s publisher issued a press statement defending and explaining the article.

On January 21 *The Saturday Evening Post* published the first installment of a six-part article by General Matthew B. Ridgway (as told to Harold H. Martin). In this initial piece entitled "Conflict in the Pentagon," General Ridgway charged that while he was army Chief of Staff military decisions were made on a basis of political expediency. Ridgway, who was outspoken in his criticisms, said in part: "I quickly learned that . . . the decisions of the Defense Department were based on . . . the advantages to be gained in the field of domestic politics by drastic reduction in military expenditures. I learned too, with a certain sense of shock, that sometimes I was not expected to present my reasoned military judgment to Secretary of Defense Charles E. Wilson. . . . I do not recall that I ever felt a greater sense of shock then when I read in President Eisenhower's State of the Union message in 1954 that: 'The defense program recommended for 1955 is based on a new program *unanimously recommended* by the Joint Chiefs of Staff.' " Most emphatically, Ridgway said, he had not concurred in the recommendation.

This forthright statement caused a second imbroglio. It gave the Democratic Party further ammunition to direct against the administration in a presidential election year. Opposition Senators demanded explanation. The Secretary of Defense and other Pentagon officials issued hurried statements and explanations. Public opinion was aroused for and against the disputants and the issues involved.

In both cases, as usually it does, the furor died away without resolving points of who said, did, or meant what; who was right, wrong, or indiscreet. The point demonstrated was the impact of the articles appearing in two powerful American magazines.

Also demonstrated was the sharp change in magazine war coverage. The magazines had enthusiastically upheld the prosecution of World War I. They had reported fully and without adverse comment on the conduct of World War II. By the time of the Korean War magazine reporting and comment reflected a changed national attitude. The attitude was more critical, and so were the magazines.

When Fidel Castro seized control of Cuba from Fulgencio Batista in 1959, American press comment was generally approving. This was the triumph of guerrilla liberalism over dictatorship. There was a tendency to see the bearded Castro and his bearded followers as romantic heroes. Not until his statements and actions made Castro's communist affiliations and designs apparent did the magazines turn against him.

Magazine coverage of the tragically unsuccessful invasion of Cuba by exiles with United States support in 1961 was sympathetic with the victims but careful. All the facts of a confused situation were not known. When the Soviet offensive buildup in Cuba was made known in the fall of 1962 and the missile crisis developed, Russia and communism were the manifest enemies, and the magazines could be forthright in their denunication, but public trust in the government's efficiency to deal with warlike gestures had been shaken, and the magazines showed it. These events and press reaction to them conditioned American attitudes toward involvement in Vietnam.

American troops became engaged in just the kind of war on the mainland of Asia so long warned against. Though men and material were poured into Vietnam year after year there were no decisive victories. There was less and less chance of any victory at all, even, finally, of settlement. Though posted at first as an incident in the U.S. policy of containing communism geographically, the war became a major conflict, long-drawn out, purposelessly expensive in American lives and in billions of taxpayers' dollars. It was a fight between democracy, which is good, and communism, which is evil. That part was all right, but few could understand the political differences within Vietnam which caused the seemingly insoluble dispute or see that they had any relevance to the United States.

The Vietnam War has provided plenty of magazine material and produced thousands of articles, but little of it concerned with the actual conflict. Instead it has been concerned with political divisiveness about the war, accusations and counter-accusations, rebellion against the military draft, protest meetings, student riots against the war and against campus recruiters for companies producing armament or ammunition, Vietnam as a testing ground for conventional weapons and tactics with a chance for professional military men to experience combat and win promotion. The weekly body count of young Americans, just as dead as if they had been killed for a cause anyone believed in, has sufficed for basic radio and newspaper reporting of the war, while the magazine subject has been in general the manifestations of unrest and dissatisfaction in the United States provoked by Vietnam. Manufacturers did not buy magazine space to boast that they produced materiel for the Vietnam War. If they did produce for it, they advertised the fact nowhere.

Previous 20th century wars acted to concentrate magazine editorial effort. They increased magazine circulations and added to their incomes. Vietnam benefited the magazines no more than it did anybody or anything else.

Chapter 27

Magazine Variety

The two decades following World War I saw the establishment of many of today's leading magazines: *Time, The Reader's Digest, The New Yorker, Fortune,* and *Business Week* in the 1920's; *Life* and *Look* in the 1930's. Few magazines which have attained national significance were founded in the early years after World War II. Instead, flushed with wartime prosperity and faced with a future which seemed to promise only more of it, the extant magazines drove for larger circulations and each for a larger share of the lucrative advertising which it was comparatively easy to get as business set out to reestablish and widen its markets. To bring in the reader-customers the magazines went in for a general refurbishing and a streamlining of content and appearance.

When he visited the United States in 1908, Lord Northcliffe, originator of the tabloid and astute publisher of the London *Daily Mail* and *The Times,* was outspoken in his opinion that even then American magazines were "infinitely better than those of England." He prophesied that the next great advance in American magazine production would take place when some method of printing photographs in color could be devised. *Life* and *Look* proved Northcliffe correct, and the general and women's magazines went in for greater use of color and of graphics generally. Other changes came. Type faces were modernized. New logotypes were devised to replace the older ones. Margins disappeared with the increased use of bleed for color and picture pages.

Editorial changes were made to match the changes in appearance. The whole appeal of many of the mass magazines became one of speed and the suggestion of easy reading or riffling. General weeklies increased the number of articles in an issue and shortened them to balance the quickness of impression provided by pictures. When they did not drop fiction completely, they reduced the number of short stories and shortened those they retained. *The New Yorker* went the opposite way with more and longer fiction, and the women's monthly magazines continued with the kind of romantic escape fiction they had made their own, often running cut versions of complete novels by popular writers in a single issue.

A greater variety of short features, cartoons, quips, puzzles, and amusements was introduced, and the accent on timeliness was stressed. As they still do, the magazines competed with each other for the memoirs of public men, for stories about celebrities, for exclusive, inside, never-before-told features. A magazine paid $60,000 for "Admiral Halsey Tells His Story," $175,000 for the war diary of General Eisenhower, and $102,000 to another general and his collaborator for a series of six articles on World War II. Though no price was announced, *Life, The New York Times,* and a book publisher are reported to have paid $1,000,000 for Sir Winston Churchill's war memoirs. *The Saturday Evening Post* paid $100,000 for Lindbergh's "33 Hours to Paris," and $75,000 for Bing Crosby's "Call Me Lucky." This competition for manuscripts by or about the great or the near-great continues.

As a result of the millions of dollars worth of free publicity obtained when the assassinated President's widow sued to prevent magazine serialization and book publication, *Look* reached what it claims as the largest audience ever obtained by four consecutive issues of a magazine when it published in 1967 William Manchester's *Death of a President. Look* has never divulged the price it paid for the serial rights, but it was probably more than the $300 or so which the class magazines or the $1,500 or more which the mass magazines pay for the ordinary article. *McCall's* advertised widely that it paid more than $1,000,000 for an article by Robert F. Kennedy, assassinated five months before, which it ran in November, 1968.

In the late 1940's and early 1950's the day seemed far past when a magazine editor and publisher could almost count, as could Noah Webster, on the early financial failure of his venture. It is a far cry, too, from the days when magazine contributors were unpaid, or the days, a little later, when Edgar Allan Poe was paid ten dollars for "The Raven" by the *American Review*. Longfellow sometimes received twenty dollars a poem from *Graham's*, and Lowell got ten dollars at first, more somewhat later. When Lowell himself became an editor, he paid such contributors as Emerson, Longfellow, and Bryant about five dollars a page for their work in the *Atlantic*. "Couldn't you," he wrote in 1864, as editor of *The North American Review*, to John Lothrop Motley, who was then minister to Austria, "write on the natural history of the diplomatic cuttlefish of Schleswig-Holstein without forfeiting your ministerial equanimity?" Again he offered five dollars a page.

Editorial salaries had also improved somewhat. Rufus Wilmot Griswold's salary as editor of the very successful *Graham's* was $1,000 a year. James Russell Lowell received what was at the time the very large salary of $2,500 a year as editor of the *Atlantic*. A chief reason for supplanting Lowell with James T. Fields, a member of the firm which then published the magazine, was to save this ruinous outlay. A hundred years later the still flourishing Curtis Publishing Company was paying its top editors over $100,000 a year.

Editorial research was rampant by this early post-World War II period. It promised to substitute infallible science for fallible art in editing, and its possibilities seemed inexhaustible. An editor knew immediately what subjects and treatments had worked in past issues so what might work well in the future. He knew the kinds of articles and stories men preferred, which women preferred. The women's magazines surveyed their readers to find out what they thought about divorce, birth control, moral standards, and subjects outside the purely domestic sphere so that they could edit accordingly. With this weapon at his disposal it seemed that an editor could almost put out his magazine by simple arithmetic or a slide rule or let the computers do it by themselves.

Much research, editorial, economic, and social, was conducted before *Holiday,* one of the few new magazines to emerge after World War II, began publication. The publishers and *Holiday's* first editors had masses of facts about leisure, recreation, travel, eating, drinking, and decorous reveling to start with.

Holiday fumbled to a start in 1946. It steadied and picked up when after the first few issues Ted Patrick was made editor. A Young & Rubicam copywriter who had published a magazine for the Office of War Information, Patrick had been hired from the Compton advertising agency to develop a pictorial magazine after the *Life* manner—it never appeared—for Curtis. Under Patrick, *Holiday* caught on. Its circulation was over 1,000,000 in 1968.

Holiday had trouble defining itself. Strenuously it insisted that, despite all internal indications to the contrary, it was not a travel magazine. Instead, it was "the magazine of creative leisure." Its earnest purpose was to instruct people how best to use the new leisure with which they were blessed or confounded. In the words of Ted Patrick, "Creative use of leisure time includes travel, but also other activities . . . all sports, the theater, movies, television, and radio, music, painting or writing indulged as a pastime, the reading of good books, the preparation and pursuit of food, party-giving and attending, the fixing of one's home to make it more rewarding and relaxing to live in, and the making or acquisition of the clothing best designed for any of these activities." Patrick made his list all-inclusive, the beachcombing dilettante's delight.

Though it shows some of the aspects of them all, lushly dressed *Holiday* is not a travel magazine, a shelter book, or a literary monthly. It has some of the glamour of *Vogue,* some of the substance of the *National Geographic,* a touch of *The*

New Yorker's urbanity, and wears them all unsurely. It has always just missed being smart, but it is knowing about foods, wines, resorts, and night clubs. There are usually plenty of bikinis (inhabited) and bits of stage business gossip. In fact, *Holiday* was and, though he died in 1962, still is the good life as Ted Patrick saw the good life—jet-set travel, expensive restaurants, tennis, the correct wines, European nobility and the American rich posed in their photogenic habitats. Served for the aspiring epicure and *bon vivant,* the correctly attired lawn or field sportsman, the self-conscious cosmopolitan, and the suburbanite who would be socially sophisticated, *Holiday* offers caviar, the approved wines, and some more substantial fare, usually in a night-club setting.

Place articles are the *Holiday pièces de résistance.* They are full, informative, sometimes charming, sometimes pretentious, often seductive—objective and subjective descriptions of Atlanta or Rome, café and resort society in Philadelphia or on Capri, the romance of Africa, Asia, Indianapolis, or Kansas City. Most of these pieces are pleasantly and skillfully written. Some are superficial and brilliant; others, like the E. B. White piece on New York (April, 1949), J. B. Marquand on Boston (November, 1953), and Frank O'Connor on Ireland (December, 1949), had greater depth, strength, and virtue.

Holiday has returned to many places more than once, each time making the country, city, or resort the focal point of an issue. There are only so many plush playgrounds and so many glamor cities. This treatment serves to bring together *Holiday's* otherwise rather scattered offering; in addition, the issues are highly promotable for circulation purposes in the favored spot.

Holiday, which does not consider unsolicited contributions and assigns all of the pieces not staff written or purchased from the agents of established writers—Patrick liked to use novelists for non-fiction pieces—uses as many big names as it can get. It has used Faulkner, Dunsany, Hemingway, Steinbeck, O'Faolain, Joyce Cary. More characteristic of the magazine's tone and attempt are Bemelmans, Perelman, Fadiman,

A mounted trooper of the Blues stands guard over an issue of *Holiday* devoted entirely to London—London scenes, shops, royalty, restaurants, hotels, clubs, and crime. *Holiday's* dominant theme is "The New Leisure."

Lucius Beebe, Stong, Michener, Guthrie, Schulberg, Wechsberg, and Jerome Weidman. *Holiday* has published notable issues on Paris (April, 1953), on Italy (April, 1955), on London (April, 1956). From the standpoint of layout, illustration, and reproduction, every issue of *Holiday* is attractive.

As one of its properties, *Holiday* was affected by the ups and downs, after 1960 mostly the downs, of The Curtis Publishing Company. It lost some of its top staff during the upheaval, saw a succession of business executives come and hastily go, and has had several changes of editor since Patrick's death. Possibly because of its essential subject or, despite all the defining words, its essential lack of central concept, *Holiday* has always seemed more veneer than substance. A smooth performance, it lacks warmth and other than poolside and cabana reality. Perhaps this and gracious living by graciously well-heeled people are the reality for *Holiday* and the ideal of its suburbanite readers.

The United States had been developed. World conflict had been resolved. Unimaginable leisure for everyone was forecast after the close of World War II. Automation could take over the labor and everyone could play. *Holiday* was founded to exploit the market for all the toys and diversions which people would consume in enjoying themselves; which is why it had to deny so vigorously that it was merely a travel magazine and why Ted Patrick had to insist so laboriously that it was much, much more. Most people have more free time than they did, but in actuality the new leisure has proved to be mostly the possession of organized labor and of teachers and students, who have always had it. There was that flaw in the basic idea, and the same weakness of unrealized basic idea shows in *Holiday*. It has never quite become what someone must once have thought it would be.

Play is at one pole of most people's interest, work at the opposite. Here a weekly magazine founded in the unpropitious year of 1929 has done well for itself and its giant publisher, McGraw-Hill, Inc. Its other magazines deal with specific management, engineering, production, maintenance, and selling functions in business. They are intended as vehicles to communicate applicable information to men at work within given industries or professions. *Business Week,* described by its publishers as "essentially a news service," has by the nature of its coverage a wider appeal. Because business in some form is the primary American occupation and preoccupation, the magazine's emphasis on business and its handling of most subjects from an economic viewpoint makes it function in some degrees as an important news weekly. Timely, accurate, authoritative, *Business Week* covers production, marketing, labor, finance, management, transport, government, business abroad and has departments on the Business Outlook and the Washington Outlook.

Business Week goes a little further. Many of its articles are as well done of their kind as those in *Fortune* or *The Wall Street Journal.* McGraw-Hill has also shown a kind of missionary zeal—and staked out a kind of ownership—in recognition of the economic and social plight of American cities. In February, 1968, it published "Business and the Urban Crisis," a 33-page insert prepared by a team of its editors, in 33 of its publications, including *Business Week.* About ten per cent of all the articles which *Business Week* published in 1967 were concerned with some aspect of the urban problem. The magazine also goes in for pieces on civil rights, the Supreme Court, federal anti-trust policy, and the like, as well as for routine coverage of its standard business departments. Commercially, *Business Week* is by far the most successful of the large-circulation business periodicals, *Forbes, Fortune, Nation's Business,* and the others which it resembles in subject, but does not really resemble because of its news weekly character. Like all the other McGraw-Hill periodicals, it is a special-interest magazine but the nearest to a general interest magazine of them all. Standard Rate and Data Service lists it among consumer magazines as well as among business publications.

Business Week is not sold on the newsstands, and its subscription circulation is controlled. The masthead states, "Subscriptions to Business Week solicited only from management men in business and industry," and applicants are required to give the names of their companies and the titles of their position. This makes for a valuable list and a circulation attractive to advertisers. Every year *Business Week,* with over 600,000 chosen subscribers and many of its issues running over 200 pages, vies with *The New Yorker* for the largest amount of advertising and the highest advertising revenue among weekly magazines.

Somewhere between the two poles of work and play, about midway for most people, lies another center of interest, the home.

There are a number of handsome shelter books. Some are older and more pretentious, affect a more patrician pose and appeal. Though it slipped for a time, none has achieved greater popular success since World War II than *Better Homes & Gardens,* founded 1922 and published in Des Moines by the Meredith Corporation. Heavy, thick with advertising, *Better Homes & Gardens* with a circulation of over 7,500,000 stands about sixth in size currently among all American magazines. It carried over $19,000,000 in advertising in the first six months of 1969. It is published in about 64 different editions, and one 1967 edition was published in 78.

Since World War II, home ownership, particularly in suburbs and small towns and cities, has become widespread. Made easier by higher wages, government subsidies of one kind and another, mortgage guarantees, comparatively small down payments and the rest through rental installments, it seems to have become the rule rather than the exception, even among people of an age and income which previously would have caused delay in the acquisition of a house and grounds. Innumerable appliances and devices have been produced and marketed for the building, then the maintenance and repair of the house and its plot of lawn or garden. These changed economic and social conditions are such that an attractive and practical magazine about the home appeals to a wide audience, and *Better Homes* has capitalized on the situation. Founded by E. T. Meredith, who had been Woodrow Wilson's

Secretary of Agriculture, *Better Homes* began with idealistic pronouncements about the home and its place in American life. It has capitalized on the change in the domestic sphere to become a useful magazine as well as a practical success.

When the magazine was twenty-five years old it printed a folksy editorial statement in which it could claim that for years it had printed more about food than any other magazine in the world, that one out of four subscribers clipped and saved its recipes—560,000,000 clipped recipes in ten years. A study had found it the magazine gardeners most often turned to for help. It was the magazine most read by families building new homes. More than a million families had used the complete homeplanning centers set up by the magazine with department stores in various cities. Five to six thousand people wrote the magazine monthly "for help on anything from smoky fireplaces to keeping frogs through the winter." Every month *Better Homes* describes in detail a "Five Star" home. Complete plans and specifications after designs by leading architects are offered. Hundreds of thousands of these plans have been sold. Most popular of all was Number 2001, published in January, 1950. By March, 1955, 28,982 sets of plans for this house had been sold. This one house plan has accounted for the building of almost 6,000 homes for a total building cost of nearly $120,000,000. Some 3,600 families still planned to build Number 2001 at a future estimated building cost of another $73,000,000.

Better Homes runs contests, gives advice and suggestions on home building, decorating, and household activities. It promotes community beautification programs. It gives its readers plenty of luscious illustrations, plenty of how-to-do-it hints, plenty of home remodelling ideas, plenty of articles on family problems, green-thumb tips on bulbs, perennials, parasites, and sprays, and takes in plenty of profitable advertising. It can and does promote itself with some accuracy as "the family idea magazine," and Meredith has called itself "America's largest publisher of ideas for today's living and tomorrow's plans." It exploits its magazine material in paperbound cookbooks, sewing books, garden books, home handyman's books that it sells by the millions in supermarkets.

The American public has proved that it will read, at least tolerate and support, a great variety of magazines. It has shown its favor to long-established periodicals, to certain that are relatively new, and to some so changed in content and format as to seem new. It has responded to magazines concerned with the basic interests of work, play, and the home. It will also patronize, if not extravagantly in every instance, publication of a very different kind from *Holiday, Business Week,* and *Better Homes & Gardens.* Some of these publications are intellectual. They appeal to limited numbers of readers. Others are subliterate. If estimated circulations of the second group are an indication, they appeal to everybody.

Take a look first at what are still called class magazines, though "class" has been adopted as a flattering designation by many magazines which can claim it only on the basis of small circulation and not at all on quality. In the United States at the present time there are exactly three major periodicals which are generally so categorized. In the order of their founding they are *Harper's,* the *Atlantic,* and *The Saturday Review.*

Of the great literary monthlies dominant among American magazines in the last quarter of the 19th century, only *Harper's* and the *Atlantic* survive. They maintain their prestige and influence today, in large part, because while still directed to the literate educated minority, they began to present more diversified material in more lively fashion.

Harper's is the more vigorous, worldly, and varied of the two. Despite its "Atlantic Reports on the World Today" and pages devoted to Washington and other capitals after the manner of a news weekly, the *Atlantic* is still the more genteel-literary, the more Boston-Harvard Square-Anglophilic-parochial. As prestige magazines, both command the occasional serious work of distinguished writers. They also command attention far beyond the audience suggested by their comparatively small circulations.

Harper's does not shrink from controversial subjects. In October, 1954, it ran a very long piece, five times the length of an ordinary *Harper's* article, "The Case of J. Robert Oppenheimer" by Joseph and Stewart Alsop. In December, 1955, *Harper's* published "Pay by the Year: Can the Unions Afford it?" by a businessman who had earlier been a CIO economist. In January, 1956, the magazine published a piece it had deliberately sought out, "The Southern Case Against Desegregation" by Thomas R. Waring, editor of the Charleston *News and Courier*. "One of the duties of an independent magazine, allied to no party or interest group, is to give a hearing to significant bodies of opinion which cannot find expression elsewhere—even when the editors disagree," an editorial note explained. *Harper's* for February, 1956, contained even more explosive matter, a brief letter in which the Secretary of Agriculture commended as excellent a December, 1955, article by *Harper's* editor-in-chief, "The Country Slicker Takes Us Again." The article had described the American farmer as a pampered tyrant. Segments of public opinion did not believe the Secretary should agree with such a description of his charges, and the dispute was front-page controversy before the Secretary could hastily explain that his commendation was all a mistake.

Atlantic and *Harper's* covers were once monochromes, one issue, except for date and table of contents, looking much like the last or one of ten years before. Both are splashy now. The two wish visibility on the newsstands and in the home as much as less quality-conscious periodicals.

Partly designs in color, partly scare-head advertisements for the articles inside, *Harper's* covers are particularly noisy. They testify to the magazine's dominant interest in public affairs and current events. A typical issue contains one short story, two or three poems, and the rest articles on government, race, and the contemporary political scene. As he has done for many years, Russell Lynes appears frequently with his essays. John Fischer, *Harper's* editor-in-chief, 1953–1967, now occupies the "Easy Chair," a department made famous by some of its previous incumbents. Even in its use of English *Harper's* is less literary than it was. Many of its pieces are in slangy journalese. They read smartly and *Harper's* itself reads smartly and intelligently.

An editor who can write, a rare phenomenon, John Fischer held forth cogently in August, 1968, on the student revolt. *Harper's* likes the subject and made its position clear in the cover blurb for "They Are Taking My Letters, A Story about Revolution at Good Old Columbia U." in October, 1968. The lead piece in the issue was "The Politics of Violence" by Arthur M. Schlesinger, Jr. It was followed by articles on Mayor Richard J. Daley of Chicago and Mayor John Vliet Lindsay of New York.

In a long, long "Open Letter to the Next President," September, 1968, John Fischer was characteristically knowledgeable, pro-Johnson, and clear-headed. After a learned comparison of the political and social situation with that faced by Diocletian in 282 A.D., he condemned the "near paralysis of the federal bureaucracy" and pled with Johnson's still unchosen successor for administrative reform. *Harper's* has departments on books, music, theatre, the arts, but comment on politics and the social spectacle, particularly politics, is *Harper's* subject. It really splurged in November, 1968, both on cover and in content. "Norman Mailer, Miami and Chicago" in huge red, white, and blue capitals covered the cover, and Mailer's book preempted 89 pages of the interior. Most *Harper's* issues run a little over 100 pages.

Edward Weeks took over the editorship of *The Atlantic Monthly* in 1938 and held it until 1966. When he assumed office, his predecessor, Ellery Sedgwick, told him that the fastidious element was the permanent core of the *Atlantic* audience, and for 28 years Weeks,[1] who continues in the magazine

[1] Weeks told the "Great Editors Seminar" of the American Society of Magazine Editors, November 20, 1967, that Sedgwick also told him to get the personal philosophy of life kind of article. He got it from men like James B. Conant and Alfred North Whitehead.

as its "Peripatetic Reviewer," edited fastidiously for the fastidious.

During his editorship, though over his objections, the *Atlantic* rejected Thornton Wilder's *The Bridge of San Luis Rey,* but Weeks brought George F. Kennan, Edwin O'Connor, Albert Camus, the Sitwells, Dylan Thomas, Evelyn Waugh, and Albert Einstein into the *Atlantic.* He published Roland Hayes, Ethel Waters, and Fred Allen. He instituted the "Atlantic Firsts," first short stories by writers, some of whom later attained fame. Because the *Atlantic* had accepted one of his early contributions in 1927, Ernest Hemingway contributed two short stories to the 100th anniversary issue of the *Atlantic* in 1957. In 1957 and 1958 the Atlantic published in ten installments what deservedly became its most popular series to that time, James Thurber's *The Years with Ross,* published in book form by The Atlantic Monthly Press in association with Little, Brown and Company, a long-standing arrangement.

The *Atlantic* first dared pictorial covers with a picture, fittingly, of T. S. Eliot. The issue sold well. It did so well with Robert Frost on the newsstands that it used his likeness a second time. Its covers now are almost as vivid as *Harper's.*

A professional talker and almost a professional fisherman, Weeks speaks often at colleges. To the fall of 1967 he had spoken on "every campus that would have me as a lecturer," about 200 colleges and universities. He loves it, and the *Atlantic* has long seemed to be edited largely for school and college consumption. As well as making for impeccable English and literary sensitivity this makes it sometimes sound priggish and inevitably schoolteacherish, though to attract young readers Weeks introduced writers like August Heckscher, McGeorge Bundy, and William Buckley.

The *Atlantic* dared punning humor when, in April, 1968, it ran "What Makes Bill Buckley Run." Author of the piece was William F. Buckley, Jr., once, like Henry Luce, editor of the *Yale Daily News.* In this instance the imperturbable and often disdainful Mr. Buckley of television, his syndicated newspaper column, and his own conservative periodical was running for election to the Yale Corporation. As in 1966 when he ran for mayor of New York, he was out-run.

The academic persists in the *Atlantic*. Its lead article in October, 1958—after 54 pages of mixed advertising, reports, letters to the editor, and promotion for forthcoming issues—was "The War Against the Young" by a Rutgers professor. As the *Atlantic* is, he was for the young. The Atlantic First in the same issue was set, as so many of them seem to have been, on the college campus. In September McGeorge Bundy had written on "Faculty Power," but someone else on "Politics and Death."

The presumption is that there will be more politics and public affairs in the *Atlantic*. Its present editor had been an assistant Secretary of State, appointed by President John F. Kennedy, and before that a senior editor of *Time* who for several years was in charge of the London Bureau for *Time, Life*, and *Fortune*.

The *Atlantic* is one of the few major magazines that still publishes unsolicited manuscripts, more, it says, than any other magazine of national circulation in the United States. As the number of articles, poems, and short stories it can use in twelve issues yearly is limited, this cannot be very many. *Harper's* receives about 20,000 manuscripts a year and accepts about 30. Like most modern magazines, it has its own staff writers.

From 1920 to 1924 Yale professor of English Henry Seidel Canby edited the Saturday night *Literary Review*, a supplement of the New York *Evening Post*. On the staff of the Post, writing a column called "The Bowling Green," was Christopher Morley. In 1924 the *Literary Review* broke away from the *Post* and, published by Briton Hadden and Henry Luce for their Yale professor to edit, became *The Saturday Review of Literature* with Canby as editor and Morley and William Rose Benét as associates. Under Canby, who retired as editor in 1936 but remained as chairman of the editorial board, the SRL, which had a difficult time financially, was a thin scholarly paper on newsprint, primarily a collection of book reviews. Bernard De Voto succeeded Canby as editor. In 1942 the editorship went to Norman Cousins, who had graduated from Teachers College, Columbia, then spent two years on *Current History* and another two as executive editor of *SRL*. Soon the magazine dropped "of Literature" from its title and bravely took all culture within reach for its province.

The Saturday Review covers travel, music, recordings, television and movies, as well as the new books. It has liberal opinions. It fights for causes. It seems to consider its mission the dispensation of knowledge and the generation of ideas. It is still very literary but seems more vital. Page size cut down, on slick paper, illustrated, it looks more like a magazine than the supplement from which it stemmed. Popular opinion used to link *The Saturday Review* with the Sunday *Herald Tribune* "Books" and *The New York Times Book Review*. *The Saturday Review* became a periodical entity. It carried signed articles as well as reviews, the humor of Bennett Cerf, anagrams, cryptograms, the mellow conversation of bibliophiles, and pieces which its table of contents listed proudly as "SR Ideas." Even its book reviews are not merely reviews. *The Saturday Review* takes literary criticism seriously as an art in itself. The "personals" in its classified advertising columns, long the warmest and most amusing page of the publication, seem less colorful. The magazine calls itself now a "magazine of ideas, entertainment, and the arts." *Time* has called it a bookworm that turned and described it as "a sort of last haven for the sprightly American essay." [2] Like the *Atlantic* and *Harper's*, *The Saturday Review* carries a kind of hallmark of prestige for readers who take their culture seriously in conversation. A point at issue when Henry Seidel Canby and his fellows started the periodical was to see whether the United States would support a purely literary weekly. The answer, apparent in the revamped magazine, is that it can and does; in moderation, of course. It is in great moderation that nationally circu-

[2] "A Bookworm Turned," August 1, 1949. The bookworm has really not turned much.

lated magazines of literature, ideas, and the arts are tolerated in the United States.

Traveler, platform talker, and vocal internationalist with a kind of proprietary interest in the atom bomb as article and editorial subject, Norman Cousins raised the circulation of *The Saturday Review* from 40,000 in 1940 to about 250,000 in 1961 when he sold the magazine to the McCall Corporation but retained the editorship. Under McCall's that circulation has doubled to well over 500,000, most of it subscription, almost twice that of either *Harper's* or the *Atlantic*. High among the weekly magazines in pages of advertising, the *Review* raised its advertising base rate to 550,000 in January, 1969.

The Saturday Review is very conscious of the nuclear age, talks about it, and tries to do some things about it. In 1955 its project "Hiroshima Maidens" brought young women to this country who had been disfigured by the atom bomb for plastic surgery and other medical treatment. The magazine did the same thing in 1958 and 1959 for 38 Polish women who had been mutilated in Nazi medical and surgical experiments during World War II.

Though it covers science and engages in brisk editorial comment on foreign policy, had the humor of Bennett Cerf, and has the poetry of John Ciardi, *The Saturday Review* is still long on book reviews and book trade gossip. It carries a long list of "Editors at Large," including Herbert R. Mayes of McCall's; and another list of Contributing Editors, including the bibliophile John T. Winterich, its managing editor of some twenty years ago and one-time associate of Harold Ross on the AEF's *Stars and Stripes*. *The Saturday Review* is essentially critical rather than creative. Criticism and creation are not necessarily antipathetic or always distinct, but they often seem so here. Perhaps it is that which makes the magazine seem a little pretentious, academic, and prosaic with dullness not always too far away.

One quality magazine defies classification as class, mass, or as anything else but itself. Revered by its readers, who seldom discard a copy, and the envy of many publishers, it has no newsstand sales and no subscribers, but it has a circulation of more than 5,500,000 and yearly takes in more than $10 million in advertising. The magazine is the *National Geographic Magazine.* Property of the National Geographic Society, a nonprofit scientific and education organization in Washington, D.C., the *Geographic* goes only to accredited members of the Society.

Since 1888 when the National Geographic Society was founded at a meeting in Washington's Cosmos Club of explorers and travelers, the *National Geographic* has been the teacher of geography to the nation. That is not quite true, for it was only a scholarly brochure in 1888. It is certainly true since April 1, 1899, when Alexander Graham Bell appointed 23-year old Gilbert Hovey Grosvenor, soon to become his son-in-law, to the editorship of the monthly periodical.

One of the identical twin sons of an Amherst College professor of history and a cousin of William Howard Taft, young Grosvenor went to Washington from a teaching job in Englewood, New Jersey. As the sole employee of the National Geographic Society, he put out his first issue of the *National Geographic,* addressed mailing wrappers to the society's 1,000 members, and carried the entire edition to the post office himself. From that point Gilbert Grosvenor actually created the *National Geographic.*

President of the Society, wealthy, popular, and energetic, Alexander Graham Bell wanted it to have a magazine like the *Century, McClure's,* the *Review of Reviews,* the popular magazines of the time. He had editorial consultants come down from New York to advise his editorial committee. Famous editor of the famous *Century,* Richard Watson Gilder warned against using photographs. He said they were vulgar. The very successful S. S. McClure proposed a whole list of essential changes. He advised that the magazine be moved to New York, that its name be changed, that it make no mention of the National Geographic Society because people considered geography a dull school subject, that it be placed for sale on the newsstands, and that efforts to extend circulation through canvassing for members to the National Geographic Society be stopped.

Though he had to buck the conservative geographers who were impressed by McClure's expertness, Grosvenor violated every one of McClure's strictures. An avid promoter as well as a clear-eyed editor—born in Constantinople when his father was teaching in Roberts College, he had something of the same kind of missionary background as Henry Luce and DeWitt Wallace—Grosvenor knew just what he wanted to do. He used all of his distinguished connections, and he had many, in campaign after campaign for memberships. He kept the magazine in Washington, though two issues were printed in New York, and kept it off the newsstands. He began to use photographs in profusion.

Ably supported by John Oliver La Gcrce, who joined him in 1905, Grosvenor edited and promoted his magazine to the ends he visualized. He decided early that his magazine would have absolute accuracy and that its articles would have permanent value. It would discuss nothing of a partisan or controversial nature. It would always speak kindly of nations and people.

He wished vivid eyewitness accounts in straighforward language, bountifully illustrated with good photographs, that would make geography romance and adventure. Geography is a specific and limited subject. Grosvenor could have created, undoubtedly with success, a special-interest magazine of limited circulation. His conception made for a different and much larger effort. "I thought of geography in terms of the Greek root *geographia*—a description of the world. It thus became the most catholic of subjects, universal in appeal and embracing nations, people, plants, animals, birds, fish." [3]

Grosvenor's dual work as editor and assiduous promoter succeeded quickly. By 1907, out of profits from the magazine, the National Geographic Society was able to make its first grant.

[3] Grosvenor, Gilbert Hovey, "Romance of the Geographic," 75th Anniversary Issue, the *National Geographic Magazine*, October 1963.

It gave $1,000 to Commodore Robert E. Peary for his final assault on the North Pole. Since that time the society has granted many millions of dollars for exploratory and archeological expeditions, and its blue, brown, and green flag—blue for sky, brown for earth, green for sea—has been triumphantly planted many times where men had never been before.

There is no need to stress the value of this magazine, a favorite with educators, each issue containing six to ten articles on travel, exploration, natural history, each replete with what are often magnificent photographs. The *Geographic* has carried accounts of their adventures by Peary, Roald Amundsen, Theodore Roosevelt, Vilhjálmur Stefánsson, Sir Ernest Shackleton, Charles A. Lindbergh, and how many other heroes. From the first Roosevelt through John F. Kennedy, Presidents have bestowed National Geographic medals on successful explorers in special White House ceremonies, and many Presidents have written for the *Geographic.*

The *National Geographic* began to prepare and distribute its maps by the millions in 1915. They proved invaluable in two world wars when often they were the only accurate maps available. The magazine has made world travelers and explorers of its readers. The authenticity of its editorial content, its many distinctions, and the many distinguished names attached to it have established the repute of the *National Geographic* and fixed it in popular esteem. In 1964 the National Geographic Society moved from 16th Street, North West, in Washington to a striking new building at 17th and M Streets. The Explorers Hall on its main floor has a huge, slowly rotating globe of the world and exhibits of Arctic, Antarctic, and space explorations. There is little doubt that many tourists, like many readers of the magazine, believe the *National Geographic* to be part—one of the more reputable parts—of the federal government.

The *National Geographic* in its familiar yellow covers, and still in *Century-McClure's-Review of Reviews* format, manages to be at once staid, authoritative, and exciting; which is a neat trick if you can do it, and the *Geographic* has been doing it

James Whittaker plants the American and National Geographic flags atop Mount Everest in an action photograph from the *National Geographic Magazine*. (Courtesy National Geographic Magazine. Copyright © National Geographic Society.)

for a long time. It sells the romance of faraway places, polar wastes, ocean floors, the conquest of snow-topped mountains and the moon, intrepid courage, scientific investigation, and reader education all at the same time, and it invests the whole with an aura of high purpose under august sponsorship.

Gilbert Grosvenor was its editor for 55 years. Not until 1954 did he retire to become chairman of the board with La Gorce, who had been his associate, succeeding him as editor. Pictured in the *National Geographic* article by his father in 1963 both as an infant in arms in 1903 and as a Naval Academy midshipman at a later date, Melville Bell Grosvenor became editor of the magazine in 1957.

Chapter 28

The Comic Magazines; The Little Magazines

In the 1950's shrill outcry arose against what, given their huge audience, were the most popular and prevalent magazines in the United States. Harried and bedevilled, attacked as depraved, violent, sadistic, obscene, as fomenting juvenile delinquency, preying on the immaturity of adults, and pandering to the lowest instincts and impulses of the human animal, the comic magazines were selling at the rate of 60 to 90 million copies a month. The higher figure was used in hearings before the Senate Subcommittee to Investigate Juvenile Delinquency in 1954.[1]

The comic magazines are an offshoot of the newspaper comic strips and pages which began late in the last century in the New York *World* with R. F. Outcault's "Yellow Kid." He took the Kid to the *New York Journal,* later developed the famous Buster Brown for the *New York Herald.* Today's Superman, L'il Abner, Blondie, Orphan Annie, *et al.* are direct descendants of Buster Brown, Foxy Grandpa, Happy Hooligan, and the rest. The comics have been powerful circulation builders for the newspapers for a long time. The comic monthly magazine originated in the 1930's when the Eastern Color Printing Company in New York, printers of Sunday

[1] *Barron's,* January 17, 1955, said 60 to 90 million, *Time,* September 27, 1954, said 80 million; the New York *Herald-Tribune,* December 29, 1954, said 60 million. Accurate circulation figures are available only for those comic magazines reporting to the Audit Bureau of Circulations.

newspaper comic supplements, conceived the idea of printing comics in book form in small page size. They successfully published *Funnies on Parade,* and followed that with *Famous Funnies,* issued for distribution through variety stores. The book proved so popular that the publishers began to put it out monthly. Then came the deluge. By 1950 a Fawcett Comics Group advertisement (in *Advertising Age,* May 8) could be headlined in true comic book style: "The comic magazines bought each month laid end to end would reach 1/25th the space from the earth to the moon."

The agitation against the worst of the comic books started in magazines.[2] Horror and crime comics were condemned in the newspaper press. Parents' groups rose in protest against them. The comics were legislated against in a dozen states, banned from the newsstands of some large cities, policed in others. Leading comic book publishers were quizzed by the Senate subcommittee on juvenile delinquency. Under fire and complaining bitterly that their attackers did not discriminate between good and bad comic magazines, they formed the Comics Magazine Association of America and appointed a New York magistrate, who had specialized in juvenile delinquency, to act as czar and censor for the industry.

As a result of all this agitation by outraged public opinion, some of the worst of the horror comics ceased publication. Others edited out some of their more offensive material. In England, where millions of copies of American comic magazines had been reprinted each month, the activity came to an end.[3] There has been a considerable reduction in the number

[2] "What Parents Don't Know About Comic Books," by Frederic Wertham, M.D., *Ladies' Home Journal,* November, 1953. The article came out in book form as *Seduction of the Innocent* and was condensed by *Reader's Digest,* May, 1954. The *Digest* also published another exposé, "The Face of Violence" by T. E. Murphy, in November, 1954. In the horror comics, magazines had an example of magazine influence which they would gladly disavow.

[3] One of the two big English publishers of comic magazines said the outcry against his wares had made it so difficult to get comics printed and distributed that his costs had become prohibitive. He pointed out that the comic magazines were not intended for children anyway. Among his customers, he said, were two army colonels, some majors, and a number of people in public life. "An analysis of my sales would almost certainly reveal that the main readers are young married women with too much time on their hands." "Britons Drop Publication of Horror Comics," *Advertising Age,* December 6, 1954.

of comic book titles reaching the newsstands. There had been overproduction, anyway, both in number of titles—as many as 350 in one month—and in number of copies of a title printed. The newsstands could not handle them all.

The comics have been seriously defended as a new kind of American folklore, as a survival of primitive adventure narrative. They have been looked upon as inheritors of the tradition of the dime novel, now sanctified in wreaths of nostalgia. The comic technique has been praised for its educational uses. The comic magazine idea has been used as a teaching device by both the army and the navy and for purposes of government propaganda. Literary classics and Bible stories are presented in comic magazines. Used in these ways, the comics have been defended as exerting a benevolent social force.[4] As it usually is when censorship is applied or threatened, "the freedom of the press" has been invoked, this time by the indignant publishers of "good" comic books. The one thing which, in all the dispute, no one has called the comic magazines is comical. Humor is seldom their intent.

The comic books provide breathtaking, fantastic adventure, prolonging suspense until the hero finally triumphs over a long, long series of obstacles. The comics, a psychologist explains, are picture-story fantasies appealing directly to human desires and aspirations, to wish fulfillment. "Superman and his innumerable followers satisfy the universal human longing to be stronger than all opposing obstacles . . . to experience vicariously the supreme gratification of the *deus ex machina* who accomplishes these monthly miracles of right triumphing over not-so-mighty might.[5] It all depends, the moralist might add, on what kinds of wishes are to be fulfilled and what kinds of obstacles overcome.

Whatever the ethical, moral, or civic solution to the problem, the comic magazines prevailed. Dell, the largest publisher, had a circulation of over 9,000,000 for its group, which included: *Gene Autry, Tom and Jerry, Little Lulu, Mickey*

[4] Sidonie Matsner Gruenberg, "The Comics as a Social Force," *The Journal of Educational Sociology*, December, 1944.

[5] William Moulton Marston, "Why 100,000,000 Americans Read Comics," *The American Scholar*, Winter 1943–44.

Mouse, Donald Duck, Lone Ranger, Roy Rogers, and *Tarzan* —all very respectable characters. National Comics, which issued 49 titles, has a circulation of over 6,000,000. *Bob Hope, Nutsy Squirrel, Martin and Lewis,* and *Mr. District Attorney* were all in the National Comics stable. Marvel Comics, with 59 titles, among them *Annie Oakley, Black Rider, My Friend Irma,* and *Cowboy Action,* had a circulation of nearly 5,000,000. Harvey Comics, with *Joe Palooka, Little Audrey, Dick Tracy, Blondie, Dagwood, Ripley's Believe It Or Not,* and 20 other titles, went to over 4,000,000 buyers for each issue.

Whether the comic magazines are the textbooks in crime and wickedness many think them or educational periodicals with traditions going back to paleolithic times, as their admirers claim, they are read. These crudely written, crudely illustrated and reproduced magazines gratify the literary and artistic tastes of a large part of the population. In 1946 Professor Harvey Zorbaugh of the School of Education, New York University, stated that at post exchanges during World War II comic books outsold *The Saturday Evening Post, Life,* and *Reader's Digest* combined by ten to one. A study done by *Puck* in 1948 showed that four out of five American adults read comics. No more than in England are comic magazines read only by children and adolescents, though one study by Marvel Comics showed over 90 per cent readership for boys and girls aged eight to sixteen. According to survey results released by the Bureau of Public Administration of the University of California in 1955, about $100 million was spent yearly for about one billion copies of comic magazines. They were read by one quarter of American high school graduates, 16 per cent of the country's college graduates, and 12 per cent of its teachers.[6]

A decade after the concerted indignation against them and defense by the industry and some scholarly commentators the comic magazines have fallen in number to about 200. Their

[6] Survey findings reported in *Time,* March 1, 1955, and *The Reader's Digest,* June, 1955.

circulation has decreased by about two-thirds, but some 30,000,000 copies are still sold every month. As most copies are read by at least three people, this means a total audience of somewhere around 90,000,000 a month.[7]

The National Comics Group publishes a host of magazines: *Adventures of Jerry Lewis; Bob Hope; Brave and Bold; Captain Storm; G. I. Combat; Sea Devils; Superman; Superboy; Batman; Wonder Woman; The Flash; Blackhawk; Dawn Patrol* . . . for a total monthly circulation of nearly 6,000,000.[8] The Dell Comics Group has *Flying Nun; Garrison's Gorillas; Gentle Ben; Legend of Custer.* Harvey Comics Group has a full stable of bi-monthly magazines (*Sad Sack; Devil Kids; Hot Stuff; Hot Stuff Sizzlers; Little Dot Dotland; Richie Rich* . . .) with a total circulation of over 5,000,000.

Some titles have changed as one hero of legend or imagination bites the dust and another mounts his white steed, but the general content of adventure, romance, detective exploits, mystery, fantasy, science fiction, and western fiction gallops on. The comics technique is still used in training manuals and for biography, history, scientific explanations, and the teaching of religion.[9] The comics magazine publishers claim a dissipation of the worst of the evils of which their periodicals stood accused and condemned. They see this as a triumph of self-regulation under the Comics Code Authority set up in October, 1954.

This code forbids liquor, sex, knives and handguns, fireworks, and nudity in comics magazine advertising. In the editorial content of the magazines no sympathy is to be shown for criminals, and police and judges are to be treated with respect. Paragraph Six, Part A of the General Standards established by the code says flatly, "In every instance good shall

[7] Goldwater, John L. *Americana in Four Colors.* New York: Comics Magazine Association of America, 1964.

[8] *Ayer's Directory, 1968.*

[9] *Pix,* one of the scores of Sunday School publications of huge circulation put out by the David C. Cook Publishing Company of Elgin, Illinois, is a magazine in the comic book manner, and its *Pix Magazette* tells Bible stories in comic-strip sequences with balloon dialogue. The comics technique is not in itself a guarantee of depravity.

triumph over evil and the criminal punished for his misdeeds" [sic].

Here, obviously, the comics magazines do a little better than life itself. The outcry against the comic magazines has died out. They are better behaved. It has to seem ironic that since the virtuous attack on the excesses of the worst of them the actualities of political assassination, wanton murder, arson, mugging, drug addiction, and a few other comparable diversions have greatly increased and seem socially accepted. It was the representation of these popular amusements on paper in color and in picture and print that critics resented.

The so-called "little magazines" are not for the masses and not always for the classes. They are not for publishers or in general for readers. They are for writers, for cults, for groups who have something to say and wish to say it or for groups which have nothing to say but wish to say it anyway.

The little magazines are a numerous and varied group of periodicals. With new ones appearing when older ones, their funds exhausted or their motivating ideas abandoned, cease publication, they perform a service for letters, sometimes for ideas, which the national magazines cannot, at least do not, attempt. Subsidized in some way, controlled often by a group interested in experimental writing of some kind, the typical little magazine can be published without regard to the tastes of a large reading audience or the necessity of providing an effective vehicle for advertisers. It is used solely as a medium of expression for the linguistic, poetic, critical, and increasingly the political ideas of the group controlling it. It pays nothing to its contributors, or gives only token payments. Its real service is in providing publication for writers who would otherwise find it difficult or impossible to get their work before any public. Many of the little magazines exhibit an unmistakable vanity and snobbishness. They parade eccentricities and deliberate variations from the accepted norms in subject matter and style. Specific little magazines are annoying and often unintelligible to the lay reader, who suspects affectation for the sake of affectation. Their editors and writers would be displeased if they were understood by the vulgar.

The best of them have a more serious intent, and the little magazines as a whole have amassed a record of reputable accomplishment.

In 1946 three investigators who looked thoroughly into the little magazines came to the conclusion that these unsung periodicals had discovered and sponsored about 80 per cent of the important novelists, poets, and critics who began to write after 1912, and that they not only introduced but also remained the basic magazines to publish 95 per cent of the poets of this period.[10] Poetry has little or no commercial value. The larger magazines want little or none of it. It is probably not too much of an exaggeration to say that the renascence of poetry in the United States after the close of World War I could not have occurred without the help of the little magazines. The reputations of Robert Frost, Edwin Arlington Robinson, Carl Sandburg, Vachel Lindsay, and John Gould Fletcher were established in part through the appearance of their verse in the little magazines. The little magazines published many of the poets whose work is now recognized as some of the best of our poetic production in the twentieth century at a time when these writers were being ignored by the larger literary monthlies, such as *Harper's* and the *Atlantic,* which might have been expected to encourage them. Novelists such as Erskine Caldwell, Albert Halper, and James Farrell, all used the little magazines to get started on their careers. The *Double Dealer* in New Orleans gave early publication to Hart Crane and introduced Ernest Hemingway, probably the most successful commercially of any of the novelists to emerge from the little magazine movement, in 1922. The same *Double Dealer* printed the early work of the critic Edmund Wilson and of the prize-winning novelist Robert Penn Warren.

The expatriate T. S. Eliot, whose long poem of poetic despair, *The Waste Land* (1922), made him the poet of the "lost generation," as Hemingway was its novelist, edited a

[10] Frederick J. Hoffman, Charles Allen, and Carolyn F. Ulrich, *The Little Magazine, A History and a Bibliography* (Princeton, N.J.: Princeton University Press, 1946), p. 8.

little magazine, *Criterion,* in England. In it he published the poetry on which his fame depends. Ezra Pound, expatriate poet of the most advanced school, who made a cult of obscurity, and whose ideas in other directions brought him a new notoriety in World War II, emerged from the little magazines. Richard Aldington, English poet and novelist, and Wyndham Lewis, refreshingly individualistic literary critic, came up through the little magazines. Max Eastman, later (so greatly do ideas and people change) an editor of *The Reader's Digest,* was once, with Floyd Dell, an editor of the left-wing little magazine *The Masses.* Many more of our best writers had to obtain periodical publication in one or another of the little magazines.

Poetry: A Magazine of Verse, founded in Chicago by Harriet Monroe in 1912 and still extant, published for a time by the University of Chicago Press, had more to do with the rise of modern poetry in this country than any other magazine, large or small. *Poetry* was near extinction for lack of operating funds in 1955. In November a fifty-dollars-a-plate banquet and an auction of rare books and manuscripts was held in the Blackstone Theatre in Chicago as a benefit for the magazine. Robert Frost, whose first poem appeared in *Poetry,* recited some of his verse. A rare edition of one of Siegfried Sassoon's volumes of poetry was auctioned off. The benefit netted about $30,000, which was enough to float the magazine another year.

The Little Review, published first in Chicago, but for most of its life, 1912–1929, in New York, ran James Joyce's *Ulysses* in installments for three years. For introducing American readers to one of the literary classics of the twentieth century, the magazine was prosecuted on the grounds of circulating obscene material. In Paris, *transition,* founded in 1927, published parts of Joyce's *Finnegan's Wake* as "Work in Progress," and published also Gertrude Stein, Hemingway, and William Carlos Williams. This famous little magazine was discontinued in 1930 because, as one of its editors said, it "threatened to become a mercantile success." Publication was later resumed at Mt. Vernon, Iowa.

The *Partisan Review*, a bimonthly of literature and politics, was associated with the Communist Party at its 1934 founding but was independent and anti-Communist from 1938. A proponent of intellectual freedom, it opposed regimentation of any kind, was generally liberal and critical in tone. The *Review*, which featured modern short stories, essays, poems, and sound, clear-headed literary criticism, published T. S. Eliot, John Dos Passos, Archibald MacLeish, William Carlos Williams, and Edmund Wilson at one time and another. Such comparable writers as Conrad Aiken, Cyril Connolly, Andre Malraux, and John Crowe Ransom appeared in its pages.

Many of the little magazines, their purpose served, bankruptcy or near-bankruptcy achieved, or their writers successful in breaking into the larger magazines or commercially published books, have disappeared. They are not supplanted as fast as they once seemed to be. Printing, paper, and mailing costs make them in general an insupportable luxury. Their nearest equivalents as magazines of arts and letters or of the sciences are the subsidized academic or learned society periodicals.

Chapter 29

Collier's

In 1936, in an address at the University of Virginia, William Ludlow Chenery, then editor, later publisher, of *Collier's,* pointed out that from the very beginning magazines were founded, published, and edited by men intensely concerned with public affairs and public good: "The desire to serve the public interest or participate in public affairs is warp and woof of magazine history." The history of Chenery's own magazine can be used to illustrate his claim.

Under Norman Hapgood *Collier's* had been one of the powerful muckraking weeklies. Hapgood boasted that it stood first in influence with the public. Mark Sullivan, Hapgood's associate on *Collier's* and then his successor as editor, said much the same thing in 1938, calling the *Collier's* of that period the most influential magazine in the country and one of the most distinguished. The achievements of *Collier's* in the magazine fight against the patent-medicine industry and against the foisting of adulterated food on the public have been noted. Finley Peter Dunne was the magazine's last editor under the management of Robert Collier.

In 1919 the Crowell Publishing Company purchased control of *Collier's,* which was in difficulties as a business venture, for about $1,750,000. As Cyrus Curtis had poured *Ladies' Home Journal* money into establishing *The Saturday Evening Post,* the Crowell Company in promoting *Collier's* spent about $15,000,000 earned by the *Woman's Home Companion,* highly successful under the veteran Gertrude Battles Lane, and by the *American Magazine,* which was thriving with John Siddall as editor and Bruce Barton as chief writer of the success stories and inspirational articles it purveyed under the slogan "Not Literature But Life." William Ludlow Chenery, a Virginia newspaperman, was made *Collier's* editor in 1925, and quickly brought to the magazine a staff of first-line writers and reporters, including William G. Shepherd, William B. Courtney, John B. Kennedy, and Walter Davenport. More writers, whose names are now well known, were added to the *Collier's* staff: Quentin Reynolds to write reports; Kyle Crichton to do the theater and the motion pictures; other men to cover Washington, Europe, and the Orient.

The reinvigorated *Collier's* attacked the Ku Klux Klan when that organization was growing in power as a dangerous threat to the civilized community. It reported fully on the activities of Huey Long, attacking his fascistic ideas and operations. *Collier's* had originally supported Prohibition. When thorough investigation around the United States by its reporters showed that Prohibition was not only not working, but was also creating a situation worse than that which it had been designed to cure, *Collier's* began to fight for its repeal. It even drafted a model constitutional amendment which would abolish it. *Collier's* lost 3,000 angered subscribers as a result of its attack on Prohibition. It gained 400,000 new ones.

Some of these social achievements of his magazine Chenery reviewed. He also pointed honestly and accurately to the limitations which large circulation then imposed on the national magazine:

> Many conditions of great importance are . . . outside the scope of a national magazine. To be magazine material it must be possible without violence to the facts to contrive an interesting and, therefore, a dramatic story. . . . It [the national magazine] is not an endowed educational institution. It is a business operated primarily for profit. If it does not interest its readers, it cannot endure.[1]

Collier's was no longer the muckraking, strident reform magazine it once had been. For a time after William Chenery ceased to be either editor or publisher—he resigned in March,

[1] William L. Chenery, "The Magazine and Public Opinion," *Vital Speeches*, August 15, 1936.

1949—the magazine, though straining to increase its stature, seemed to lack coordinated planning and direction. *Collier's* looked to be wavering and slipping. It suffered both circulation and advertising losses and apparently was declining in public favor. A succession of editors and businessmen strove, each by various means, to relieve the situation. After weaving, wavering, and pitching, *Collier's* seemed to be righting itself again.

Despite all the surface agitation the essential *Collier's* was there. With a mixture of defensiveness and self-congratulation, it said of itself in 1949 that it was a popular magazine, its chief function to entertain, and that it intended to remain just that; but it pointed out also that it intended to face up to the facts of our day, stating the problems that confront people, even if it did not have all the answers.[2]

About this time, though the magazine had said it was not interested in sensation for sensation's sake, *Collier's* began to run many sensational articles. "An Exposé an Issue" was the slogan attributed to its editor from 1949 to 1952. Much of this was done in an obvious effort to bolster circulation.

Most sensational of all during this period was the October 29, 1951, issue which was devoted wholly to a "Preview of the War We Do Not Want." This was a detailed account of an imagined World War III in articles, all on aspects of the same subject, by many big-name contributors. Vividly described and illustrated were the atomic bombing of New York, Washington, and Moscow, the disappearance of Stalin, the defeat of Russia, and the occupation of that country by the Western allies. The spectacular offering was noisily ballyhooed in advance. "This issue . . . may change the course of history." *Collier's* is reported to have spent an additional $40,000 for editorial costs. The issue proved the sensation that was planned. A press run of 3,900,000 copies was a quick sell out.

The issue attracted the attention it clamored for, but much of the comment was unfavorable. *Collier's* was accused of war-mongering, irresponsibility, disturbing the delicate international situation, and of other peccadilloes. Greatly hurt,

[2] "What *Collier's* Stands For," *Collier's*, June 18, 1949.

it found itself having to defend an attempt which it felt had been misunderstood and misinterpreted. Reader opinion was sampled. Seventy-one per cent, *Collier's* reported, thought the issue a "good idea." So did Henry Luce, publisher of *Time* and *Life,* who wrote *Collier's* editor, "There is no question that you made a great impact with that issue and, in my personal opinion, a useful one." [3]

In December, 1952, Crowell-Collier Research made public the long-awaited results of a major survey—interviews with 33,452 respondents in 16,000 homes—conducted with an outside agency on "reading in depth." It surprised few that *Collier's* was found to have depth of reading. It emerged from the study as "practically TV-proof." It had lost only three per cent of the public's reading time to television where competitive magazines had lost much more. *The Saturday Evening Post,* the study showed, had lost 13 per cent.

Razzle-dazzle tactics continued on both the editorial and the business side of *Collier's.* In 1953 youthful Paul C. Smith, a story of many instant successes behind him and a spectacular record as the young editor of the San Francisco *Chronicle,* was imported from California to become a Crowell-Collier vice president. He became president January 1, 1954, then chairman of the board and editor-in-chief of all three of the company's magazines, *Collier's, The American Magazine,* and *Woman's Home Companion.*

May 7, 1953 Crowell-Collier announced that with its issue of August 7 *Collier's,* which had been a weekly magazine for 65 years, would become a biweekly.

Throughout the newspaper and trade press, the magazine's publishers were quoted as blaming television for necessitating the change.[4] *Collier's* publishers quickly denied what was reported. The real reason for their decision, they said, was that *Collier's* had been losing circulation, advertising, thus money.[5]

[3] "Time Out of Mind," *Collier's,* February 10, 1952.

[4] *The New York Times* said, May 8, 1953: "The publishers of *Collier's* announced yesterday that the magazine would be published every other week in a move made necessary by television's inroads on the reading audience."

[5] *Collier's* was losing $400,000 a week in April, 1953. Its loss for the year was over $4 million ("Can *Collier's* Come Back?" *Forbes,* September 15, 1955).

The change to biweekly publication would take the magazine out of direct competition as an advertising medium with the long firmly entrenched *Saturday Evening Post* in the general weekly field and place it in competition with *Look.* A biweekly has a longer on-sale period and, because it is current longer, has that much more chance of being read by more people. The new *Collier's* would be launched with a guarantee of at least 112 pages in each issue and a circulation guarantee of 3,500,000.

The biweekly *Collier's* was planned to reverse one trend apparent in most of the general mass magazines. It would run more, rather than less, fiction and would restore the practice, dropped some time previously, of publishing serialized fiction. Deliberately, many of these stories would be slanted to appeal to women readers. To accomplish this, a male fiction editor was replaced by a woman.

When the August 7, 1953, issue of *Collier's* appeared, it proved to be 50 per cent larger than previous weekly issues. It contained a substantial number of advertising pages, most advertisers in the weekly issue continuing their schedules. An editorial reaffirmed, verbatim, the *Collier's* policy stated in 1949:

> *Collier's* is a popular magazine, first and last, and it means to remain one. It knows that a major function of a popular magazine is to entertain. All of us have to have some escape in these troubled times....
>
> But we must also face up to the facts.
>
> *Collier's* intends to face the facts and to state the problems that confront us, even if it doesn't have all the answers. It is not interested in sensation for sensation's sake....*Collier's* believes in change, but only within the framework of American institutions and traditions. . . .
>
> *Collier's* is not buying any new political systems....It is allergic to stuffiness. . . . It believes there are times when kidding can be more effective than crusading. . . .
>
> *Collier's* believes that it is just as important to appreciate and perpetuate all that is good in our national life as it is to correct what is wrong.[6]

The first biweekly *Collier's* carried on the cover a cartoon treatment in color of William O'Dwyer, ex-mayor of New York and ex-ambassador to Mexico. Its lead story was on "William

[6] "A Restatement of What *Collier's* Stands For," *Collier's,* August 7, 1953.

O'Dwyer—The Man Who Won't Come Home," a description of the private life of a mysterious and controversial expatriate. The issue featured "the dramatic story of Saint Paul" from a new religious book by the late Fulton Oursler, and a love story by Pearl Buck. A lively article described Frank Sinatra in a new role as a dramatic actor in "From Here to Eternity"; another, with vivid photographic illustrations in color, was "Forest Fire." There was plenty of light fiction, the beginning of a new serial and a short-short story, a literary form which *Collier's* could claim to have originated. These, together with such standard *Collier's* features as "*Collier's* Credits" (item about contributors), Walter Davenport's "48 States of Mind," and a plenitude of *Collier's* popular cartoons, set the pace for the changed magazine. It retained much the same tone and content in succeeding biweekly issues—articles, special pieces, short stories, serials, and continuing features, adding such regular departments as "Appointment with O'Hara," chatty columnist material, and titling its last-page editorial "*Collier's* Comment."

People, behind-the-scenes articles, adventure and romantic stories, and sensational exposés were the *Collier's* staples, as, to a large extent, they had been for many years. Big-name writers, many of whom *Collier's* developed over the years, appeared often. The magazine carried solid fiction by writers as good as John Steinbeck, and as popular as Erich Maria Remarque, as well as Ellery Queen mysteries and Luke Short westerns. Yet, through all its changes and with its avowed purpose of entertaining as a popular magazine, *Collier's* retained its position as a national paper of serious intent. For journalistic purposes, its presentations were usually more flamboyant than those of its long-time rival, *The Saturday Evening Post,* for its appeal was, generally, to the man in the street and the middle-class man and woman at home. Yet *Collier's* exerted its influence strongly on public opinion. It made no immoderate claims, one year-end editorial said, yet the magazine's part in some causes and effects was more than coincidence. It pointed out that it had revealed the connections between remnants of the Capone gangs and politicians, had exposed gambling and gangsterism before Marcantonio's defeat when he ran for re-election from New York, and that certain pertinent articles had preceded Robert Taft's re-election to the Senate in 1950.[7] *Collier's* might have pointed to many more examples of its keeping ahead of public opinion as well as reflecting it.

It has spoken out forthrightly on public questions, on big business, its responsibilities, dangers, and value to the country; it has treated race problems and the problems of minority groups courageously. It attacked Prohibition when the abuses which flourished under it had become manifest. Its articles on the conservation of natural resources from 1910 through 1955 have been informative and effective. It has paid its share of attention and had its share of influence on national and international affairs.

Watched closely by the press, the struggle continued. New men, financial trouble shooters rather than men from publishing, were placed on the board of directors. In all the company borrowed about $10,000,000 to keep its magazines going, yet it was forced to drop the once popular *American Magazine* in the summer of 1956, "incorporating it with" *Woman's Home Companion. Collier's* and *Woman's Home* were popular with readers, each having a circulation of over 4,000,000, but not with advertisers. *Collier's* got thinner and thinner. Crowell-Collier lost $7,500,000 in 1956.

Often it is not what a magazine is or is not but the impression of it which ordinary people have that decides its fate. An unnamed advertising agency media director said, "We'd go along with a company's sales manager when he was holding his annual sales meeting. If he got up and announced that this year his company was making its big advertising push in *Collier's,* the salesmen just sat there. If he said Life, they'd get up on their feet and cheer." [8] This reaction had become fixed.

Collier's for January 4, 1957, had a picture in full color of Grace Kelly on its cover to introduce "Princess Grace Prepares

[7] "Causes and Effects," *Collier's,* December 30, 1950.
[8] Quoted in "Magazine Paradox," *Business Week,* January 19, 1957.

for Her Baby." It carried a "Special Report on NON-delinquency," proving that 18,000,000 teen-agers could not be wrong. There was a complete Nero Wolfe mystery thriller in the issue, part of another western serial by "Luke Short." There were articles on pipe lines, hockey, missionaries, and a Hollywood starlet, a diversified and lively offering. Editorial comment was on the Russian invasion of Hungary. There was nothing in the 74 pages of the magazine to indicate that this was the final *Collier's*.

Woman's Home Companion for January, 1957, "125 Ways To Stay on a Diet" featured on its cover, began a new novel, *Blue Camellia* by Frances Parkinson Keyes. Readers would never be able to finish it in *Woman's Home*. Bound into this final issue was a special-offer order card, 14 issues of *Woman's Home* for only $2.45. Anyone who filled out the order got some other magazine instead.

Look bought the Crowell-Collier circulation subsidiaries and took on fulfillment of unexpired *Collier's* subscriptions, thereby increasing its own circulation by about 1,000,000. Crowell was left with its long-profitable book publishing—Collier's Encyclopedia and the Harvard Classics among its list leaders—long established under its P. F. Collier & Son imprint.

The collapse of *Collier's* and *Woman's Home* shook the magazine world. Magazine net profit after taxes as a percentage of sales had stood at about 6.7 per cent in the middle 1930's. It had climbed during the profitable war years to 8.3 per cent in 1946, then fallen to an average of 2.8 per cent in 1954 and was still sinking.[9] What many feared had begun to happen.

Disappearance of the two long-established and still popular magazines was bitter enough story for Crowell-Collier employees. They had had warning enough, but there is always hope, and a magazine with its regular periodical publication seems a living thing. Its death is hard to realize. The plight of these employees in their fight for severance pay was duly reported in the press and did nothing to hearten others in

[9] *Sales Management,* October 15, 1955.

magazine publishing in New York and Philadelphia. The worst had happened. It had happened there, and it could happen here.

Though it carried the usual announcement that characters and events were imaginary, and the author said he had witnessed the collapse of three great publishing enterprises from the inside, Theodore H. White's *View from the Fortieth Floor* was read popularly as a fictional account of the Collier's tragedy. The story concerned the "General American Publishing Company" with its two magazines, "Trumpet" and "Gentlewoman."

The *Collier's* story has not been forgotten in magazine circles. Citing it, John Fischer of *Harper's* said, October 23, 1967, "I think it is a fairly safe generalization that magazines are built by editors and killed by business men." [10] Speaking at the University of Kansas, February 10, 1959, Ben Hibbs, editor of *The Saturday Evening Post* and a Kansan, spoke sorrowfully and comfortably of the passing of *Collier's*. The *Post* itself was losing advertising in 1959, but The Curtis Publishing Company was showing an annual profit of about $4,000,000.

Hibbs said that he had known six of the *Collier's* editors-in-chief personally and that at least two of them (not an imposing percentage) had been able men who could have continued successful publication of the magazine had it not been for interference from the business office. "I am fully aware that it is bad taste to speak critically of the dear departed, but in this case I don't apologize. It is one of the tragic stories of publishing, and it should be known." [11]

[10] "Great Editors Seminar," American Society of Magazine Editors, 1968.
[11] William Allen White Memorial Lecture, 1959.

Chapter 30

The Curtis Publishing Company

Played center stage to press fanfare and catcalls, the painfully drawn out Curtis debacle has to be the sickest and saddest performance in magazine publishing since appearance of the *General Magazine* in 1741. When in 1968 an unnamed Curtis director called it "the greatest corporate disaster in American history," he badly understated the case.[1] The jobs of thousands of men and women disappeared, as did the investments of other thousands. Millions of readers of the Curtis publications were hurt and confused. Communications suffered. The dying throes of this particular giant added to more than mere corporate disaster.

It was the failure of men and ideas, the inadequacies of well-intentioned men and the machinations of other men who reserved their good intentions for themselves. Complacency, stupidity, inefficiency, then callowness and callousness, ineptitude, vulgarity, and sleeziness were all poured into a witches' brew which makes the distillation at the opening of *Macbeth* seem as innocent as the punch at a children's dancing school party.

The founding generation of astute and hard-headed men who understood popular magazine publishing and editing built an unmatched magazine empire. The next generation of Curtis editors and executives, imitative and timid servants of

[1] Quoted in "Curtis Publishing: The Last Act," Forbes, May 1, 1968.

absentee owners, let it drool away. *Après moi le déluge,* and the deluge came with seizure and direction of control by men who knew nothing of magazine publishing and, better yet, seemed to have no intention of finding out about it.

Though tables of figures seldom tell a complete or even a completely accurate story, the basic fact about The Curtis Publishing Company in recent years is imbedded somewhere in these.[2]

	Net Profit	*Loss*
1953	$4,403,396	
1954	4,516,682	
1955	4,080,788	
1956	6,234,398	
1957	6,239,292	
1958	2,786,207	
1959	3,960,810	
1960	1,079,361	
1961		$4,193,585
1962		18,917,000
1963		3,393,000
1964		13,947,000
1965		3,352,000
1966	347,000	
1967		4,839,000
1968		20,900,000

In the 1920's when *Life* and *Look* did not exist, *The Reader's Digest* did not take advertising, and there was no television, Curtis was the great, the virtually unique, magazine publishing house. *The Saturday Evening Post* and the *Ladies' Home Journal* seemed as fixed in the American scene as Independence Hall across the park from the huge, pillared Curtis building on Independence Square or as the Declaration of Independence itself. The *Post* was "the magazine reflection of a nation." It was a glorious five-cent weekly announcement of the commonplace, irrefutable, unassailable. Its advertising manager could and did accept space orders much as he pleased. The *Ladies' Home Journal* was almost equally revered. They did not have to solicit business. Business sought them. In 1929 the *Post* and *Journal* together carried 40 per

[2] Annual reports of The Curtis Publishing Company for these years.

cent of all U. S. magazine advertising, and The Curtis Publishing Company showed a net profit for the year of $21,000,000 on a gross of $84,000,000.

The company showed a substantial profit for 79 consecutive years. Its first loss, $4,193,585 in 1961, was kept to that figure only by the sale of securities. From 1961 to 1968 it lost over $55,000,000.

Increased manufacturing and production costs, greatly increased second-class mailing rates, and television did not help, but all the mass magazines have suffered these. Curtis had other ailments, and the symptoms showed long before it was stricken.

When *Life* passed *The Saturday Evening Post* in circulation in 1942, Curtis was at first disbelieving, then affronted and indignant. It was the *Post* and had always been at the top. It frowned on *lèse majesté*. It maintained a hurt dignity and went on as it had always done for some years. *Ladies' Home Journal* still queened it from the top of the pile. Established in 1946, *Holiday* was catching on. Run on a very small budget, *Jack and Jill* stayed atop the hill and showed a small profit every year. In 1960 after a bitter competitive struggle, *McCall's* passed the *Journal* in circulation.

By this time Curtis was bewildered and alarmed. It had got rid of the always unprofitable *Country Gentleman*. The *Post* was continuing to lose advertising. Curtis, which had consistently refused to diversify into radio or television or specialized magazines, tried to regain solid ground by more and louder promotion of its magazines. It tried to publish a television weekly and another magazine directed to the bridal market. Both failed.

For too long the *Post* remained unperturbed. It was old, and it valued its age and repute. It was old, and it was also, in the eyes of the powerful advertising agencies, old-fashioned. George Horace Lorimer's *Post* had fitted its world perfectly. It had kept pace with it, even, in some ways, led. People and events had outdistanced it. The *Post* had lost touch. It was competent William Allen White journalism and viewpoint in a world no longer bucolic. Outside there were atom bombs, Sputnik, social unrest, international bickering, emerging Africa, domestic strife, and Asiatic involvements, but behind the tall pillars, upstairs over the marble lobby with its Maxfield Parrish mosaic and the goldfish pool it was still a Clarence Buddington Kelland world.

When uneasiness did penetrate the *Post,* it tried to recognize change, only it did not know how to recognize it. Hurriedly the *Post* began to imitate *Life, Look,* and every other successful magazine. With its familiar covers the *Post* still looked like the *Post,* but it lost much of its long-established identity as a conservative, Republican, businessman's magazine in a hasty effort to attract women readers, liberals, younger readers, and even Democrats. Imitation is usually fatal. *The Saturday Evening Post* lost its identity and failed to establish another.

Walter Deane Fuller, who had sold dress patterns door-to-door for the Butterick Publishing Company when he was a young man, joined Curtis in 1908. He was president of the company 1934–1950, then board chairman until 1957. Robert E. MacNeal, who had gone to work in a glass factory in southern New Jersey when he was 13, began as a scheduling clerk at Curtis in 1923, worked up through industrial engineering to become secretary of the company, and succeeded Walter D. Fuller as its president in 1950.

MacNeal inherited a weakened company structure and an activity that was already beginning to show signs of malfunctioning, a weekly magazine still published much on the formula devised for an earlier generation of readers and advertisers, and an entrenched hierarchy of editors and executives whose Curtis complacency had not yet been noticeably jarred. Schooled in conservative Curtis traditions, which included reverence for "editorial integrity" and letting the Curtis editors run their magazines without interference from outside, MacNeal himself did not have a free hand for some years. As chairman of the Curtis board, Walter Fuller, who spent in all

56 years with the company, was still a dominant force in company councils and the formation of policy.

MacNeal was capable and hardworking. Curtis was his life. He tried to do too much himself and he made what proved unwise appointments to key positions in advertising and circulation, but by the time he was free to exercise his own judgment and authority it was almost too late anyway. Television and Curtis' magazine competition were making further inroads. The Curtis magazines were not improving either editorially or in favor with the large advertising agencies. Outsiders who had scented Curtis weakness were fighting first to gain representation on the Curtis board and then to control it. MacNeal had little chance to mend matters that by this time were really unmendable or even to survive.

For years Curtis had boasted that it was the only fully integrated magazine publishing company. It grew its own trees for its own wood pulp, made its own paper, printed its own magazines on its high-speed presses at Sharon Hill just outside Philadelphia, and distributed them along with the magazines of many client publishers through its own circulation company. The completely integrated publishing company began rapidly to disintegrate as completely.

The Saturday Evening Post, which had long been the company's principal moneymaker, continued to slip. It began to take liquor advertising in 1958. The familiar script "The Saturday Evening Post" was dropped (it was later replaced) and the monosyllabic "Post" printed in the logotype with "The Saturday Evening" in miniscule type above it. Even this subtle maneuver did not seem to help. Ben Hibbs, its editor since 1942, resigned and was succeeded by Robert Fuoss, who had come with Hibbs from *Country Gentleman* and been first managing editor, then executive editor of the *Post*. The "New Post," which was such a resounding failure when it appeared in September, 1961, was concocted during this period.

Bruce and Beatrice Gould resigned as *Ladies' Home Journal* editors in March, 1962. Fuoss resigned from the *Post* after a policy dispute in early 1962. In June, 1962, Robert E. MacNeal, in Europe at the time for the company, was removed as president of The Curtis Company. Wholesale firings, forced retirements, and the wiping out of entire departments were now the order of the day in Philadelphia. Some 2,000 of the total 8,000 Curtis employees were dismissed in what proved to be only the first round.

A fast-talking supersalesman out of broadcasting and advertising was swept into the Curtis presidency to succeed MacNeal. With him be brought an entourage of new editors and executives, most of them from the National Broadcasting Company or the Radio Corporation of America. With all the publicity he could obtain, and it was a lot, he flew about—literally, for he commuted from the New York suburbs to Philadelphia in a helicopter which Curtis provided for his transport—promising complete reform and miraculous recovery for The Curtis Publishing Company. An ex-*Time* reporter was made or made himself editor-in-chief of all the Curtis magazines. All of them except the unimportant *Jack and Jill,* both editorial and advertising, were moved from Philadelphia where they had been established for so many years to New York where they were not established at all. Personnel decimation continued until departments were ravaged and only skeletal forces remained in many.

Financial loss was lowered, but there was no gain except through the sale of subsidiaries. Exploitation continued frenziedly. New executives were given high salaries and contracts binding Curtis to large compensatory payments in case of dismissal or failure. New editors followed in rapid succession on all the Curtis magazines, new publishers were appointed for them. Even the publisher of tiny *Jack and Jill* was dismissed and supplanted by a superannuated state supervisor of education from New York. Once dignified Curtis now had all the sobriety of opportunists jostling to freeload at the bar and knifing each other between drinks.

Climax of this performance came in 1964 when two senior executives and more than a dozen adherents publicly accused the Curtis president who had appointed them of gross mismanagement. They petitioned the Curtis board for his removal. The president was ousted, but the two chief protesters, who were being paid about $1,500 a week each, were also dismissed. The president was moved up to the chairmanship of the board, then reverted to space salesman before he left the company. The two ousted vice presidents sued the company for nearly $500,000, but accepted settlements eventually of much smaller sums.

The internal quarrel at Curtis was headlined across the United States. Its shabbiness shocked even the hardened advertising press. Curtis was now getting more publicity than the public relations department which it had once had could ever have hoped for. The "sophisticated muckraking" which the now dismissed editor-in-chief of all the Curtis magazines had instituted in the now every other Saturday evening *Post* backfired explosively and expensively. "The Story of a Football Fix" in its issue for March 23, 1963 accused the University of Georgia's football coach of telephoning his team's plays to the coach of the University of Alabama before a game which Alabama won 35–0. Both men sued and were awarded judgments. The Alabama coach accepted a settlement of $300,000 tax free. After additional litigation which took the case to the Supreme Court, the Georgia coach got $460,000 plus interest which brought the total to a supposed $600,000. As a result of statements made in "The Automakers and their Mighty Works," *Post,* September 19, 1964, the president of Chrysler brought a $2,000,000 libel suit against Curtis. There were other suits.

While *Printer's Ink* deplored the Curtis "front-page brawling" and the advertising agencies decided not to place schedules with Curtis magazines that might cease publication before the advertising appeared, Curtis lost its contract for the offset printing of some 12,000,000 *Reader's Digest* condensed books a year. Misfortune piled atop misfortune, but there was one stroke of good fortune. The Texas Gulf Sulphur Company found ore on its lands adjacent to Curtis acreage in Ontario.

Curtis stock jumped up as a result. While the clownish antics of management continued to make headline news, copper and zinc were discovered on its holdings, and Curtis sold its timber and mineral properties in Ontario and Pennsylvania to Texas Gulf Sulphur for $24,000,000. This was in 1965.

This manna kept Curtis going. It sold its Lock Haven, Pennsylvania, paper mill to Hammermill Paper Company this same year. It sold various subsidiaries, National Analysts, a research organization, and Data Processing.

Because no one else would take the job the Curtis presidency went to a former RCA executive who had come in with the new regime and outlasted the man who had employed him. He had been in office only a few months when he was faced with an ultimatum from *Holiday's* four top editors. Either the editor appointed by the short-term "editor-in-chief" of all the Curtis magazines to succeed Ted Patrick went or they would go. The new president accepted their resignations, and Curtis was treated to more unfavorable newspaper publicity.

This second post-1961 Curtis administration lasted only from November, 1964, to early 1968. A bookkeeper's administration responsible in reality to the banks which had lent Curtis large sums, it was comparatively quiet. It was marked only by the rapid entrances and exits of editors and executive personnel, continued financial loss, the falling off further of advertising in all of the Curtis magazines—though *Ladies' Home Journal* showed some signs of recovery in 1967—and further decimation of Curtis staff in repeated purges. The big Curtis building on Independence Square in Philadelphia seemed virtually deserted. One followed his echoing footsteps down empty halls past what seemed miles of empty offices. The splendid block-long building with its 1,000,000 square feet of floor space and one of the most renowned addresses in the country was sold in the spring of 1968. Where there had been thousands at work, with whole departments spilling over into nearby office buildings, there were now a handful of Curtis employees in leased space on parts of three floors.

In April, 1968, another dazzling sea change struck Curtis. The energetic young lawyer-president of a film processing company in Manhasset, Long Island, lent Curtis $5,000,000, borrowed another $5,000,000 from Time, Inc., and moved in as Curtis president. Every year there had been rumors of new purchasers of Curtis or one or another of its magazines. The newest Curtis president announced quickly and sharply that none of the magazines was for sale. A financial manipulator whose successes had proved his skill, he had other plans for Curtis and its properties.

Curtis posted another deficit of $1,600,000 in the first quarter of 1968 and a far greater loss for the entire year was forecast at its annual stockholder's meeting in May. In July another 450 Curtis employees in New York and Philadelphia were dismissed, as more were dismissed in the late summer. In August, Curtis sold both the *Ladies' Home Journal* and *American Home,* which it had purchased ten years previously. It acquired the failing and small-circulation *Status,* reportedly in payment of a debt to its subsidiary Curtis Circulation Company. The Circulation Company was then sold to Perfect Film.

The most spectacular maneuver was undoubtedly the halving of the circulation of *The Saturday Evening Post* from its approximately 7,000,000 count. Subscribers whose age, income, or address did not meet standards set for what was presented as a new-new *Saturday Evening Post,* a quality magazine which could be purchased only by the elect and select, were arbitrarily dropped. They could have *Life,* which as a mass magazine, they presumably would not mind.[3] The long familiar *Saturday Evening Post,* "Big, Believed, Beloved," as Curtis

[3] This got Curtis more free publicity. Many newspapers carried mocking comment. Art Buchwald satirized the ploy in his syndicated column as "The Post Dropouts." Longtime subscribers who considered themselves well enough educated, respectably housed, of sufficient income and even intelligence to cope with the *Post* were incensed. An electrochemist of some repute in the scientific world, a man in his late sixties with a suburban Maryland address, his laboratory in Washington, D.C., was proud of the fact that he had been a *Post* boy salesman. He had read the *Post* all of his mature life. He was expelled. Two or three months later his elder sister, unmarried, a retired casualty insurance broker, received a hard-sell direct-mail piece urging her to subscribe to the new high-priced select-audience *Saturday Evening Post.*

promotion long insisted—"The Saturday Evening Pest," "The Moron's Bible," for it had its detractors too—had ceased to exist. Because it could no longer meet its assets and earnings requirements, the New York Stock Exchange delisted The

Mayor Richard Daley and *Playboy* publisher Hugh M. Hefner in effigy bestride a model of Chicago on the cover of the final issue of *The Saturday Evening Post*.

Curtis Publishing Company in May, 1968. Legally Curtis still existed, but a new Saturday Evening Post Company became the publisher of the *Post, Holiday, Status,* and *Jack and Jill.* In effect the Sharon Hill printing plant was all that was left of the Curtis Publishing Company. By court action the three last-named magazines were restored to Curtis control in January, 1970.

The Saturday Evening Post dribbled to its inglorious end Friday, January 10, 1969, when its demise was made official. No Clarence Buddington Kelland, no Tutt and Mr. Tutt, no Tish, no Norman Rockwell disported themselves in the final issue of February 8, 1969, which was still in press, but "Founded in 1728 by Benjamin Franklin" still sat snugly under Franklin's profile on the contents page. The captain went down with the ship he had never really commanded. Ironically the *Post* had ended 1968 with a December 28 bright poster cover from which the words "Happy . . . Happy . . . Happy" leaped out.

The New York Times carried a suitable obituary across four columns of the bottom of its front page when the *Post* died. Inside it ran a nostalgic half page replete with reproductions of old *Post* covers. At the last moment an avant garde publisher dramatically offered to take over the *Post.* He offered no money, would assume none of the *Post*'s obligations, but asked majority ownership of the stock in a company he suggested be formed. The offer could hardly be taken seriously and it was not, but there may well have been truth, if not as he intended, in part of the rejected benefactor's aggrieved comment: "It has been said that a good magazine never just dies, it commits suicide." [4]

[4] Barney Rosset, quoted in *The Wall Street Journal,* January 10, 1969.

Chapter 31

The Change in Magazine Publishing

There are 10,204 publications described as periodicals published in the United States.[1] Many of these are magazines only because they appear at regular intervals. When it has need to mention a number at all, the trade usually says there are about 8,000 magazines. The Library of Congress receives about 35,000 different periodicals, about half of them published in this country.[2]

About five billion copies of these magazines published weekly, biweekly, monthly, or quarterly permeate contemporary America every year. Every time they are issued the combined circulations of the magazines of the United States exceed the population of the country, men, women, and children, by about 25,000,000. Yet the magazine publishing industry is comparatively small. The large magazines represent and look like Big Business, but the Magazine Publishers Association, to which most of the large publishers of the magazines which dominate and account for most of the circulation and advertising figures belong, has only about 100 members who publish some 250 magazines.

About 70,000 men and women are engaged in the actual printing and publishing of magazines, and they account for an

[1] *N. W. Ayer & Son's Directory Newspapers and Periodicals, 1968.*

[2] Estimate, October, 1968, by the Chief, Serial Division, Library of Congress, Washington, D.C.

annual payroll of nearly a half-billion dollars.[3] This may sound like a considerable enterprise, but it is hardly comparable in size to many other segments of manufacturing industry. A number of individual corporations employ more people than the whole of magazine publishing: Union Carbide Corporation, for instance, employs 80,000 people in the United States and another 46,000 abroad.

Total magazine circulation goes up every year. It was 44,095,000 in 1920; 94,871,000 in 1940; 147,260,000 in 1950; 190,432,000 in 1960; 225,262,000 in 1966; 237,101,335 in 1968.[4] Total advertising revenue in 1969 reached $1,245,321,982, up seven per cent over 1968 with *The Saturday Evening Post* figures excluded from the 1968 count. Magazine advertising revenue also rises yearly but part of the increase in 1969 was due to increased space charges.[5]

Despite these primary indicators of magazine publishing growth and despite the omnipresence of glossy magazines in the home, public libraries, the classroom, doctors' offices, and beautician's parlors, the large-circulation magazines are not prospering. Profits have declined almost yearly. The net profits of 35 major magazines averaged only 1.7 per cent of gross income in 1960, and there is little reason to suspect that—as an industry average—the percentage has increased.[6]

The loss of advertising to television, multiplied production and distribution costs, the fierce competition for circulation have all contributed to this cut in profits. So has the federal government. A series of substantial increases in second-class mailing rates has effectively abrogated the intent of the Postal Act of 1879. Second-class mailing rates were increased 89 per

3 Basing its count on Labor Department statistics, Table No. 323 of the *Statistical Abstract of the United States, 1967,* gives 73,000 as an average annual number employed; using Department of Commerce figures, Table No. 1114 of the *Abstract* gives 67,000 as the number employed in 1965 and shows the number to have been fairly constant since 1958.

4 Reports of the Magazine Advertising Bureau of the Magazine Publishers Association for all A. B. C. magazines, general and farm, excluding comics.

5 Publishers Information Bureau, Inc., New York, N.Y., 1968, 1969, 1970.

6 "New Magazines," *The Wall Street Journal,* October 19, 1961.

cent between 1945 and 1962.[7] Despite sharp protests by the magazines they went up again. Millions were added to the postage bills of the magazines. The editor of *Harper's* exclaimed, "I just can't believe that the government actually intends to destroy such magazines as Harper's, the Atlantic Monthly . . ."[8]

Second-class mailing rates were raised in 1967 by three annual increases through 1970 by another 23 per cent. Because of the maze of special regulations and rate considerations and the way in which these are stated by Post Office rulings it seems impossible to determine how much they have risen on the average for the average magazine, but in April, 1967, the Magazine Publishers Association estimated 147 per cent since 1953.

Assuming a hypothetical magazine with a mix of one-half pound of editorial and one-half pound of advertising going to the fourth of the eight postal zones, which is the general experience of most publishers, Kent Rhodes, *Reader's Digest* vice president directly concerned with mailing, gives 156 per cent as the increase from the end of World War II to January 1, 1969. The same hypothetical magazine that cost 2.25 cents to mail in 1945 now costs 6.10 cents to mail.

As does the public for other classes of mail, the magazines are paying in this instance for political preferment and bureaucratic muddle. In a July 16, 1968, editorial, "Back to the Pony Express," *The New York Times* commented that the mail service appeared to be near the point of total collapse. *Life*, September 13, 1968, used the same phrase, ". . . while the postal service may once have been the strand that bound the nation together, it is now antiquated, inefficient, in constant danger of total collapse, and its service, as a result, is awful." *Life* quoted one of ex-President Johnson's appointees to the Postmaster Generalship—his tenure was very brief—

[7] "Post-War Postal Rate Trends Percent Change, Second Class, Half-Pound Magazines, 50% editorial/50% advertising, Mailed to Fourth Zone, 1945–1961," U.S. Post Office Department, Washington, D.C., n.d.

[8] Quoted in "Second-Class Mail Rates Can Ruin First-Class Magazines," *The Reader's Digest*, April, 1962.

who said, "No human being can efficiently manage the nation's postal service as it is now constituted." [9]

The President already knew the truth of his appointee's dismay. His own Commission on Postal Organization reported in 1968 that the Post Office was wasting almost $1,000,000,000 annually in inefficient operation. It recommended elimination of all the political patronage jobs in the postal system (an unlikely eventuality) and turning the Post Office over to a non-profit corporation.[10]

The immediate result of these postal raises has been higher magazine subscription and cover prices. It is usual, of course, for an industry to pass on cost increases to the consumer, but in this case an industry hard pressed for the profits which allow continued operation had little choice. Virtually all of the leading magazines have gone up, many of them doubling prices. The news weeklies, *The New Yorker, McCall's, Look,* even *The Reader's Digest,* which maintained its original twenty-five cent price from its founding in 1922 until 1957, are all fifty cents a copy. *The Saturday Evening Post,* sold at five cents a copy from 1897 to 1942, was fifty cents at its demise, a price increase of 900 per cent. The *Atlantic, Harper's,* and *Holiday,* and others are seventy-five cents a copy.[11]

Magazine publishing is a business which depends upon profits to live. It is not, or not yet, government-operated or government-subsidized. From the viewpoint of the publisher, magazines are not media of public communications or periodical journalism. Magazines are a product. Their editorial content is incidental, an expense, even a necessary evil, of importance only becauses it induces circulation, hence advertising space sales. Magazine publishing has to make its own way and, despite all the appearance of success, is having a difficult

[9] Lawrence F. O'Brien.

[10] *National Observer,* July 22, 1968. In "The Awful Truth About the U.S. Post Office," November, 1968, *The Reader's Digest* described its rates and the postal accounting system as chaotic.

[11] Mailing and production costs are basically responsible for these increases, but there is also the fact that chronic inflation has made comparatively small sums of money seem inconsequential. There is little else the purchaser can do with fifty, seventy-five, or one hundred cents.

time doing it. This situation brought about the major change in magazine publishing in the 1960's.

The New Yorker Magazine, Inc., publishes, and very successfully, a magazine, *The New Yorker.* It publishes nothing else, and it sells nothing else. It seems almost alone among the major magazines in this single-hearted concentration.

The Reader's Digest, which *The Wall Street Journal,* March 17, 1966, headlined as the "top publishing success since the Scriptures," also publishes, internationally, just one magazine, but the Digest has become a giant sales organization. In the multi-millions it sells condensed book club memberships, phonograph records, textbooks, school readers, dictionaries, almanacs, anthologies, children's classics, and handsomely produced special books such as *Wonders of the Animal World, The Reader's Digest Great World Atlas, The Reader's Digest Complete Book of the Garden.* In 1968 it even published a complete history, geography, panorama, and inventory, *These United States,* in one volume—a digestive feat even for the *Digest.* The inescapable *Digest* uses high-pressure, hard-sell, direct-mail gimmicks of many kinds, and even stages lotteries to sell all of these related items bearing the widely respected *Digest* name.

In 1965 *The Reader's Digest* purchased Funk and Wagnalls and Wilfred Funk, Inc. together with their entire line of encyclopedias, dictionaries, and reference books, and, greatly expanding the operation, went into general book publishing. In 1967 the *Digest* even went into the mutual fund investment business in Germany and may well extend this interest to other countries.

The world's largest magazine publishing company, Time, Inc., publishes *Time, Life, Fortune,* and *Sports Illustrated.* Still primarily a magazine publisher, it also publishes Time-Life books, most of them graphically handsome display volumes from the contents of the magazines. The mail-order sale of these books, in fourteen languages, came to $60,000,000 in 1967. In January, 1968, Time, Inc., for $17,000,000 acquired

Little, Brown and Company of Boston, one of the country's oldest and most reputable book publishers.

Operating internationally, Time, Inc. has a one-third interest in a paperback book company in Germany. It owns one-half of the General Learning Corporation of which Silver-Burdett is a part. As Time-Life Broadcast it operates five large television stations. With Crown Zellerbach it is joint owner of the St. Francisville Paper Company. As Eastex Incorporated it makes paper. It has Printing Developments, Inc., which operates in the United States, Europe, and Latin America. In 1967 it began to service the food industry with the reports of its Selling Areas-Marketing, Inc. Time, Inc., owns the Newark *Evening News* and the *Sunday News* and has heavy investments in Metro-Goldwyn-Mayer, Inc.

Thirty-five per cent of the gross revenue of $506,268,000 and net profit of $30,423,000 which Time, Inc., showed in 1967 came from other than magazine publishing. Its net profit was down $3,000,000 from 1966. Fall-off in magazine advertising, *Life* hardest hit with a drop for the year of 8.2 per cent, accounted for much of the loss. Profit came from diversification and a corporate mix.[12] Though its circulation is tremendous, over 7,800,000, *Life* dropped 17 per cent in number of pages of advertising for the first half of 1969.

Look once stood by itself, its only acknowledged companions the Des Moines newspapers of its founders. *Look* is now part of Cowles Communications, Inc., which publishes *Look, Venture, Family Circle* (in Great Britain and West Germany as well as in the United States), *Living* (in Great Britain), *Modern Medicine, Geriatrics, Dental Survey, Dental Industry, Dental Laboratory Review, Nursing Homes,* and *Neurology.* As well as this long list of general and special interest magazines it published newspapers in Puerto Rico; Gainesville, Florida; Lakeland, Florida; and Suffolk County, Long Island. It publishes the Cowles Comprehensive Encyclopedia, textbooks, reference books, and one-shot books for school distribu-

[12] "Time Incorporated: Annual Report to Stockholders, 1967."

tion or newsstand sale. Its Education Division publishes a bi-weekly news magazine, *Education News,* directed to the schools. Cowles owns the Cambridge Book Company which issues paperback textbooks. It is in printing with its Xograph 3-D process. It has television and radio stations in Des Moines and Memphis and another television station in Orlando-Daytona Beach.

In 1966 Cowles Communications, Inc. had earnings of $3,786,000. In 1967 it had a loss of $3,434,000. Costs of expansion and diversification—all within the communications field—accounted for much of the loss, but *Look* showed a seven per cent drop in advertising in 1967 and despite a raise in rates a five per cent drop in advertising revenue.[13] Cowles posted another substantial loss in 1968 and in October, 1969, dropped the *Suffolk Sun,* a Long Island newspaper on which it had expended large sums. *Look*'s circulation in 1968 almost 7,800,000, it showed a drop of 3 per cent in advertising pages and 2 per cent in revenue for the first six months of 1969.

Always high on the list of the leading magazines with a circulation in excess of 7,000,000, *Better Homes and Gardens* is the property of the Meredith Corporation in Des Moines. Meredith, which has changed its corporate name from Meredith Publishing Company to indicate the greater range of its interests, publishes numerous cookbooks, garden books, home repair books, many paperbound books on such domestic subjects as Christmas ideas and birthday celebration hints all emanating from *Better Homes.* Emanating from its *Successful Farming* are more books, these on such subjects as animal health, weed and insect control, and machinery management.

In New York the Meredith Press (which absorbed Appleton-Century and Duell, Sloan and Pearce) was in general book publishing. In December, 1969, the Meredith Corporation sold all rights in the general trade list of the Meredith Press but retained its *Better Homes and Gardens* titles. Meredith will concentrate on how-to-do-it and reference books compatible with the *Better Homes* line but not publish them under a

13 "Cowles Communications Inc., Annual Report 1967."

Meredith imprint. Meredith is in broadcasting with stations in Syracuse, Omaha, Phoenix, and Kansas City, Missouri. Jointly with Avco it owns a television cable company. In Chicago it manufactures geographical globes. It produces and sells educational programming devices. In Des Moines it does high-speed-full-color printing for the magazines of client publishers, among the magazines, *Vogue, House & Garden,* and *Brides.* Meredith, which does an annual business of over $110,000,000 is not dependent on *Better Homes and Gardens* and *Successful Farming.*[14]

In 1961 *The Saturday Review* was sold to the McCall Corporation, a giant printing company which publishes the top-circulation women's magazine, *McCall's.* The McCall Corporation publishes *Redbook* as well. It publishes McCall books on gardens, sewing, a "Needlework Treasury." The McCall Pattern Company does a huge business in dress patterns. The McCall Printing Company with divisions and operating plants in Dayton, Prince George's County, Maryland, and in Doraville, an Atlanta Suburb, also has a lithographing plant in Menlo Park, California. Among many other magazines it prints *The Reader's Digest* and *Newsweek.* In Jersey City, McCall's Pennland Printing is the largest producer of Bell System telephone directories. Among others it prints all those for New York City, Philadelphia, Baltimore, and Washington, D.C. as well as for all of New Jersey, and Westchester County, New York. McCall's owns the Plimpton Press, printer of hardcover books, with large plants in Norwood, Massachusetts, and Pinola, Indiana.

In July, 1968, this huge corporation, whose 1967 sales totaled $209,631,000 despite a decline in advertising revenue from *McCall's,* became part of a still larger corporate entity.[15] Norton Simon, Inc. was formed through the merger of Hunt Food & Industries, Inc. (tomato catsup) and the Canada Dry Corporation (mostly ginger ale) with the McCall Corporation. Norton Simon then purchased a television and motion picture

[14] "Meredith Publishing Company Annual Report, 1967."
[15] "McCall Corporation 1967 Annual Report."

producing company. Big as it is, *McCall's* magazine is now only a detail in an industrial complex. With such financing behind it, *McCall's* could afford to pay the estate of Robert F. Kennedy more than $1,000,000 for the 25,000-word manuscript of "Thirteen Days," story of the Cuban missile crisis in 1962, getting a big name, an "inside story," and another jump on its magazine competitors all at the same time, but the conclusion is inescapable that *McCall's* could drop out of this much mixed corporate mix and that nobody might notice its absence for some time.

The New Yorker has refused many merger offers. Still privately owned, *The Reader's Digest* shows no public signs of considering sale, merger, public ownership, or immersion in some still larger enterprise. The H. M. H. Publishing Company still owns *Playboy* and its other activities bearing the Playboy name. Most of the other large magazine publishers have gone in either for failure, consolidation, expansion, or some device which can save them from the present perils of major magazine publishing. Even the much smaller "class" monthlies have sought protection. They have long been subsidized by book publishers, but in 1965 John Cowles, Jr., of the *Look* and Cowles Communications family, editor of the Minneapolis *Star* and the Minneapolis *Tribune,* became president of Harper's Magazine, Inc., and its principal stockholder. He became board chairman in July, 1968.

The organization which *Advertising Age* called "the largest communications empire in the world," and which well may be, has not gone in for major change in recent years.[16] The Hearst Corporation has been much the way it is for a long time. Privately owned by the Hearst Foundation in New York and the William Randolph Hearst Foundation in San Francisco, it is under no legal obligation to issue an annual report, and it is chary of releasing information of any kind about itself. Where Hearst was once synonymous with yellow journalism, scream-

[16] Quoted by Albert Bermel in "The Future of the Hearst Empire," *Harper's,* January, 1962.

ing newspaper headlines, and sensationalism at its most sensational, Hearst is modestly quiet about its own business.

Though it once had many more, Hearst owns nine large newspapers: the Los Angeles *Herald-Examiner,* Baltimore *News American,* Boston *Record American,* Boston *Advertiser,* Albany *Times-Union,* Albany *Knickerbocker News,* San Antonio *Light,* San Francisco *Examiner,* and Seattle *Post-Intelligencer.* It owns 550,000 acres of timberland and a silver mine in Mexico and 212,000 acres of California. It has King Features Syndicate, Avon paperback books, and is in radio and television in Pittsburgh, Milwaukee, Baltimore, and San Juan.

With a long list of subsidiary companies and organizations and enterprises of many kinds, Hearst is also a major publisher of magazines. It publishes thirteen of them in the United States: *American Druggist, Bride & Home, Cosmopolitan, eye, Good Housekeeping, Harper's Bazaar, House Beautiful, Motor, Motor Boating, Popular Mechanics, Town & Country, Science Digest,* and *Sports Afield.* In addition it publishes five magazines in Great Britain.[17]

Some of the long-established Hearst magazines are among the leaders in circulation and in advertising revenue. With a net paid circulation of over 5,600,000 *Good Housekeeping* ranks near the top among the women's books. It took in more than $17,000,000 in advertising during the first half of 1969. *Cosmopolitan* with a circulation just over 1,000,000 showed a gain of 22 per cent for this same period.[18] *Popular Mechanics* is the leader in its field. *Harper's Bazaar* is one of the exclusive two top high-fashion magazines, and *Town & Country* one of the most opulent in appearance of American magazines.

It is doubtful if some of the other Hearst magazines do anywhere nearly as well as these, but that can hardly make much difference to the Hearst Corporation. It is credited with assets of over $500,000,000, and it is believed that these may reach $1,000,000,000 before too long. It is estimated that Hearst

[17] "Hearst Lives," *Newsweek*, January 22, 1968.
[18] M.A.B. and P.I.B. reports.

makes an annual net profit of from $8,000,000 to $10,000,000 and that its magazine properties are worth at least $100,000,000.[19]

One of the largest publishers in the country, McGraw-Hill, Inc., is in the business of business. Functioning like a machine, it publishes 48 trade, industrial, and business magazines and three daily construction newspapers. Many of its magazines—*American Machinist, Chemical Engineering, Coal Age, Electrical World, Engineering News-Record, Textile World,* and some of the others—are as standard in their field as the micrometer, slide rule, test tube or whatever else characterizes the trade.

Originally the McGraw-Hill Book Company, offshoot of McGraw-Hill Publishing which issued the magazines, published only textbooks in the physical and then the social sciences. It is now a large publisher of trade books, fiction, biography, juveniles as well as texts from the lower school grades through the university. With over 12,000 employees, 800 of them editors, and some 250 offices in 175 cities around the world, news bureaus in ten American cities and ten cities abroad, McGraw-Hill is a fairly sizable enterprise, big enough to be leaving its blue tile skyscraper on West Forty-second Street in New York for a new 50-story building in Rockefeller Center.

McGraw-Hill has scores of subsidiaries or affiliates, some of them in Canada, Mexico, Panama, Australia and other foreign countries as well as in the United States. It sells films and instructional systems, investment services, computerized services. Among many other organizations it owns Standard & Poor's Corporation. McGraw-Hill's operating revenue in 1958 was $96,241,000; in 1967 it was $328,284,260. Of this amount $126,515,000 came from advertising placed in its magazines with their combined circulation of about 2,750,000. The point here is that this gain of 3.4 per cent in 1967 following on a gain of 15.4 per cent in 1966 came from advertising in special interest magazines going to firm circulations limited by busi-

[19] "A Nest Egg for the Grandchildren," *Forbes,* December 1, 1967.

ness or professional interests, not from mass advertising to mass audiences in mass magazines.[20]

Outside of magazine publishing but still within communications there are other large concentrations of properties and power. In book publishing, for instance, Random House which embraces Pantheon Books, Alfred A. Knopf, Modern Library, and other subsidiaries is now part of the Radio Corporation of America which owns the National Broadcasting Company. The once independent Macmillan Company is now part of Crowell-Collier. Formed by the amalgamation of two book publishers in New York and one in Philadelphia, Holt, Rinehart & Winston is also a magazine publisher with representation on the board of directors of the Magazine Publishers Association.

The danger in all of these and comparable concentrations of media power is manifest. Of course, it has not gone unnoticed. In June, 1968, the *Atlantic* ran an article on the "Media Barons" by a member of the Federal Communications Commission. In a piece choked with admiring references to the good deeds of various federal regulatory agencies he naturally advocated greater government control of communications in the public interest by limiting concentrations of media ownership.

Just as manifest to the general observer is the danger of any more government control of anything, particularly the press in any of its forms. Happily, the bureaucrat empowered to decide what is or is not in the public interest here has not yet been designated—though obviously a few hundred thousand who feel fully qualified for the task are ready to sacrifice themselves to the burden of such office.

Magazines have achieved and maintained national penetration. As the industry likes to point out, 85 per cent of the nation's families read at least one magazine. The college-educated read more magazines than those who have not attended some college. With college education more and more widespread, there will be more educated readers. Largely through

[20] McGraw-Hill, Inc., Annual Report, 1967.

sectional advertising, magazine advertising revenue rose forty per cent between 1961 and 1967. None of this means that every magazine and every magazine publisher shares in these benefits. With the abrupt disappearance of *Collier's*, the *American*, and *Woman's Home Companion* fresh in memory and the Curtis cadaver still dangling, there are pervasive fears.

Other factors contribute, but the compelling reason behind the mergers, diversifications, expansions, and takeovers is undoubtedly the realization that, in general, it is no longer economically feasible to publish just one magazine, no matter how large or ostensibly successful, or even a group of such magazines. Publishers fear carrying all their eggs in one paper and print basket even when it has a varnished color cover. Thus many major magazines are now but parts of complexes engaged in related, tangential, or completely unrelated activities. Some of them seem only the house organs of homogenous or heterogenous agglomerations.

The Reader's Digest made it from an idea and some petty cash. Thirty years later the strongly contrasting *Playboy* did the same thing. Some unusual combination of individual acuteness, circumstance, and good fortune may bring another successful magazine crashing through, but the same reasons which have impelled the magazine media concentrations—increased production and mailing costs, television, merciless magazine competition for both circulation and advertising—mitigate against the possibility of starting a new major general or consumer magazine and keeping it going.

Chapter 32

Editorial Considerations

Magazine editors are irritatingly and erroneously convinced of their omniscience. They buy material only from Big Names and from their friends. They cannot write themselves yet they consider themselves to be judges of writing. They reject an author's best work and mutilate beyond recognition the few manuscripts they accept from outside their own offices. Ask any writer.

A novelist and one-time *Saturday Evening Post* humorist, Caskie Stinnett, the current editor of *Holiday,* said ruefully in one of his signed editorials that readers consider the editor an albatross hung around a writer's neck.[1] Certainly writers do.

Writers are conceited, stubbornly wrong-headed, undependable, and generally impossible to work with. Ask any editor. Mellowed by an alcoholic lunch one editor recently confided that all writers are children and have to be treated as children. They should be praised when they are well-behaved and punished when they are not. When Curtis was still flourishing, one of its top editors had a set speech which began with his looking out his office window toward Independence Hall through the Philadelphia gloaming after the day's work had been done, the last manuscript had been read, and "the last starving author has been seen." As the editor was being paid over $100,000 a year and few of them make an appreciable fraction of that amount, writers who heard him resented the sneer, so

[1] "Speaking of Holiday," *Holiday,* November, 1968.

when he gave the speech on later occasions the editor changed the derisive phrase to "the last fractious author" and felt he had paid them a compliment.

Behind all the statistics, graphs, and percentage points used to describe and appraise mass magazine publishing there is always a simple and human situation, and not much else. The composing room and the presses are usually somewhere else, sometimes in plants owned by the publisher. More often printing, binding, and shipping are contracted out. All there is at the offices of the magazine are the editorial, advertising, and circulation departments with their supporting units.

Editorial, advertising, and circulation make a nice triumvirate. Usually at odds among themselves, they make it difficult to fix responsibility for the success or failure of an issue or even for the success or failure of a magazine. The advertising salesmen say they could sell space by the skyful if only circulation would get them the numbers and kinds of readers advertisers and advertising agencies demand. Circulation says it could double the number of subscribers and newsstand buyers if only the editorial content of the magazine were attractive to readers and the cover illustrations were big enough and bright enough to attract attention. Editorial says it is running features so startling and so frightening to competitive magazines—and they have the clippings to prove it—that anybody should be able to sell the issues and space in them, and it has even more startling features scheduled. It is using more illustrations, more color, more cartoons . . .

Circulation, editorial, and advertising men don't always say these things this bluntly to each other, for they are gingerly polite when they meet, but they make themselves violently and profanely clear among themselves.

Actually it has to come down to the editorial, for as far as the public is concerned that is all there is. Here the subject is not that simple. A magazine is not a drop-forge thudding out engine parts or metal tools. It is not a Battle Creek cereal manufacturer shooting helpless grains of rice or oats through giant compressed air guns and making a lot of noise doing it.

No substantial or durable physical product emerges from all the concentrated effort which, issue after issue in an unending series, goes into the production of a magazine.

All a magazine had to begin with is people and ideas that must be expressed in words and pictures. Each issue starts from nothing or only from editorial prescience, accumulated experience, skill with words, and feel for design. There are few rules, and most of them are flexible. There are no templates or reliable gauges. The ultimate ingredients of a magazine are invisible. They come down to imagination, skill, intuition, judgment, possibly intelligence, and a few other attributes; and in combinations of them biologically and psychologically assembled in one individual or a small group of individuals.

Strong editors make strong magazines. Bok, Bonner, Hale, Lorimer, Luce, Mencken, Ross, and Wallace—strictly in alphabetical order—are cases in point. A magazine editor need not be right or even bright. He need not be intellectual, fair-minded, of good will, or even likeable. What he has to be is distinct and somehow to be able to transfer that distinctness to his magazine, making it consistently recognizable and different from every other magazine. If he is fortunate, he feels an empathy with his readers; and if he is particularly fortunate, he is like a few thousand or a few million of them.

Few things can be successfully faked, and a magazine can never be. To keep the illustrations safely in the past, Sarah Josepha Hale could not have edited *The North American Review* successfully, and James Russell Lowell could not have done well with *Godey's*. An editor cannot edit up or down. He has to be what he is and what he is doing. George Horace Lorimer was convinced, dogmatic, and autocratic. Edward Bok was almost rapturously self-assured. Except that its issues are thicker and its short stories are not short, *The New Yorker* looks much the same now as it did in 1946. Yet it is not the same as it was under Harold Ross. *The Reader's Digest,* on the other hand, is still DeWitt Wallace and the editors he has gathered about him, who are even more so.

In many of the mass magazines strongly marked editors with convictions and decided tastes have been supplanted by editors of a more modern type. They are capable men, often with journalism school backgrounds, who know the elements of their demanding trade thoroughly. They are aware of the broad field of communications, sloughs as well as fair green meadow. They know what attractions a feature article should contain and how a lead paragraph should be written. They are career men safeguarding their jobs in large, impersonal organizations. These men are functional. They are products of the industry and conform to what they understand as competent practice. They have few eccentricities or, if they do, they conceal them. It does not do to risk the generous pensions toward which most of them are working.

Individuality, of course, is harder to attain and more dangerous to parade than it once was, but the lack of it shows in the similarity of the magazines these men produce. One remarked wistfully that reader research is a great leveller among editors, but reader research is not the cause. These editors are the kind of people, professionally competent but without marked characteristics, which our kind of society produces. Strong and distinctive magazines are seldom produced by such men. It is always easy to look back and say there were giants in those days, but the fact is that there were and that in many cases their editorial successors seem men and editors of lesser stature and paler coloring.

More and more the mass magazines are staff written. The news weeklies are entirely staff written, and what were once the predominantly pictorial magazines are very nearly so. *Holiday* is completely and the contrasting *Harper's* partially written by its own writers or those to whom pieces have been assigned. The original writing in *The Reader's Digest* is done mostly by its roving editors and a few others long connected with the magazine. The magazine market for the independent writer has greatly diminished, though public figures, sports and stage personalities, and the survivors of celebrated crimes, with their ghosts, can almost name their own price.

There is sense behind all this. Editors are no more idealistic than publishers and, if they intend to remain editors, they are as realistic as their employers. They must use writers, staff or retained, of whose competence they are assured and upon whose performance they can depend. For public relations purposes most of the mass magazines proclaim that they earnestly seek new writers and that all manuscripts are read by someone. Issues, they point out, must be filled. Some of the magazines sometimes do look for new writers and fresh material, but in reality little that comes in "over the transom" ever gets into print. The magazines usually deny that they seek out famous names, but they do. The literary quality or even the intelligence of a piece has little to do with acceptance or rejection. Whether it will attract attention, build circulation, win approval from sources whose approval is valued has much to do with it.

All magazine editors have to have adequate amounts of passable materal, and they can find little of it in the unsolicited manuscripts which pour into their offices. Some editors file large inventories of manuscripts against future issues or various contingencies, and keep some of them in lead with galleys in the office for quick editing, cutting, and makeup. They keep many stories on the shelf until they are outdated or otherwise unpublishable, then write them off, or sell them at cut rates to other editors who think they can use them. Where their subject does not tie them to a date, some editors prepare issues many months or even a year in advance. Others live from issue to issue in the belief that pressure will produce a livelier issue or in the hope of a startling new piece on some startling new development, which usually they do not get.

Television, of course, has complicated the magazine editor's operation. He had always to outstrip and defeat his fellows on the next periodical. Now he has also to outwit the insatiable electronic monster—which, he insists, has already gobbled up all the best stories. Television is now. Except for the news weeklies the content of the newest issue of a magazine can be months old before the public sees it. Television is life happening, not life inspected, considered, and passed upon. Reflection can seldom be as exciting as actuality. Television is also a spectator sport, and watching rather than participating is American habit. Reading itself is no longer an admired skill. Advertisers of eyeglasses assure people that their spectacles will not make them look studious.

The ordinary magazine piece is journalistic, not belletristic. It is ephemeral, not lasting. It is of the week or of the month, at least of the prevailing mood and mode. Next week or next month will see another world-shaking piece in its stead, and it will be promoted just as hard by the publisher.

The main purpose of the piece is generally to hold the attention of the reader long enough so that purposefully or accidentally he will look at the advertising which surrounds it. It is hoped that some of the interest generated by the piece will be transferred to the advertisements. If the article has stimulated, there is at least the chance that, through the accident of planned contiguity, the advertisement will stimulate to purchase. The pervasive glamor, humor, naiveté, intellectualism, or ribaldry will operate to make an identical advertisement produce a different effect in different periodicals. The advertisement will partake of the aura and repute of the magazine in which it appears.

The thing to remember about mass magazines—and their editors have to remember it even if they resent it—is that their primary purpose is profit. Only incidentally do they perform a service. They convey the news, display the fashions, provide inspiration, parade the movie and television starlets, clown, offer decorator hints and political advice, they give the inside dope on this and the outside dope on that, so that you will buy them. Preferably more people will buy more copies of one magazine than another. The publisher of the favored magazine can then tell the advertiser that he has the most readers or the most valuable readers or the most susceptible readers, and, of course, will have to charge a little more or a lot more for advertising space.

Given all of these considerations, the job of the mass magazine editor is a little more complicated than it once was. To accomplish the ends to which he is committed, he must always provide information and entertainment. By definition that is magazine objective. He must both provide escape and seem to interpret reality. The proportions differ, but facts and fancy are in most magazines. There is more escape in the *Digest* than in *Time*, but there is also escape in *Time* and reality in the *Digest*. Both are in most of the mass magazines. In one way or another all seem to cover much the same subjects, the problems—they are always "the problems"—of government, business, race, politics, morality, the home, education, religion, war, peace, diet. . . . The magazines seem more and more alike. They lack the distinctiveness given them by distinctive editors.

The manufacturer of an automobile, a razor blade, or a can of soup can perfect his product and then stop. He may have to make stylistic modifications as time goes on, but he has made what he set out to make, and the basic job is done. The magazine editor never knows this peace. There is always the next issue to get out. He has to start fresh again and please anew. The last issue has been forgotten. Deadlines are relentless. He must be brilliant again on schedule. There is stimulation in this. It is like getting a second chance every week or every two weeks or every month. The rewards are elation when some piece attracts wide and favorable attention or depression when an article or a whole issue falls flat. There are difficulties of a hundred kinds, and increasingly there is the dark threat of complete extinction.

No magazine has a guarantee of immortality. Often, for no discernible reason or from a complex of many causes over which the editor has little or no control, a magazine seems simply to age, wilt, wither, and die. A magazine is a sensitive plant. A change in public taste can kill it. The mere rumor of possible cessation can shake advertiser confidence to the point of abstention or withdrawal. The editor can then whip himself and his staff into a frenzy of experiment, originality or imitation and win only fatigue or more enfevered panic. You cannot bring a dead aspidistra back to life by pouring water on it, even a lot of water. Editors have learned these facts even if they cannot always act on them.

It seems unlikely that any magazine will ever again have the hold on its readers that Lorimer's *Saturday Evening Post* had from early in the 20th century into the 1930's and by lasting effect and accepted tradition for perhaps another twenty years. *The Youth's Companion* and *St. Nicholas* had something of the same hold for many years. They inspired affection as well as respect and eager interest. The only current magazine with anything like the same hold is *The Reader's Digest.*

Magazines do not exist in and of themselves. God, if you like, is the only uncaused cause. Magazines are produced by editors and the circumstances of a given time. Great editors make great magazines and make them commercially as well as editorially successful. The one follows the other without their having to bother too much about it. There are few such editors now, and the likelihood is that there will not be many more. The conditions of late 20th century life mitigate against their appearance.

The best magazines have a durability that is better described as a property in the minds and attitudes of their readers than as inherent in the publications themselves. *The North American Review* was serious, eloquent, sometimes incisive, often ponderous. It lasted for 129 years because it was consistently addressed to readers who enjoyed literary and intellectual qualities akin to those the magazine displayed. The magazine disappeared with the disappearance of the class of readers for whom it was edited.

Basically unchanged for many years, *Blackwood's* has been coming out of Edinburgh since 1817. The British Empire which it long celebrated in heroic tales is gone, but 'Maga,' as it is fondly called, endures because adventure and narratives of adventure are durable. *Blackwood's* has one simple element, story; and complicated and confused as they may have become, men still listen to story.

The recognizable appeal in most large magazines today is to youth. The reason is simple. They are struggling to obtain younger readers, and proportionately there are more people of younger age in the population than there were. Advertisers demand these young readers as they are the chief buyers of homes, cars, appliances, and most other products. They constitute the profitable market. The newer "liberalism" of many of the mass magazines stems from their attempts to entice young readers; the basic reason for it is not ideological but economic.

Chapter 33

Conclusion

In 1941 Frederick Lewis Allen commented on the revolution that had taken place in magazine publishing within fifty years. In 1891 a small group of monthly magazines, all with circulations of between 100,000 and 200,000 were dominant. Only two of them, *The Atlantic Monthly* and *Harper's,* survive, and these partly because they have imitated the national magazines which took over the leadership by inserting more information on vital subjects and more human interest material in their pages. Commenting on the changes between 1891 and 1941, Allen said:

> The revolution of which I have been speaking has undoubtedly had its bad side. It has brought us much vulgarity and evasion. It has brought us too much pseudo-information, pellets of half-truths designed to be consumed on the run. . . . Yet the existence of this mass reading public offers more than a gigantic demonstration of the bare literacy of the American public, or of its wish for easy entertainment. It offers a demonstration also of the American appetite for information —practical information—for tips on how to do one's job better, on how other people have succeeded at the same sort of job, on what is going on in the community and beyond its borders. These innumerable magazines of ours appeal to—and satisfy—a tremendous and undying urge to get on, to escape from provincial limitations, to acquire a sense of taste and style and at least outward distinction, to widen the horizon, to become . . . in some degree citizens of the world. In that sense our American magazines of today, considered as a broad group, give us a very impressive exhibit of democracy working.[1]

[1] Frederick Lewis Allen, "American Magazines, 1741–1941," *Bulletin of The New York Public Library,* June, 1941.

Twenty years later another observer, with less knowledge of magazines but the wider perspective offered by a more distant view, numbered magazines among the forces making for a standardized and vulgarized civilization in Europe as well as in the United States. After listing with vehement distaste the most repellant of its manifestations—neon lights, quizzes, crooners, the Bible in comic strip sequences, and a few more —Arthur Koestler blamed the mass communications media for making this stereotyped culture pattern irresistible.[2] Radio and television can claim part of the credit, but Koestler did not exempt American magazines. He gave special credit to the largest of them all.

What one man saw as reasonably good another man saw as unreasonably bad. As they are about most other things, moral judgments about magazines are subjective. A man's emotional reactions are determined by his background and his tastes, and he picks up his prejudices where he can. The point of interest here is that both Allen and Koestler assumed that the influence of the magazines of the United States is strong.

The force of magazines is reflected not only in legislative reforms following magazine campaigns once fought to bring them about, but also in what we eat, what we wear, what we plant in the garden or buy from the automobile dealer and the refrigerator manufacturer, what we think about foreign and domestic affairs, and how we judge our neighbors. We measure our own accomplishments or lack of them by those of men whose lives and actions are described in magazine articles; we desire and buy the necessities and gadgets enticingly displayed in magazine advertisements; we note and forget or unconsciously store the facts of current happenings as these are given in magazine accounts and imbibe magazine opinions about them. We even react pleasurably or with distaste to the visual and tactile stimuli offered by the physical properties of various periodicals. Magazines are a continual and almost inescapable pressure exerted on our minds and our emotions.

[2] Koestler, Arthur. *The Lotus and the Robot.* New York: The Macmillan Co., 1961.

Although this influence is difficult to isolate and prove, cause and effect are discernible in given instances. In 1928 *Harper's Magazine* printed an article on "The Possibilities of Large Telescopes" by George Ellery Hale. The article led directly to the construction and erection of the 200-inch telescope on Mount Palomar in California.

Alva Johnston, who had earlier written *New Yorker* "Profiles," first introduced Wendell Willkie to a national audience when he wrote "The Man Who Talked Back" for *The Saturday Evening Post* of February 25, 1939. This was a biography of Willkie as president of the Commonwealth and Southern Corporation, a private utilities company, and as an opponent of the Tennessee Valley Authority. Wendell Willkie himself wrote "Idle Money—Idle Men" for the *Post* of June 17, 1939. A poll taken by George Gallup's American Institute of Public Opinion in March, 1940, disclosed that Willkie was well enough and favorably enough known to be mentioned in answer to the question, "Whom would you like to see elected President this year?" But Willkie, then, was named by fewer than 1 per cent of those answering the question. Three days before the opening of the Republican national convention in 1940, a second Gallup poll showed 29 per cent favoring Wendell Willkie for the Republican nomination for President. Two days later *The Saturday Evening Post* of June 22, 1940, was published. Its two lead articles were "Five Minutes to Midnight" by Wendell L. Willkie and "I Am Not Nominating Him" by General Hugh S. Johnson, an early and enthusiastic Willkie supporter. Eight days after the appearance of these articles, with the convention still in session, a third poll by the American Institute of Public Opinion showed that 44 per cent of Republican voters wished Willkie to receive the nomination. These widely read magazine articles undoubtedly contributed greatly to Willkie's growing popularity.

The first full news of the discovery of atomic power and an appraisal of the significance of the discovery reached the public through two contrasting magazines. Only a few days after newspaper announcements that atomic fission had been effected, *Harper's Magazine* published in its issue of June, 1940, "Enter Atomic Power" by J. J. O'Neill. *The Saturday Evening Post,* September 9, 1940, published "The Atom Gives Up" by William L. Laurence, the same writer on scientific subjects who was later selected to write the official War Department releases when Hiroshima was bombed in August, 1945, and announcements of atom bomb experiments in New Mexico were made. "The Atom Gives Up" described in detail the discovery of U-235. It told of the work of Professor Arthur J. Dempster at the University of Chicago, of Professor Enrico Fermi's work first in Italy, then at Columbia, of the investigations of Lise Meitner and Dr. Otto Hahn in Germany, and of the contribution of other nuclear scientists to the ultimate discovery. The splitting of the uranium atom and the release of atomic power were fully described; so was the power of the force newly released. One pound of pure U-235, wrote William Laurence, would have the explosive power of 15,000 tons of TNT, or 300 carloads of fifty tons each.[3] So important and so revealing was this article considered that during World War II the Federal Bureau of Investigation forbade *The Saturday Evening Post* to send out reprints of the article or any copies of the issue containing it. The names of people requesting it had to be turned over to the War Department.

In February, 1947, *Harper's Magazine* published former Secretary of War Henry L. Stimson's statement on why the United States had used the atom bomb in the war with Japan, a document that was both major news and a record important in world history. Knowledge of the newly discovered atomic force, and realization of what its influence on their lives and on the future of the world might be, thus came first and most fully to the public, couched in terms understandable to the lay reader, through America's magazines.

Brevity and sharpness characterize today's magazine. They are timed to nervousness and hurry, styled to modern conceptions of swift design. More and more their appeal is visual.

[3] The article ventured a prophecy that, unfortunately, was incorrect: ". . . such a substance would not be likely to be wasted on explosives."

Increasingly they deal with the pressing social and economic problems of the day. The format, typography, and editorial style of some of the leaders are imitated by their competitors, but the similarity goes beyond mere imitation. Edward Bok once remarked that a picture is as good as a page of text. Others have made the same remark with the same air of discovery and finality, but a picture has certain limitations. It can arrest the reader's attention; it can dramatize, convey static reality, give heightened color to a written account, sometimes, in a very limited sense, tell a story; but it cannot discuss or explain. Realizing the values of pictures, editors of the general magazines have used them more and more, but have continued to place their chief reliance on words to convey ideas. The pictorial magazines, given over almost entirely to pictures at first, have used an ever greater proportion of text.

The women's general and service magazines, all of them good when judged by the standards they have set for themselves, are scarcely distinguishable in purpose or type of contents. The pattern for these magazines was set by Louis Godey and Sarah Joseph Hale in *Godey's Lady's Book* in the nineteenth century. Edward Bok enlarged and vastly improved the contents of all women's magazines through the influence of the *Ladies' Home Journal,* but he did not change the basic pattern. Editors of women's magazines since Bok's time have added more material of general interest to their pages, keeping pace with women's widened social and political interest in the twentieth century, but have retained the *Godey's* pattern built around fashions, home decoration, recipes, house plans, hints on decorum and etiquette, and all the rest. Today's shelter magazines, with their full-color pictures of the beautiful interiors and the beautiful exteriors of beautiful homes, seem all cut from the same bolt of glitter. The same terse news item, or the same magnificent or subtle advertisement, appears in an urban weekly, a small-town news magazine, or a rural monthly. A politician's views on world politics are as apt to appear in one of the women's magazines as in one of the pictorial magazines or in one of the general magazines. No magazine, no group of magazines, now has a monopoly on significant material. Despite their changed appearance, magazines now are not fundamentally different from what they were more than a century ago, and they are more and more alike.

Certain formulae of magazine journalism persist: success stories, slick fiction, the glib superficiality of newspaper-like feature articles. Yet today's magazines seem compact of a marked seriousness, almost a grimness. After all, because like any kind of public communication they cannot avoid it, they reflect the world they present, Magazines cannot live in a vacuum.

Some magazines and other magazines in some issues seem unable to check a strained attempt to embrace and explain the scientific, the economic, the sublime, and the less sublime in one gasping issue which will at the same time acknowledge art, literature, and all of history. Usually the result is as confusing as the attempt is admirable. Other magazines sometimes smother their real substance with so much froth that the sterner stuff goes almost unnoticed.

If a magazine is not read, its influence, its force of any kind, is nil. If it continues to go unread, the magazine is soon extinct. The larger the audience at which a magazine is directed, the greater the concessions it must make to the education and intelligence of its readers. The more thoughtful as well as the more frivolous magazines must observe this fact. They have to divert as well as to advise. Men and women are under no compulsion to read America's magazines. They read magazines, on their own declaration, to amuse themselves and "to keep well informed." As part of an elaborate pilot study made in 1944 to determine the feasibility of launching a new magazine, a survey was made in an east coast city. The sample of magazine readers questioned answered that they read magazines for these reasons in this order: entertainment, increase in knowledge, conversational material, escape, practical information, inspiration.

There must be variety in mood, variety in writing, and variety in the kind and extent of mental effort exacted of the reader. The popular magazines provide it. When an overly enthusiastic "constant reader" told Cyrus H. K. Curtis that he read every issue of *The Saturday Evening Post* from cover to cover and enjoyed everything in it, the publisher replied that he would have to check on his editors. If they were so perfectly matching the tastes and interests of this one reader, it was obvious that they were not putting a sufficient variety of interests into the magazine. The quality magazines which are still extant learned this lesson too. The staid *Atlantic,* not the *Ladies' Home Journal,* published *The Egg and I*—and *The New Yorker,* not one of the country's more ostensibly serious magazines, devoted an entire issue to John Hershey's 30,000-word account of the devastation wrought at Hiroshima by the first atom bomb used.

The past of the magazines of the United States is fixed, and their accomplishments stand firm.

When the United States was a handful of separated colonies scattered along the eastern seaboard, magazines helped create the feeling of their being a colonial entity. During and after the Revolution (as part of the "immense exhalation of periodical trash" which Mrs. Trollope deplored) they helped develop the hesitant national consciousness. Magazines were as potent a force in the abolition of slavery as in the lessening of sectionalism and insularity.

Magazines helped develop writers and readers for those writers. Henry Thoreau's *Ktaadn,* originally published in the *Union Magazine* in 1848 when no one was paying much attention to Thoreau, was the subject of magazine articles one hundred years later. The content of the first few years of *The Atlantic Monthly,* writings of Emerson, Holmes, Longfellow, Lowell, and their contemporaries, affect new readers every year.

When they began to take advertising the nationally distributed magazines opened national markets for manufacturers who previously had been able to produce only for local or sectional consumption.

Early in this century magazines, led by the muckraking *McClure's*, raised a furor with sensational exposés that resulted in needed reforms. Magazines deliberately crusaded for legislation, such as the Food and Drug Act of 1906, which effectuated social gain. More and more the magazines became what Colonel George Harvey called them in 1910, the country's "national newspapers." The mass magazines purveyed—and some of them still purvey—sex in its most glamorous aspects, violence which is made to appear more romantic and exciting than cruel and painful, saccharine optimism, pretense of intellectuality where there is only glibness, articles shining with polished mediocrity, and dishonest fiction.[4] At the same time the monthlies and general weeklies, as well as the weekly news magazines which assumed it as a business, began to publish an increasing proportion of material dealing in some way with what is essentially news and comment on the news.

By 1921, when he was professor of American literature at the University of Wisconsin, William B. Cairns could write:

> The reading of magazines has come to be far more common than the reading of books. Thousands of persons who would resent the imputation that they are lacking in culture read almost no books at all. . . . No home, however, in which there is a pretense of intellectual interest is without magazines, which are usually read by all members of the family.[5]

The prevalence and acceptance of magazines multiplied many times after 1921, and two world wars forced readers into awareness of people, places, and ideas beyond Sandy Hook and the Golden Gate. World War II particularly enabled the

[4] Though "mass magazine" has been used often throughout this discussion as a generally understood convenient term of reference, the composite, of course, does not exist. The large-circulation magazines have many characteristics in common, but the virtues of some are not the virtues of all, nor are the deficiencies. When it ran the stories of Frank Norris, Booth Tarkington, Mary Roberts Rinehart, Earl Derr Biggers, J. P. Marquand, Kenneth Roberts, and their few peers, *The Saturday Evening Post* published some of the best popular fiction written in this country.

[5] *Cambridge History of American Literature.* New York: The Macmillan Co., 1943, Vol. II, p. 229. Used by permission of The Macmillan Company, publishers.

magazines, and they made the most of their opportunity, to present explanation and discussion of political, geographical, economic, ideological, and a myriad of other subjects which they could not have published successfully earlier. Since the end of the last war the magazines have been compelled to maintain the high reportorial and educational standards they reached between 1939 and 1945, when, incidentally, their circulations multiplied.

Magazines were the favorite reading of millions of men and women in the armed forces; often they were the only reading matter available. These men and women, their knowledge of the war limited to what was happening in their own sectors or at their own posts, read primarily for information about the progress of the war and the kind of peace that might be expected to follow, and secondly for recreation. Often, in Europe and in the South Pacific, magazines were the most typically American product obtainable. Their contents were devoured. Sight and feel of the magazines themselves provided comfort and reassurance. In this country, their publishers hampered by paper shortages, magazines were at a premium. Copies of new issues of the large magazines disappeared from the newsstands in a matter of minutes. American dependence on magazines increased greatly during World War II.

The tense international situation, relieved only by wars in Korea, Vietnam, and the Middle East, which has obtained ever since World War II, has resulted in continued magazine emphasis on international affairs and on social and political action in the United States. There is lighter material about people and places, but serious discussions of serious subjects predominate.

An outside force has had its effect on magazines generally. The wide and rapid spread of higher education has brought the majority of magazine readers to acceptance of more thoughtful material. The educational and intellectual level of the population has been raised to the point where the large general magazines can and must present subjects and treatments of these subjects which their audience would have rejected as boring, unnecessary, or highbrow a few years ago. The magazines can hold their huge circulations with serious discussions which would not have been tolerated by the earlier magazine audience. It is a more critical audience, less easily deluded, less apt to be hypnotized by phrases, or content with standardized, colorless treatment of vital subjects. It is a fact-hungry audience which has learned to evaluate facts and their significance, to form its own opinions, and to judge those proffered by magazine writers.

This is true only in part. As education has spread, it has also spread thin. It has been said often enough that more people can read today but fewer can think. A literate population does not constitute a critically intelligent one. The tolerance of most mass magazine readers for thoughtful material is low. They read mostly to be amused; they do not wish to be shocked or made unhappily aware of unpleasant facts when what they are seeking is the kind of escape they have gone to popular magazines to find. These magazines can run substantial material in many instances only if they treat it lightly, make it diverting, avoid taboos, and sweeten the material sufficiently to make it palatable. Television came into being as a communications medium with astounding swiftness. As quickly as it came it conditioned its vast audience to undiluted light entertainment, little of better than mediocre quality. The continuing appeal of the comic books is reassuring guarantee that American magazines have not become too serious and informative.

A magazine is a perishable product. It has to do with the contemporary. It is meant for ready and relatively quick perusal. Essentially a compromise between the newspaper and the book, the magazine lacks the relative permanence of the book but has more than the highly transient value of the newspaper. Normally it is kept for some time after purchase and original reading. Usually it is read by the entire family, picked up and read by visitors to the household, often passed on to friends. Its influence, its potential as a social and economic force, is not limited to the subscriber or newsstand purchaser.

The active life of one issue of a periodical, the duration of its spreading influence, may well be a matter of weeks, months, or even years. The time varies with the periodical and the contents of a particular issue. A news magazine may well be discarded after a week, whereas a fashion magazine may be of use for an entire season.

Today's magazine is shiny and brightly colored to attract the attention of men and women who have other sources of information and amusement competing for their attention. Their surface glitter attracts, but it takes substance to hold. Most adults have had the experience of buying a magazine at a railroad station, expecting its contents to interest for most of a journey of several hours, then found they had exhausted its possibilities in ten minutes and had to stare out of the train window, usually at the unkempt back yards of discouraged looking houses, for the rest of their journey. This is not always the fault of the magazine. It can be the state of the reader's mind or body. But in one short trip I have seen the same new copy of a very popular magazine discarded by its businessman purchaser after a brief and obviously unsatisfactory perusal, likewise discarded by a bored sailor, then scanned for only a few minutes by the housewife who took the seat after the sailor got off the train. The magazine was finally utilized by a small child, who, staggering up the aisle of the swaying coach, espied the magazine and enthusiastically tore out most of the pages. It ate one.

More often the magazine is read, read by more than one person; then, whether that copy is kept for a day or five years, it becomes an important part of the written record of American civilization. The bound files of magazines maintained by libraries throughout the United States are invaluable to the investigator into the tastes, manners, habits, interests, and achievements of any period of our history. The social historian has no richer source. He can discover and check facts in the newspapers of the time. For contemporary opinion of that time, for comment revealing how the news of the day appeared to those who made or were first affected by it, for discovery of what was approved in popular fiction and art, he must go to the magazines. Our present will some day be the quaint past at which possible survivors of future wars can be amused or aghast, but which they cannot neglect, in the pages of our magazines.

The present of the mass magazines is not fixed at all, and there is little that is firm about their entire situation. Though they have the mammoth circulations for which they fought the internecine wars which have been the chief characteristic of magazine publishing since World War II, and these circulations seem only to get larger every year, they are no longer the chief source nationally of public information and entertainment or the dominant national advertising medium. Where they exist at all, profits are in most cases small. As minor components of leviathan corporate enterprises in which a number of them have taken refuge about all that is asked of them is that they carry their share of the overhead.

To some, even within the industry, the mass consumer magazine now seems an anachronism in its own time, as dated as the stereopticon and about as useful. To others, who are a little more sanguine or cautious in the phrasing of their opinions, the mass magazine is on the wane. For a dozen years it has been a commonplace among men in magazine publishing that the day of the big magazines is at least in its late afternoon. The usual comment is that the large-circulation general magazine is through or nearly through while special-interest periodicals edited to small circulations of readers engaged in an activity or engrossed in a subject will become stronger.

No magazine publisher can be assured that he will always be able to continue publication at profit enough to make it possible, and it is true that major activities wax and then some of them disappear. The buggy, the bicycle, luxury liners, the icebox, the coal furnace, the fountain pen, the novel, to an extent motion pictures, and enough other items all had their periods of acceptance and dominance, then fell away. It is entirely possible that, beset by many difficulties, supplanted in part by television, unsure of their function in the total communications structure, magazines based commercially on the advertising of a mass-production, mass-consumption society and editorially on the purveyance of information and entertainment to great audiences will fall away, too. The big magazines served their purpose during the years when the United States was developing as an industrial and commercial country with a free-enterprise economy and a society which accepted it. With that system severely modified the magazines which expressed and encouraged it have less reason for being.

The magazines seem to be going through an experience much like that enjoyed by the newspaper press since early in this century. Where large American cities had ten or a dozen newspapers they have one or two. Failures, mergers, discontinuances for a tangle of reasons killed many of them and many good ones. Horace Greeley's *Tribune,* James Gordon Bennett's *Herald,* Joseph Pulitzer's *World,* Philadelphia's *Public Ledger,* Boston's *Transcript,* and how many more are all gone.

In the same way important and once very successful magazines have gone: *Delineator, Woman's Home Companion, Collier's, World's Work, Review of Reviews, Literary Digest, American, Forum, Century, Outlook, Independent, The Saturday Evening Post* . . . it is a long, long list. Sometimes the death of a magazine comes with the death of an editor or the lapse of his powers or with a publisher's death and sale or liquidation of the property by his estate—the ordinary concomitants of any commercial enterprise. Sometimes, though no one quite knows why, a magazine simply loses its hold on its readers and its appeal to advertisers.

Undoubtedly more important magazines will disappear in what used to be called the ordinary course of human events, though the course is seldom ordinary and many of the events seem rather inhuman. As with the newspapers, the strong or the strongly financed will survive. Whether mass magazine publishing as a journalistic phenomenon will survive, show further decline, or suddenly take a new and firmer grasp on life—which means reader popularity and advertising agency approval—no one knows. All that anyone can know is that the activity is badgered by perplexities and forebodings which it did not know and could not suspect during and immediately after World War II.

The mass magazines bear internal evidence of the insecurity and uncertainty they feel and exhibit a strange paradox.

Long conservative and staunch upholders of their conceptions of democracy, most of the weekly news magazines and the weekly, bi-weekly, and monthly general magazines now generally back the forces leading to increased socialization in an already socialized United States. In their anxiety to attract young readers and win "minority group" approval they strive to be more and more "liberal," though few of them, as few people, seem longer sure of what liberalism means. They are determined to be "with it" whether the issue is social, racial, political, academic, or whether there is any real issue at all.

In general, magazine sympathy is with the protesters against whatever is being protested against. It is for rebellion against authority whatever the authority. The assumption they seem to make is that the authority of the law, an industry, a corporation, the trustees and executives of a university, or whatever institution was gained by suspect means and is being unjustly exerted. Whether the magazines do this to curry favor or because they are written and edited by men and women who share the human dislike of all authority it is impossible to say. What is certain is that many of the large magazines reflect the confusion—call it the chaos, if you like—of the times, share a dislike of what is and a wish for they are not quite sure what. Some of these magazines seem to be basically against "the Establishment" (which means whatever you dislike at the moment) and to be riding off in all directions to dozens of contradictory conclusions in widely scattered places and doing it with indiscriminate enthusiasm.

At the same time the mass magazines are completely dependent for financial support on advertising which is part, parcel, possibly the relic, of the diminishing free-enterprise economy for which they have long been the outspoken spokesman. Advertising is the articulation for the same established social, governmental, and business system which their editorial content often attacks and derides. That the magazines feel some uneasiness in the performance is sometimes manifest in their pages.

The right or wrong, the reason or unreason, of this situation is not the point here. Someone else may decide that. Certainly the future will. The point here is that the popular consumer magazines seem to stand essentially divided against themselves. They are trying to serve two masters, biting the hand that feeds them, and expecting the goose to continue to lay golden eggs for those intent on wringing its neck. One of all of these bits of proverbial wisdom must fit. All of them indicate that the position in which the magazines have been placed or have placed themselves is uncomfortable.

Magazines helped make the world which now they cannot fully attack or completely defend, but they sound one hopeful note. They will be glad to help form any brave new world that comes along, if one comes, or even one that is not too brave and not too new if they can find one. Meanwhile, as part of the aggressively seething indecisiveness they helped cause and which they share, they can only report and comment upon the alarms, discontent, and disasters and hope that through mergers, diversification or diffusion, good fortune or magic they can keep on publishing.

They have one other choice. They can stay with hairdos, lyric descriptions of the beauties of Rome, diet, the newest news of Mrs. Aristotle Onassis, directions for things to make while you watch television or announce a new miracle in medicine, science, hope or life itself once a month. Some of them do.

If there are uncertainties leading only to dusty answers in mass magazine publishing and in the magazines themselves, there seems to be, as so many magazine people feel, indications of strength and growth in special-interest magazines. The mass magazines which are closest to being one-subject magazines do best. Fashion, geography, news, sports, wit, sex . . . you have little difficulty attaching a popular magazine name to each broad category. In addition there are thousands of small business, trade, vocational, and hobby magazines—magazines for numismatists, obstetricians, kindergarten teachers, conservationists, orthodontists, postal employees, and embalmers—which do very well.

They may carry a little, but most of these magazines do not depend on advertising. They are financed by trade associations, professional societies, universities or other nonprofit institutions, or are paid for out of membership fees. These magazines tell their readers what they wish to know about, and they can be independent in their views. They can afford luxuries of expression which often the mass magazines cannot. They have fixed subjects and, if limited, reasonably fixed circulation markets. Many of the scientific, literary, and philosophical magazines of this kind are of very high quality. Long-established academic periodicals like the *Kenyon Review, Yale Review, Georgia Review, Sewanee Review* and their peers are really small-circulation class magazines.

Whether literary quarterlies or professional journals these magazines have wider readership and stronger influence than their limited circulations indicate. Many are standard library references. University and college libraries take them regularly. Amherst receives about 1,300 different periodicals; Haverford about the same number; Macalester 1,400; Middlebury nearly 1,400; Smith 2,400; Wellesley over 1,800. The universities with their graduate and professional schools subscribe to many more. These libraries do not purchase these magazines because they are popular with readers. They buy them because they believe their contents are significant and file them because they believe they are of lasting scholarly, technical, or informational value.

It is just possible that under duress American magazines are finding their way back to what they were originally. The failure of some consumer magazines and the jeopardy in which others quake is one indication. The endurance of subsidized or reader-supported quality magazines is another. The idea of magazines of great circulation supported by advertisers and published primarily to provide a channel by which business could reach its markets flourished for well over a half century, which is a long time for anything to flourish. The idea which produced magazines that were both prosperous and widely influential was a good one for its time, but, if much that the magazines now report and comment upon is accurately indicative, that time may be past or passing. Business has other ways of reaching its customers now, and business itself and the social system which business built do not stand unquestioned.

Magazines may become again primarily editorial vehicles with modest advertising content which will regain stability through finding their place in total public communications made up of newspapers, magazines, books, pamphlets, brochures, television, radio, doctoral dissertations, and the photocopying and recording devices, the computers and punched cards which are rapidly putting town criers and sandwich men out of business.

Magazines have been doing an imperfect, perhaps, but certainly a useful job in the United States for a long time, and there are those who are fond of them. This does not mean that magazines are or should be impervious to change. Especially as it has been established for some time that the more things change the more they remain the same.

SELECTED BIBLIOGRAPHY

Books and Pamphlets

ALDEN, HENRY MILLS. *Magazine Writing and the New Literature.* New York: Harper & Bros., 1908.

ALLEN, FREDERICK L. *Harper's Magazine, 1850–1950.* New York: The Newcomen Society in North America, 1950.

ATKINSON, WILMER. *An Autobiography.* Philadelphia: Wilmer Atkinson Co., 1920.

BAINBRIDGE, JOHN. *Little Wonder and How It Grew.* New York: Reynal & Hitchcock, 1946.

BAKER, RAY STANNARD. *American Chronicle.* New York: Charles Scribner's Sons, 1945.

BOK, EDWARD. *The Americanization of Edward Bok.* New York: Charles Scribner's Sons, 1920.

———. *A Man from Maine.* New York: Charles Scribner's Sons, 1923.

BORDEN, NEIL H. *The Economic Effects of Advertising.* Homewood, Ill.: Richard D. Irwin, Inc., 1942.

Country Gentleman, A Brief History of. Philadelphia: The Curtis Publishing Co., 1954.

DREWRY, JOHN E. *Some Magazines and Their Makers.* Boston: The Stratford Co., 1924.

Editors of *Life. Project Mercury.* New York: Time, Inc., 1964.

ELLIS, HAROLD MILTON. *Joseph Dennie and His Circle.* Austin, Texas: Bulletin of the University of Texas, No. 40, 1915.

FAULKNER, HAROLD UNDERWOOD. *The Quest for Social Justice, 1898–1914.* (*A History of American Life,* Vol. XI.) New York: The Macmillan Co., 1931.

Great Editors Seminar. New York: American Society of Magazine Editors, 1968.

HARPER, J. HENRY. *The House of Harper.* New York: Harper & Bros., 1912.

HODGINS, ERIC. *The Span of Time* (Reprint of a Speech delivered at the Chautauqua Institution). New York, 1946.

HOFFMAN, FREDERIC J., CHARLES ALLEN, and CAROLYN F. ULRICH. *The Little Magazine, A History and a Bibliography.* Princeton, N.J.: Princeton University Press, 1946.

HOWE, M. A. DEWOLFE. *The Atlantic Monthly and Its Makers.* Boston: Atlantic Monthly Press, 1919.

HOWER, RALPH M. *The History of an Advertising Agency, N. W. Ayer & Son at Work.* Cambridge, Mass.: Harvard University Press, 1939.

JOHNSON, WALTER. *William Allen White's America.* New York: Henry Holt & Co., 1947.

KABLER, JOHN. *Luce: His Time, Life, and Fortune.* Garden City, N.Y.: Doubleday & Co., Inc., 1968.

KLAPPER, JOSEPH T. *The Effects of Mass Media.* New York: Bureau of Applied Social Research, Columbia University, 1949.

KLEPPNER, OTTO. *Advertising Procedure.* 4th ed. Englewood Cliffs, N.J.: Prentice-Hall, Inc., 1950.

LYNCH, DENIS T. *Boss Tweed.* New York: Boni and Liveright, 1927.

MORRIS, LLOYD. *Postscript to Yesterday.* New York: Random House, Inc., 1947.

MOTT, FRANK LUTHER. *American Journalism, A History of Newspapers in the United States.* New York: The Macmillan Co., 1942.

———. *A History of American Magazines, 1741–1905.* 4 vols. New York: Appleton-Century-Crofts, Inc., 1930, and Cambridge, Mass.: Harvard University Press, 1938–1939, 1957.

NOEL, MARY. *Villains Galore—The Heyday of the Popular Story Weekly.* New York: The Macmillan Co., 1954.

PATTEE, FRED LEWIS. *The First Century of American Literature, 1770–1870.* New York: Appleton-Century-Crofts, Inc., 1935.

Printers' Ink, Fifty Years: 1888 to 1938. New York: Printers' Ink Publishing Co., 1938.

RAYFIELD, STANLEY. *Life Photographers, Their Careers and Favorite Pictures.* Garden City, N.Y.: Doubleday & Co., Inc., 1957.

———. *How Life Gets the Picture.* Garden City, N.Y.: Doubleday & Co., Inc., 1955.

RICHARDSON, LYON. *A History of Early American Magazines.* New York: Thomas Nelson and Sons, 1931.

ROWELL, GEORGE P. *Forty Years an Advertising Agent.* New York: Franklin Publishing Co., 1926.

Saturday Evening Post, A Short History of The. Philadelphia: The Curtis Publishing Co., 1949.

SCHLESINGER, ARTHUR MEIER. *Political and Social Growth of the American People, 1865–1940.* New York: The Macmillan Co., 1941.

———. *Political and Social History of the United States. 1829–1925.* New York: The Macmillan Co., 1925.

SCHRAMM, WILBUR (ed.). *Mass Communications.* Urbana, Ill.: The University of Illinois Press, 1949.

SEDGWICK, ELLERY. *The Happy Profession.* Boston: Little Brown & Co., 1946.

SELDES, GILBERT. *The Great Audience.* New York: The Viking Press, 1950.

SLOSSON, WILLIAM PRESTON. *The Great Crusade and After, 1914–1928.* (*A History of American Life,* Vol. XII.) New York: The Macmillan Co., 1930.

SMYTH, ALBERT H. *Philadelphia Magazines and Their Contributors, 1741–1850.* Philadelphia: Robert M. Lindsay, 1892.

STEPHENS, ETHEL A. (comp.). *American Popular Magazines, A Bibliography.* Boston: The Boston Book Co., 1916.

STODDARD, HENRY LUTHER. *Horace Greeley, Printer, Editor, Crusader.* New York: G. P. Putnam's Sons, 1946.

Story of an Experiment, The. New York: Time, Inc., 1948.

SULLIVAN, MARK. *The Education of an American.* New York: Doubleday, Doran & Co., 1928.

———. *Our Times.* Vol. I, *The Turn of the Century,* and Vol. II, *America Finding Herself.* New York: Charles Scribner's Sons, 1926, 1927.

TARBELL, IDA. *The Nationalizing of Business, 1878–1898.* (*A History of American Life,* Vol. IX.) New York: The Macmillan Co., 1944.

TASSIN, ALGERNON. *The Magazine in America.* New York: Dodd, Mead & Co., 1916.

TEBBEL, JOHN. *George Horace Lorimer and The Saturday Evening Post.* Garden City, N.Y.: Doubleday & Co., Inc., 1948.

THURBER, JAMES. *The Years With Ross.* New York: Grosset & Dunlap, Inc., 1959.

TOOKER, L. FRANK. *The Joys and Tribulations of an Editor.* New York: Appleton-Century-Crofts, Inc., 1920.

TRENT, W. P., SHERMAN ERSKINE, and CARL VAN DOREN (eds.). *Cambridge History of American Literature.* New York: The Macmillan Co., 1943.

WAPLES, DOUGLAS, BERNARD BERELSON, and FRANKLIN BRADSHAW. *What Reading Does to People.* Chicago: University of Chicago Press, 1940.

WARD, A. W., and A. R. WALLER (eds.). *The Cambridge History of English Literature,* Vols. IX and X. New York: G. P. Putnam's Sons, 1913.

What Makes Time Tick. New York: Time, Inc., n.d.

WHITE, WILLIAM ALLEN. *Autobiography.* New York: The Macmillan Co., 1946.

WOLSELEY, ROLAND E. *The Magazine World.* Englewood Cliffs, N.J.: Prentice-Hall, Inc., 1951.

WOOD, JAMES PLAYSTED. *Of Lasting Interest.* Garden City, N.Y.: Doubleday & Co., Inc., 1967.

———. *The Story of Advertising.* New York: The Ronald Press Co., 1958.

———. *This Is Advertising.* New York: Crown Publishers, Inc., 1968.

MAGAZINE ARTICLES

ALLEN, FREDERICK LEWIS. "American Magazines, 1741–1941," *Bulletin of The New York Public Library,* XLV, No. 5 (June, 1941).

———. "The American Magazine Grows Up," *The Atlantic Monthly,* November, 1947.

"American Magazine—Literature of the Last Century," *The Atlantic Monthly.* April, 1860.

"American Men of Letters and Periodical Literature," *Harper's Magazine,* April, 1907.

BRAY, THOMAS V. "Cowles' Woes," *The Wall Street Journal,* January 21, 1970.

BUTTERFIELD, ROGER. "What Pocket Magazines Feed On," *The Saturday Review of Literature,* March 9, 1946.

CALKINS, ERNEST ELMO. "Fifty Years of Advertising," *Printers' Ink,* October 10, 1947.

CHENERY, WILLIAM L. "American Magazines, 1741–1941," *Bulletin of The New York Public Library,* June, 1941.

———. "Magazines and Public Opinion," *Vital Speeches,* August 15, 1936.

CHURCHILL, ALLEN. "Harold Ross, Editor of The New Yorker," *Cosmopolitan,* May, 1948.

"Crowell," *Fortune,* August, 1937.

DAVIDSON, BILL. "Czar of the Bunny," *The Saturday Evening Post,* April 28, 1962.

Editors of *The Reader's Digest.* "Second-Class Mail Rates Can Ruin First-Class Magazines," *The Reader's Digest,* April, 1962.

EDWARDS, JACKSON. "One Every Minute; The Picture Magazines," *Scribner's Magazine,* May, 1938.

ELLISON, JEROME. "Selling Dreams in Marble Halls," *The New Republic,* October 13, 1947.

FRANCIS, C. M. "Fighting Magazines," *Bookman,* July, 1910.

"Freedom of the Press," *Survey,* June 4, 1910.

GIBBS, WOLCOTT. "Time . . . Fortune . . . Life . . . Luce," *The New Yorker,* November 28, 1936.

GILDER, RICHARD WATSON. "Century's Twentieth Anniversary," *Century Magazine,* November, 1890.

"Glance at the World's Periodicals," *Review of Reviews,* January, 1911.
GROSVENOR, GILBERT HOVEY. "The Romance of the Geographic," *National Geographic Magazine,* October, 1963.
HARMSWORTH, ALFRED (Lord Northcliffe). "The Future of Magazines," *The Independent,* November 19, 1908.
HARRIMAN, MARGARET CASE. "The Candor Kid," *The New Yorker,* January 4 and 11, 1941.
HARTMAN, E. P. "Magazines; Moulders of Opinion," *Wilson Library Bulletin,* April, 1947.
HARVEY, GEORGE. "Magazines in Journalism," *Harper's Weekly,* March 19, 1910.
HAVILAND, THOMAS P. "Franklin's General Magazine," *General Magazine and Historical Chronicle* (University of Pennsylvania), Winter, 1946.
HICKMAN, POWELL. "Collier's," *Scribner's Magazine,* May, 1939.
"History of a Publishing House, The," *Scribner's Magazine,* December, 1894.
HUGHES, LAWRENCE M. "North American Steppes Yield Gold to Mr. Tilley," *Advertising Age,* December 1, 1947.
HUTCHENS, JOHN K. "The New Yorker," *Herald-Tribune Books,* June 2, 1963.
IVERSEN, WILLIAM ("Ivor Williams"). "The Pious Pornographers," *Playboy,* October, 1957.
——. "The Pious Pornographers Revisited," *Playboy,* November, 1957.
KERR, W. A., and H. H. REMMERS. "Cultural Value of 100 Representative American Magazines," *School and Society,* November 22, 1941.
"Literature of Business," *The Nation,* November 15, 1906.
LYDGATE, WILLIAM A. "Romantic Business," *Scribner's Magazine,* September, 1938.
"Magazine Literature," *Harper's Magazine,* February, 1903.
"Magazines, Their Scope and Influence," *The Independent,* October 1, 1908.
MANCHESTER, HARLAND. "Farm Magazines," *Scribner's Magazine,* October, 1938.
MILLER, MERLE. "Freedom to Read; Magazines," *Survey Graphic,* December, 1946.
MIZENER, ARTHUR. "The Voice is Quiet, the Eye is Sharp," *The New York Times Book Review,* December 18, 1960.
MULLER, EDWIN. "Radio versus Reading," *The New Republic,* February 19, 1940.
"A Nest Egg for the Grandchildren," *Forbes,* December 1, 1967.
"New Yorker, The," *Fortune,* August, 1934.
"The New Yorker at 40," *Newsweek,* March 1, 1965.
"Norman Hapgood and Collier's Weekly," *Outlook,* November 2, 1912.
OURSLER, FULTON. "American Magazines, 1741–1941," *Bulletin of The New York Public Library,* June, 1941.
PRINGLE, HENRY F. "High Hat; The Luxury Magazines," *Scribner's Magazine,* July, 1938.
———. "Ross of The New Yorker," *'48,* March and April, 1948.
REPPLIER, AGNES. "American Magazines," *Yale Review,* XVI (1926–1927).
ROSS, ISHBEL. "Geography, Inc.," *Scribner's Magazine,* June, 1938.
"Story of an Experiment, The." *Time,* March 8, 1948.
"Strangling the Magazines," *The Nation,* May 2, 1912.
TARBELL, I. M. "Sarah Josepha Hale," *American Magazine,* March, 1910.
WHIPPLE, LEON. "SatEvePost," *Survey,* March 1, 1928.
WHITNEY, ALAN. "The Story of Playboy," *Chicago Magazine,* October, 1955.

Index